D1602835

V&R

Religion, Theologie und Naturwissenschaft/ Religion, Theology, and Natural Science

Herausgegeben von
Antje Jackelén, Gebhard Löhr, Ted Peters
und Nicolaas A. Rupke

Band 8

Vandenhoeck & Ruprecht

Gaymon Bennett / Martinez J. Hewlett
Ted Peters / Robert John Russell (ed.)

The Evolution of Evil

Vandenhoeck & Ruprecht

Bibliografische Information der Deutschen Nationalbibliothek

Die Deutsche Nationalbibliothek verzeichnet diese Publikation in der Deutschen Nationalbibliografie; detaillierte bibliografische Daten sind im Internet über http://dnb.d-nb.de abrufbar.

ISBN 978-3-525-56979-5

Satz: OLD-Media OHG, Neckarsteinach.
Druck und Bindung: ⊕ Hubert & Co, Göttingen.

Gedruckt auf alterungsbeständigem Papier.

Table of Contents

Introduction: Evil and Evolution
Gaymon Bennett   7

I. Evolution and Evil: Framing the Problem

The Evolution of Evil
Ted Peters   19

Creation as "Very Good" and "Groaning in Travail": An Exploration
in Evolutionary Theodicy
Christopher Southgate   53

Darwinism and Christianity. Does Evil Spoil a Beautiful Friendship?
Michael Ruse.   86

Nature and Nurture: The Irony of the Sociobiology Debate
James W. Haag   99

The Groaning of Creation: Does God Suffer with All Life?
Robert John Russell   120

II. Evolution and God: Theodicy

Evolutionary Evil and Dawkins' Black Box: Changing the Parameters
of the Problem
Joshua Moritz   143

Evolution and The Suffering of Sentient Life: Theodicy After Darwin
John F. Haught   189

How Evil Entered the World: An Exploration Through Deep Time
Patricia A. Williams   204

Making the Task of Theodocy Impossible? Intelligent Design and the
Problem of Evil
William A. Dembski.   218

Evolution, Suffering, and the God of Hope in Roman Catholic
Thought after Darwin
Peter M. J. Hess.   234

III. Evolution and the Human: Anthropodicy

"What A Piece of Work Is Man!" The Impact of Modern Biology on
Philosophical and Theological Anthropology
Martinez J. Hewlett 257

Biology, Rhetoric, Genocide: Assembling Concepts for Theological
Inquiry
Gaymon Bennett 275

Eugenics and the Question of Religion
Nathan Hallanger 301

Sins of Commission, Sins of Omission: Girard, Ricoeur, and the
Armenian Genocide
Derek Nelson 318

Violence, Scapegoating and the Cross
René Girard 334

Cross, Evolution, and Theodicy: Telling It Like It Is
George Murphy 349

Contributors. 367

Introduction
Evil and Evolution

Gaymon Bennett

Darwinian evolution and the history of associated scientific, cultural, and philosophical developments, challenge the adequacy of classical theological responses to the problem of evil. The Darwinian challenge calls for reformulation, both in terms of theodicy and theological anthropology. This volume presents a range of responses and proposed reformulations. Taken together the chapters offer a multivalent diagnosis of the problem of evil in an evolutionary context. This diagnosis consists of analysis of what is at stake, scientifically and theologically. More importantly, it offers an array of synthetic proposals for how theology might move beyond current difficulties, opening new directions for thought, and clearer understandings of evil.

The Evolution of Evil

When Charles Darwin published *The Origin of Species by Natural Selection* in 1859, he drew a picture of the natural world replete with the struggle for existence, predation, suffering, death, and even extinction. That Darwin could find a thread of nobility in the progressive development from the realm of the brutes to the realm of the human intellect did not mitigate the long predecessor history of seemingly meaningless pain and death. Within Darwin's own lifetime his view of nature as a "struggle for existence" was interpreted as a "survival of the fittest", and nature portrayed as "red in tooth and claw".

Though such interpretations were extrinsic to Darwin's theory, they were echoed in Darwin's own meditations on the implications of his explanations. Darwin referred to extinct species as waste. Such waste raised the theodicy question with new urgency: how can we attribute such enormous waste over deep time to a creator, a creator thought to be benevolent or caring? Darwin effectively answered this question by removing responsibility from God's shoulders. He provided a strictly natural explanation: variation in inheritance combined with natural selection. Natural processes explain natural waste. Science need not thank or blame God for the eons of bloodshed. But in fact, the problem of evil, seemingly made worse by Darwin's explanations, is not resolved. It is simply bracketed. Needless to say, this bracketing has not sufficed.

The appearance of Darwin's theory of evolution altered the course of Western culture. Though initially developed as an attempt to explain speciation,

Darwin's thought has had an enormous influence on developments in social theory, economics, technology, politics, ethics, and in some cases has contributed to racism, war, and even genocide. Concepts such as "struggle for existence" or "survival of the fittest" escaped the biological sciences and became generative ideas in multiple domains of contemporary thought and practice. To cite just one example, today sociobiologists and evolutionary psychologists are asking whether the human race can or should imitate or defy the impulses of our evolutionary heritage. Such questions, and the formative role of evolutionary thought, inform the context within which the theologians and philosophers writing in this book ask: just how should we understand the relationship between evolution and evil?

In order to answer this question, the authors in this book have had to consider a range of factors. A first set of factors concerns the conceptual and scientific events connected to the development of evolutionary biology. If Darwinian evolution challenges the sufficiency of prior ways of thinking about the problem evil, it does so in the first place because of the ways in which it refigures the natural world and the human place in it. From the publication of *The Origin of Species*, the Darwinian account of nature has figured violence, predation, and victimage as structurally integral to the way in which the biosphere regenerates and thrives. For theology, such an account raises both the question of God's creative justice as well as the question of human evil. Did God create a world that relies on suffering and death as a motor of regeneration? And to what extent are human behaviors and capacities determined by the dynamics of natural selection? Might human behavior be so genetically constrained that significant human evils such as war or genocide can be best explained in evolutionary terms?

Developments in evolutionary biology thus pose a significant challenge to some long held theological assumptions. Theologians have long distinguished between human sin and natural evil. Sin is the result of human choice, we have assumed. Suffering among nature's creatures has been thought to be something separate. Separate theological categories seemed warranted. With Darwinian evolution, however, thoroughly naturalized interpretations of human nature became far more plausible. Humans are descended from common ancestors shared with other primates. Further back we share common ancestry with all of life. This fact raises questions concerning whether or not sin derives from our animal ancestry and is not in fact a strictly human phenomenon. Should theologians look for the preconditions for what we know as sin in the remote evolutionary past of our biological inheritance? In light of evolution the relation of human evil and natural evil needs to be rethought.

Other factors which the authors in this book have confronted are more practical and political than conceptual or scientific. If evil is a problem for contemporary theology because of scientific developments, it is all the more so because evil continues to characterize so much of human life. Over the last century and a half we have witnessed more needless suffering and death than at any time in previous recorded history. Wars have never been bloodier; and the human relation to the non-human world has never been more destructive. Among these events, many have involved direct conjunctions of evolutionary biology and political power. Political and social programs have been justified in the name of biology—eugenics, racism, genocide, militarism, and the like. In the premodern chapters of Western history, religion was appealed to as justification for despotism and military aggression. In our Enlightenment era, science has largely replaced religion as that which certifies and enables power. Power politics wants science on its side. In some of the most conspicuous moments of political evil in the 20th century—such as eugenics and Nazi "racial hygiene"—the theory of evolution and the logic of survival-of-the-fittest was taken up to justify the ethics of racism, imperialism, and domination. While recognizing that social and political conditions have changed dramatically in the past century, evolutionary biology and the wide range of biological sciences connected to it continue to play a formative role in contemporary life. As such, theology must continue to be attentive to the political and ethical significance of science.

As editors, we assembled the material in this book as a team of theologians, scientists, and philosophers for whom both theology and evolutionary biology possess integrity. We seek to build bridges between science at its best and theology at its best. We argue that when these two are at their best, they attend carefully to the data and concepts of inquiry, committed to a rigorous and honest understanding of reality. They aspire to be directed and governed by truth. Although modes and practices are distinct, problems and commitments converge.

It is our judgment that the science associated with Darwin's theory of evolution is sound science. It is not apodictic truth. Nothing scientific is. Yet, after a century and a half of confirmation, the Darwinian model of evolution has demonstrated its fertility. Combined with the field of genetics, the neo-Darwinian synthesis has become the most reliable theory regarding speciation and related biological phenomena. Today it provides foundational conceptual orientation for the most exciting and productive areas of genomic and post-genomic biological research and engineering. Theologians dealing with the problem of evil and the natural world must take up the challenges of an evolutionary perspective. This we attempt to do.

The Problem of Evil in Evolutionary Perspective

The problem of evil is frequently characterized as a logical dilemma: the challenge of reconciling claims about God's power and goodness with the reality of evil in the created world (typically understood in terms of human or non-human suffering). Perhaps God is sufficiently powerful to create our world; but God does not love creatures enough to protect them from predation, victimage, and suffering. Or, perhaps God loves creatures totally; but God is not powerful enough to overcome natural forces or sinful proclivities to prevent victimage and death. The stakes of such a dilemma are frequently taken to consist of the proof or disproof of God's existence. The principal task of this volume is not to resolve the logical dilemma, nor is it to prove or disprove God's existence. Rather, it is to intensify the problem of evil by assessing it in light of what we now know about the natural world due to the theory of evolution.

It goes without saying that the nature of evil has long been disputed in Christian thought. It bears noting, however, that despite disagreements, Christian theologians have, by and large, connected evil to such things as violence, predation, suffering, victimage, death, and extinction. Darwinian evolution, by contrast, takes these phenomena as simply the way the natural world operates. Biology simply does not use the concept of evil. Evil is not a scientific category.

Because violence and suffering are natural, they become morally neutral. To refer to them as evil seems to be a human value imposed on non-human phenomena. In short, these phenomena are a problem for Christian thought in a way that they are not for evolutionary science. Theology, in contrast, judges them antithetical to God's vision for creation. Theological topics such as creation, sin, redemption, and eschatology are sites within which theology connects suffering and death to the problem of evil on the one hand, and to the hope of salvation on the other. Where theology sees a broken creation, evolutionary biology sees nature as value neutral.

Following classical approaches, the problem of evil as it is addressed in this book develops around two poles. The first pole centers on God and the problem of evil—the problem of theodicy. In the context of evolution, the problem of theodicy becomes acute. Understandings of God's relationship to the world are encumbered by tensions between Christian claims of God's justice on the one hand and the apparent injustice of a creation characterized by death and waste on the other.

The second pole, centers on the problem of evil and human nature—what some have called anthropodicy. Several analytically distinct questions about human nature are especially relevant. The human as a moral animal is the first: how do we make sense of human capacities for good and for evil, however those terms are defined? The second follows closely: to what extent is the human a self-determining animal? to what extent is the moral animal capable and incapable of fostering good? As crucial as these two is a third, the relationship among humans, God, and the non-human world: in what ways does this matrix of relations enter into our thinking about the problem of evil?

Three Approaches to the Problem of Evil

In what specific ways does evolutionary biology challenge classical formulations of the problem of evil? Several key examples can be offered as an initial response. Working schematically, we can identify three moments in the development of Christian approaches to the problem of evil; and we can show how evolution calls for possible reformulation in each. It is important to note that the three approaches or conceptual models overlap in significant ways, and share many of the same elements—indeed, the second two follow from and build on the first. However, salient differences can be distinguished.

A first theological approach to the problem of evil identifies death with God's wrath and human sin. This approach, which can be termed "the Fall from Life to Death", is the classical basis of theodicies developed in the Pauline tradition. In this approach suffering and death (both in humans and in non-human nature) are introduced into the world as God's righteous judgment on human sin. God judges human sin unacceptable, and gives humans over to depravity and even death. All of creation groans awaiting God's redemption in Christ. Two elements bear underscoring. The first is causal: death results from God's judgment on human sin. The second is historical: originally the world was not characterized by suffering and death. Adam sins; God judges; death ensues.

Evolutionary biology would seem to challenge this approach. In biology death is part of the natural world long before humans arrived on the scene. Death precedes human sin. Over deep time, predators began to eat prey and some species survived while others went extinct. It is difficult to hold that a human event would have a retroactive affect on pre-human history. Many scholars have recommended that Christian theologians free themselves from belief in a literal historical Garden of Eden followed by a fall. Suffering and death are realities with which we must deal, to be sure; but the human race was born into these already established realities. This raises old questions in a new form: did God create the natural world already with predation and death and extinction built in? And if so, what affect might this have on a Pauline approach to the problem of evil?

A second theological approach to the problem of evil identifies death and suffering with the exercise of human freedom in an ordered cosmos. This approach, which can be referred to as "the Fall from Order to Disorder", is usually associated with Augustine and Anselm. Like the first, this second approach looks to past events to explain suffering and death in the present: death enters the world in the Fall, and is subsequently passed on through history. However, this second approach provides an expanded causal account of how this history unfolds: by locating human sin within a classical view of the cosmos, understood as an integrated, complete and harmonious reality. If in the first approach death and suffering are accounted for as the relation between human sin and God's judgment, in this approach the emphasis is on human sin as the introduction of disorder on an otherwise ordered cosmos. The problem of evil is thus a problem of disorder caused by human freedom. Augustine argues that the cosmos is naturally ordered to and by God.

Humans, by freely choosing to order their lives away from God introduced disorder into the cosmos.

How is the Augustinian and Anselmian approach challenged by evolutionary biology? The classical view of nature as a harmonious and complete cosmos is difficult to reconcile with the vision offered by contemporary evolutionary biology. Evolution describes the natural world as epigenetic, as unfolding over time. The language of order-disorder, harmony-disharmony, has been replaced by language of development, inheritance, selection, context, and emergence. As such an explanation of evil as the disordering effects of human sin across an integrated cosmos appears unpersuasive from an evolutionary point of view. Without a classical view of nature, how might we take seriously Augustine's insight that suffering is connected to disorder? How does the evolutionary view of the human place in nature adjust such a classic approach? Do conceptions of genetic inheritance and biological determinism provide a vocabulary for rethinking Augustinian notions of original sin?

A third theological approach to the problem of evil identifies death and suffering with historical immaturity. This approach, which can be termed "the Climb from Immaturity to Maturity", can be associated with the work of Friedrich Schleiermacher, though some scholars connect this approach to the thought of Irenaeus as well. Where an Augustinian approach adds a classical view of the cosmos to the problem of evil, this third approach adds a philosophy of history in which the future is different from the past. Unlike the other first two approaches, Schleiermacher's theodicy does not posit a historical paradise from which humankind fell. Rather, it offers a developmental view according to which history is moving toward future consummation. If the first approach figures suffering and death as God's righteous judgment, and the second approach figures suffering and death as the disorder of a cosmos, suffering and death in this approach are figured as artifacts of historical underdevelopment. That is to say, evil is the result of historical immaturity. The dynamics of history are moving the world toward a better future.

At first glance the view of history offered in this third approach would appear to be more consonant with evolution. Like evolution, it provides a view of nature and history that emphasizes change over time. However, a Schleiermachian view of history is both teleological and progressive; it discerns a unifying purpose built into the dynamics of historical change. And while many 19th and early 20th century Darwinians thought that natural evolution may have agreed with this teleological view, we must ask: does evolutionary biology see nature this way? Is purpose built into the natural world? Is evolutionary development teleological? Many biologists would grant that there are multiple functional purposes *within* nature; but they would also argue that an overall guiding purpose cannot be discerned. Many would note the qualities of irreversibility and complexification, but they certainly do not perceive a master design or single guiding direction to evolutionary history. Theologians see nature as God's purposeful creation; yet it appears that contemporary evolutionary biology would resist any theological attempt to discern divine purpose in natural processes.

Darwinian evolution suggests that the future will be different from the past. But this Darwinian future will still be a product of past causation. As such, the basic dynamics of evolutionary change, which involve suffering and death, will remain in place. Evolutionary biology resists an understanding of nature with a guiding trajectory let alone a redemptive purpose. Where does this leave theology? How should theologians think about the problem of evil and the Christian vision of a redeemed world? How should theologians make sense of God's promises of a new creation in an evolutionary world?

The editors' response (although our view is not shared by all of the contributors in this volume) relies upon the logic of divine promise. We can see a purpose *for* nature, even if we cannot see a purpose *in* nature. When it comes to the Christian vision, the future new creation will be different from the present creation in many respects, to be sure. But, the future Christian theologians envision will not be the effect of present causes alone. In the New Testament God promises the arrival of the new kingdom, the new creation. This suggests to us that the Garden of Eden is a future promise rather than past and lost reality. It suggests to us that the new creation comes first in rank even if second in the sequence of God's creative action with our world. This understanding of the eschatological renewal of all things will be the result of a divine act, not a growth of nature over evolutionary time.

Overview of Content

The chapters in the book are arranged under three principle sections. The first section, *Evolution of Evil: Framing the Problem*, takes up the orienting question for the volume: how is it that evolutionary biology and related developments intensify the problem of evil? Addressing this question, each of the chapters in this section offers a proposal for how theology might reframe the problem and thereby respond more adequately.

In chapter 1 Ted Peters asks how the theological concept of original sin might be reworked in light of evolutionary biology. Might evolutionary accounts of the human condition, especially evolution seen through the eyes of sociobiology, provide a more scientifically sufficient explanation for the doctrine of original sin? No, is his answer.

In chapter 2 Christopher Southgate poses the problem of theodicy in light of the vast non-human suffering in the natural world that appears to be a fundamental part of how the biosphere develops and even thrives. In response he offers a strategy for moving beyond anthropocentric formulations so as to develop an evolutionary theodicy that begins in biology and ends in environmental ethics.

In chapter 3 Michael Ruse asks whether or not the problem of theodicy in an evolutionary context preclude Christian faith. Does the problem of evil prevent a constructive relation between Darwinism and Christianity? Could theology find a friend in Darwin?

In chapter 4 James Haag argues that the neo-Darwinian synthesis has provided the foundation for the far-reaching scientific and philosophic re-evaluation of human life known as *sociobiology*. His chapter provides theologians and philosophers with a base-line understanding of developments in sociobiology that bear on questions of anthropology, evolution, and evil.

In the last chapter in the first section of the book, Robert John Russell underscores that today the theological explanation of the two sides of life—as created good and consequentially evil—is severely challenged. The challenge comes from new understandings of the biological history of life on earth in which death is integral to multicellular life and extinction is integral to the evolution of species. He poses a question at the core of this volume: how can we believe in the goodness and power of the God who creates life through the very processes of evolution which in turn constitutively involve natural evil?

The chapters in the second section of the book, *Evolution and God: Theodicy*, take up the challenge of developing distinctive approaches to theodicy and evolution. In chapter 6 Joshua Moritz proposes to examine and thereby reject several foundational assumptions underlying the challenge of evolutionary theodicy in its current state. Moritz's approach is distinctive in that he responds to the challenge of evolutionary theodicy on scientific grounds, suggesting that recent developments in evolutionary biology shift the parameters of the problem, opening new ways forward.

In chapter 7 John Haught poses the question: Now that evolutionary science can plausibly account for suffering as a purely natural adaptation, what possible meaning or truth could religious myths about the origin and end of suffering, or theological explanations of God's goodness and suffering, still claim to have? He responds by identifying the limitations of Darwinian explanations of suffering and in so doing establishes the terms for a theodicy after Darwin.

In chapter 8 Patricia Williams proposes a focused approach to the theodicy problem: an evolutionary explanation of how pain and death—typically understood as evils in theology—came into the world. Williams argues that in an evolutionary world goods and evils are inextricably linked, but that there is a predominance of good, a predominance that offers a hopeful response to the problem of evil.

In chapter 9 William Dembski offers a reassessment of evolutionary theodicy from the perspective of Intelligent Design. Responding to critics, Dembski argues that far from making the theodicy problem hopeless, the concept of intelligent design helps highlight God's purposefulness in creation and thereby provides new ways of thinking about how God brings good out of evil.

In the final chapter of section two, Peter Hess traces the development of Roman Catholic responses to evolution and the problem of evil. Hess' historical review demonstrates ways in which Catholic theology has worked to sustain integrity and coherence even while taking seriously the challenges of evolutionary biology.

The third section of the book, *Evolution and the Human: Anthropodicy*, takes up the problem of evil in view of the relation between evolutionary biology and the question of human life. The chapters in this section consist both of theoretical approaches to evolution, evil, and human nature as well as several case studies that analyze the role of evolutionary thought in modern political life. In chapter 11 Martinez Hewlett provides an overview of specific challenges that developments in biological anthropology pose to philosophical and theological anthropology. As significantly, he also notes ways in which philosophical and theological anthropology extend beyond and enrich biological explanations of human life.

In chapter 12 Nathan Hallanger offers a case study of the relation of American religion to the eugenics movement of the early 20th century. Hallanger's examination demonstrates that both eugenic scientists, who were largely naturalists, as well as theologians and clergy viewed eugenics as a religious endeavor, appealing to the highest aims and desires for humanity's future.

In chapter 13 Gaymon Bennett poses the question of what conceptual tools theology needs for thinking about the relation of biology and the problem of evil today. He proposes to develop such tools through an examination of the relations among rhetoric, biology, and genocide.

In chapter 14 Derek Nelson introduces the distinction between sins of commission and omission as an analytic grid through which to examine the evil of genocide. Offering the Armenian genocide as a case example, Nelson proposes the work of René Girard as a theoretical frame for understanding how the sin of commission is at work in genocide and the work of Paul Ricoeur as a frame for understanding genocide and the sin of omission.

In chapter 15 René Girard argues that the Christian religion provides a unique and definitive understanding of the nature of human evil by uncovering the operations of the scapegoat mechanism. Girard argues that in distinction to all other archaic myths the cross reveals to us the self-delusion of myths of violence and thereby moves us from self-delusion to the truth about who we as human beings are.

In the final chapter of the volume George Murphy approaches evolution and the problem of evil through Luther's Theology of the Cross. Taking the evolutionary account of the natural world with utter seriousness, Murphy argues that any sufficient theodicy today must not only makes sense of how God creates through evolution, but must begin and end in the Christian claim that God shares in and even bears the suffering of the world.

Before closing, let me report on the origin of this volume. It is the product of six plus years of work by a small research group, the "Theodicy, Evolution, and Genocide" group, which we affectionately nickname "TEG". This research project itself evolved from within the Science and Religion Course Program (SRCP) conducted by the Center for Theology and the Natural Sciences at the Graduate Theological Union, funded by a grant from the John Templeton Foundation. Long after SRCP had completed its formal work in 2000, TEG continued for another half decade, until the participating graduate students obtained their Ph.D.s and began to emigrate. This book is the fittest of the products to survive the now extinct TEG. Included in the TEG project were Gaymon Bennett, Mary Anne Cooney, James Haag, Nathan Hallanger, Peter M.J. Hess, Martinez Hewlett, Carol Jacobson, Joshua Moritz, Derek Nelson, Ted Peters, and Robert John Russell. We the editors, on behalf of all the members of TEG, wish to thank Jörg Persch and Tina Bruns at Vandenhoeck & Ruprecht for working so encouragingly and patiently with us in the struggle to bring this book into existence.

I close this introduction with a final observation. This book is not meant to be the last word on evolution and the problem of evil. Nor can it be. The problem is still pressing and unfolding. Things are still in flux. Conceptual and pragmatic challenges abound, as evidenced by the flurry of publications associated with this problem, by the ongoing cultural and legal debates over the ways in which evolutionary biology does and does not inform thinking about God, the world, and human life, and by the myriad ways in which evolutionary biology continues to shape the contemporary world. This book thus confronts a straightforward if difficult task: characterizing the problem of evolution and evil today, and proposing ways forward. We hope our efforts have been adequate to the significance of the task.

I. Evolution and Evil: Framing the Problem

The Evolution of Evil

Ted Peters

Nothing is more practical than a good theory. This is especially the case with a theory of human nature. On the basis of our conceptual model of what a human being is we make decisions and plans regarding how as parents we will raise our children, what we expect from our school system, what incentives we need to motivate, what to predict will happen in time of scarcity or time of plenty, what makes war necessary or avoidable, what life means, and what death means. Our theory of human nature helps us understand what is happening within our own inner nature; and it helps us forecast what others around us will think and do.[1]

Christians and other theists are firmly convinced that our relationship to God defines who we are as human beings. Even if all the elements of what makes us human are not visible day to day, we believe that the essence of who we are is determined by how God relates to us. In fact, we can not be our authentic selves except in harmonious relationship with God. No theory of human nature that fails to include our relationship with God is adequate, at least from a theological point of view.[2]

A tension strains our relationship with God. As we can see from the creation story in Genesis 2, we human beings live in the tension between soil and

---

[1] This chapter continues where a previous discussion left off. See: Ted Peters, "Genes and Sin", ch. 10 of *Sin: Radical Evil in Soul and Society* (Grand Rapids MI: Eerdmans, 1994). This chapter's argument overlaps with the content of lectures delivered at Goshen College, March 2007. See: Ted Peters, *The Evolution of Terrestrial and Extraterrestrial Life: Where in the World is God?* forthcoming from Pandora Press and the Australian Theological Forum.

[2] Steven Pinker complains that the dominant theory of human nature in Western society has been that of the Judeo-Christian tradition. He describes the Judeo-Christian anthropology in trivial almost laughable terms, then he cites an opinion poll showing that 76 percent of Americans believe in the biblical account of creation. This popular religious anthropology which he belittles should be surpassed by a scientific anthropology, he proposes. "The modern sciences of cosmology, geology, biology, and archaeology have made it impossible for a scientifically literate person to believe that the biblical story of creation actually took place. As a result, the Judeo-Christian theory of human nature is no longer explicitly avowed by most academics, journalists, social analysts, and other intellectually engaged people." *The Blank Slate: The Modern Denial of Human Nature* (New York: Viking, 2002) 2. Pinker compares an opinion poll version of religious anthropology with a sophisticated version of science for "intellectually engaged" academics. This is like rejecting little league baseball because one plays for the Detroit Tigers or Oakland Athletics. Our challenge here is to explicate a theological anthropology at the level of the Boston Red Sox or New York Yankees.

spirit, between what is mundane and what is transcendent. This tension is reflected in the two essential elements within Christian anthropology, namely, the *imago dei* and the fall into sin. Our harmony with God is emphasized in the concept of the image of God [*imago dei* in Latin or *eikon tou Theou* in Greek] where the resurrected Christ fulfills on our behalf the image of God. As we participate with Christ in resurrection and new creation, we too take on and fulfill the image of God in us.

It is the other element within Christian anthropology which will occupy us in this chapter and in this book, namely, the understanding of the human being as estranged from God due to our sinful condition. We begin not with a story of a temporal event: Adam and Eve falling from paradise into the wilderness of malice and perdition. Rather, we start with the observation that human beings individually and in groups are violent, seeking to prop up their own communities with social harmony by demonizing outsiders and telling lies to make their own home life secure and prosperous. We will ask: what accounts for this characteristic of the human condition? Perhaps evolution accounts for it, especially evolution seen through the eyes of sociobiology.

In what follows we will explicate the central thesis of sociobiology (along with that of evolutionary psychology), namely: genetic replication is the force that directs and drives evolutionary history and generates human culture, including ethics and religion. We will refer to this core thesis as the "selfish gene" theory.[3] We will also call this "genetic determinism", but with qualifications. We will ask: can we attribute the origin of human sin and our inherited propensity for violence to genetic determinism? Our answer will be an exploratory and hypothetical "yes". The selfish gene thesis is here a hypothesis worth testing.

Our explication of sociobiology will include doubts regarding its scientific credibility. Proponents of sociobiology like to think of themselves as doing science. It is not clear that this field qualifies as a science, however, because it avoids empirical experimentation on its subject matter, namely, human persons in culture. Be that as it may, we wish for theology to become informed by this field. Even if it turns out that sociobiology is eventually discredited as a science, this exercise in dialogue with theology is still worth pursuing. The concept of original sin in the form of inherited sin needs to place itself in conversation with the concept of biological determinism in principle, and sociobiology provides a sufficiently good example.

Genes and Genocide

When I think of the worst of human evils, the medieval list of the seven deadly sins—greed, gluttony, lust, sloth, pride, envy, and wrath—does not come to

---

[3] The selfish gene theory appears on the stage of discussion with the 1976 publication of Richard Dawkins, *The Selfish Gene* (Oxford and New York: Oxford University Press, [2]1989).

mind. All these are character distortions; and, to be sure, they deserve biological as well as psychological and theological attention. But into my mind enters the image of graver evils, horrendous evils, unspeakable evils, unfathomable evils. Cruelty nears the top slot of the worst of the worst for me. Yet, there is something even worse. In my mind, the worst evil I can think of is genocide. Following World War II in 1948, the United Nations General Assembly adopted the *Convention on the Prevention and Punishment of the Crime of Genocide*. The UN defined genocide as an act or acts "committed with intent to destroy, in whole or in part, a national, ethnic, racial, or religious group". The historical genocides we know about include cruelty right along with a plan to eliminate an entire group of human beings defined as outsiders, at least outsiders to the group of killers.

What is so significant for theology is the fact that the murderers in a genocide are not pursuing evil for the sake of evil. They are pursuing violence and destruction and cruelty and elimination of an entire group of persons in the name of something they deem to be good, usually the welfare of their own group. Jesus referred to such self-justification as hypocrisy. Genocide is found together with hypocrisy, although the former is more deadly than the latter.

Up until recently theologians could routinely distinguish between moral evil and natural evil. Moral evil is what free human beings do; so we are told. Natural evil refers to human suffering that results from an uncontrollable event in nature—a flood, tornado, earthquake, drought, or such. Because it is natural, it is amoral, even though people suffer. Insurance companies refer to natural evil as "acts of God".

What happens with sociobiology is that moral evil and natural evil become conflated, undistinguishable. By removing primary agency from the decisions of allegedly free human persons, what we previously thought was moral perversion becomes an expression of a more basic biological nature. The agenda of genetic replication now explains why people engage in familial, ethnic, racial, social, cultural, and religious activities that occupy us. Because each gene seeks its immortality at the expense of competing genes, we now have a natural explanation for genocide, literally, the killing of genes. When one national, ethnic, racial, or religious group attempts to murder and eliminate an entire competitor group, we can now explain this according to Darwinian principles: it is simply the way that the fittest genes survive. Human genocides can now be understood as natural, as obeying the bidding of our genes.

Now that genocide has a genetic explanation, we might ask whether it remains in the category of moral evil or not. Does it dissolve into natural evil? Does all that we believe human morality to be dissolve into naturalistic categories? This may be an interesting question, but simply deciding which category to employ is not my agenda here. Whether we call it moral evil or natural evil, theologically speaking, a genocide remains a horrendous evil. More than an explanation, we need salvation.

Methodological Preliminaries

I forecast that I will find consonance between what we learn scientifically and what we find important theologically. That is to say, I begin with the assumption that serious theology and honest science are compatible. More specifically, I begin with the assumption that a Darwinian model of human evolution will, upon investigation, turn out to be compatible with Christian anthropology. I do not share a conflictual predisposition on this issue, according to which the success of a biological explanation for human behavior would diminish a theological explanation and vice versa. I do not expect theology to automatically gain if sociobiology loses in the race to provide explanatory adequacy. Rather, I assume that, if genuine science provides us with an accurate picture of human biological history and human nature, we will find it is consonant with the best insights of the Christian tradition.

Now for a caveat. I must confess, I actually do not believe sociobiology counts as good science. The best I can say about the field is that it might turn out to be a good guess. But, because it has no empirical evidence produced by genetic studies of human beings to support it, it remains in the category of a guess at best, an ideology at worst. Be that as it may, I still would like to explore its implications just in case this guess turns out to be right. Even if the selfish gene theory within sociobiology fails to obtain empirical confirmation, we may still discover other significant biological determinants for human nature and human behavior. With that eventuality in mind, I would like to invest theological energy in drawing out the potential significance of this representative field for Christian anthropology.

Does Sin Originate with Selfish Genes?

The field of sociobiology and its second generation heir, evolutionary psychology, prompts theological reflection on two counts. The first is the hypothesis of genetic determinism or, more precisely, genetic reductionism. Theologians need to ask: are classical conflicts such as that between flesh and spirit better understood within the single domain of the flesh? The second is the hypothesis that specific forms of human consciousness and behavior such as the propensity for tribalism and bloodshed are genetically determined. Theologians need to ask: might we have here a scientific explanation for original sin or, more accurately, inherited sin? If the answer to these two questions is affirmative, then this leads to a third: how does this fit with the Christian understanding of God making a good creation?

Robert Wright sets the evolutionary dinner right before the theologian's eyes. On the plate is the challenge that original sin can be explained genetically, or at least in terms of Charles Darwin's theory of natural selection. "The roots of all evil can be seen in natural selection, and are expressed (along with much that is good) in human nature. The enemy of justice and decency does indeed lie in our genes."[4] Gregory Peterson makes the turn to theology. "In sociobiology, original sin becomes naturalized, providing both an origins story and an account of human behavior."[5] To try to determine just what the theologian should imbibe from the sociobiologist or evolutionary psychologist is the task to which we now turn.

Richard Dawkins and Edward O. Wilson have been the progenitors of the sociobiological agenda and have continued to nurture its development for three decades. They provide the paradigm within which additional reasoning and expansion are emitted. The hard core center of the paradigm is the concept of the *selfish gene*.

According to the selfish gene theory, the driving force of evolutionary history is the driving force of DNA which wants to replicate itself. The incessant and aggressive advance of in tact DNA sequences provides the explanatory principle for the history of life on our planet, for the behavior of all organisms, and for human culture, ethics, and religion. It is the DNA sequence (or gene in the loose sense of the word) which employs reproduction for the purposes of its own perpetuation into future individuals and gaining protection through the establishment of new species that will carry on this particular genetic code. The adjective "selfish" applied to "gene" indicates the hegemony over biological development exercised by DNA self-replication.[6]

The organism is DNA's way of making more DNA. One might think that an egg is a chicken's way of making more chickens. But, the reverse is the case. A chicken is an egg's way of making more eggs. Organisms and populations of organisms are transport vehicles for DNA sequences to attain their own immortality through replication. "We, and all other animals, are machines created by our genes", writes Richard Dawkins.[7]

Reproductive success is the goal of genes in making machines, such as us. "Successful genes are genes that, in the environment influenced by all the other genes in a shared embryo, have beneficial effects on that embryo. Beneficial means that they make the embryo likely to develop into a successful adult, an adult likely to reproduce and pass those very same genes on to future generations."[8]

---

[4] Robert Wright, *The Moral Animal* (New York: Pantheon Books, 1994) 151.
[5] Gregory R. Peterson, "Falling Up: Evolution and Original Sin", in: Philip Clayton and Jeffrey Schloss (ed.), *Evolution and Ethics*, (Grand Rapids MI: Eerdmans, 2004) 273.
[6] What is taking place here is that agency is being removed from the organism and located in the gene, or more accurately, in the DNA sequence. This is not necessarily a moral understanding of "selfish", because it describes the drive for replication at any and all cost. It may or may not make the organism selfish. For Richard Dawkins, the idea of the selfish gene explains why we have selfish people. However, Michael Ruse says, "selfish genes do not necessarily cash out as selfish people", in: "Evolutionary Ethics Past and Present", in: *Evolution and Ethics*, 44.
[7] Dawkins, *Selfish Gene*, 2.
[8] Ibid., 235.

DNA sequences compete with one another for immortality. "Genes are immortals, or rather, they are defined as genetic entities that come close to deserving the title."[9] The concept of "survival-of-the-fittest" coming from Herbert Spencer and Charles Darwin is now applied to the fittest DNA sequence, not to the organisms or species that live longer. Reproductive fitness now refers to the achievement of a particular genetic code to produce organisms that reach reproductive age, produce babies, and thereby perpetuate their genetic code into immortality. If organisms compete with one another, and if one population decimates a competitor, then the genes of the victor live on. The winning genes will have defined themselves as more reproductively fit.

What the field of evolutionary psychology adds to the initial sociobiological model is a more creative role for the human brain and an emphasis on decisive events in the history of natural selection, referred to as the EEA or Environment of Evolutionary Adaptedness. The adaptationist approach therefore associates specific human behaviors with the result of a natural selection process in a period during which those behaviors would have given our distant ancestors a survival advantage. Jerome Barkow, Leda Cosmides and John Tooby, authors of *The Adapted Mind*, identify the key assumptions of the field: "there is a universal human nature, but…this universality exists primarily at the level of evolved psychological mechanisms, not of expressed cultural behaviors…cultural variability is not a challenge to claims of universality…the human mind is adapted to the way of the Pleistocene hunter-gatherers, and not necessarily to our modern circumstances."[10] Because our physical brains and hence our minds were formed during the decisive Pleistocene EEA thousands of years ago during a much more primitive time in which human beings were adapting to a quite different environment, we understand why we see maladaptations to our modern industrialized society. Our modern skulls house a stone age mind.[11] Genes are still firmly in the driver's seat, to be sure; but the human brain has become a complex vehicle for helping to ensure reproductive fitness.[12]

---

[9] Ibid., 34.

[10] Jerome Barkow, Leda Cosmides, and John Tooby, *The Adapted Mind: Evolutionary Psychology and the Generation of Culture* (New York: Oxford University Press, 1992) 5.

[11] Taken from "Evolutionary Psychology: A Primer" found online at http://www.psych.ucsb.edu/research/cep/primer.html. One might ask: how did our stone age minds produce a culture that transcends the stone age? The environment did not change all by itself; we altered the environment. If we have stone age minds, how did we build the modern world to which we are now maladapted?

[12] Philip Clayton believes we develop a sense of self that cannot be reduced to either gene or brain activity. "I maintain, the world of subjective awareness is neither equivalent to, nor reducible to, the physical structures of the brain." "Conclusion: Biology and Purpose: Altruism, Morality, and Human Nature in Evolutionary Perspective", in: *Evolution and Ethics*, 327. Gregory Peterson elaborates on this point. He is reluctant to grant, based on molecular biology, that genes have a direct relationship to human behavior. Why? Because gene expression passes through brain activity, and the variety of brain options is disproportionately vast. "While there are about thirty thousand

Human Pawns in the Genetic Chess Game

Whether using the sociobiology model or the evolutionary psychology model, the central thesis is this: we human beings as individuals and as families are pawns in this giant genetic chess game. When we try to defeat *our* competitors, we are being used by our genes to checkmate *their* competitors. Every aspect of our lives—our loving and hating, our fighting and cooperating, our giving and stealing, our greed and generosity—are but subplots in the larger evolutionary drama. When in our daily life we experience ourselves acting selfishly, we can appeal to an underlying biological explanation. We are selfish because our genes are selfish.

Human daily life is by no means limited to selfish behavior, to be sure. We have our moments of caring, of devotion, of high minded sharing and cooperation. This too finds a sociobiological explanation, the same explanation. Our caring and sharing are explained as "kin altruism" and "reciprocal altruism". The selfish gene uses our altruistic behavior to perpetuate itself. How? Because the selfish gene can use groups: kin, families, tribes, races. Within a kinship group which shares the same DNA sequence, individuals can cooperate with one another and even in rare instances sacrifice themselves on behalf of their loved ones' safety. The sacrifice of one individual so that other individuals can reach reproductive age and have babies still counts as a success for the selfish gene. The gene will successfully replicate itself as long as the survivor of a crisis bears the preferred genetic code.

The logic here demands careful scrutiny. Altruism occurs within a range of genetic continuity, so that those showing altruistic behavior towards one another share the specific DNA sequence. Outsiders—that is, organisms or tribes that do not share the DNA sequence in question—do not deserve self-sacrificial service. Self-sacrificial service remains within genetic limits.

Outside the kin group where genes are not shared, one group might cooperate with another for survival. Both groups survive because of this cooperation. The genes of both persist through reproduction. This has been called "reciprocal altruism", since introduced by Robert Trivers.[13]

This model is based on the concept of "inclusive fitness". Survival-of-the-fittest is measured here in terms of the number of copies of a gene or DNA sequence that is passed on to subsequent generations. This passing on can be direct or indirect. An organism can pass on genes directly by making more babies. Or, an organism can assist another organism with the same or similar

---

to forty thousand genes in the human genome, there are on the order of 100 billion neurons in the human brain. Not only is it impossible for so few genes to program instructions for every neuron, it is unlikely that genes program the brain in the narrowly specific way that is sometimes suggested by evolutionary psychology." "Falling Up", 281.

[13] See: Robert L. Trivers, "The Evolution of Reciprocal Altruism", Quarterly Review of Biology, 46, 1971, 35–57.

genome to have more babies. This indirect form of fitness is called "altruism" (in both its kin and reciprocal forms). Inclusive fitness includes both the direct and indirect.

Further, within the range of genetic kinhsip, a hierarchy is constructed. Those closest to us in kinship are more deserving of self-sacrificial love than those who are genetically more distant. A parent, for example, is more likely to sacrifice his or her own well being on behalf of a child who shares fifty percent of his or her genes than for a distant cousin who shares a lower percentage.[14]

This leads to a formula that distinguishes between genetic insiders and genetic outsiders. Outsiders are seen as genetic competitors, subject to elimination. Within the group of insiders, those more genetically proximate benefit most from one's altruistic behavior; and those more genetically distant will receive proportionately less loyalty. According to this logic, the most altruistic individuals would be clones or identical twins, who serve one another because the net result is the passing on to the next generation of their entire genome. Parents would be somewhat less devoted to their biological children—not adopted children—because fifty percent of their genome will get passed on. Devotion to service decreases proportionately for nieces and nephews. No altruism is expected for strangers or aliens or anyone outside the genetically determined family, clan, tribe, or race.

In 1964 a precursor to what would become sociobiology, William Hamilton, produced an actual formula (rB > C) calculating that a sacrificial action could be identified if the cost (C) to the actor would be less than the benefit (B) to the recipient, times the degree of genetic relatedness (r).[15] If the individuals are unrelated (r = 0), then no altruism should occur. *Hamilton's Rule*

---

[14] When sociobiologists or evolutionary psychologists say it this way, it is misleading. Molecular biologists would point out that all human beings share more than 99 % of their genes with the human race generally. The fraction that distinguishes one individual is less than one percent. So, the 50 % genetic continuity between parents and children is only 50 % of that fraction, not 50 % of the entire human genome.

[15] William D. Hamilton, "The Genetical Evolution of Social Behavior I", The Journal of Theoretical Biology 7 1964, 1–16. For more on Hamilton's Rule, see:Louise Barrett, Robin Dunbar and Jon Lycett, *Human Evolutionary Psychology* (Princeton and Oxford: Princeton University Press, 2002) 26 f. It appears that the widespread practice of adoption would falsify the predictions of kin selection theory, because parents who love their adopted children and raise them to reproductive age would not be promoting their own genes. But, upon closer look, researchers found "adopted children were often discriminated against in favour of the couple's own biological children". Ibid., 50. Whew. A close call, but the theory still stands. What could be included in future studies might be the reason for adoption: why would parents allegedly driven by the selfish gene toward inclusive fitness give up their children before insuring they have reached reproductive age? Why is it that genetically proximate parents abandon children and genetically distant parents invest themselves in raising these children? It must be admitted that no "simple unitary adaptive explanation for adoption" exists. So, evolutionary psychologists speculate: "[...] it may be that adoption in western society is possibly an instance where modern behaviour has been forced off-track with

combined with Triver's phrase, "reciprocal altruism", laid the foundation for what would become sociobiology. The point is that, allegedly, the further the genetic distance the less likely acts of sacrificial altruism will occur. For those whose genetic code is very distant and who are seen as DNA competitors, war and murder and even genocide become the order of the day.

Groups can serve other groups, and they can receive protection from groups that are genetically other or different. Such group selection and co-operation can occur when the reciprocity is viewed as genetically beneficial for both groups. The sociobiological model needs to be expanded to include indirect reciprocity. Ultimately, still, what furthers gene immortality governs even complex social arrangements at the organism level.

Altruistic behavior is actually selfish behavior. It promotes the long term goal of the selfish gene, namely, to perpetuate its own DNA sequence. Even though at the level of the organism altruism may appear to us to be virtuous, the underlying drive of the gene to replicate is relentless and pitiless. "Scratch an 'altruist', and watch a 'hypocrite' bleed", has become a motto.[16]

Significant in its implications for theological anthropology is the possibility of genetic factors underlying the human propensity for dividing the human race into insiders and outsiders, accompanied by the justification for treating outsiders violently. Oh yes, by "genetic determinism" we refer to the entire interaction of genes and environment necessary for the mechanism of natural selection to work; but what is important for the theologian here is that we apparently are born with a biology inherited from evolution that predisposes us to divide the human race into friends and foes. Edward O. Wilson writes, "human beings are strongly predisposed to respond with unreasoning hatred to external threats and to escalate their hostility sufficiently to overwhelm the source of threat by a respectable wide margin of safety. Our brains do appear to be programmed to the following extent: we are inclined to partition other people into friends and aliens."[17]

When we apply this to Christian values such as self-sacrificial love or *agape*, we find a theological idea that simply does not fit into the selfish gene scheme. Kin altruism within a family, clan, or tribe or perhaps even a race fits the selfish gene theory, because love and care within the kin group would promote reproductive fitness for the DNA sequence in question. Reciprocal altruism accomplishes the same end, even if a bit more indirectly. But to extend this loving service to someone who is other, to someone outside the kinship circle or outside the circle of reciprocators, simply does not fit this explanatory

---

negative consequences for inclusive fitness". Ibid., 51. Whew. By declaring adoption to be "off-track" the theory is saved again.

[16] M. Ghiselin, *The Economy of Nature and the Evolution of Sex* (Berkeley and Los Angeles: University of California Press, 1974) 247.

[17] Edward O. Wilson, *On Human Nature* (New York: Bantam Books, 1978) 122.

model. "Much as we wish to believe otherwise", comments Dawkins, "universal love and the welfare of the species as a whole are concepts that simply do not make evolutionary sense".[18] The theologian must ask: is this genetic explanation accurate? If so, does it reinforce the Christian understanding of sin as an inherited disposition toward selfishness? Does it render as hopelessly idealistic the Christian ethic of self-sacrificial love?

Regardless of our connecting the Christian ethic of *agape* love to this discussion, it seems that the central claims of sociobiology and evolutionary psychology should command the interest of the theological community. "The origins of sinfulness, it would seem", says Gregory Peterson, "are rooted not in the act of an original, historical couple, but in the complicated evolutionary process itself…Yet, strictly speaking, such a perspective is not in direct conflict with the theological tradition, and further reflection suggests that there is much to commend it."[19]

Molecular Biology vs. Sociobiology

At this point we need to interrupt our exposition and analysis to clarify four items. First, we need to distinguish between two types of genetic determinism. One type would derive from molecular biology. Molecular biologists study DNA sequences in the laboratory and try to determine which gene produces which protein for the body. These are empirical scientists who study specific gene expression. This is not what we find at work in the sociobiological approach.

"What is a selfish gene?" asks Dawkins. "It is not just one single physical bit of DNA […] it is *all replicas* of a particular bit of DNA."[20] Any DNA sequence, with any number of genes, can be engaged in DNA replication. This is the core principle of sociobiology. What a specific gene does for our body is not relevant; what is relevant is that each and every gene or DNA sequence drives toward replication from generation to generation.

Sociobiologists do not study any genes directly. Rather, sociobiologists along with evolutionary psychologists advance a hard core hypothesis that DNA sequences seek to replicate themselves regardless of which genes appear within those DNA sequences. The brute force of gene replication is the explanatory principle. *Human behavior is explained as the result of gene replication, not as the result of gene expression.* It is this replication theory that occupies our attention in this discussion. In the event that molecular biologists would find specific gene complexes which in their expression lead to either sinful or altruistic behavior, it would not count in the sociobiological calculus. All that counts is brute replication, regardless of which genes are in question.

---

[18] Dawkins, *Selfish Gene*, 2.
[19] Peterson, "Falling Up", 283.
[20] Ibid., 88.

The field of molecular biology would stimulate a very different theological analysis from one beginning with sociobiology.

Second, the phrase "genetic determinism" should be employed somewhat loosely, though seriously. It refers to a focus of study; it should not connote independence of genes over against their interaction with the environment.[21] Sociobiology sets genetic determinism within the larger Darwinian model of evolution, which automatically incorporates the role of natural selection; hence, it presupposes an interaction between genes and environment. Environmental interaction is an important factor in the selection of which DNA sequences get replicated.[22] The concept of genetic determinism is inclusive of environmental factors in natural selection as well as translation through brain activity. The opposites of genetic determinism are not environmental determinism but rather such items as self-determination or mind or spirit or culture or even God.

We should further note that for molecular biologists as well as behavioral geneticists the term "determinism" refers to the search for naturalistic explanations. "In truth", writes behavioral geneticist Lindon Eaves, "genetic theories of human bevhaviour are neither more nor less 'deterministic' than environmental theories. Determinism is a theoretical construct implicit in most, if not all, scientific theories of behaviour because they seek to explain behavioural phenomena in terms of underlying biological and social causes."[23] More important to the theologian than genetic determinism is genetic reductionism— that is, asking whether the method can account for non-materialistic factors such as selfhood or personhood.[24] Theologians can live comfortably with genetic determinism; it is genetic reductionism that poses the challenge.

---

[21] With reference to the Human Genome Project, Matt Ridley writes, "I believe human behavior has to be explained by both nature and nurture [...] the more we lift the lid on the genome, the more vulnerable to experience genes appear". *Nature via Nurture* (San Francisco: Harper, 2003) 3f.

[22] Gregory Peterson makes it even more complex. "Any genetic programming that does go on is a complex interaction of genes, body, environment, and self that is difficult to disentangle." "Falling Up", 281. Even so, one must ask whether Sociobiology fits the Darwinian model. According to the original Darwin model, random variation in inheritance gave natural selection the opportunity to cultivate new species over time. When in the Twentieth Century the field of molecular biology explained random variation in terms of unpredictable genetic mutations, the Neo-Darwinian synthesis became the dominant theory of evolutionary biology. The sociobiologists, to the contrary, presuppose a principle of DNA stability that precludes random variation. The gene wants to replicate itself in tact. If the genes are in biological control of the replication process, then how can a sociogiologist account for what is observable under a microscope, namely, random genetic mutations?

[23] Lindon Eaves, "'Ought' in a World that Just 'Is'", in: Willem B. Drees (ed.), *Is Nature Ever Evil?* (London and New York: Routledge, 2003) 305.

[24] Biologist Jeffrey P. Schloss locates the methodological concern: "What is significant here is not the determinism but the reductive reconceptualization from organism as agent to organism as instrument." "Surveying the Issues", Evolution and Ethics, 5.

Third, an observation about methodology. How, we might ask, do sociobiologists arrive at theories such as the selfish gene or reciprocal altruism or a formula for kin preference in the human race? What is their method of study? The answer is: analogy. Wilson studies social behavior in non-human animals such as insects—behavior such as aggression, sexual habits, reciprocal altruism, and such—and then by analogy he applies this to human society. Because human beings share with nonhuman animals common descent in Darwinian terms, what we witness as human social organization is one more form of adaptation for the purpose of extending the future of the genes we carry. Note that he does not perform empirical research on human beings, even though he draws conclusions about human beings. Does an argument by analogy count as science?

Michael Ruse finds this satisfactory. "The sociobiologists argue that in some cases it is legitimate to argue from non-humans to humans. Hence, we have analogical support for the genetic basis of human behavior."[25] Now, Ruse believes "analogsy *per se* is not a bad argument".[26] Yet I would like to ask: if sociobiology claims to be a science, then why does it not provide empirical study on the subject matter it deals with, namely, the connection between human gene replication and human behavior at the level of culture? Could sociobiological researchers conduct the same experiments with human beings that they already conduct with ants? If so, and if the theory generates progressive knowledge, then it could be admitted into the halls of science. In the meantime, I for one find an argument by analogy insufficient to count as reliable knowledge about human behavior.

Despite my demure, sociobiology along with its child, evolutionary psychology, is popular. However, the popularity of the field ought not count in favor of its scientific veracity. Still, Steven Pinker brags about its popularity as if this should give it intellectual respect. "In the study of animal behavior, no one even talks about 'sociobiology' or 'selfish genes' anymore, because the ideas are part and parcel of the science. In the study of humans, there are major spheres of human experience—beauty, motherhood, kinship, morality, cooperation, sexuality, violence—in which evolutionary psychology provides the only coherent theory and has spawned vibrant new areas of empirical research."[27] Until these new areas of research find empirical corroboration for the basic theory in molecular and genetic studies or in sociological studies, we simply cannot know if this is science or snake oil.

Fourth, one more item requires clarification. Although purpose language is used by sociobiologists to describe the drive toward replication, they say this

---

[25] Michael Ruse, *Sociobiology: Sense or Nonsense?* (Dordrecht, Boston, and Lancaster: D. Reidel, ²1985) 61.

[26] Ibid., 142. "In theory one can argue analogically from the primates to humans; but in practice I am far from convinced that the sociobiologists have yet provided enough evidence to do so." Ibid., 145.

[27] Pinker, *Blank Slate*, 135.

is only metaphorical. Dawkins denies purpose at the biological level. "Natural selection favours replicators that are good at building survival machines, genes that are skilled in the art of controlling embryonic development. In this, the replicators are no more conscious or purposeful than they ever were. The same old processes of automatic selection between rival molecules by reason of their longevity, fecundity, and copying fidelity, still go on…blindly."[28] This is no small point for sociobiology. Nihilism is an integral assumption. "The universe we observe has precisely the properties we should expect if there is, at bottom, no design, no purpose, no evil and no good, nothing but blind, pitiless indifference."[29] The combination of genetic reductionism with materialist nihilism ought to wake theologians up so that they take notice of the picture of the world being painted by this field of thought.

With these four observations in mind, let us return to our exposition and analysis.

Gene Replication and Human Ethics

We might want to ask Edward O. Wilson whether religious ethics might have the power to reverse the direction of our genetic determinism and guide us successfully toward loving outsiders, strangers, and aliens. This would be impossible according to Wilson's version of sociobiology. The genetic determinism is too strong. "Can the cultural evolution of higher ethical values gain a direction and momentum of its own and completely replace genetic evolution? I think not. The genes hold culture on a leash. The leash is very long, but inevitably values will be constrained in accordance with their effects on the human gene pool."[30]

Regardless of the length of the leash, it holds securely to all of human culture, including ethics, morality, and religion. Although Wilson "favors a purely material origin of ethics",[31] he does not advocate the brutal social ideology of Spencerism or Nazism. Instead of an ethic of dog eat dog, Wilson believes our society ought to embrace altruism and cooperation. On what grounds? Because "cooperative individuals generally survive longer and leave more offspring", he argues.[32] He tethers his ethic of social cooperation to the leash of reproductive fitness. Despite the selfish gene and survival-of-the-fittest, he contends we ought to support modern liberal values such as human rights over against premodern tribalism and xenophobia. Is there a contradiction

---

[28] Dawkins, *Selfish Gene*, 24.
[29] Richard Dawkins, *River Out of Eden* (New York: HarperCollins, Basic Books, 1995) 133.
[30] Edward O. Wilson, "Ethics, Evolution, and the Milk of Human Kindness", in: Arthur Caplan (ed.), *The Sociobiology* (New York: Harper & Row, 1978) 313.
[31] Edward O. Wilson, *Consilience: The Unity of Knowledge* (New York: Alfred A. Knopf, 1998) 241.
[32] Ibid., 253.

operative here? Does striving for universal human rights run counter to kin preference and the tribal values that serve the selfish gene? Is this an expression of genetic determinism or an override? "Human nature can adapt to more encompassing forms of altruism and social justice. Genetic biases can be trespassed" in favor of universal social cooperation, says Wilson.[33]

Wilson is inconsistent, complains Holmes Rolston III. How can a sociobiologist tether all ethics to the genetic leash and then suddenly cut the leash? "Just where is Wilson getting these *oughts* that cannot be derived from biology, unless from the insights of ethicists (or theologians) that transcend biology? This no longer sounds like a biologist biologicizing ethics and philosophy. It sounds like a biologist philosophizing without acknowledging his sources."[34] It would seem that any biologist who is serious about grounding ethics in evolution would have to follow in the footsteps of Spencer and draw the conclusions of Hitler. To advocate such things as altruism, cooperation, or universal human rights would require appeal to ethical norms that are extra-biological, perhaps even theological. Intellectual honesty would require such acknowledgement, says Rolston.

Dawkins might diverge slightly from Wilson on just how to move from sociobiology to ethics. Whereas Wilson wants to hold that his liberal values derive from his animal nature, Dawkins will allow some slippage between biology and values. According to Dawkins, we can defy our genes. We can lift our cultural values off from their original biological substrate. "We, alone on earth, can rebel against the tyranny of the selfish replicators."[35]. This implies that religion, which is a form of culture, is capable of successfully promoting liberal values applicable to the universal human race. We are not foredoomed to serve the division of the human race into insiders and outsiders. We are capable of overcoming racial and ethnic prejudice and establishing social justice.

What seems curious as we draw out the implications of sociobiological theory is the tug of war between genetic determinism and cultural transcendence. If all of human culture, including religion and ethics, was invented by our genes for the purpose of promoting reproductive fitness, then how could an ethic arise such as the Christian ethic of self-sacrificial love for the outsider or the Enlightenment ethic of universal human dignity? Is such an ethic still

---

[33] Edward O. Wilson, "Human Decency is Animal", New York Times Magazine, October 12, 1975, 50. Actually, Wilson gives two incompatible arguments for valuing universal human rights. On the one hand, he argues that such a valuing takes us beyond kin preference and, hence, beyond genetic influence. On the other hand, he also argues that valuing universal human rights is an extension of kin preference in mammals. See: *On Human Nature*, 198 f. For a critique of the latter argument, see Mikael Stenmark, *Scientism* (Aldershot UK: Ashgate, 2001) 68–77.

[34] Holmes Rolston, III, *Genes, Genesis, and God* (Cambridge: Cambridge University Press, 1999) 267.

[35] Dawkins, *Selfish Gene*, 201. Despite the similarity of the two versions of sociobiology, Dawkins claims that he and Wilson arrived at the theory simultaneously yet independently. "Wilson and I had independently introduced the same mutant meme!" Ibid., 328.

invisibly in service of the selfish genes; or is it an example of culture transcending its evolutionary history? Dawkins admits that such an ethic makes no evolutionary sense; yet he encourages us to rebel against the tyranny of our genes and rise up to embrace modern liberal ethics. Just how we get from where we came from to where Dawkins would like us to go is unclear.

Is Racial Prejudice Genetic?

Among molecular biologists in the era of the Human Genome Project, a theory regarding the variety of races within the human species began developing and gaining empirical confirmation. The essential hypothesis is that racial divisions are not due to wide divergences in genomes. To date, the genetic reasons for racial divisions have not been found. It appears from empirical examination that the genetic difference between two individuals is greater than the collective genetic difference between members of one race and those of another race. Sharp lines cannot be drawn between racial groups.[36]

The implications are significant. It appears that the lines between insiders and outsiders cannot be due to the quantity of shared genes. The formula with which Dawkins and other sociobiologists work cannot be confirmed by counting the genes. The insider group, for all practical purposes, is the entire human race.

Dawkins admits this. Despite Dawkins' reliance upon a formula that says organisms will protect those genetically more proximate and wish genocide on those more genetically distant, he refrains from applying it at the human level to ethnic rivalry and racial prejudice. He cannot deny that the entire human race is a single species; we can mate with one another regardless of race.

How does this factual knowledge influence the application of sociobiological theory to the actual human situation? Dawkins resorts to explaining human tribalism and ethnic rivalry as a product of culture, not gene replication. He attributes it to mating patterns established by ethnic and religious traditions. "Because our mating decisions are so heavily influenced by cultural tradition, and because our cultures, and sometimes our religions, encourage us to discriminate against outsiders, especially in choosing mates, those superficial differences that helped our ancestors to prefer insiders over outsiders have been enhanced out of all proportion to the real genetic differences between us."[37]

In struggling for integrating this molecular observation into his explanatory model, Dawkins comes up with two alternatives, a strong theory and a weak theory. According to the strong theory, skin color and other conspicuous ge-

---

[36] See my earlier discussion of genes and race in *Playing God? Genetic Determinism and Human Freedom* (London and New York: Routledge, ²2002) 84.

[37] Richard Dawkins, *The Ancestor's Tale: A Pilgrimage to the Dawn of Evolution* (Boston and New York: Houghton Mifflin Co., 2004) 411.

netic badges evolved actively as discriminators in selecting mates. According to the weak theory, geographical distances along with cultural differences such as language and religion led to the eventual separation of the single human race into multiple racial groups. The two theories could be combined, of course. Original genetic determinism in dialectical relation to natural selection eventually evolved into cultural determinism which, in turn, now influences which genes survive and become immortal. At some point, culture took leave of its biological origin and now returns to influence biological evolution.

Susan Blackmore extends the Dawkins auxiliary hypothesis to the point of saying that culture in the form of religion actually influences genetic selection. In tribal society, the genetic formula for kin preference governs. In multi-tribal society or modern city life, effective governments reduce the bloodshed due to tribal rivalry. Cities are safe. Yet, nations go to war. Why? Because religion redraws the lines between insiders and outsiders. Now soldiers without proximate genes fight side by side with enemies of their shared religion. "The history of warfare is largely a history of people killing each other for religious reasons. Religions give people a motive, other than genetic self-interest, for self-sacrificing their lives for others—something that does not happen in band and tribal societies."[38] With Dawkins and Blackmore, the selfish gene fixed the paradigm that has been copied by culture; and now culture in the form of religion behaves genetically but no longer for genetic reasons. This seems to be the logic of this branch of sociobiology.

The ethical import of this is what we want to focus on. It appears that Dawkins followed by Blackmore are telling us that back in earlier stages of evolutionary history it was the formula for DNA sequence survival that created the differences between insiders and outsiders. The selfish genes gave rise to culture and to religion and to ethnic traditions which favored one genetic code over its competitors. Then, at some point, human intelligence became an independent force and culture lifted itself off its biological base. Not entirely, however. The legacy of preferring insiders over outsiders persists, even though now the justification is no longer genetic but only apparently genetic. Racial differences, if I understand Dawkins correctly, are due to apparent genetic differences but not actual differences.

This position is accompanied by an egregious anti-religious bias. Blackmore fears that evolution has so molded the human brain that we have become genetically receptive to religious ideas or memes. This saddens Blackmore. Yet, she does not give up hope. "Perhaps our brains and minds have been molded to be naturally religious and it really is difficult to see logic and scientific evidence to change the way we think—difficult, but not impossible."[39] Black-

---

[38] Susan Blackmore, *The Meme Machine* (Oxford and New York: Oxford University Press, 1999) 199.
[39] Ibid., 202.

more's insiders include her friend Richard Dawkins and perhaps others; all religious people have become outsiders. Her hope is evidently that through the power of culture scientific ideas will render religious ideas extinct and her favorite memes will become immortal. According to this revised version of sociobiology, culture parallels genetics while transcending its genetic history.

What we see here is an attempt to patch up the original sociobiological theory with auxiliary hypotheses that take into account countervailing evidence. Had today's molecular biologists been able to prove that racial differences are due to significant genetic differences, then Dawkins could have used this to support his formula. But, because today's molecular biologists suggest that all human beings, regardless of race, are genetically proximate, Dawkins resorts to culture and religion to explain apparent genetic conflict. Sociobiological theory just does not want to admit failure at providing an explanation, no matter how disconfirming the empirical evidence.

Chimps and Men as Killers

Regardless of the credibility of the theory of sociobiology, what it observes about human violence cries out for explanation. When we look at the archaeological record, we see human beings have been engaged in violent if not genocidal behavior for as far back as evidence provides. "Buried in the ground and hidden in caves lie silent witnesses to a bloody prehistory stretching back hundreds of thousands of years. They include skeletons with scalping marks, ax-shaped dents, and arrowheads embedded in them; weapons like tomahawks and maces that are useless for hunting but specialized for homicide; fortification defenses such as palisades of sharpened sticks; and paintings from several continents showing men firing arrows, spears, or boomerangs at one another and being felled by these weapons."[40] This suggests that our human propensity for violence is rooted in our evolutionary history.

This leads to the question of our relationship to partner species. It is becoming increasingly recognized and accepted that we human beings share common descent with primates such as gorillas, orangutans, bonobos, and chimpanzees. With chimpanzees, molecular biologists tell us we share 98.5 percent of our genetic material. With only a 1.5 percent difference, this makes chimps an obvious species for us to study if we want to make educated guesses about our own evolutionary past. What we find in chimpanzee culture shockingly parallels what we find in our own. Especially relevant, is that the male gender engages in rape and bands together in groups to commit murder.

Might this have been predicted by sociobiological theory? Perhaps. Male rape could confirm direct fitness—that is, spreading around the male's genes as far as they'll go. Male murder could confirm the idea of genetic compe-

---

[40] Pinker, *Blank Slate*, 306.

tition. Human society today continues to carry on this biologically driven pattern.

Richard Wrangham and Dale Peterson see a continuity in "demonic males" between today's men and our closest cousins, the primates. "We cloaked our own species' violence in culture and reason, two distinctly human attributes, and wondered what kind of original sin condemned us to this strange habit. And suddenly we found this event in the ape world...Did it imply that human killing is rooted in prehuman history?"[41] The answer seems to be affirmative. "Primate communities organized around male interests naturally tend to follow male strategies and, thanks to sexual selection, tend to seek power with an almost unbounded enthusiasm. In a nutshell: Patriotism breeds aggression."[42] Chimpanzees provide a mirror in which we can see human nature at an earlier evolutionary stage. "Party-gangs and bonded males—suffice to account for natural selection's ugly legacy, the tendency to look for killing opportunities when hostile neighbors meet."[43] This is our heritage. "If we start with ancestors like chimpanzees and end up with modern humans building walls and fighting platforms, the 5 million-year-long trail to our modern selves was lined, along its full stretch, by a male aggression that structured our ancestors' social lives and technology and minds."[44]

When we turn to evolutionary theory to explain human behavior, it looks a great deal like sin. Because our evolutionary history is our only history, we could not have developed otherwise. We are chained to this legacy. "Why are human males given to vicious, lethal aggression? Thinking only of war, putting aside for the moment rape and battering and murder, the curse stems from our species' own special party-gang traits: coalitionary bonds among males, male dominion over an expandable territory, and variable party size. The combination of these traits means that killing a neighboring male is usually worthwhile, and can often be done safely."[45]

Jared Diamond concludes, "of all our human hallmarks...the one that has been derived most straightforwardly from animal precursors is genocide. Common chimps already carried out planned killings, extermination of neighboring bands, wars of territorial conquest, and abduction of young nubile females. If chimps were given spears and some instruction in their use, their killings would undoubtedly begin to approach ours in efficiency."[46] What Diamond provides here is an analogy between chimp and human behavior.

---

[41] Richard Wrangham and Dale Peterson, *Demonic Males: Apes and the Origins of Human Violence* (New York: Houghton Mifflin Company, 1996) 6f.

[42] Ibid., 233.

[43] Ibid., 168.

[44] Ibid., 172.

[45] Ibid., 167.

[46] Jared Diamond, *The Third Chimpanzee: The Evolution and Future of the Human Animal* (New York: Harper, 1993) 294.

There is no causative relationship. Yet, if we surmise that both chimps and humans share a common ancestor, then it is reasonable to consider the following: we have inherited an inborn propensity for genocide. No wonder that genocides occur, and continue to occur.

Is Nature Friend or Foe?

Is nature friend or foe? The challenge to a theological doctrine of creation, says Philip Hefner, is to demonstrate that our "world is 'a planned and purposed enterprise'…that its processes are so reliable and trustworthy that we can say the created world is a home for humans and other forms of life, rather than an uncaring or even hostile environment."[47]

What does nature say? We get one perspective from Steven Weinberg akin to that of Dawkins: we live in "an overwhelmingly hostile universe […] The more the universe seems comprehensible, the more it also seems pointless."[48] We get another perspective from Mary Midgley: "evolution is not actually just a simple sequence of dog eating dog, that co-operation is just as important in it as competition. Evolution is a much wider process which has produced sociality, generating love and altruism just as much as competition."[49] Holmes Rolston, III, adds, "in nature too there is surprising goodness."[50]

Despite the total governance of evolution by genetic determinism accompanied natural selection, what some call "psychological altruism" is possible. Some individuals on some occasions are in fact motivated by the welfare of others without expectation of return. Elliot Sober and David Sloan Wilson make this distinction. "Group selection favors within-group niceness *and* between-group nastiness…Not only do individuals compete with other individuals in the same group; in addition, groups compete with other groups… [Nevertheless] concern for others is *one* of the ultimate motives that people *sometimes* have."[51] Individuals, on occasion, exhibit psychological altruism—that is, they are motivated to care for another person without reciprocal expectations—even though the group to which such individuals belong continues to be subject to comprehensive evolutionary principles.

Perhaps nature when speaking all by itself is ambiguous. "The message that we receive from nature, both in daily experience and in scientific knowledge, is ambiguous; we may turn our attention either to its bounty and aptitude for

[47] Philip Hefner, "The Creation", in: Carl E. Braaten and Robert W. Jenson (ed.), *Christian Dogmatics*, 2 vol. (Minneapolis: Fortress Press, 1984) 1:271.
[48] Steven Weinberg, *The First Three Minutes* (London: Andre Deutsch, 1977) 154.
[49] Mary Midgley, "Criticizing the Cosmos", in: Willem B. Drees (ed.), *Is Nature Ever Evil? Religion, Science, and Value,* (London and New York: Routledge, 2003) 17.
[50] Holmes Rolston, III, "Naturalizing and Systematizing Evil", ibid., 81.
[51] Elliott Sober and David Sloan Wilson, *Unto Others: The Evolution and Psychology of Unselfish Behavior* (Cambridge MA: Harvard University Press, 1998) 9.

life, or to its ruthlessness", writes Eduardo Cruz.[52] Perhaps we need to listen
to nature through theological ears.

The Theobiology of Sin: Peacocke, Williams, Hefner

Some theologians have found ways to incorporate the proposed findings of
sociobiology into their anthropologies and doctrines of creation. When in-
corporating biology into theology, however, theologians are reluctant to grant
exhaustive genetic determinism. They want to make room for cultural transcendence of our biological determinants and for human freedom. Arthur
Peacocke, for example, asserts that God works through the bio-evolutionary
process. "God has made human beings thus with their genetically constrained
behaviour—but, through the freedom God has allowed to evolve in such
creatures, he has also opened up new possibilities of self-fulfillment, creativity, and openness to the future that requires a language other than that of
genetics to elaborate and express."[53] Peacocke wants to absorb evolutionary
biology into his theological anthropology, but only if he can downplay the
genetic determinism and rely on a modicum of human freedom at the cultural
level. Theology requires free will; and he can absorb only a science with room
for free will.

Patricia Williams, like Peacocke, accepts the challenges posed by evolutionary science in the form of sociobiology; but, in contrast, she recommends
that theologians revise their accounts of creation and human nature accordingly. Because the evolutionary story makes no room for a single moment
of creation in an original paradise where human beings were morally virtuous, she recommends that theologians eliminate Adam and Eve and original
virtue from their scheme. Science—by science she means sociobiology—will
provide a new substitute view of human nature. The sociobiological view of
human nature is better than the biblical view, says Williams, because the biblical view is false and the scientific view is true. Even so, Christian theology
can find a partner in sociobiology because both are concerned about the same
topic, namely, original sin. "Because sin remains central, science and Christianity can be united."[54] Just how? "I replace the doctrines of original sin with
sociobiology's theory of human nature."[55]

---

[52] Eduardo R. Cruz, "The Quest for Perfection: Insights from Paul Tillich", in: *Is Nature Ever Evil*, 215.

[53] Arthur R. Peacocke, *God and the New Biology* (San Francisco: Harper, 1986) 110f. See also Peacocke's Bampton Lectures, *Creation and the World of Science* (Oxford: Clarendon Press, 1979) 161–164. Ronald Cole-turner's position is similar, but Cole-Turner emphasizes more the ethical use of molecular biology to influence human behavior for good. *The New Genesis: Theology and the Genetic Revolution* (Louisville: Westminster John Knox Press, 1993).

[54] Patricia A. Williams, *Doing without Adam and Eve: Sociobiology and Original Sin* (Minne-apolis: Fortress Press, 2001) xv.

[55] Ibid., 141.

Williams draws upon the genetic mechanism for cultural distinctions between insiders and outsiders. We have inherited this propensity from our evolutionary history; natural selection has brought the human race to this point. Our specific genomes compete with other genomes for survival; and even our altruism serves our kin group while discriminating against outsiders or aliens. "Under both group selection and kin selection, racism and genocide are natural. Only within groups is charity likely to flourish…So altruism does not result in charity toward all, but charity to close kin, sometimes."[56]

Racism and genocide are explained as natural. And, this explains more subtle social phenomena such as nepotism. "Parents showing favoritism were our ancestors, and we carry copies of their altruistic genes…Nepotism is favoritism toward adult relatives by people who hold power or high office in the community…Its existence is a lesson in how evolution works. Evolution has neither morals nor designs. A tinkerer by trade, it cares only for survival to reproduce."[57]

Because of our biologically inherited preference for our own kin even when expressing charity, it is difficult for Christians to mount a universal ethic or one that encourages us to love our enemies. When Christians try to justify *agape* love, they may even use language that capitalizes on kin preference, by calling aliens kin. "When we want universal cooperation, we invent fictive kin, proclaiming all people brothers and sisters."[58] Ultimately, then, altruism is so nepotistic an ethic that it cannot be considered love in the Christian sense of devotion to someone who is other. Sociobiology agrees with classic Christian anthropology: by nature, we lack charity.

Williams denies that sociobiology teaches genetic determinism.[59] Genes all by themselves govern nothing, she says. Rather, we look at statistical trends and overall patterns, not at individual gene expression. These larger aggregates are affected by interactions with the environment. The interaction of genes with environment that leads to the consolidation of species is natural selection. The determinism of which we speak is better thought of as a combination of genes and environment. Williams believes that this slight opening beyond the limits of genetic determinism can become foundational for human freedom and for a Christian ethic that carries us beyond where evolution has brought us. Williams enjoins us: "nepotism must be fought, charity nurtured."[60] Here she locates a glimmer of ethical hope.

Philip Hefner expands the opening between genes and culture to develop a bio-cultural framework—a coevolution of genetic and cultural information—for integrating sociobiology with theological anthropology. Even if genetic

---

[56] Ibid., 134.
[57] Ibid., 139.
[58] Ibid., 140.
[59] Ibid., 143 f.
[60] Ibid., 154.

replication has been deterministic in our biological past, the genes did determine that we would become free. In our freedom, we humans now shoulder responsibility for the future of the evolutionary process.

"Biology enriches our understanding of the inherent character of sin", writes Hefner. This enrichment applies in five areas. "(1) Sin is an inherent factor in human awareness. (2) We participate in sin as a condition pertaining to our very origin as person. (3) Sin seems to be inherited in some fashion. (4) Sin is associated with our freedom. (5) Sin is marked by a sense of guilt and estrangement, thus requiring the gift of grace."[61] When it comes to the knotty problem of connecting reciprocal altruism to the expansive Christian notion of *agape* love, Hefner warns us that all of us on the planet belong together, society demands altruism beyond the kin group for its survival. "The fact that Christianity elevates the sacrificial action of Jesus on the cross to a central position, in symbol, in faith, and in ethics is of striking significance against the sociobiological background."[62] Hefner thanks evolution for determining that we human beings would be free. He now admonishes us to use our freedom to make the world a better place. Who we are as humans has not been already determined by our evolutionary past; it is still contingent on who we will become in the eschatological future.

Genes, Culture, and Freedom in Theology

One thing I would like from our theologians reflecting on the significance of sociobiology is the following: an assessment of the validity of the claim that DNA replication is the driving force in causing human beings to draw lines between insiders and outsiders. Peacocke simply admits into his theological anthropology from science only what will pass through his theological filter; only a genetic determinism with free will passes through. Williams simply accepts sociobiological theory as true; then she proceeds to revise Christian theology accordingly. Hefner also works with the assumption that the sociobiological claim is true; then with greater elaboration he shows how the cultural component to bio-cultural evolution permits human beings to transcend our genetic history.

Whether for good or ill, theologians seem to want to gain some leverage on behalf of culture over against the limitations of genetic determinism. Wentzel van Huyssteen provides another vivid example. "Cultural evolution has its own dynamics, going beyond the dynamics of biological organic change. Ex-

[61] Philip Hefner, *The Human Factor* (Minneapolis: Fortress Press, 1993) 129.
[62] Philip Hefner, "Sociobiology, Ethics, and Theology", Zygon, 19 (June 1984) 201. Hefner is followed by Hubert Meisinger in placing the human being described by sociobiology into a larger eschatological framework. "Soziobiologie der Liebe. Neutestamentliches Liebesgebot und soziobiologische Altruismusforschung", in: Uwe Gerber and Hubert Meisinger (ed.), *Das Gen als Maß aller Menschen?* (Frankfurt am Main: Peter Lang, 2004) 43–64.

actly on this point evolutionary epistemology differs seriously from the genetic determinism of sociobiology."[63] Do we have at work here an incompatibilist assumption? Do theologians tend to assume that a thorough genetic determinism is incompatible with the Christian understanding of human nature?

To my reading, the liberation of culture from genetic determinism may not be necessary to pursue an adequate theology of original sin; because Christian anthropology for the most part is compatible with other forms of determinism. If in the liturgy we confess that "we are in bondage to sin", we would be no strangers to what Dawkins calls the "tyranny" of our genes. A certain level of consonance obtains. Sociobiology and evolutionary psychology may fall short of providing an exhaustive explanation of human behavior due to weaknesses within the theory; yet, one need not necessarily find weaknesses in the doctrine of genetic determinism in order to connect theological with sociobiological insights. Partial consonance establishes partial value for theology.

The battle between genetic tyranny and cultural liberty is a secularized version of the now marginalized religious battles between body and soul or flesh and spirit. Nothing is to be gained theologically with a victory for cultural freedom over genetic tyranny. To cheer for cultural independence out of fear of genetic hegemony is to cheer for the wrong horse. Theologians ought to be able to ride along with genetic determinism in its most stringent form for two reasons: first, because Christianity positively affirms the physical realm as God's beloved creation; and, second, because of theological precedents for dealing with sin as physically inherited.

It is not my self-assigned task here to confirm or disconfirm the theory of sociobiology. What I am trying to do here is highlight an observation made by sociobiologists, namely, human beings regularly distinguish between insiders and outsiders. And within the group of insiders, some receive more altruistic devotion than others. Outsiders are subject to demonization and decimation. This is what theologians observe in the human phenomenon as well. What is consonant between sociobiology and theology is the observation that this propensity seems to be inherited. We are born into it. Whether it comes with our genes or some other aspect of our evolutionary biology, our present experience suggests that its origin predates us. We inherit a sinfulness we did not author, even while we perpetuate its consequences by inventing ever new forms of violence and victimage.

From Mimesis to Scapegoating

In the late nineteenth century when Thomas Huxley, "Darwin's High Priest",[64] was drawing out the ethical implications of natural selection, he identified a

---

[63] J. Wentzel van Huyssteen, *Duet or Duel? Theology and Science in a Postmodern World* (Harrisburg PA: Trinity Press International, 1998) 157.

[64] Adrian Desmond, *Huxley: Evolution's High Priest* (London: Michael Joseph, 1997).

key characteristic of the human being. That characteristic is mimesis. "Man is the most consummate of all mimics in the animal world", he wrote.[65] Perhaps an analysis of the role played by mimesis is called for here.

When it comes to an analysis of mimesis, no one is more thorough than René Girard. Girard connects mimesis to his scapegoat theory of culture. What he says about mimesis and scapegoating illuminate the human phenomenon we know theologically as sin. Not only does Girard describe well the structure of human behavior, he provides the kind of analysis that makes sense out of atonement theology.[66]

By "mimesis" we refer to imitation. Human desire is fueled by, even inflamed by, the desire to acquire what others desire. Far more than mere survival, what motivates mass human movements is acquisitive desire turned into conflictual desire. This becomes central to explaining human division, rivalry between individuals and between groups. "If *acquisitive mimesis* divides by leading two or more individuals to converge on one and the same object with a view to appropriating it, *conflictual mimesis* will inevitably unify by leading two or more individuals to converge on one and the same adversary that all wish to strike down."[67] Conflictual desire leads to scapegoating, murder, even genocide.

What follows is what I have labeled self-justification. Girard calls it "myth", referring to the social lie that founds a society. Once the "other" or the enemy has been sacrificed, murdered, or eliminated, the surviving society orders or organizes itself around the story it tells about its own founding. When telling the story, it depicts its own founders as heroes or valiant victors; and it describes the vanquished as inferior or even evil. The insiders are good; and the outsiders are evil. The rise of religion and its corresponding ethic derives from this division of the good and the evil; and it places all the insiders on the good side of the line. I have tried in another work to show in greater detail how this mechanism of self-justification maintains social delusion.[68]

Due to the character of the crucifixion of Jesus and the way it is remembered in Scripture, Girard finds within the Christian tradition a prophetic judgment against mimetic desire, violence, scapegoating, and the justification of violence. The key is Christian love and concern for the victims, the victims everywhere. The Christian faith lifts up and celebrates and commemorates

---

[65] Thomas Huxley, *Evolution and Ethics; Science and Morals* (Amherst NY: Prometheus Books, 1896, 2004) 28.

[66] I have tried to explicate my theological appropriation of Girard in *GOD—The World's Future* (Minneapolis: Fortress Press, ²2000) chapters two and seven; and also in "Atonement and the Final Scapegoat", in: Perspectives in Religious Studies, 19:2 (Summer 1992), 151–181 and "Sin, Scapegoating, and Justifying Faith", Dialog, 39:2, Summer 2000, 84–92.

[67] René Girard, *Things Hidden Since the Foundation of the World,* tr. by Stephen Bann and Michael Metteer (Stanford CA: Stanford University Press, 1987) 26.

[68] Peters, *Sin*, ch. 6.

the victims. Whereas Adolf Hitler adopted the evolutionary ethics of Herbert Spencer and Francis Galton when formulating the Nazi program of racial hygiene (*Rassenhygiene*) that led to the death camps, the Christian concern for the victims stands in stark contradiction to the survival-of-the-fittest and its adepts. Reflecting on Adolph Hitler's genocide, Girard remarks, "the spiritual goal of Hitler's ideology was to root out of Germany, then all of Europe, that calling that the Christian tradition places upon all of us, the concern for victims."[69] Although religion in general functions to hide and justify violence, this prophetic interpretation of the atoning work of Jesus Christ provides divine judgment against mimesis and violence along with ethical and religious justification of violence.

Now, does this theory preclude interpreting the rise of religion and ethics as servants of the selfish gene? What it adds, to be sure, is that religion and ethics establish social order based on self-deceit, on a lie. While presenting the criterion of good and bad or right and wrong, religion usually does so hypocritically so that it can justify its own right to scapegoat victims without feeling guilt. What Girard adds to the mix of interpretive constructs is the notion of the delusion, the social lie, the self-deceit, the justification of violence without which social order cannot be established. No account arising from sociobiology or evolutionary psychology to date has incorporated this massive and universal human trait into their analysis.[70]

Is the human propensity for mimesis the result of natural selection? Thomas Huxley would answer in the affirmative. We human beings have inherited from our evolutionary past the ability to be sympathetic, to intuit the feelings of others. We can experience in ourselves the joy or suffering of another. The human being is an "emotional chameleon."[71] In reverse, we can anticipate what others think of us; and we may construct our own positive self-image in order to attain respect or avoid shame due to the way others see us. Conscience is the introjection of how others view us. "We judge the acts of others by our own sympathies, and we judge our own acts by the sympathies of others, every day and all day long."[72] Huxley interpreted this evolutionary inheritance positively, as the birth of the Golden Rule: to do unto others as you would have others do unto you. Within the matrix of the Girardian theory of sacrifice, however, mimesis is the prelude to violence, even to genocidal violence.

S. Mark Heim tries to integrate Girardian social theory with evolutionary theory. He argues that it is possible to posit a "mimetic transition" in the emergence of human nature at some point in our biological history, in a previous

---

[69] René Girard, *I See Satan Fall Like Lightning* (Maryknoll NY: Orbis, 2001) 171.

[70] Steven Pinker is aware of the mechanism of self-justification in the *lex talionis*, the law of clan revenge. "The law of retaliation requires that the vengeance have a moralistic pretext to distinguish it from a raw assault." *Blank Slate*, 325.

[71] Huxley, *Evolution and Ethics*, 28.

[72] Ibid., 30.

Environment of Evolutionary Adaptedness. Prior to this EEA we human beings were strictly subject to our genetic drive for reproductive fitness. Then, when larger brains capable of considering alternatives evolved, an EEA event bequeathed us the capacity for mimesis. "Research is revealing a genetically selected neurological and cognitive structure for imitation, an in-built program that introduces a truly open-ended interaction with the social environment… Recent work in the cognitive sciences suggests imitation is a rare, perhaps even uniquely human ability, which may be fundamental to what is distinctive about human learning, intelligence, rationality, and culture."[73] Heim grants that "mimetic desire and mimetic rivalry are already present among animals in a rudimentary sense."[74] Nevertheless, he contends that this mimetic transition in our evolutionary history offered something new: it made it possible for us humans to imagine what is happening in other people's minds. It makes insight into minds possible. It thereby makes possible understanding other people's desires. The mimetic transition gave a "quantum boost to cultural evolution."[75]

The work of Philip Clayton might be drawn in here. Clayton recognizes that the human brain represents a new level of emergent complexity; and this has made human life as we know it possible. Yet, "inner complexity has another downside: self-deception…Biologically as well as socially, it's often advantageous to deceive yourself into believing that you are fully innocent, since others are then more likely to believe you as well."[76]

With mimesis came mimetic desire, rivalry, self-deception, and large scale war. Religion, according to Heim, then developed as a means for "curbing and overcoming mimetic conflict and violence."[77] Whereas to be consistent with Girard one might view religion as a means for mimetic desire and its accompanying violence to become morally justified; Heim, in contrast, sees religion as countering mimesis and violence. The larger point, however, is that Heim is proposing a convergence of Girardian scapegoat theory with evolutionary psychology. "The interaction of evolutionary thought and Girard's mimetic theory provides the background for a renewed formulation of the Christian understanding of Christ's reconciling work."[78]

Original Sin and Inherited Sin

I am quite sympathetic to the task of relating an inherited biological propensity toward violence with the Christian concept of original sin. The obser-

---

[73] S. Mark Heim, "A Cross-Section of Sin: The Mimetic Character of Human Nature in Biological and Theological Perspective", in: *Evolution and Ethics*, 256.
[74] Ibid., 262.
[75] Ibid., 260.
[76] Philip Clayton, "Conclusion", 328.
[77] Heim, "Cross-Section of Sin", 255.
[78] Ibid., 264.

vations about human nature are consistent with sociobiological theory, even if sociobiological theory still needs confirmation. Yet, looking for biological prompts for human behavior does not exhaust what is important in the doctrine of original sin. Our relationship with God is also important. In fact, the concept of original sin derives primarily out of reflection on a double relationship, one to Adam and one to Christ, one to death and the other to life. The relational dimension to sin carries our discussion well beyond the scope of evolutionary biology.

The Christian concept of original sin begins with an attempt to interpret not Genesis 2, as is popularly thought, but rather Romans 5:12–21 (NRS):

> Therefore, just as sin came into the world through one man, and death came through sin, and so death spread to all because all have sinned –[13] sin was indeed in the world before the law, but sin is not reckoned when there is no law.[14] Yet death exercised dominion from Adam to Moses, even over those whose sins were not like the transgression of Adam, who is a type of the one who was to come.[15] But the free gift is not like the trespass. For if the many died through the one man's trespass, much more surely have the grace of God and the free gift in the grace of the one man, Jesus Christ, abounded for the many.[16] And the free gift is not like the effect of the one man's sin. For the judgment following one trespass brought condemnation, but the free gift following many trespasses brings justification.[17] If, because of the one man's trespass, death exercised dominion through that one, much more surely will those who receive the abundance of grace and the free gift of righteousness exercise dominion in life through the one man, Jesus Christ.[18] Therefore just as one man's trespass led to condemnation for all, so one man's act of righteousness leads to justification and life for all.[19] For just as by the one man's disobedience the many were made sinners, so by the one man's obedience the many will be made righteous.[20] But law came in, with the result that the trespass multiplied; but where sin increased, grace abounded all the more,[21] so that, just as sin exercised dominion in death, so grace might also exercise dominion through justification leading to eternal life through Jesus Christ our Lord.

What is obvious in this text is the dialectic between death and life, between injustice and justification, between sin and grace. The anthropology of St. Paul does not describe sinfulness all by itself; rather, he describes the human condition under its double dimension of estrangement and reconciliation. The figures of Adam and Christ provide the rhetorical vehicle for describing the dialectic.

When St. Augustine sought to interpret such biblical passages, he tried to discern just what it means to be "in" Adam. The result is a unified picture of the human race. All human beings are one in Adam. We are one with Adam in sin and death. "For we all were in that one man, since we all were that one man, who fell into sin by the woman who was made from him before the sin […] And thus, from the bad use of free will, there originated the whole train of evil, which, with its concatenation of miseries, convoys the human race from its depraved origin, as from a corrupt root, on to the destruction of the

second death, which has no end, those only being excepted who are freed by
the grace of God."[79] To explicate what it means to be "in" Adam and to make
sense of our inheritance of Adam's guilt, Augustine declared that original sin
has been passed on physically from generation to generation through pro-
creation. Our physical nature becomes the bearer of sin's history. The free
will exercised by Adam and Eve is now lost as we inherit the legacy of their
sin, namely, concupiscence or the desire to pursue our own ends in a manner
that produces evil in the world.

As the doctrine of original sin grew it began to look like a three leaf clover.
One leaf, *peccatum originans* or first sin refers to what the one man, Adam—
actually the one couple of Adam and Eve—did to introduce sin into an otherwise felicitous creation. A second leaf, *peccatum originatum* refers to the
state of estrangement from God into which we in the human race are born.
John Calvin describes this inborn alienation as natural depravity. "The natural
depravity which we bring from our mother's womb, though it bring not forth
immediately its own fruits, is yet sin before God, and deserves his vengeance:
and this is that sin which they call original."[80] The third leaf is *concupiscen-
tia* or concupiscence, our in-born disposition or inclination to pursue selfish
desire, especially mimetic desire. When we receive baptism, this sacrament re-
moves the second leaf; it replaces estrangement with reconciliation.[81] Those of
us who are baptized are still motivated by concupiscence, however. Both the
baptized and unbaptized among us must struggle to get mimetic desire under
control. Ethics and morality help us in this regard.

Some theologians embrace the concept of original sin but are uneasy with
the idea of inherited sin. The idea of original sin adequately describes the state
or condition in which the human race undisputably finds itself; yet, to explain
this as something we have physically inherited makes them uneasy. Reinhold
Niebuhr belongs in this camp. He believes human sinning is inevitable; but it
is not determined. We are still responsible. He fears that by calling sin inherited we will exculpate us from responsibility.

It is the dimension of inheritance rather than historical origin that requires
attention here. When asking whether a bridge can be built from evolutionary
biology in general or sociobiology in particular to the Christian understanding of original sin, many see the fundamental problem as the historicity of
Adam and Eve in a paradise of primordial harmony. The fall is thought to
be a temporal event, a shift from paradise to our present wilderness of sin.
The great theologians of the past—Augustine, Thomas, Luther, Calvin—all
presumed the historicity of the Eden account. So, when the theory of evolu-

[79] Augustine, *City of God*, XIII: 14.
[80] John Calvin, *Commentaries on the Epistle of Paul and the Apostle to the Romans 5:12*, trans.
and ed. by John Owen (Grand Rapids MI: Baker Book House, 1996) 200.
[81] See: Jerry D. Korsmeyer, *Evolution and Eden* (New York: Paulist Press, 1998) 23 f.

tion provides us with an apparent alternative account which makes no room for an ancient paradise, we ask whether or not we have a conflict. However, if temporal location is the sole problem, it appears to me that we have a very small problem indeed.

Roman Catholic scientist Jerry D. Korsmeyer provides a case in point. If biblical critics can say that the book of Genesis does not provide a history, then we can borrow the history given us by evolutionary theology. "Therefore, we need not take as literal truth that human beings began their existence in a paradise…nor conclude that there was an offense committed by the first human beings so horrible that the justice of God demanded that henceforth they and their descendants be punished with suffering and death, and declared guilty of eternal damnation."[82] Yet, we still need to account for the human phenomenon we observe as inherited sin. Korsmeyer drafts evolution into this service. "The sins of the world flow from our genetic heritage which has evolved in a struggle for survival, from human relationships that seek the security of the local group, and from human institutions designed to stabilize power for the interests of their founders."[83] That is, Adam and Eve can be replaced with our genetic history.

I find this satisfactory, though in itself it does not account for the entire phenomenon of sin. We understand sin dialectically. We understand sin over against its alternatives, over against perfection or paradise or salvation or heaven. The image of the biblical Garden of Eden or the coming Kingdom of God stand out in sharp contrast to the situation in which human beings find themselves. Reinhold Niebuhr, standing squarely in the Augustinian tradition gives up on the historicity of Adam and Eve; but he keeps the *justitia originalis*, the original perfection, of the Garden of Eden. We in the human race operate daily with the image of ourselves as just, as perfect, as healthy. We live in ambiguity, with a combination of awareness of who we are as sinners plus a vision of ourselves in paradise. "This righteousness […] is not completely lost in the Fall but remains with sinful man as the knowledge of what he ought to be, as the law of his freedom."[84]

In sum, we stand judged by paradise, because we fall short of paradise. Inherent in the doctrine of sin is the sense that reality demands something different than what has existed or presently exists. We have a mandate to become better than we are. Dividing the human race into insiders versus outsiders and then justifying prejudice, gossip, hatred, murder, and genocide is sinful, even though it is an every day occurrence. Sin is accompanied by guilt because we can imagine a human existence that is sinless. Whether we look to paradise

---

[82] Ibid., 121.
[83] Ibid., 125.
[84] Reinhold Niebuhr, *The Nature and Destiny of Man,* 2 vol. (New York: Charles Scribner's Sons, 1941) 1:280.

back in time in the Garden of Eden (Genesis 2) or forward in time in the New Jerusalem (Revelation 21), it is the contrast with the present situation that is decisive to our self-understanding.

The Self Curved in on the Gene

Most theologians, it seems to me, respond to the stimulus of genetic determinism with a defense of free will. For some reason, they feel a need to preserve free will with its accompanying moral responsibility against a threat that science might remove it. Frankly, I find this a non-issue. It is a non-issue on two counts. First, genetic determinism or even environmental determinism does not need to dissolve free will; nor does it necessarily eliminate moral responsibility. What appears to be the problem is this, in the words of Steven Pinker, "if someone tries to explain an act as an effect of some cause, the explainer is saying that the act was not freely chosen and that the actor cannot be held responsible". However, a description of causes does not eliminate human freedom; nor does it eliminate moral responsibility. "It is a confusion of *explanation* with *exculpation*", says Pinker.[85] On this point, I agree with Pinker. I would add that there exists such an entity as the human self, and what we know as freedom consists of self-determination. As long as self-determinism is in the picture, genetic determinism or even environmental determinism is not a threat to human freedom.

Second, defending free will ought not to be front and center on the theologian's mind when dealing with original sin. Part of the character of sin is bondage, the opposite of freedom. We are in bondage to forces and pressures and desires and drives. We are in bondage to an inheritance we have been born with. Evolutionary psychology could in principle aid us in getting a handle on understanding such bondage. The word "sin" describes an imprisonment from which we want to be set free.

St. Augustine followed by Martin Luther described this bondage as enslavement to one's self. Because every action is a form of self-expression and ultimately serves the self, I am unable not to sin, *non posse non peccare*. What God's grace entering our lives does is liberate us from ourselves, liberate us to love another for the sake of the other. Grace liberates us from our selves so we can love God for Godself. Luther calls this "Christian Liberty."[86] Standard defenses of free will have virtually no relationship to Christian liberty, regrettably.

One way to interpret sociobiology would be to place the selfish gene in the role of the tyrant that holds us in bondage. Certainly this is the image

---

[85] Pinker, *Blank Slate*, 179.

[86] See: Martin Luther, "Treatise on Christina Liberty", in: *Luther's Works*, American Edition, vol. 1–30, Jaroslav Pelikan (ed.) (St. Louis: Concordia Publishing Company, 1955–1967); vol. 31–55, Helmut T. Lehmann (ed.) (Minneapolis: Fortress Press, 1955–1986) 31:327–378.

Richard Dawkins gives us, and to some extent E.O. Wilson. This places the self curved in upon itself back one step, to the DNA sequence rather than the person. The self is curved in on the gene, so to speak.

To explore this much further, we would need to know if sociobiological theory can be confirmed scientifically or not. The jury is still out. If this theory gets confirmed, then we might want to see our inborn selfishness as a derivative of our inherited evolutionary history. We might want to interpret grace's liberation in terms of liberation from our evolutionary past. Perhaps Douglas John Hall would pave this road to lead all the way to ethics. "It is well, Christianly speaking, when a religious community manifests a sufficient degree of the knowledge of the love of God to see the world from the perspective of its nation's real or alleged enemies; when it is sufficiently liberated from the immodest behavior of its own racial, ethnic, cultural, and cultic loyalties to consider the rights of 'the other'."[87]

Theology of the Cross

Rather than go further down this road, I would like to turn now toward a different question: how should we understand God as creator and redeemer in light of the nihilism and unfeeling brutality of evolutionary history? Is this God's world?

I would like to explore the possibility of applying the *Theology of the Cross* to the natural world. Deriving from Martin Luther, the theology of the cross emphasizes two things. First, as a theory of revelation, it insists that God's presence and action in the world are not immediately obvious. In fact, what God actually does might be contrary to what we expect. God is hidden. God's majesty and power are hidden behind the masks of humility and weakness. God's eternal life is hidden behind the mask of death, healing behind a mask of suffering. "The manifest and visible things of God are placed in opposition to the invisible, namely, his human nature, weakness, foolishness…in the humility and shame of the cross."[88] To understand God, says Luther, we must look at the cross and recognize that we do not understand God.

A second characteristic of God comes through the cross, namely, God's life shares in the suffering of the world. In the person of Jesus, the triune God suffers. "When the crucified Jesus is called the 'image of the invisible God'", writes Jürgen Moltmann, "the meaning is that *this* is God, and God is like *this*…The Christ event on the cross is a God event."[89] One might say that all the suffering of this world is taken up in this representative person, Jesus Christ, who is both the embodiment of the physical world and the image of God. God experiences what we experience, both suffering and estrangement.

---

[87] Douglas John Hall, *The Cross in Our Context* (Minneapolis: Fortress Press, 2003) 5.

[88] *Luther's Works*, 31: 53.

[89] Jürgen Moltmann, *The Crucified God* (San Francisco: Harper, 1974) 205.

This experience of God with suffering and even estrangement in the crucifixion of Christ is ordinarily thought of by theologians as a historical event. It
is a human event. But, we might ask, could it be a natural event as well? Could
we apply what we learn about God from the cross to how we understand the
natural world, and even how we understand human nature?

George L. Murphy would answer "yes". He sees the cross as a pattern with
which to interpret creation. "The crosslike pattern of creation means that
Christ crucified has cosmic significance."[90] Murphy would like the suffering
of God within the creation to supply him with a theodicy, with an answer to
the question of the relationship of a good God to a creation replete with sin,
suffering, and death. "God suffers *with* the world from whatever evil takes
place…We begin with the fact that God suffered on the cross, but we do not
have to stop with that. God's voluntary self-limitation that enables the world
to have its own existence and integrity keeps God from simply preventing all
evil in miraculous ways. Evil is then the 'dark side' of an aspect of the goodness of creation, its functional integrity."[91]

One thrust of the theology of the cross is to face reality realistically, even
to face our own human nature realistically. "It belongs to the theology of the
cross…that it permits and demands—demands and permits—an exceptional
realism",[92] writes Douglas John Hall. Spiritually, we must face the reality of
the contingency of our existence, our being subject at any moment to accident
or disease, the inevitability of our death; and we must face our own participation and complicity in the violence that pervades our world. Theologically,
we must face the reality that our God does not depend on triumph and victory along with the genocide of enemies to accomplish the divine will. This
permits us to face the reality about ourselves as human beings. We must face
the fact that, as the German text of the Augsburg Confession says, "all human
beings who are born in the natural way are conceived and born in sin. This
means that from birth they are full of evil lust and inclination and cannot by
nature possess true fear of God and true faith in God."[93]

If we are unable to face this reality, then we turn to a theology of glory. In
our own minds we picture God as triumphant, and we use our belief in God
to justify pursuing our own triumphalism—survival-of-the-fittest—at the expense of those we consider "other". A theology of glory allows us to paint
ourselves good and our enemies bad. A theology of glory draws our religion
into the mechanism of self-justification for pursuing victory over our enemies

---

[90] George L. Murphy, *The Cosmos in Light of the Cross* (Harrisburg PA: Trinity Press International, 2003) 33.

[91] Ibid., 87.

[92] Hall, *Cross in Our Context*, 212.

[93] Augsburg Confession, Article II, in: Robert Kolb and Timothy J. Wengert (ed.), *The Book
of Concord: The Confessions of the Evangelical Lutheran Church* (Minneapolis: Fortress Press,
2000) 36 ff.

and disenfranchising if not eliminating them. A theology of the cross, in contrast, asks us to look at ourselves in the mirror next to the victim of someone's glory hanging on the cross. It reveals our nature. It also reveals God's compassion for us, as we are without our triumphs and without victory over our alleged enemies.

Not Possible Not to Sin

Does the genetic determinism of sociobiology or even the brain determinism of evolutionary psychology provide an explanation for Augustine's description of the inborn human condition, *non posse non peccare*, not possible not to sin? If so, Christian theology could be thought of as consonant.

What then does this do to Jesus telling us to love the other, to love even our enemies? Luke 6:35 (NRS) "But love your enemies, do good, and lend, expecting nothing in return." Jesus' ethic is explicitly non-reciprocal. Is Jesus asking us to do something that is impossible? Is it impossible for us to follow Jesus because we are genetically determined to orient our productive lives around our reproductive lives? As slaves to the tyranny of our genes, do we lack the freedom to follow Jesus? If the answer is "yes", this ought not to be surprising.

We might want to distinguish somewhat between what we do each day as individuals from the composite behavior of the human race. Each of us can have an occasional good day—that is, during Christmas season we might find ourselves giving extra money to charities that will benefit people we will never meet. Each of us individually is not given over to greed and genocide twenty-four/seven. Yet, as a society, or as a globe of internationally cooperative and competing societies, we just might be subject to the law of the selfish gene, unable to transcend our service to the dictates of inclusive fitness. If so, then, we should heed the advice of Jesus. NRS Mark 13:7 "When you hear of wars and rumors of wars, do not be alarmed; this must take place, but the end is still to come."

Is love for the other as other possible? Douglas John Hall thinks so. "It is possible—and now it is absolutely necessary—to hold firmly to a faith that not only does *not* kill but opens a community to life-enhancing communion with others of our own kind, and of the other kind as well. *At base*, that is precisely what the 'theology of the cross' means to me."[94] Because we can envision *agape* love or psychological altruism, Hall seems to assume we can accomplish it. Yet, if what the sociobiologist says is correct, then it is not possible. This would imply that Jesus has given us an ethic that is impossible to fulfill.

Reinhold Niebuhr would disagree flatly with Hall, on the grounds that groups cannot love in the way Hall would want them to. Oh yes, individuals can have their moments of psychological altruism; but groups always—that

---

[94] Hall, *Cross in Our Context*, 6.

is, always!—orient themselves around self-interest and domination. "As individuals, men believe that they ought to love and serve each other and establish justice between each other. As racial, economic and national groups, they take for themselves, whatever their power can command."[95] If Niebuhr's observation is accurate, it is significant that the selfish groups are not necessarily limited to genetic groups. Racial groups could appear to be genetically united, to be sure; but certainly economic classes and nations are agglomerations of individuals without regard to genetic identity. What seems to be the case is that human nature is constituted by the propensity to divide between insiders and outsiders; and sociobiology provides an alleged biological explanation for this propensity. Whether or not sociobiology is explanatorily adequate, it appears that the doctrine of original sin sees us human beings—at least in groups—as unable not to sin.

Jeffry Schloss, in his haste to reconcile theology with sociobiology, enlists Jesus as a disciple. "Jesus almost sounds like a sociobiologist in the synoptic gospel accounts that exhort us not to restrict our greetings or dinner invitations or lending to those who do the same in return."[96] Jesus is a champion of sociobiology here. Really? Now, on the one hand, I see Jesus as just the opposite. Jesus is repudiating reciprocal altruism. In fact, Jesus would undoubtedly decry the hypocrisy we employ culturally to hide our own reproductive advantage when pretending to follow his ethic of loving the other. On the other hand, perhaps Jesus asks us to love outsiders without reciprocity simply to challenge us with an understanding of God. God can love his enemies, even if we cannot.

Our human condition does not have to remain the way it is. One of the bright spots in this otherwise dark picture is that evolution implies change. The future will not remain what the past was or the present is. In fact, the New Testament prophecies significant changes ahead. The New Testament promises transformation. Philip Hefner looks forward to eschatological renewal. "Within the framework of Christian theology, the dynamic of nature is to be explained as its trajectory toward communion with God, according to God's intentions…Nature is a realm of becoming, and its underlying thrust, its *cantus firma*, if you will, is communion of its parts with each other and with God."[97]

---

[95] Reinhold Niebuhr, *Moral Man and Immoral Society* (New York: Charles Scribner's Sons, 1932, 1960) 9.
[96] Schloss, in: *Evolution and Ethics*, 19.
[97] Philip Hefner, "Nature Good and Evil: A Theological Palatte", in: *Is Nature Ever Evil?*, 197.

Creation as "Very Good" and "Groaning in Travail"

An Exploration in Evolutionary Theodicy

Christopher Southgate

The affirmation that "God saw all that he had made, and behold, it was very good" (Genesis 1:31) is not only the culmination of the first account of creation in the Book of Genesis, but a conviction to which Christian orthodoxy has held since the early days of its struggle with Gnosticism and Manichaeanism.[1] The modern Darwinian portrayal of the natural world, however, is characterized (among other types of interplay) by competition, struggle, suffering, death and extinction. These facets of biological existence might well remind any reader of the New Testament of Paul's "we know that creation is groaning in travail" (Romans 8:22). What is so interestingly reminiscent of those enigmatic verses 19 to 22 of Romans 8 is the recognition by evolutionary theorists that it is precisely the process of natural selection of inherited variation—the competition that prevents the less successful organisms from reproducing—that gives rise to the beauty and diversity of the biosphere as we know it. The natural world appears to be marked by an inherent coupling of value and disvalue: the suffering of very many creatures produces benefits for the adaptedness of their species as a whole. In Holmes Roston III's resonant phrase: "the cougar's fang has carved the limbs of the fleet-footed deer".[2] Moreover, it is the extinction of the vast majority of the species that have ever lived which has permitted the evolution of the species and ecosystems of the contemporary biosphere (including the human "project"). The natural world seems "subjected" (to return to the terminology of Romans 8) to travail by God in order that values may be enhanced within that world.[3] The Darwinian account of nature therefore poses a theological problem: did the God of the Bible create a world in which violence and suffering—disvalue—are the means by which good—value—is realized? Darwin himself recognized the theological difficulties produced by a view of life in which "horror" is linked

---

[1] Colin E. Gunton, *The Triune Creator: A Historical and Systematic Study* (Edinburgh: Edinburgh University Press, 1998) 47–50, 74.

[2] Holmes Rolston, III, *Science and Religion: A Critical Survey* (New York: Random House, 1987) 134, republished in 2006 by the Templeton Foundation Press (Philadelphia and London).

[3] 'The great majority of commentators agree that the one who subjected the world [in Romans 8:20] was God himself'—so John Ziesler, *Paul's Letter to the Romans* (London: SCM Press and Philadelphia: Trinity Press International, 1989) 220.

to "grandeur". Yet a century and a half later the problem in theodicy in light of the suffering of non-human creation has been little addressed.[4]

This surprising lack of theological response to the problem of evolutionary theodicy[5] partly reflects the profound anthropocentricity that so many ecological writers have noted in Christianity. Theodicy has been a human-focused science, giving little attention to the sufferings of the non-human world. But in the context of a Darwinian understanding that pain, suffering, death and extinction are intrinsic to the life-process, and to the evolutionary history that has led to the arising of human beings, the challenge to the contemporary theodicist cannot be escaped.

The theodicy problem as informed by such an evolutionary view in nature has three main aspects. The first is *ontological*, in respect of the fact of God's giving existence to a world containing non-human suffering, death and extinction. This fact of (non-human-induced) suffering within the non-human creation extends the theological problem posed by human suffering.

The second is *teleological*. The problem of God's responsibility for a world containing so much creaturely suffering, death and extinction is intensified in any scheme which imputes teleology to this process of divine creation, in the sense of God desiring certain values to arise through the process. G. W. Leibniz' famous phrase that this is the "best of all possible worlds" begs in this connection the question—best for what? I freely concede that this may be the best possible world for the evolution of creatures like humans, and yet the question remains as to whether the creation of such a world, full of suffering and extinction, is the activity of a God worthy of worship.[6] If, for example, God particularly desired the outcome that there be freely-choosing self-conscious beings able to come into conscious reciprocal relationship with God, then other creatures, for example those whose extinction made possible the rise of the mammals, begin to seem no more than means to the divine end.[7] And the more God is considered to be directly involved in steering the process of evolution towards God's long-term ends, the more problematic it is to account for God's permitting so much suffering during the process (a point clearly realized by Robert J. Russell in his exploration of the possibility of special divine action within evolution, and one which needs more consideration by proponents of "intelligent design"[8]).

---

[4] Even John Hick, who in his *Evil and the God of Love* (Glasgow: Fount, 1979) first published 1966, acknowledges the "sufferings of animals [to] constitute one of the most baffling aspects of the problem of evil" (109), goes on to downplay those sufferings (349f).

[5] For a summary of recent responses see Christopher Southgate, "God and Evolutionary Evil: theodicy in the light of Darwinism", Zygon 37, 4, 2002, 803–824, esp. 808–816.

[6] A question sharply posed by David Hull in his "God of the Galapagos", Nature 352, 1992, 485f.

[7] Which seems to be the implication of the view of, for example, Keith Ward in his *God, Chance and Necessity* (Oxford: Oneworld, 1996).

[8] See Russell's "Divine Action and Quantum Mechanics: A Fresh Assessment", in: R. J. Russell, P. Clayton, K. Wegter-McNelly and J. Polkinghorne (ed.), *Quantum Mechanics: Scientific Perspec-*

The third is *soteriological*. If some scheme of redemption of non-human species is used to compensate for these difficulties, there is work to do at the level of soteriology, since traditional Christian redemption theory has focused on one event in the history of humanity—a particular crucifixion of a particular member of a historically contingent species, lately arrived after 3.8 billion years of evolution had already passed by. What place, it must be asked, does this view of redemption have when our focus widens to embrace the whole of evolutionary history?

This essay proposes a strategy for an evolutionary theodicy.[9] This strategy is founded on four primary claims: (1) the ontological claim that it was God who created and continues to sustain both the matter and the natural processes of the universe; (2) the teleological claim that humans' freely chosen response to the grace of God is *a* principal goal—*though not the only one*—of God in creation; (3) the claim that God suffers with God's creation through self-giving love, of which Christ's Cross is indicative; and (4) the soteriological claim that (i) God does not abandon the victims of evolution, and (ii) that humans have a calling, stemming from the transformative power of Christ's action on the Cross, to participate in the healing of the world. Several authors have proposed strategies which take seriously the first three of these claims.[10] However, without the fourth element evolutionary theodicy remains preg-

---

tives on Divine Action, 293–328 (Vatican City: Vatican Observatory and Berkeley, CA: Center for Theology and the Natural Sciences), 318 ff. For a survey of the debate on intelligent design see Ted Peters and Martinez Hewlett, *Evolution from Creation to New Creation* (Nashville, TN: Abingdon Press, 2003), ch. 5, or Niall Shanks, *God, the Devil and Darwin: A Critique of Intelligent Design Theory* (Oxford: Oxford University Press, 2004).

[9] I develop this strategy at greater length in my book, *The Good and the Groaning: Evolution, the Problem of Evil, and the Call of Humanity* (Louisville, KY, Westminster/John Knox Press, 2008).

[10] See for example Arthur Peacocke "The Cost of New Life", in: John Polkinghorne (ed.), *The Work of Love: Creation as Kenosis* (London, SPCK and Cambridge and Grand Rapids, MI, Eerdmans, 2001) 21–42, and Holmes Rolston, III, "Naturalizing and Systematizing Evil", in: Willem B. Drees (ed.), *Is Nature Ever Evil? Religion, Science and Value* (London: Routledge, 2003) 67–86. Also Richard Kropf's *Evil and Evolution: A Theodicy*. Eugene, Oregon: Wipf and Stock Publications, 2004, first published 1984. Niels Gregersen similarly concludes that there is a case to answer *in re* evolutionary theodicy, and that merely to say that pain, suffering and death are necessary to the complexification and refinement of living things is not adequate theodicy (Niels H. Gregersen, "The Cross of Christ in an Evolutionary World", Dialog: A Journal of Theology, 40:3, 2001, 192–207. He seems to accept 1) to 3) on my list and to take up, though not in any very developed way, the soteriological point 4)i). Important insights in his article include: the concept of "deep incarnation"—Christ is incarnate in putting on not only human nature but "also a scorned social being and a human-animal body, at once vibrant and vital and yet vulnerable to disease and decay" (193); the perception that Christ is in solidarity with victims of the evolutionary arms race, as one put to death without genetic offspring; lastly, and in accord with my own conclusion, that this form of theodicy must rest on an objective theory of the atonement—reality must be transformed by this identification of the Crucified One with creaturely suffering, since in the case of non-human creatures the force of Christ's love cannot be appropriated merely through his example.

nant with the charge that God used non-human creatures as merely means to an end, allowing the intrinsic value of myriad creatures to be cast aside by the very processes God had set in train.[11]

The strategy proposed here faces head-on the problem of a good God and a groaning world. It does this through four steps. First, it provides a new classification of approaches to theodicy, and uses this classification to assess the sufficiency of current evolutionary theodicies. Second, it explores God's relation to the non-human world in terms of a model of Trinitarian creation and divine co-suffering with the suffering of creatures. Third, it considers the eschatological dimension to non-human suffering in terms of God's ultimate purposes. And fourth, it reconsiders the human relationship to the non-human creation in terms of humans' call to participate in God's ultimate purposes.

My proposal begins in biology and ends in environmental ethics. It is informed throughout by a single problem: how can creation be regarded as "very good", and as the work of a sublimely good God, and at the same time be a place where values are realized only and obligatorily in the context of the disvalues of suffering and extinction? It bears noting that mine is an exploration within Christian theology. It will therefore take as core hypothesis that Trinitarian creation and redemption are valid ways of speaking (in however partial and incomplete a way) of God's relation to the world. Specifically, it will explore the possibilities afforded by the formulation of Irenaeus that the Son and the Spirit are the two "hands" of the Father in creation[12], and a theological anthropology in which human beings may not only grow into freedom and be drawn into the fellowship of the divine life, but have an eschatological role in the healing of creation (see the sections on eschatology and ethical kenosis below).

A New Classification of Approaches to Theodicy

I have considered the precise nature of the problem of evolutionary theodicy in an earlier article.[13] I showed there that the crucial issue is not *pain* — a necessary concomitant of a richer experience of the world in higher animals[14], or

---

[11] John F. Haught in *God After Darwin* (Oxford and Boulder, CO: Westview Press, 2000) comes closest to assembling a theodicy comparable to one offered here. Haught's own solution can be seen as a fusion of 1) and 3) above, with a process-influenced version of 4(i). See also a fine essay by Robert J. Russell, "Natural Theodicy in an Evolutionary Context", in: Bruce Barber and David Neville (ed.), *Theodicy and Eschatology*, (Adelaide: Australian Theological Forum, 2005) 121–152, stressing the necessity for an eschatological dimension to an evolutionary theodicy.

[12] See Gunton, *The Triune Creator*, 54.

[13] Southgate. "God and Evolutionary Evil", 804 ff.

[14] Arthur Peacocke, "Biological Evolution — A Positive Theological Appraisal", in: Robert J. Russell, William R. Stoeger SJ and Francisco J. Ayala (ed.), *Evolutionary and Molecular Biology: Scientific Perspectives on Divine Action*, 357–376, (Vatican City, Vatican Observatory and Berkeley, CA, CTNS) 366 f.

death—a thermodynamic necessity—and, I would argue, no "evil" if it follows a fulfilled life[15], or *the loss of non-living entities*. The heart of the problem is that the experience of many individual creatures, such as the new-born impala torn apart alive by hyena, seems to be all suffering and no richness. There are innumerable sufferers of the processes of predation and parasitism, including organisms for which life seems to contain no fullness, no expression of what it is to reach the potential inherent in being that creature. Indeed the "overproduction" typical of biological organisms virtually guarantees this. These unfulfilled organisms may be regarded as in some sense the victims or casualties of evolution.

The classical theological view of the problem of violence and suffering in nature is to see it as a product of the human fall into sin. However, if standard evolutionary accounts of nature are correct, then predation, violence, parasitism, suffering, and extinction were integral parts of the natural order long before *Homo sapiens*. As every T-Rex-loving six-year-old knows, there is evidence of these natural dynamics from the age of dinosaurs, which came to an end some 65 million years ago. Even the longest estimate of the time for which creatures that might be recognized as human have existed is no more than one million years at the very outside.[16] However, despite its complete

---

[15] Death is also the prerequisite of "regeneration" (so Rolston) and of "biological creativity", cf. Peacocke, "Biological Evolution", 369, also Denis Edwards, *The God of Evolution: A Trinitarian Theology* (Mahwah, NJ: Paulist Press, 1999) 38 f. I am aware that what I refer to as a "fulfilled life" depends on guesses about the experience of non-human creatures; it rests on a strong instinct about human life which sees death, in many instances, as a natural and fitting end to a consummated life (despite the additional stress and suffering that humans know through living lives full of a conscious awareness of mortality). It seems reasonable to suppose that there can be a corresponding fulfillment of an animal life. I explore this further below.

[16] For vehement rejections of the traditional form of the Doctrine of the Fall see Arthur Peacocke, *Theology for a Scientific Age* (Oxford, Blackwell, expanded edition 1993) 222f and John Polkinghorne, *Reason and Reality* (London: SPCK, 1991), 99ff. So far from the universe being fallen through human action from a perfection initially given it by God, I suggest firstly that the sort of universe we have, in which complexity emerges in a process governed by thermodynamic necessity and Darwinian natural selection, is the only sort of universe that could give rise to freely-choosing self-conscious beings. Secondly that such beings are one goal (though not the only or the final goal) of God's creation. But reflection on the long history of life on Earth does lead to conundra in the divine action debate. For example, the extinction event at the K/T boundary, although it must have caused huge quantities of distress in the dominant creatures of the biosphere, might be regarded as a "good" event in terms of the evolution of freely-choosing self-conscious life-forms. Indeed the extinction event could even be seen as an instrument of God's purpose. Whereas an ecological catastrophe destroying the hominids of East Africa 2 million years ago would presumably have been a "bad" event in not only causing great suffering but also ending a particular set of possibilities for conscious life. How are we to construe divine action, and theodicy, in respect of these cases? Might we not think of God permitting the first event, but preventing—if the possibility arose—the second? (Cf. my chapter "A Test Case—Divine Action", in: Christopher Southgate (ed.), *God, Humanity and the Cosmos: a companion to the science-religion debate*, 260–299, (Edinburgh: T&T Clark International, 2005), esp. 286–290.

lack of congruity with the scientific narrative of the unfolding of the biosphere, a sense that human sin is responsible for factors in the natural world
quite beyond our power to influence remains strong.[17]

Attempts to think beyond this sin-preoccupied approach can already be
seen in the work of Thomas Aquinas. Taxed by the problem of non-human
suffering Aquinas writes: "Since God, then, provides universally for all being,
it belongs to His providence to permit certain defects in particular effects,
that the perfect good of the universe may not be hindered, for if all evil were
prevented, much good would be absent from the universe. A lion would cease
to live, if there were no slaying of animals; and there would be no patience
of martyrs if there were no tyrannical persecutions."[18] For Thomas, then, the
goodness of the world is axiomatic, and necessary evils must be seen in that
larger context.

A related effort to contextualize the suffering of non-human nature can
be seen in the work of Holmes Rolston. Rolston has argued that being the
locus for the exchange of value is the respect in which an ecosystem may itself
be considered of value.[19] Within ecosystems, the disvalue of suffering is "redeemed" by the value of regeneration that it offers to other creatures in the
ecosystem.[20] I would submit however (contrary to Rolston's view) that the *regeneration* of life out of the suffering of other life does not of itself "redeem"
the suffering experienced by individuals, be they dying impala calves or lame
cheetahs succumbing slowly to hunger. Regeneration does not comprehend
all that is connoted by the word "redemption", and the suffering of individual
organisms, even it promotes the flourishing of others, must still remain a challenge for theodicy. Moreover, I would argue that *extinction* must be conceded
to be an evil for any species, and always a loss of value to the biosphere as a
whole. A whole strategy of being alive on the planet, a whole quality of living
experience is lost when any organism becomes extinct.

Both Aquinas and Rolston attempt to justify harms experienced within
creation on the basis of goods thereby made possible. This is a key strategy in
theodicy, and warrants careful analysis. With my colleague Andrew Robinson

---

[17] See for example its intrusion into the otherwise very sophisticated treatment of the theodicy
problem in David Bentley Hart's *The Doors of the Sea: Where was God in the Indian Ocean
Tsunami?* (Grand Rapids, MI and Cambridge: Eerdmans, 2005) 63. The appeal to human sin as an
explanation for suffering in nature also remains strong among so-called "young earth creationists".
For a patient and careful evaluation of creationist approaches against those of theologians engaging
with evolutionary theory see Peters and Hewlett, *Evolution from Creation to New Creation*.

[18] Aquinas, Thomas. 1947. *Summa Theologica*, transl. by the Fathers of the English Dominican
Province, New York: Benziger Brothers, The quotation is from pt1.Q.xxii.art.2.

[19] Holmes Rolston, III, *Environmental Ethics: Duties to and Values in the Natural World* (Temple University Press: Philadelphia, 1988), *Conserving Natural Value* (New York: Columbia University Press, 1994).

[20] Rolston, "Naturalizing and Systematizing Evil", 83 ff.

I identify three ways in which such a "good-harm analysis" (GHA) may be formulated:[21]

(1) Property-consequence GHAs: a consequence of the *existence* of a good is the *possibility* of it causing harms. The classic instance of this is the free-will defense in respect of moral evil.

(2) Developmental GHAs: the good is a goal which can only *develop* through a *process* which includes the possibility (or necessity) of harm. The most familiar version of this is John Hick's "Irenaean" theodicy of the world as a "vale of soul-making" in which virtue is learned through a process that involves suffering.[22] Another type of developmental argument would be one in which harms are unavoidable by-products of a process which also gives rise to goods. This we term a "developmental by-product" defence.

(3) Constitutive GHAs: The existence of a good is *inherently, constitutively, inseparable* from the experience of harm or suffering.

Each of these "categories" of good-harm analysis may have three types of "reference": human (the relevant goods and harms are restricted to humans); anthropocentric (the good accrues to humans, but the harm to a range of creatures), or biotic (both the goods and the harms may be experienced throughout the biosphere). My concern in the present article is "biophysical evil", harms to non-human creatures which have no human cause, and whether it is possible to frame a satisfactory theodicy with a "biotic" reference.

Drawing on examples offered by Rolston we can understand how this reference is elaborated differently in each kind of GHA. Rolston describes the behaviour of certain kinds of orca which, in killing sealions, will toss their victims playfully in the air, prolonging their agony.[23] This type of orca is so feared by its prey animals that dolphins will drag themselves onto land and suffocate rather than face their predators.[24] As we consider this behaviour our focus may be on the orcas themselves. The freedom of behaviour involved in their lifestyle as predators *can* lead to what seems to human observers like the gratuitous infliction of suffering, but it does not necessarily do so. Other types of orca do not show this behaviour, and often predators (unless teaching their young to hunt) kill their prey with the minimum of energy and fuss. Focus on this behaviour in orcas, then, would lead to a property-consequence approach

---

[21] Christopher Southgate and Andrew Robinson, "Varieties of Theodicy: An Exploration of Responses to the Problem of Evil based on a Typology of Good-Harm Analyses" forthcoming in: Robert J. Russell, Nancey Murphy and William Stoeger SJ (ed.), *Physics and Cosmology: Scientific Perspectives on the Problem of Evil in Nature* (Berkeley, CA and Vatican City: CTNS and Vatican Observatory, 2006).

[22] See Hick, *Evil and the God of Love*.

[23] Rolston, "Naturalizing and Systematizing Evil", 67.

[24] Douglas H. Chadwick, "Investigating a Killer", National Geographic, April 2005, 86–105.

to the analysis of goods and harms. Certain properties in created entities can lead—but need not necessarily lead—to suffering in the biotic world.

We could choose to focus instead on the orca's prey, the sealion. We could conclude, with this focus, that the fact of predation progressively develops the abilities of sealions as a species and leads to greater abilities and greater flourishing. Though individuals suffer, the species as a whole becomes better adapted—a developmental approach to goods and harms, one in which suffering is instrumental to the development of creatures.

We could broaden our focus still further and consider the whole ecosystem of this part of the ocean. It is a system in which eating and being eaten is of the essence. An elaborate chain of interdependent relationships builds up around this dynamic (with the pain that is necessarily caused to various creatures within the process). Focus on this chain of relationships might lead to a constitutive type of understanding of goods and harms. Indeed Rolston also uses this type of language, calling nature "cruciform". "The secret of life", he goes on to say, is that it is a *passion play*.[25] By this he presumably means that, as at the passion of Christ, the good does not have its meaning without the suffering intrinsic to it.

Another of Rolston's examples offers more insight into the dynamic between types of argument. He notes the way in which the white pelican, like a number of other predatory birds, hatches a second chick as an "insurance". The insurance chick is normally driven to the edge of the nest by its sibling, and once displaced is ignored by its parents. Its "purpose" is merely to ensure that one viable chick survives. It has only a 10 % chance of fledging.[26]

Again, if the focus is on the pelican species as a whole, this strategy, "careless" and "wasteful" of individuals as it might seem, has "worked" for the white pelican, which as Rolston points out has lived successfully on Earth for thirty million years. The process of natural selection has developed in pelicans a strategy which is successful, although in many cases it leads to suffering. A defence based on this analysis would regard the harm as a by-product of the good, and would therefore be a developmental-byproduct defence.

But if we shift our focus to the individual that suffers, the "insurance" chick itself, the language of tragedy returns. Rolston talks of "the slaughter

---

[25] Rolston, *Science and Religion*, 144, italics in original. Humans' sense of the beauty and importance of these interdependent systems is shown in many films of wildlife. The camera operator does not intervene to rescue the limping impala calf from the hyenas, any more than US National Park officials intervene in cases of non-anthropogenic suffering in animals under their care (see Lisa H. Sideris, *Environmental Ethics, Ecological Theology, and Natural Selection* (New York: Columbia University Press, 2003) 179–182, drawing on further examples given by Rolston). Though it operates by way of suffering that on occasion seems tragic, the system tends to be depicted by the film-makers as good and necessary—if a theodicy were being mounted, it would be a constitutive-based one.

[26] Rolston, *Science and Religion,* 137 ff.

of the innocents"[27]; the process "sacrifices" the second chick to the good of the whole—it is intrinsic to the system that new life is regenerated out of the chick's death. The victims of the evolutionary process "share the labor of the divinity. In their lives, beautiful, tragic, and perpetually incomplete, they speak for God, they prophesy as they participate in the divine pathos".[28] "Long before humans arrived, the way of nature was already a *via dolorosa*."[29] Southgate and Robinson suggest that there is a tension here. Rolston's understanding of goods and harms, we suggest, remains a developmental one, but the rhetoric by which he elaborates his evolutionary theodicy (here and in the preceding case) implies a constitutive approach.[30]

It may be seen from these examples that specific foci within the system can lead to the formulation of property-consequence or developmental arguments, but concentration either on the ills of the individual sufferer, or on the beauty and value of the system as a whole, will take the analysis back in the direction of a constitutive approach.

Jay McDaniel's response to Rolston's analysis is very instructive. He quotes Rolston's remark that, "If God watches the sparrows fall, God does so from a great distance".[31] McDaniel is convinced this must be wrong—God's care is present to every sparrow,[32] and it is not enough simply to say of the back-up pelican chick that its suffering benefits the species as a whole. Redemption, McDaniel argues, must be of the particular creature concerned itself, and must involve a context in which it can respond to God's redeeming initiative. Hence his hope of "pelican heaven", and that "kindred creatures, given their propensities and needs, find fulfilment in life after death too".[33] This is a recourse not only to divine fellow-suffering (as also in Rolston) but also to eschatological compensation for the victims of evolution. As such it differs from the drama of non-human redemption that Rolston formulates, in which redemption is understood to occur through regeneration of life in other creatures. By focussing on the suffering creature itself, McDaniel questions whether a developmental defence based on the flourishing of other creatures, or the adaptedness of the species as a whole, can be deemed sufficient. Rolston makes much use of the language of sacrifice, but this only sharpens the point that it is not

---

[27] Ibid., 144.

[28] Ibid., 145.

[29] Holmes Rolston, III, "Kenosis and Nature", in: J. Polkinghorne (ed.), *The Work of Love*, 43–65 (London, SPCK and Grand Rapids, MI and Cambridge, Eerdmans, 2001) 60.

[30] To say this is not to detract from Rolston's important achievement in drawing attention to the evolutionary dimension of creaturely suffering, but simply to indicate the profoundly difficult character of this branch of theodicy.

[31] Rolston, *Science and Religion*, 140.

[32] Cf also Denis Edwards, "Every Sparrow that falls to the Ground: The Cost of Evolution and the Christ-event", Ecotheology 11:1, 2006, 103–123.

[33] Jay McDaniel, *Of God and Pelicans: A Theology of Reverence for Life* (Louisville, KY: Westminster John Knox Press, 1989) 45.

the evolutionary victim (such as the backup pelican chick) that has *chosen* the good of others over its own. It is the *process* that has "sacrificed" the victim's interests to the interests of the larger whole.

Ways of Thinking the Relation of the Creator God to an Evolutionary World

In setting out my approach in evolutionary theodicy in Section I I indicated that it would be based on the ontological claim that God gave rise to the creation (and continually sustains it as it unfolds), the teleological claim that God has goals within the creation, one—though only one—of which is the evolution of freely-choosing self-conscious creatures such as ourselves, and the claim that God suffers with the suffering of every created creature. I showed in section above that it is inappropriate to fall back on the traditional understanding of suffering in creation being the result of human sin.[34] It is therefore necessary to find some formulation of the theology of creation which allows for a God who creates an ambiguous world, a biosphere based on an inherent coupling of values and disvalues, and who suffers with that world even as the divine love draws it on.

I consider first the strategy of "kenosis in creation"[35], and in what way the concept of divine self-emptying can be helpful in understanding the relation of the Creator to an evolutionary creation. That relation has to be such as to give rise to biological "selves" with their own interests and behaviours. I explore how the states of those biological selves may be described both scientifically and within a theology of "deep intratrinitarian kenosis". I then explore how creaturely response to the creator may be characterized within such a theology. I note the work of two theologians, Hans Jonas and Ruth Page, whom I consider to have taken this problem of theodicy with the utmost seriousness, and indicate what I see as the strengths and weaknesses of their approaches. Finally, I show how my understanding of the Creator-creature relation affects our understanding of the nature of human being.

An important way in which God has been described as giving rise to a quasi-autonomous creation, in which there is disvalue as well as value, and which may be a cause of divine suffering with suffering creatures, is through a kenotic theology of creation, based on divine self-emptying. This concept, which in Christian thought derives originally from the description of Christ's self-emptying in Philippians 2:7, is used in kenotic theologies of creation to account for God's permitting of processes which give rise to disvalue, and also to imply a way in which the divine love suffers with that disvalue. It is

---

[34] For a recent survey of literature on a "cosmic Fall" see John J. Bimson, "Reconsidering a 'Cosmic Fall'", Science and Christian Belief, 18:1, 2006, 63–81.

[35] See in particular John Polkinghorne (ed.), *The Work of Love: creation as kenosis* (Grand Rapids, MI and Cambridge: Eerdmans and London: SPCK, 2001).

now my contention[36] that the language of kenosis in creation tends to arise out of commitment to a questionable spatial metaphor for the God-world relation—the alleged need for God to "make space" within Godself for the created world[37] and/or an (also questionable) commitment to incompatibilism—the notion that the free actions of creatures are incompatible with the involvement of God in every event[38], and is largely unnecessary to express the theological motivation underlying its use. What is being described in self-emptying terms can be redescribed in terms of the self-offering love of the Creator, through the activity of the Word and Spirit.[39]

However, I consider that kenosis *can* be extended from its original application in Philippians 2:7 in two helpful directions, which themselves mirror two important senses in which the self-emptying of Christ in Philippians can be read. "Ekenōsen", "he emptied himself", can be taken with the preceding clauses about Christ not seeking to snatch at equality with God. That leads naturally to an incarnational reading in which the divine Son empties himself of divine equality to take the form of a human. Or it can be taken with the following clause, "taking the form of a servant", which leads to more of an ethical reading, attesting to the sacrificial self-giving in Jesus' life. In what follows I shall develop both of these understandings of kenosis. In this section I shall draw on the work of the Roman Catholic theologian Hans Urs von Balthasar in providing language for that movement of the inner life of the Trinity that enables us to understand God as the creative, suffering origin of all things.[40] This is a theory of what might be termed "deep intratrinitarian kenosis". The self-abandoning love of the Father in begetting the Son establishes an otherness that enables God's creatures to be "selves". In the final section I shall consider what ethical response in humans liberated from the power of sin might lead to an appropriate response to the "groaning" of the non-human creation (Romans 8:22)

---

[36] A shift in my position from my 2002 article in Zygon.

[37] Most notably in Jürgen Moltmann's *God in Creation: An Ecological Doctrine of Creation, The Gifford Lectures 1984–85* transl. by M. Kohl (London: SCM Press, 1985) 87 ff.

[38] See my "'The Creatures' Yes and No to their creator: a proposal in evolutionary theology, kenotic trinitarianism, and environmental ethics", in: *Issues in Science and Theology* (London and New York: T&T Clark/Continuum, 2008, forthcoming), also Sarah Coakley, "Kenosis: Theological Meanings and Gender Connotations", in: J. Polkinghorne (ed.), *The Work of Love* (London: SPCK and Grand Rapids, MI and Cambridge: Eerdmans, 2001) 192–210.

[39] I have been influenced in my shift of position by the comment of Peters and Hewlett in *Evolution from Creation to New Creation* that creator-creature relations are not necessarily a zero-sum game, a "fixed pie of power" (143), and by valuable discussions with Dr Robert J. Russell. Cf. also Gunton, *The Triune Creator*, 141, "[...] there is no suggestion in the Bible that the act of creation is anything but the joyful giving of reality to the other".

[40] E. g. Hans Urs von Balthasar, *Theodrama: Theological Dramatic Theory, Vol. IV, The Action*, trans. G. Harrison, San Francisco: Ignatius Press, 1994, see also Paul S. Fiddes, *Participating in God: A Pastoral Doctrine of the Trinity* (London: Darton, Longman and Todd, 2000) 184.

First, then, kenosis within the Trinity. It is useful to distinguish von
Balthasar's formulation from the "divine withdrawal" model of Moltmann
(cf. note 37). Both theologians are wrestling with the problem of how a perfectly self-sufficient Trinitarian God can give rise to a creation that is other
than Godself. Both would want to see the self-sacrifice of Christ on the Cross
as deeply indicative of the character of God's gracious nature from all eternity.
Moltmann's kenotic model of creation uses the imagery of divine withdrawal,
making a space of non-existence within which existence can be formed. One
of the weaknesses of the model is the implication that there might be ontological "space" to which God is not present.[41] Von Balthasar takes kenosis
"back" a stage further—it is the self-emptying love of the Father in begetting
the Son that makes "space" within which other selves can be formed. That
separation of Father from Son of which Moltmann wrote with such power in
his *The Crucified God*[42] is for von Balthasar inherent, in some measure, in the
very character of a God who gives existence to the other and exposes Godself
to the other in vulnerable love. Otherness in the Trinity is the basis for the
otherness of creation.

But the existence of entities other than God is only the first stage of the
problem of engaging theologically with an evolutionary creation. Non-living
entities have existence, but it is a characteristic of living organisms that in
some sense they have "agency", they have "interests" that their behaviour
promotes.[43] This is crucial to our exploration of the inherent ambiguity of
creation, the intrinsic link between values and disvalues. The ambiguity of
the creation, its apparent "groaning", relates to the disvalues experienced by
living creatures. There is no waste in the "death" of stars by supernova or the
erosion of great mountains to hummocks[44], no evil in the changes in the surface of Jupiter owing to the impact of the comet Shoemaker-Levy.[45] Outside
living organisms there are no selves, no discrete entities with interests (except
on a process metaphysic) to which "evils" can occur.[46]

Biological selves, then, have interests that their behaviour seeks to promote.
At its simplest level this means that they derive energy from their environment
and seek to avoid harmful elements in that environment . As they grow and

---

[41] Cf. Gunton, *The Triune Creator*, 141.

[42] Jürgen Moltmann, *The Crucified God*, transl. by R. A. Wilson and J. Bowden (London: SCM
Press, 1974).

[43] Rolston, *Environmental Ethics*, also Stuart Kauffman, *Investigations* (Oxford: Oxford University Press) 2000.

[44] Southgate, "God and Evolutionary Evil", 806.

[45] Rolston, "Naturalizing and Systematizing Evil", 67.

[46] Which is not of course to say that there are not great *values* in aspects of the non-living
world, even that God may delight hugely in those aspects, whether they be the Antarctic ice-sheet
or the rings of Saturn. But the values are there by dint of others' valuing them, not—as we are
arguing here for living organisms—because there are evaluating selves that are themselves centres
of value.

mature the behaviour by which they exercise agency and promote their own self-interest is both a function of the species to which they belong and of their own individual identity. Drawing on an expression of the nineteenth-century Jesuit poet Gerard Manley Hopkins, I designate the process by which living creatures' behaviour promotes their flourishing and establishes their identity by the term "selving". On the model I am elaborating, then, the relationships within the creator God are such as make space not only for creaturely existence but for creaturely "selves" and their response to their environment. The Father whose self-abandonment begets the Son, the Son whose self-emptying gives glory to the Father, these in the power of the Spirit give rise to living selves whose character is typically not that of self-giving but of self-assertion, for that, in a Darwinian world, is the only way biological selves can survive and flourish.

I now develop this theology of creation further, aware of the speculative nature of this material, but regarding this engagement with the ambiguous character of evolutionary creation as essential to a proper dialogue between Trinitarian theology and contemporary science. A starting premise is that in the context of such an evolutionary creation it is still meaningful to talk of creation originating by the will of God the Father and occurring through the agency of the divine Logos and the Holy Spirit, a formulation which Gunton traces back to Irenaeus' phrase about the Son and the Spirit being the two "hands" of the Father in creation (see note 12). I therefore explore here how this "two-hands" formulation might be applied to a biosphere understood as evolving by natural selection, with all the problems of theodicy—ontological, teleological and soteriological—that that entails.

Hopkins writes in what is arguably his finest sonnet, "As kingfishers catch fire":

> As kingfishers catch fire, dragonflies draw flame;
> As tumbled over rim in roundy wells
> Stones ring; like each tucked string tells, each hung bell's
> Bow swung finds tongue to fling out broad its name;
> Each mortal thing does one thing and the same;
> Deals out that being indoors each one dwells;
> Selves—goes itself; *myself* it speaks and spells,
> Crying *What I do is me: for that I came.*[47]

What I want to argue, in linking the creation of biological selves to the theology of Trinitarian creation, is that when a living creature "selves" in the sense of Hopkins' kingfishers, behaving in its most characteristic way, and flourishing in so doing, it is conforming to the pattern offered by the divine Logos, the pattern of that type of selfhood imagined by the divine Word, and begot-

---

[47] *Poems and Prose of Gerard Manley Hopkins: selected with and introduction and notes by W. H. Gardner* (Harmondsworth: Penguin, 1953) 51.

ten in the Spirit out of the perfect self-abandoning love of the Father. Selving, then, takes place within what I have called "deep intratrinitarian kenosis". It is from the love of the Father for the world, and for the glory of the Son, that other selves gain their existence, beauty and meaning, that which prevents them collapsing into nothingness. It is from the self-sacrificial love of the Son for the Father and all his works that each created entity gains the distinctive pattern of its existence, that which prevents the creation from collapsing back into an undifferentiated unity. It is from the power of the Spirit, predictable only in its continual creativity and love, which is the same self-transcending and self-renewing love as is between the Father and the Son, that each creature receives its particularity. Within each pattern or "logos"[48] of created entities is a diversity of individual being, a "thisness" which is the distinctive gift of the Spirit In its moment of "catching fire" the kingfisher is in that moment the pattern of "kingfisher". Hopkins sees this as a kind of profound creaturely "yes"—"what I do is me, for that I came". It is a yes of identity, but also of particularity.

We can imagine these moments of creaturely yes, of the creature perfectly expressing its identity, the pattern and particularity of its existence to their full potential, most easily in higher animals, in the moments in which the creature seems perfectly to fulfil what it is to be that animal, that bird, whether it be the moment of eating the best food, accomplishing the perfect hunt, the moment of pure play. More generally, any creature's yes comes when it is perfectly itself, both in terms of the species to which it belongs and in its own individuality. The creature perfectly sounding the "hung bell" of its existence perfectly "selves". We can associate this language of perfect selving with the concept of creaturely praise of God, a concept which has been strong in various parts of the Christian tradition.[49] This language of creaturely praise finds support in the Psalms, in particular 19:1–4, 145:10–14, 148.

I am well aware that to many biologists this account of creaturely existence will seem essentialist and outdated. A more familiar scientific description would be to see the properties of every organism as plottable on a "fitness landscape". This is a helpful way to understand evolving systems, and I adopt it into my model as follows. I see a species as representing a peak on a fitness landscape, as biologists describe. I see every such peak as a possibility imagined in the mind of God, hence possessing in Maximus' terms "logoi", divinely-given patterns of being. I see the work of the Holy Spirit as constantly affirming every organism in its particularity, and constantly offering

---

[48] On this terminology from Maximus the Confessor see Andrew Louth, "The Cosmic Vision of Saint Maximus the Confessor", in: Philip Clayton and Arthur Peacocke (ed.), *In Whom We Live and Move and Have our Being: Panentheistic Reflections on God's Presence in a Scientific World* (Grand Rapids, MI and Cambridge: Eerdmans, 2004) 184–196.

[49] See Ian Bradley, *God is Green: Christianity and the Environmen* (London: Darton, Longman and Todd, 1990) 39–45.

new possibilities of being. So I do not see species as static or unchanging, nor do I imagine all members of the species as clustered on the fitness peak.[50] The work of the two hands of the Father in creation both draws onwards the ever-shifting distribution of peaks in the fitness landscape, through the unfolding creative work of the Logos, and encourages organisms, through the power of the Spirit, in their exploration of that landscape, giving rise to new possibilities of selving. This model of divine creativity has something in common with the work of the late Arthur Peacocke, in his use of metaphors such as God the improvisatory composer,[51] and also with the model of divine lure in process theology. My model, only sketched at this stage in its development, is distinguished from these firstly in being explicitly Trinitarian in its formulation, and secondly in giving an account of how organisms are both valued by God in their nature, but also are able to resist the divine invitation to transcend that nature (see below).

What is vital to a treatment of evolutionary theodicy is to acknowledge that the character of the creation is such that many individual creatures never "selve" in any fulfilled way. I gave above Rolston's classic example of the "insurance" chick that birds such as white pelicans hatch.[52] Typically this younger chick is edged out of the nest by its elder, and then ignored by the parents. It has only a 10 % chance of fledging. The insurance pelican chick rarely has the chance to manifest the pattern "pelicanness"—instead its life, typically, is one of starvation, pain and abandonment to early death.

To gain some theological purchase on this view of evolved creation, shot through as it is with ambiguity and implicit question as to the goodness of God, we can analyse the possible states of living creatures as follows:

i)   "fulfilled"—a state in which the creature is utterly being itself, in an environment in which it flourishes (including an appropriate network of relationships with other organisms), with access to the appropriate energy sources and reproductive opportunities[53]

ii)   "growing towards fulfillment"—not yet mature, but still with the possibility of attaining state i)

iii)   "frustrated"—held back in some way from fulfillment, whether by adverse mutation or environmental change, or through old age, or being

---

[50] Louth, op. cit., notes that it is the dynamic quality in Maximus' concept that makes it more helpful in the dialogue with contemporary science than its Platonic antecedents.

[51] Arthur Peacocke, *Paths from Science towards God: the end of all our exploring* (Oxford: Oneworld, 2001) 77 f, 136 f.

[52] Rolston, *Science and Religion*, 137 ff. As noted above, the predicament of the insurance pelican chick has also attracted analysis by McDaniel, *Of God and Pelicans*, ch. 1.

[53] I note that not all creatures have reproductive opportunities, also that in some sexually-reproducing species there may be social roles which may constitute "fulfillment" for that organism without the need to be reproductively active.

predated upon or parasitised, or being unable to find a mate through
competition or species scarcity

iv) "transcending itself"—through some new pattern of behaviour, whether
as a result of a favourable mutation, or a chance exploration of a new possibility or relating to its own or another species

The first state is the state of true "selving", the state Hopkins talks about in
his poem, and it is the "sound" of "praise" from creature to Creator, "what
I do is me, for that I came". Scientifically, it is made possible by the flux of
energy through the biosphere, both from the sun and from the hot interior of
the Earth, and by the recycling of energy from other life-forms.

Theologically, we might say that this fulfillment in the creature is the gift of
existence from the Father, form and pattern from the Son, particularity from
the Holy Spirit, and that the creature's praise, in being itself, is offered by the
Son to the Father, in the delight of the Spirit. As I indicated above, I hold that
these states of fulfillment consummate a creaturely life, such that the death
that inevitably follows them may be considered a natural end rather than itself
being evil.

The second state is scientifically describable in terms of the interaction
of the genome with intraorganismic and environmental factors, again made
possible by the flux of energy through a dissipative system. It will include
pain, in many organisms, because of the need to learn an aversion to negative
stimuli. As I noted above this is a necessary, rather than a negative, aspect of
the growth of sentient life. The Godhead that is so committed to the creation
as ultimately to experience birth and infancy as a human may be imagined to
take an especial delight in the growth of young organisms.

The third state, that of frustration, is one which Darwin's model of natural
selection brings very much to the fore. Darwin recognised that biotic systems
will be limit-sum games, that evolutionary strategies often involve the overproduction of offspring, and necessarily imply that state iii) is a precondition
for states i) and ii). In the current creation "frustration", including the actual
pain caused to organisms by disease, competition, and being the victim of
predators, is a necessary cost of selving. Indeed it is a characteristic of nature
that the full flourishing of some individuals is at the expense of that of other
individuals, either of the same species or of others. Predation is the most obvious example; competition for reproductive success is another.

Theologically we may posit that the frustration of the creature, be it of the
insurance pelican chick, or the sheep parasitized by the worm *Redia*[54], or the
aging lion beaten for the first time in a fight with a younger male, is received
by the Son through the brooding immanence of the Spirit, and uttered in that

---

[54] An example given by John F. Haught, "Darwin, Design and the Promise of Nature, The
Boyle Lecture 2004" (available on the internet).

Spirit as a song of lament to the Father. All that the frustrated creature suffers, and all it might have been but for frustration, is retained in the memory of the Trinity, and the creature is given fulfillment in a form appropriate to it at the eschaton.[55]. Given that the same processes lead to full selving and to frustration, we must imagine this ambiguity held deep in the loving relationships within God.

I indicated above that we might (tentatively) identify perfect selving with creaturely praise, drawing on Hopkins' line "What I do is me, for that I came". But I regard the position as more complex than that, and develop here a fuller picture of creaturely response to the Creator, which will incorporate the fourth of the possibilities given above, that of creaturely self-transcendence. I indicated above that I saw the invitation to self-transcendence in the exploration of new possibilities of being as particularly the gift of the Holy Spirit in creation. The Spirit longs for creatures to transcend themselves, to find new ways of relating. Evolutionary self-transcendence is dramatically illustrated in such cruxes as the symbioses that gave rise to the first eukaryotic cells, or the Middle to Upper Palaeolithic "Transition" in *H. Sapiens*, by which the human being emerged from being an animal of relatively modest technological skills[56] to a being not just capable of great linguistic, social, economic and artistic sophistication[57], but also of worship and of genuine self-sacrifice. Indeed a form of self-transcendence occurs whenever co-operation between organisms, either within a species or across species, produces new types of "selves". The various forms of "altruism" that have been described for non-human species are expressions of that transcendence of mere self-interest.[58] But clearly such co-operations are limited, and take place within a larger context of competition among the extended selves for scarce resources.

I have long been fascinated by a passage in Paul Fiddes' book *The Creative Suffering of God* (1988). He writes of God's relation to the creation, "Some overall vision of the 'responsiveness' and 'resistance' of creation to the Spirit of God is needed for a doctrine of creative evolution, (and) for a proper the-

---

[55] I follow here McDaniel's suggestion of "pelican heaven" (cf. *Of God and Pelicans* 46f), noting also Denis Edwards' judicious agnosticism as to this proposal in "Every Sparrow that falls to the ground". Cf. also Keith Ward, *The Concept of God* (Oxford: Blackwell, 1974) 223: "If there is any sentient creature which suffers pain, that being—whatever it is and however it is manifested—must find that pain transfigured by a greater joy".

[56] Cf. Jared Diamond, "The Evolution of Human Inventiveness", in: M.P. Murphy and L.A.J. O'Neill (ed.), *What is Life? The Next Fifty Years. Speculations on the Future of Biology*, 41–55 (Cambridge, Cambridge University Press, 1995) 45f.

[57] Cf. Ian Tattersall, *Becoming Human: Evolution and Human Uniqueness* (New York: Harcourt and Brace, 1998).

[58] See Holmes Rolston, III, *Genes, Genesis and God: Values and their Origins in Natural and Human History* (Cambridge: Cambridge University Press, 1999) for a listing of such evolutionary strategies, and for cautions about extending this analysis to human behaviour.

odicy…"[59] Fiddes is arguing that we must speak of some sort of "free will in creation", of resistance and responsiveness, if we are to speak of God suffering in creation. This taps into Fiddes' conclusion that suffering must be something that befalls God, not a mere logical outworking of the divine plan.

Fiddes' language of freely-chosen resistance, and of suffering that befalls God outside the divine plan, needs further exploration, particularly in the case where it is being applied outside the sphere of human choices. The sort of creation that this is presumably *is* very much part of God's plan. Indeed it is a creation, according to Paul in Romans 8:19–22, subjected to travail by God in order that eventually it may achieve the glorious liberty of the children of God. To realize this goal God must encounter the contingency and struggle of creatures' being creatures and not-being-God. Just as the Cross, in Christian tradition, is part of God's plan (so Revelation 13:8), as the only way to bring all creation to its ultimate fulfillment, so it is part of God's plan that God encounter and bear the self-seeking and communion-denying elements in what it is to be a Darwinian creature. Immanent in all things, God must be exposed to what it is for living organisms to selve in this way.

I articulated above a suggestion of how we might understand creaturely responsiveness, the creature's "Yes" to God—in the moment of eating the best food, accomplishing the perfect hunt, the moment of pure play. More generally the creature's yes comes when it is perfectly itself, both in terms of the species to which it belongs and in its own individuality. The creature perfectly sounding the "hung bell" of its existence perfectly "selves". How then might we understand a creaturely "No", a "resistance" to the divine will?

Von Balthasar places the tension between createdness and self-interest within a Trinitarian frame. He writes: "The creature's No, its wanting to be autonomous without acknowledging its origin, must be located within the Son's all-embracing Yes to the Father, in the Spirit".[60] What, though, *is* the creaturely "No"? It is, after all, not easy to associate the theologian's description of the creature "wanting to be autonomous without acknowledging its origin", with scientifically-characterised behaviour in birds, or yet bacteria. What follows is an attempt to venture onto this very difficult territory.

Contained within the behaviour of Darwinian creatures, which is understood in Christian thought to be created by God, and is the means by which the extraordinary beauty of the cheetah and the gazelle, the orca and the porpoise, the peregrine, the hummingbird, the honey-bee, all come to be the creatures that they are, is a limitation of creaturely response. The creation is "very good", but each element of it is necessarily limited. Self-transcendence is, as was noted above, limited within the non-human realm. There is within the non-human world little sign of costly self-giving to the other, or identifi-

---

[59] Paul S. Fiddes, *The Creative Suffering of God* (Oxford: Clarendon Press, 1988) 228.
[60] Von Balthasar, *Theodrama, Vol. IV*, 330.

cation with difference in community. There are some very touching examples of animal behaviour, particularly in social animals. Orcas will push an ailing pod member to the surface to breathe, elephants will surround and support a sick member of the family group. But very rarely is there care for the genuinely other. In this respect the heart-rending observations of a lioness who exhibited motherly behaviour towards a series of young oryxes[61] stands out as an example of possibilities virtually never seen (and indeed, in Darwinian terms, maladaptive). It could be argued that a lioness which nurtures and protects her prey-animal instead of feeding off it is not being a lioness. This is the true imaginative stretch of the Isaianic vision of 11:6–9. There, animals which seem defined by, and indeed beautiful in, their hurting and destroying, are pictured as not hurting or destroying on the holy mountain, but rather lying down with their prey. I take up this problem in the next section.

Of themselves, then, organisms other than the human show limited signs of self-transcendence. Non-human creatures, it might be said, then, offer a "No" to the example of the triune creator's self-giving love, to the love poured out without the cost being counted. The work of the Holy Spirit in offering possibilities of community succeeds in giving rise to ecosystemic complexity, but "fails", in most of the non-human world, in creating any community characterized by authentic altruism, true self-giving love. Only hints of this behaviour emerge, in the care given to infants in many species, in the mutual protectiveness in social groups. The non-human creature returns to God its "selving" Yes, but also a No to self-transcendence, to growing into the image of the Trinity of self-giving love.[62]

God bears this "No" in God's being—it is always new and always particular, because particularity is part of the gifting of God to the creation through the Holy Spirit. God suffers not only the suffering of myriad creatures, each one precious to the Creator, and the extinction of myriad species, each a way of being imagined within the creative Word, but also the continual refusal—beyond the creation's praise—of God's offer of self-transcendence, the continual refusal, beyond all creation's flourishing, to live by the acceptance of the divine offer which would draw the creature into the life of the Trinity itself. It will be apparent anew how paradoxical the theology of evolutionary creation must be, given the Christian affirmation that a good God has given rise to a good creation, and yet as we have seen the creation is shot through with ambiguity. The purposes of God are, and are not, realized in the life of any given creature. God delights in creatures in and for themselves, and yet longs for the response of the creature that can become more than itself, whose life can be broken and poured out in love and joy after the divine im-

---

[61] Http://www.lewa.org/oryx-lioness-facts.php.
[62] Only with the evolution of the human do we see the full extent of the possibilities inherent in a Yes which is the Yes beyond the self, the yes of the self-given self.

age. Divine purposes are, seemingly, realised, eventually, at the level of the biosphere as a whole, in the evolution of a rich variety of ecosystems and a freely-choosing self-conscious creature capable of sophisticated reflection on the planet, and hence potentially a partner for God in the care of living things. But at the level of the individual creature, the divine desire for creaturely flourishing is frequently unrealised, and where it is realised, it is only so at the expense of other possibilities, and often at the expense of the flourishing of other organisms. The pattern of the creation's flourishing, then, is an *ambiguous* pattern—"yes" to God always accompanied by "no"—full of beauty, full even of praise, but also of selving that takes place at the expense of the flourishing of other selves.[63]

It is this nexus of considerations that offers the real challenge and excitement of evolutionary theology, a challenge too often muted by creationist and other naïve readings of the narratives both of scripture and of science. Few theologians have really engaged with this. Two who have done so, reframing the problem so as to draw the sting of evolutionary suffering for a doctrine of God, are Hans Jonas and Ruth Page. Jonas, whose own mother died in a concentration camp, is particularly sensitive to the stricture that if we say anything at all about God today we should not say anything we would not also be willing to repeat in the presence of the children of Auschwitz. Although this point has already been well taken—perhaps particularly well by Kenneth Surin[64]—it bears restating and restating. But the model of God to which Jonas is driven is an extreme one—his God empties Godself of mind and power in giving the creation its existence, and then allows the interplay of chance and natural law to take its course. God's only further involvement is that God holds a memory of the experience of the creation—he receives his being back "transfigured or possibly disfigured by the chance harvest of unforeseeable temporal experience".[65] However authentically held, this position is a form of "sub-deism" (to borrow a phrase of Clare Palmer's), not a basis for a Christian theology of creation and involvement with the cosmos. Jonas' God is indeed not the sort of God to whom anyone would be inclined to pray.

The other recent account that creatively reframes the problem of evolutionary evil, but may be thought to concede ground unconcedable within Christian thought, is that of Ruth Page.[66] This is an important position which has had too little attention, one which takes on board the problem I set out in the introduction and genuinely attempts a theological solution. Page writes:

---

[63] The "yes" contains the "no" and vice versa; this is the constitutive element in my good-harm analysis (see my section on classification above).

[64] In his impressive *Theology and the Problem of Evil* (Oxford: Blackwells, 1986).

[65] Hans Jonas, *Mortality and Morality: A Search for the Good after Auschwitz*. A collection of essays ed. by Lawrence Vogel (Evanston, IL: Northwestern University Press, 1996) 125.

[66] Ruth Page, *God and the Web of Creation* (London, SCM Press, 1996) and "God, Natural Evil and the Ecological Crisis", Studies in World Christianity 3:1, 1997, 68–86.

"I cannot imagine a God responsible for natural evil any more than one responsible for moral evil…To those who wish to affirm full-blooded…(divine) making and doing, (my) version will appear anaemic. But the consequences of belief in a more virile God, who has to be responsible for the removal of around 98 % of all species ever, but who fails to do anything in millions of cases of acute suffering in nature and humanity, are scarcely to be borne."[67]

The problems of theodicy associated with any long-term teleological scheme are for Page "scarcely to be borne". So like Jonas she emphasizes that God "lets the world be"—drawing here on the Heideggerian term *Gelassenheit*. God creates possibilities, and lets them unfold. Thus far this is a clear picture, and one to which no metaphysically-aware scientist could object. But this *is* the picture for which Clare Palmer in her review of Page's book coined that term "subdeism".[68] *Gelassenheit* of itself does not do justice to the Christian vision of the God involved in the world. Page is well aware of this, and she therefore also invokes a category of divine involvement she calls *Mitsein*, God's companioning of the world at every stage and locus. I do not believe this view is entirely consistent in Page, because sometimes she speaks of *Mitsein* as a non-judging maintenance of relationship, and sometimes she uses a more familiar terminology very akin to process thought, as in her talk of "a God always present everywhere, offering both reproach and encouragement, and above all saving, forgiving, companionship".[69] Divine reproach and encouragement sound very like the steering of the cosmos to me.[70] However, Page's central point is that her divine companioning is "teleology now"—it is all for the benefit of the entity concerned, and does not use that entity as a means to an end.

It may be doubted whether this altogether relieves the theodicist's burden. After all, God is still responsible for the ontological aspect of the problem—for the existence of the world in which the suffering takes place. Moreover all life, from its most primitive, is characterised by differential selection of self-replicators—and only very primitive ecosystems, lacking all sentience, involve no significant cost to organisms in terms of pain, suffering and extinction. But Page might argue that life itself, life lived in companionship with God, is worth the sufferings intrinsic to its development. Her approach does go a great way to address the teleological problem—God using pain, suffering, death and extinction to realise other ends.

There are many points of contact between Page's thought and the view presented here—a strong awareness of the problem of evolutionary theodicy, a sense of God creating by creating possibilities, or even "possibilities of

---

[67] Page, *God and the Web of Creation*, 104.

[68] Clare Palmer, "Review of *God and the Web of Creation* by Ruth Page", Journal of Theological Studies, 48, 1997, 750–753.

[69] Page, *God and the Web of Creation*, 43 f.

[70] Moreover, Page is quite content to invoke resurrection in a fairly traditional fashion even though she is at such pains to remove any talk of the providential action of God (ibid., 61).

possibilities".[71] There is a consonance between this view and my own sense of God imagining the peaks on fitness landscapes which creatures explore, and also encouraging the creature to explore new ways of being within those landscapes.

I consider, however, that Page has not wholly apprehended the ambiguity in creation, that blend of value with disvalue, which this study explores. When she writes of "earthquakes, hurricanes and volcanoes", and "what horror a change of climate [of which there have been many[72]] may wreak over vast areas of the world". She comments, "These are instances when the world does not fit together, and the wonder they inspire is not likely to lead to immediate thought on the goodness of God".[73] But it is precisely those great geochemical events that have shaped the wonderful biosphere of the present Earth. They *are* the way the Earth "fits together" so as to generate new long-term possibilities. And Page surely underrates the divine concern with long-term possibilities. Consider the truly ancient predators of the world—the shark and the crocodile. Both groups of species arrived on remarkably stable peaks in fitness landscapes hundreds of millions of years ago. Both in their own way have their own beauty and fittingness (witness the extraordinary delicacy with which a crocodile, possessed of a bite-power approaching that of *Tyrannosaurus Rex*, holds its infants between its teeth). But it would be hard to image the Creator not desiring the further evolution of predators, just because such outstanding strategies had already evolved, any more than one could image God not desiring the evolution of the eukaryotic cell given the great sophistication of the bacteria that had evolved over the first two billion years of the history of life. The evolutionary process "is characterized by propensities towards increase in complexity, information-processing and storage, consciousness, sensitivity to pain and even self-consciousness"[74] and it is hard to concede Page's rigid "teleology now" and not imagine that these longer-term propensities are not also reflections of the divine desire. Since, as I indicated at the beginning of this essay, properties such as complexity and self-consciousness evolve by a process that denies full flourishing to a high proportion of the individuals and species that evolve, the long-term teleological problem in evolutionary theodicy is unavoidable.[75]

---

[71] Page, "God, Natural Evil and the Ecological Crisis", see also Southgate, "A Test Case—Divine Action", 284 f.

[72] Cf. Peter D. Ward and Donald Brownlee, *The Life and Death of Planet Earth: How the new science of astrobiology charts the ultimate fate of our world* (New York: Owl Books, 2004, first published 2003).

[73] Page, *God, Natural Evil and the Ecological Crisis*, 69.

[74] Peacocke, *The Palace of Glory: God's World and Science* (Adelaide: Australian Theological Forum, 2005) 66.

[75] As with process-theological schemes, moreover, the strength of Page's proposal is also its weakness: the world has been distanced a vast way from being in any direct sense God's creation.

The scheme I am developing here is a strongly teleological one—it affirms the value of every creature, both as a good of itself and as a vital component of an ecosystem (it should be remembered that these systems typically depend obligatorily on the flourishing of micro-organisms) but it prizes self-transcendence, the exploration by organisms, either through genetic mutation or new behaviours, of new possibilities of being. It acknowledges the propensities of which Peacocke writes, and regards them as divinely imparted to the biosphere. It assigns progressively greater value to more complex organisms, and more complex interrelations of organisms. It prizes interactions of care within and across kin groups, and symbioses between species (in line with understandings of the Holy Spirit as the former of and delighter in relationships). It claims that the Spirit longs for creatures to transcend themselves, to find new ways of relating.

I noted above that for the kingfisher truly to "selve" was to conform to the pattern of "kingfisher" given by the Creating Word. But for the human, a freely-choosing creature in the image and likeness of God, to "selve" is to conform (however momentarily) to the image of the Trinity. That means: to conform to the pattern of Christ, and to have accepted from the Holy Spirit the gifts both of particularity and of engagement in authentic community, community characterized by the self-giving love of neighbour in which is found the true love of self, of justice, and of God.

Within human beings, then, grows up (such is the grace of God in creation) the possibility of a larger "Yes"—of a sharing of resources with the weak and the non-kin, of reproductive processes accompanied by self-giving love and sustained companionship, of a recognizing all humans as one's neighbour, and of self-sacrificial actions.

On this model the *imago Dei* is the *imago Trinitatis*, the capacity to give love, in the power of the Spirit, to the radically other, and by that same Spirit to receive love from that other, selflessly. But we only grow into that image as we grow into God, as we learn to dwell within the triune love. We never possess the *imago* independently of that indwelling, that journeying towards God's offer of ultimate love.

Eschatology and Non-Human Nature

In the light of all the problems of suffering and extinction we have listed, Austin Farrer's question, "Poor limping world, why does not your kind Creator pull the thorn out of your paw?"[76] seems particularly pressing. I have stressed throughout this essay the way creaturely value is bound up with disvalue—

Nor is it clear why such a merely companioning God should be the object of worship, or yet the recipient of prayer.

[76] Austin Farrer, *Love Almighty and Ills Unlimited: An Essay on Providence and Evil containing the Nathaniel Taylor Lectures for 1961* (London: Collins, 1962) 51.

the "thorn" of creaturely suffering is also the "grace" that is "sufficient" for the drawing on of creation towards new heights of consciousness, beauty and diversity. The evolutionary naturalism of Holmes Rolston leads him to press the question "Does Nature Need to be Redeemed?"[77]. Rolston's sense that living things are redeemed in the new life that is regenerated out of the death of the old allows him to answer his own question in the negative. Whereas it is the strong conviction of Jürgen Moltmann that:

> A *Christus evolutor* without *Christus redemptor* is nothing other than a cruel, un-feeling *Christus selector*, a historical world-judge without compassion for the weak, and a breeder of life uninterested in the victims…Not even the best of all possible stages of evolution justifies acquiescence in evolution's victims…There is therefore no meaningful hope for the future of creation unless "the tears are wiped from every eye". But they can only be wiped out when the dead are raised, and when the victims of evolution experience justice through the resurrection of nature. Evolution in its ambiguity has no such redemptive efficacy and therefore no salvific significance either. If Christ is to be thought of in conjunction with evolution, he must become evolution's redeemer.[78]

It will be clear from the opening sections of this chapter that I do not regard God's creative activity in evolution as unfeeling or lacking in compassion. However, I regard Rolston's position as neglecting the predicament of the individual creature, and the burden of theodicy implicit in the suffering of all creatures that die without fulfilment. The fourth element in my evolutionary theodicy—the eschatological—has two parts. First, a conviction that God does not abandon the victims of evolution. Second, a suggestion that redeemed humans have a role in the healing of creation. I take up the first claim here, and the second in the next section.

The ultimate fate of created matter is an enigmatic element in Christian theology. We are dependent on a relatively few texts, profoundly mysterious in their import, whether they be the Isaianic vision of the leopard lying down with the kid (Isaiah 11:6–9), or Paul's exposition of the resurrection body in 1. Corinthians 15, or the motif of "eternal life" that is strong in the Fourth Gospel.[79]

Is heaven, then, a place for God and humans, or a broader redemption of all creation? What are we to make of certain "cosmic-Christological" texts which speak of the reconciliation of all creation taking place in Christ (e.g. Colossians 1:20, Ephesians 1:10)? There is an urgent need for a re-exploration of these texts and their implications for our understanding of our relation to the non-human creation. Gunton makes an important point when he writes:

---

[77] Holmes Rolston, III, "Does Nature Need to be Redeemed?", Zygon, 29, 1994, 205–229.
[78] Jürgen Moltmann, *The Way of Jesus Christ*, transl. M. Kohl (London: SCM Press, 1990) 296 f.
[79] John 3:15 and eight other references.

[T]here is in the Bible no redemption, no social and personal life, apart from the creation. It is therefore reasonable, especially in the light of Old Testament witness to the creation, to hold that the Bible as a whole is concerned with the future of creation...But the fact that it is Israel and Jesus who are at the centre of God's action in and towards the world means that it is the personal that is central, the nonpersonal peripheral. That does not rule out an ecological concern, but it cannot be of independent interest.[80]

Human personhood, then, is of the first importance theologically, but humanity will be redeemed, ultimately, as *part* of a new creation rather than *away* from contact with the rest of creation.

The position advanced here is close to that of McDaniel when he argues for "pelican heaven" (see the introduction above!), that "if the [insurance pelican] chick does continue in some way...it becomes imaginable that, in time, the pelican would experience his own fulfillment of needs and interests, his own redemption".[81] It may be asked, what is the evidence for such a heaven? What, for the non-human creation, corresponds to the dramatic prolepsis of the resurrection of Jesus, and his appearances in a resurrection body?

I freely concede that the evidence on which to proceed is scanty. I note Gunton's point above that humans are always envisaged, in the Bible, in the context of the rest of creation, and it would be curious if this were not carried forward into the realm in which relationships (presumably) are to be found at their richest and truest. I note the suggestive poetry of Isaiah chapters 11 and 65, itself problematic in that it envisions animals in the new creation, but in transformed relationship which nevertheless allows them to continue to be themselves,[82] and (perhaps most crucially in terms of the likely original sense of the text) safeguards the relationships of animals to human beings.

Even John Polkinghorne, who has tended to concentrate, in his writing both on theodicy and on eschatology, on the predicament and hope of human beings, has conceded that pets might be found in the new creation. Polkinghorne rebukes other theologians for too anthropocentric an attitude, and yet he himself limits the involvement of animals in the eschatological sphere. They will be there as types rather than as individuals, pets being an arguable exception.[83] This runs the risk of not doing full justice either to the richness of individual animal experience, or to the theodicy problems that evolutionary creation poses. Simple organisms may be agreed to be types rather than individuals, but it is individual animal centres of experience that are subject to intense suffering, and individual animal lives that sometimes experience little or

---

[80] Colin Gunton, *Christ and Creation* (Carlisle: Paternoster Press, 1992) 33 f.

[81] *Of God and Pelicans*, 47.

[82] There is a poem by James Dickey called "The Heaven of Animals", reproduced in: Neil Astley (ed.), *Staying Alive*, Tarset: Bloodaxe, 2002, 221 f, which offers a fine image of the unimaginable.

[83] John Polkinghorne, *Science and the Trinity* (London: SPCK, 2004) 152.

nothing of the fulfilled life that I explored above. These tortured or frustrated lives surely call for redemption by the God who gave rise to the evolutionary order. I draw here on Polkinghorne's own logic in the chapter just quoted. He writes of human beings:

> We shall all die with our lives incomplete, with possibilities unfulfilled and with hurts unhealed. This will be true even of those fortunate enough to die peacefully in honoured old age. How much more must it be true of those who die prematurely and painfully, through disease, famine, war and neglect. If God is the Father of our Lord Jesus Christ, all the generations of oppressed and exploited people must have the prospect of a life beyond death, in which they will receive what was unjustly denied them in this life.[84]

There are interesting links between this argument and the suggestion I advanced above that the character of human existence is such that humans' selving is, unlike any other creature, only found in self-transcendence; it is never wholly fulfilled, because its fulfillment is ultimately found within the life of God. I claimed that, in contrast, the life of non-human creatures—particular lives, not just the life of the type—can experience periods of fulfillment which fully consummate that life. But clearly there are very many creatures for whom there is no such fulfillment, there is only frustration, disease and famine, premature and painful death. And if we take seriously the hints in Colossians and Ephesians of the cosmic character of the redemption of creation in Christ, then all these creatures, we might equally argue, must have the prospect of fulfillment. This follows as soon as one rejects Polkinghorne's conclusion that animals are only representatives of their types, and considers instead their individual suffering.

What the above analysis does not resolve is how the eschatological fulfillment of creatures relates to their protological natures, and the limited nature of their selving. Is this fulfillment limited to the idea that "the whole story of the universe and life streams into the everlasting bosom of divine compassion"?[85] Does it extend to a form of subjective immortality such as McDaniel's "pelican heaven"[86] in which pelicanness is expressed, presumably still in relation to other creatures, without competition or frustration on the part of predator or prey? If so, does this represent only a form of compensatory selving for pelicans who experienced no such fulfillment in their own lives? Is it just that "every tear will be wiped away"? Or does such a heaven involve some sort of self-transcended pelicanness that is even harder for us to imagine, perhaps even involving an experience for the redeemed prey-animal which delights in the beauty and flourishing of the predator, and vice versa? Perhaps this is a question we shall never resolve, any more than we can say what would be

84 Ibid., 150.
85 Haught, *Darwin, Design and the Promise of Nature*.
86 McDaniel, *Of God and Pelicans*, 45.

fulfillment for the parasitic organisms that so exercised Darwin, or for the bacteria and viruses that only thrive as pathogens.[87] The best clues we can glean in respect of eschatological fulfillment will come from returning to the case of the human being, an animal among other animals, but one with such profoundly novel emergent characteristics as to engender a whole set of fresh possibilities in its relation to God.

Ethical Kenosis and the Calling of Human Beings

Another of those relatively few, tantalizing passages in which the Bible speaks of the eschatological future of the non-human creation is the one I quoted at the beginning of this essay, Romans 8:19–22. There, the creation is depicted as in travail, *awaiting the glorious liberty of the children of God*. It has a "travail", a painful birthing process to which God has subjected it in expectation of the transformation of human beings. In the sections that follow I explore a range of possible roles through which humans might express their glorious liberty, and participate in creation's release.

Humans as Contemplatives of Nature

I return here to the thought of Hopkins, whose concept of "selving" informed my analysis of God's relation to an evolving creation. Of itself, Hopkins' contemplative method is interesting, and sometimes inspiring, but it is essentially pre-modern. He shows little awareness of the ambiguities of the evolutionary world. He writes of the world as "charged with the grandeur of God" ("God's Grandeur"): Darwin too used the word "grandeur" in describing his "view of things"[88], but was acutely conscious of the ugliness of much of nature, and that its beauty only emerges in a process involving much suffering. Hopkins can celebrate "all trades, their gear and tackle and trim" ("Pied Beauty"), but nowhere explores the tension between this and the polluting effect of trades at large. So the poet offers us a model for a scientifically, poetically and theologically-informed contemplation, but little that can help us with environmental ethics in the complexities of our current world. The same might be said of Martin Buber, the Jewish contemplative philosopher with whose method he has something in common. Hopkins' comment that "when you look hard at a thing it seems to look hard at you"[89] is very close to this passage from Buber, contemplating a tree:

---

[87] An important attempt to delineate what can and cannot helpfully be said is Robert J. Russell's *Natural Theodicy in an Evolutionary Context*.

[88] In the coda of *On the Origin of Species by Means of Natural Selection, or the Preservation of Favoured Races in the Struggle for Life* (London: John Murray, 1859).

[89] Gerard Manley Hopkins, SJ, *The Journals and Papers of Gerard Manley Hopkins*, ed. Humphry House and Graham Storey (London: Oxford University Press, 1959) 140.

That living wholeness and unity of the tree, which denies itself to the sharpest glance of the mere investigator and discloses itself to the glance of one who says *Thou*, is there when he, the sayer of *Thou*, is there: it is he who vouchsafes to the tree that it manifest this unity and wholeness; and now the tree which is in being manifests them. Our habits of thought make it difficult for us to see that here, awakened by our attitude, something lights up and approaches us from the course of being.[90]

Behind both methods of engaging with the non-human world lurks a very strong sense of God as the one whose interest in all relationships cannot be ignored. Part of the strength of Buber's insight was that he saw that relationships never remain in that ideal "I-Thou" realm of true interpersonal (or inter-entity) meeting—they are constantly slipping back into the "I-It". That is the relation which allows the entity to whom the "I" relates to be used as a commodity, merely a means to an end, only a resource to be exploited. This thinking of Buber's is a very important corrective within human interaction, but hard to apply in any developed way to the non-human world, since humans continually need to use, and to trade (though not to "exploit") elements of the non-human world in order to survive.

More ethically productive is H. Paul Santmire's recent adaptation of Buber. Santmire notes Buber's own struggle to say how there can be true mutuality between a human and a non-sentient creature such as a tree.[91] He proposes instead a third type of relation beyond "I-It" and "I-Thou" which he calls "I-Ens".[92] This can be between a human and a non-human creature, or even between a human and a part of fabricated nature such as a building or a city. An Ens, for Santmire, "does not fit into a utilitarian description of the world [...] it confronts me directly with an exclusive claim, a claim that will not allow me to pass beyond it, in order to set it in a larger schema of means and ends".[93] It is a relationship which involves recognition of beauty and wonder, and of the need for humility and gratitude. Santmire quotes a Hasidic saying used by Buber: "there is no rung of being on which we cannot find the Holiness of God everywhere and at all times".[94]

There are hints here of something very generative for our relation to the non-human world. Santmire's formulation speaks of respect, but of something much more than respect, something more like priesthood. The implication of Romans 8:19–22[95] is that the consummation of nature must await humans' recognition of their true calling in respect of the creation.

---

[90] Martin Buber, *I and Thou*, transl. by Ronald Gregor Smith [London: Continuum, 1958 (first edition 1937, German original 1923)] 95.

[91] H. Paul Santmire, *Nature Reborn: The Ecological and Cosmic Promise of Christian Theology* (Minneapolis, MN: Fortress Press, 2000) 68.

[92] This term is the participle of the Latin verb *esse*, to be.

[93] Santmire, *Nature Reborn*, 69.

[94] Ibid., 72.

[95] Which also exercised Hopkins—see his use of the passage in the epigraph to his poem "Ribblesdale" (*Poems and Prose*, 51 f).

Humans, then, may be seen as the creatures with a distinctive capacity for deep contemplation of the creation. The future of that creation depends not only on our working-out of that capacity, but also on our ability to accept spiritual transformation, and come to find our freedom in its true form, in the Christ-minded service of God. These are of course profoundly theological imperatives, but our contemplation of and engagement with the non-human world must be based on a scientifically-informed understanding—not merely a romanticisation of nature, but a Darwinian appreciation of its processes. We must also take with all seriousness the way in which our attributes and perceptions are shaped by being ourselves evolved animals. But science can only take us so far. It is from theology, again, that we derive the ethical imperative to make of our lives a pattern of healing servanthood, from which the acquisitiveness that has been such a strong instinct of ours has been banished forever. Such an attitude would indeed begin to conform to "the mind that was in Christ Jesus" (Philippians 2:5), and might be termed a kenosis of appetite.

Humans as Co-Creators or Co-Redeemers[96]

Philip Hefner proposed the term "created co-creator" as an exploratory model of humans' role[97] and this has since been taken up in the work of Ted Peters.[98] Hefner defines the concept of the created co-creator as follows: "Human beings are God's created co-creators whose purpose is to be the agency, acting in freedom, to birth the future that is most wholesome for the nature that has birthed us".[99] *This is a strikingly future-oriented proposal*—as Peters comments, *there is a hope here for "a future that should be better than the past or present"*.[100]

Even more strikingly Ronald Cole-Turner proposes that humans, as co-creators, are involved in God's work of redemption as the species with the ingenuity to detect and ultimately to eliminate heritable disease.[101] At once he nuances this—in a way which is important for all those exploring this understanding of the human vocation—by adding "Not only are we *created* co-creators; we are creatures who constantly stand in need of redemption".[102]

---

[96] Some of the analysis that follows is based on my "Stewardship and its competitors: a spectrum of relationships between humans and the non-human creation", in: R.J. Berry (ed.), *Environmental Stewardship: Critical Perspectives—Past and Present* (Edinburgh: T&T Clark International, 2006) 185–195.

[97] Philip Hefner, *The Human Factor: Evolution, Culture and Religion* (Minneapolis, MN: Fortress Press, 1993).

[98] Ted Peters, *Playing God? Genetic Determinism and Human Freedom* (New York and London: Routledge, 1997); *Science, Theology and Ethics* (Aldershot and Burlington, VT: Ashgate, 2003).

[99] *The Human Factor,* 264.

[100] *Science, Theology and Ethics,* 213.

[101] Ronald Cole-Turner, *The New Genesis: Theology and the Genetic Revolution* (Louisville, KY: Westminster John Knox Press, 1993) 96 f.

[102] Ibid., 102.

Proponents of co-creator and co-redeemer approaches share a conviction that human ingenuity, with the power it gives us to modify plant species and domesticate animals, to reshape environments, to make cities and parks and farms, is a God-given part of our nature. They accept the great harm to which anthropocentric approaches have led in the past, and nevertheless suppose that part of humanity's transformation will be the discovery of the right use of humans' gifts in respect of the non-human world. Their thinking is, as indicated above, essentially future-oriented—they believe human activity can have a role in engendering a future more positive than the present.[103]

Humans as Priests

An important understanding of humans' role in relation to the non-human world, still emphasising humans' God-given specialness, is that of humans as priests of creation, the species that offers up creation's praise to God, the species that combines "the fruit of the earth and the work of human hands" in sacramental action. This has been an important motif in the Christian tradition, and has been usefully set in the context of the science-religion debate by Peacocke.[104] It is an idea strong in Eastern Orthodox theology, as in this sentence from Vladimir Lossky: "In his way to union with God, man in no way leaves creatures aside, but gathers together in his love the whole cosmos disordered by sin, that it may at last be transfigured by grace".[105] The idea is beautifully expressed in this passage from Wendell Berry:

> To live we must daily break the body and shed the blood of creation. When we do this knowingly, lovingly, skilfully and reverently it is a sacrament. When we do it ignorantly, greedily and destructively it is a desecration. In such a desecration, we condemn ourselves to spiritual and moral loneliness and others to want.[106]

We are already, on a high proportion of the Earth's land surface the ingenious innovators and managers of new ways of living in and with the non-human creation. Our calling is to bring this ingenuity, and the necessity of breaking the body of creation for our own needs and the needs of the future, humbly into our priesthood. We are in the image of God the maker and innovator. We should believe, as Hefner proposes, that our future with the non-human crea-

---

[103] Whereas it might be said that understandings of humans as stewards aim at preserving a future no worse than the present, and many biocentric approaches hark back to a romanticised past context of human life (see Southgate, "Stewardship", 188-9).

[104] Arthur Peacocke, *Creation and the World of Science: The Bampton Lectures 1978* (Oxford: Clarendon, 1979) 295 f.

[105] Vladimir Lossky, *The Mystical Theology of the Eastern Church*, transl. Members of the Fellowship of St Alban and St Sergius (London: J. Clarke, 1957) 111. For a recent study of this idea within Orthodoxy see Elizabeth Theokritoff, "Creation and Priesthood in Modern Orthodox Thinking", Ecotheology, 10:3, 2005, 344–363.

[106] Wendell Berry, *The Gift of Good Land* (San Francisco: North Point Press, 1981) 281.

tion can be better than the past or the present. But we need not see our co-creative calling solely in terms of technological innovation or biotechnological tweaking—we can create not only new strains of drought-resistant crops for use in the Sahel, but also the loving interspecies communities which are domesticated nature at its best. Our creativity can—must, if it is to be in partnership with God's—express our hope for the growth of love in the world. Our lordship and management can be expressed in service. Even within the community of domesticated nature we can exert our creativity and imagination to recognise the value and dignity of the other and to serve its needs with humility and joy. This would mean radical transformation of much current agricultural practice, but only thus could our role come to be in the image of the God who in Jesus expressed lordship—dominion—in terms of servanthood (Mark 10:43, cf. also the ideas of Douglas Hall[107])

What God alone could do, has done, once and for all, was to suffer death for the transformation of the world, to bear in the Christ not only the pain of the creation but the weight of all human sin. But our lives can side with that sacrifice in ways both ingenious and costly. I indicated above that a servant heart towards nature would mean a kenosis of appetite, a willingness to farm animals far less intensively and with a genuine desire for their welfare, transcending mere commercial gain. But there is a further sense of in which our servant-freedom might be worked out in relation to non-human nature—service in terms of preservation. If we were to grow into the fullness of our life under God we might be able to realise a further call—a call to participate more actively in the healing of a wild nature that may be seen both as "very good" *and* as (through the will of the same God who made it) "groaning in travail". In doing so we would be acting in the image of the God whom we see, in the life of the earthly Jesus, as always moved to compassion by the need for healing.

As I noted in the previous section, it is very hard to make use of the eschatological visions we find in Isaiah (e.g. 11:6, the leopard lying down with the kid). They are as Derr puts it "hope without details".[108] It is very hard to see how the leopardness of leopards could be fulfilled in eschatological co-existence with kids. Sideris therefore abandons all hope of making any use of these passages.[109] However, from the earliest known Christian writings there has been a strong eschatological emphasis to the faith, and a sense that the Cross is the hinge-point not merely of human but also of cosmic history. In this eschatological-redemptive perspective it is not enough to settle for the equation of

---

[107] For reference to these see Larry Rasmussen, *Earth Community, Earth Ethics* (Maryknoll, NY: Orbis Books, 1996) 231.

[108] Thomas Sieger Derr, "The Challenge of Biocentrism", in: Michael Cromartie (ed.), *Creation at Risk?: Religion, Science and Environmentalism*, 85–104 (Cambridge, MA: The Ethics and Public Policy Center and Grand Rapids, MI: Wm B. Eerdmans Pub. Co., 1995) 97.

[109] Sideris, *Environmental Ethics*, 119.

what-the-non-human-world-is with what it should or will be. Eschatological
hope should be a stronger influence on the Christian understanding than that.
In my 2002 article in *Zygon* I tested out a particular nuance of co-redemption.
I suggested there that humans' part in the healing of the world could involve
reducing, and ultimately eliminating, the phenomenon of extinction, which is
such a familiar part of the evolutionary process as we know it.[110]

A mark of humans' growing into the life of divine fellowship would be a
participation in the divine transformation of the biosphere, the relief of nature's "groaning". And although the reconciliation of predator-prey relationships in a way which does justice to the natures of both would clearly be a
work of God, far beyond even human imaginings (see the previous section), it
is not too much to suppose that a reduction of extinction, within the current
order of the biosphere, would be part of this healing of nature. Extinction is
an intrinsic part of the Darwinian scheme, of the operation of wild nature.
For Rolston's cruciform naturalism there is no case for preventing it, if it is
not human-induced.[111] But extinction of a species means the loss of a whole
way of being alive on the planet, a whole aspect of the goodness of creation, a
whole way of praising God. It also means particularly exquisite suffering for
the last members of a species (imagine as a thought-experiment the experience of the last members of the recently-discovered *Homo floresiensis*[112] as
they perceive that they are and will be the last of their kind). Part of fulfilled
human calling might be, by dint of our knowledge and ingenuity, to have a
share in eliminating that experience from the biosphere. That would mean a
co-redeemerly "stewarding" (informed by our experience as priests and fel-
low-praisers) even of wilderness, but one which would take a great deal more
wisdom as well as a great deal more knowledge than we currently possess.
So one great human priority at present must be to gather (non-invasively) as
much knowledge and wisdom as we can about the non-human world, and
to reduce the very high rate of *human-induced* extinction to which the biosphere is currently subject.[113]

---

[110] "God and Evolutionary Evil", 818 ff.

[111] He writes in *Naturalizing and Systematizing Evil*, 85, "'Groaning in travail' is in the nature
of things from time immemorial. Such travail is the Creator's will, productive as it is of glory".

[112] P. Brown et al., "A new small bodied hominin from the late Pleistocene in Flores, Indone-
sia", Nature 431, 2004, 1055–1061.

[113] Cf. Edward O. Wilson, *The Future of Life* (London, Little, Brown, 2002) ch. 7. Wilson is
interestingly optimistic about the prospects for a programme of dramatically reducing extinction.
Compare this with Michael Boulter's *Extinction: Evolution and the End of Man* (London: Fourth
Estate, 2003, first published 2002) 176–193. It is interesting to see Wilson's analysis, since as a
biologist he might well have taken the view that extinction continues to be part of the driver of
evolutionary adaptation, and so should not be prevented. Presumably his position is that, given the
extent of the human impact on the planet, non-human biodiversity has reached its maximum possible richness, and this needs to be preserved if at all possible. The view set out here is rather different, namely that with the coming to freedom of human beings in Christ the travail of evolution

Conclusion

In this essay I have highlighted the issue of suffering in the non-human creation as a tension within the biblical narratives and also within a scientifically-informed effort to understand God's relation to the non-human world. I indicated in the introduction what the shape of the problem of evolutionary theodicy is, and in the next section gave a way of categorizing the range of approaches necessary to tackle this problem. The next two sections elaborated central features of my own response to the problem—through exploration of creation's relation to the Triune Creator, and the possibility of their eschatological fulfillment. Finally in last section I endeavoured to show that understandings of human beings as contemplatives, priests and co-redeemers can all contribute to an ethic of relating to the non-human creation—an ethic derived from a vision of the glorious liberty of the children of God (Romans 8:21).

In the categories of Southgate and Robinson outlined above,[114] this approach to evolutionary theodicy is:

a) developmental-anthropocentric, in that it acknowledges that some of the struggle of non-human creatures in the long history of evolution has made possible the evolution of human beings, with our particular capacity for relationship with God

b) developmental-biotic, both in the sense that it accepts that pain responses are necessary for the adaptation of individual creatures to their environment, and in that it accepts that the traits of future creatures may be enhanced by the selection pressure on past populations

c) constitutive, in that it postulates a relation with the Triune Creator in which the creaturely "yes" is intimately and intrinsically bound up with a kind of "no".

d) eschatological-compensatory, in that it insists that creatures which do not achieve fulfillment in this life have further opportunities for fulfillment within the new creation.

To advance such a detailed scheme is not to "solve" the problem of evolutionary theodicy, or to deny the extent to which, in the last analysis, there is a necessary element of mystery in this area. It is merely to indicate my conviction that a *combination* of approaches is required to do any sort of justice to this neglected problem.

---

has run its course. Humans can now take responsibility for honouring all current ways of being alive, and offering them to God. [For a sense of the responsibility implicit in the "glory" of "the children of God" in Romans 8 see N.T. Wright, *The Resurrection of the Sons of God* (London: SPCK, 2003) 257f].

[114] Southgate and Robinson, "Categories of Good-Harm Analysis and Varieties of Theodicy".

Darwinism and Christianity

Does Evil Spoil a Beautiful Friendship?[1]

Michael Ruse

In a letter written just after the publication of the *Origin*, to his American friend and supporter Asa Gray, Charles Darwin wrote:

> With respect to the theological view of the question; this is always painful to me. — I am bewildered. — I had no intention to write atheistically. But I own that I cannot see, as plainly as others do, & as I should wish to do, evidence of design & beneficence on all sides of us. There seems to me too much misery in the world. I cannot persuade myself that a beneficent & omnipotent God would have designedly created the Ichneumonidae with the express intention of their feeding within the living bodies of caterpillars, or that a cat should play with mice. Not believing this, I see no necessity in the belief that the eye was expressly designed.[2]

This is the topic of my discussion: Does the problem of evil forever put a barrier between Darwinism and Christianity? If you are a follower of Charles Darwin, then is it impossible for you to follow Jesus Christ? Or was Darwin perhaps right about the science but wrong about the theology? I will put my discussion into a larger context, considering the general relationship between Darwinism and Christianity, moving as a climax to the issue of evil. I am not here considering the truth of either Darwinism or Christianity as such, but rather the relationship between the two.

Darwinism

Let us make a conventional distinction between the *fact* of evolution and the *cause* or *mechanism* of evolution. By the fact of evolution I mean the claim

---

[1] In this paper I am drawing together ideas expressed in several of my recent books, most particularly *Can a Darwinian be a Christian? The Relationship between Science and Religion*, (Cambridge: Cambridge University Press, 2001), and *Darwin and Design: Does Evolution have a Purpose?* (Cambridge: Harvard University Press, 2003). Readers who seek more extensive documentation of my claims should refer to these works. About twenty years ago, I gave a full defense of my Darwinian beliefs, in: *Darwinism Defended: A Guide to the Evolution Controversies* (Reading, MA: Benjamin/Cummings Pub. Co., 1992). I have written an updated version of that book, titled *Why I am a Darwinian* (Cambridge: Cambridge University Press, 2005).

[2] Charles Darwin, "Letter to Asa Gray, May 22, 1860", in: *The Correspondence of Charles Darwin* (Cambridge: Cambridge University Press, 1985).

that all organisms, living and dead, are the end result of a relatively slow process of development, by natural laws, from forms very different. In a sense, given that the earliest forms were probably very simple and that today we have complex as well as simple forms, I see the fact of evolution as being in some broad sense (that is, non-value-laden sense) progressive, and probably the original forms themselves came by natural processes from inorganic matter. I am not in any sense arguing that there is something necessarily progressive about evolution, and imply only that by the very nature of things if one starts at the bottom there is no way to go but up. By the mechanism or cause of evolution, I mean the process or processes that drove evolution, and probably drive it today. The force that makes things evolve.

Charles Darwin was not the first to propose or adopt the fact of evolution. The idea goes back to the eighteenth century, and indeed one of the earlier evolutionists was his own grandfather Erasmus Darwin.[3] However, it was Charles Darwin who—in his great work, *On the Origin of Species*, published in 1859—made the fact of evolution a reasonable hypothesis. His thinking, which he started to develop from the time he spent on board *HMS Beagle*, in the early 1830s, was that in order to explain many of the phenomena in the organic world—the nature of instinct, the fossil record, the distributions of organisms around the globe, the similarities of embryos of different species, the classificatory results of Linnaean taxonomy, and more—one must postulate the fact of evolution. In turn the fact of evolution helps to explain the phenomena of the organic world.

Darwin also proposed a mechanism, which (when no ambiguity will ensue) I shall refer to (as is the common practice) as "Darwinism". Drawing on his knowledge of the success of animal and plant breeders in the farmyard and among fanciers, he claimed that there is a natural counterpart in nature, and that this brings on indefinite change. Moreover, this change is of a particular kind, namely in the direction of adaptation, or as it was also known, contrivance. Things like the hand and the eye, things which aid their possessors, are the end result of evolution through *natural selection*. To make his case, also presented in the *Origin*, Darwin first drew the reader's attention to the pressure between population growth and food and space supplies, a phenomenon noted first around the beginning of the nineteenth century by the English parson, Thomas Robert Malthus:

> A struggle for existence inevitably follows from the high rate at which all organic beings tend to increase. Every being, which during its natural lifetime produces several eggs or seeds, must suffer destruction during some period of its life, and during some season or occasional year, otherwise, on the principle of geometrical increase,

---

[3] See Michael Ruse, *Monad to Man: The Concept of Progress in Evolutionary Biology* (Cambridge, MA: Harvard University Press, 1996); and *Mystery of Mysteries: Is Evolution a Social Construction?* (Cambridge, MA: Harvard University Press, 1996).

its numbers would quickly become so inordinately great that no country could support the product. Hence, as more individuals are produced than can possibly survive, there must in every case be a struggle for existence, either one individual with
another of the same species, or with the individuals of distinct species, or with the
physical conditions of life. It is the doctrine of Malthus applied with manifold force
to the whole animal and vegetable kingdoms; for in this case there can be no artificial increase of food, and no prudential restraint from marriage.[4]

Note that, even more than a struggle for existence, Darwin needed a struggle
for reproduction. But with the struggle understood in this sort of way, given
naturally occurring variation — a phenomenon that Darwin spent some time
documenting — natural selection follows at once.

Let it be borne in mind in what an endless number of strange peculiarities our
domestic productions, and, in a lesser degree, those under nature, vary; and how
strong the hereditary tendency is. Under domestication, it may be truly said that the
whole organization becomes in some degree plastic. Let it be borne in mind how
infinitely complex and close-fitting are the mutual relations of all organic beings to
each other and to their physical conditions of life. Can it, then, be thought improbable, seeing that variations useful to man have undoubtedly occurred, that other
variations useful in some way to each being in the great and complex battle of life,
should sometimes occur in the course of thousands of generations? If such do occur,
can we doubt (remembering that many more individuals are born than can possibly
survive) that individuals having any advantage, however slight, over others, would
have the best chance of surviving and of procreating their kind? On the other hand
we may feel sure that any variation in the least degree injurious would be rigidly
destroyed. This preservation of favourable variations and the rejection of injurious
variations, I call Natural Selection.[5]

I should say that Darwin's conviction of the importance of adaptation was the
influence of another Anglican clergyman, Archdeacon William Paley, whose
works Darwin studied with some care when he was an undergraduate at
Cambridge University. I am not suggesting that simply because Darwin was
influenced by ordained Anglicans that this means that his theory — his mechanism in particular — was a Christian theory, or that this means there can be no
conflict between his thinking and Christianity. This is a matter for conceptual
analysis, not historical exploration.

Christianity

I take it that Christianity is a religion that has as it central belief the existence of Jesus Christ, the son of God (in some sense, God Himself). Christianity supposes that (as the Bible tells us) God is creator of heaven and earth,
from nothing, and that we humans have a special place in the creation — we

---

[4] Charles Darwin, *On the Origin of Species* (London: John Murray, 1859) 63.
[5] Ibid., 80 f.

are made in the image of God, not physically but at least in some sense intellectually and morally. We have fallen into sin, from which we unaided cannot escape, and that is why God—in His great love for us—came to earth to free us from the bonds of sin. To this end, Jesus was crucified at Calvary, rising again on the third day. We are expected to love and worship God, and we have the promise that death is not the end, but—thanks to God's great sacrifice, for some or all of us—the beginning of an eternity that we will spend with God.

Christianity was not something that just appeared entire, but a system that was developed over time, from the beginnings with the Ancient Jews and their writings and traditions (as given in the Old Testament), through the life of Jesus and of his immediate followers (as given in the New Testament), and then particularly as developed by the great theologians of the Church, especially those in the early centuries of Christianity (men known as the Church Fathers). Thanks above all to the influence of Greek philosophy, the idea of God was extended and articulated beyond the Biblical notion, and God is seen to be a being with infinite powers—all loving, all powerful, all knowing. Whatever this might mean, He can know and do anything, and He would do only that which is in the true interests of humankind. In the deepest sense, He is our father—or in the more gender-free thinking of today—our parent, and as such has our welfare entirely at heart. That is why God was—in the person of Jesus Christ—prepared to suffer on the Cross. God is perfect, beyond sin, and it is we who need and depend on God.

Four Questions

Now against the background of these very brief sketches, I see that there are four key questions that must be asked, as we compare Darwin's thinking with the claims of Christianity. First, does the fact of evolution make Christianity impossible (that is, make it impossible for someone rationally to be a Christian)? Second, does the fact of evolution make Christianity unnecessary? (That is, even if you can rationally be a Christian, does evolution free you of the rational obligation to be a Christian?) Third, does Darwinism (the mechanism of natural selection) make Christianity unnecessary? Fourth, does Darwinism make Christianity impossible? Let us take these questions in turn.

Does the fact of evolution make Christianity impossible?
The answer is obviously "yes", if you hold to a literal reading of the Bible. God created in six days, humans came last miraculously (that is, by means outside the normal laws of nature), there was a universal flood, and much more. All of this simply contradicts the idea of a natural (that is, lawbound) origin of organisms, by a process of slow development. But of course, literal readings of the Bible, although popular in American evangelical circles (not all evangelicals are literalists), are not obligatory for the traditional—the theo-

logically conservative—Christian. From the time of Saint Augustine (around 400AD) and before, it has been clearly understood that if science contradicts a literal reading of the Bible, then the believer must be prepared to read and interpret the Bible metaphorically or allegorically. The essence of the Christian faith is in our relationship to God, not the details of Genesis, and it would indeed be an abrogation of our God-given powers of reason were we to think otherwise.[6]

Augustine himself was not an evolutionist, but he certainly prepared the way for such an understanding. For him, God lies outside time, and hence for Augustine's God the thought of creation, the act of creation, and the product of creation are as one. God created the seeds of organic being that then unfurl. So, without in any sense denying that the fact of evolution demands that the Christian think hard about his or her faith—the true meaning of Adam and Eve, for instance, and the nature of original sin—we can state unequivocally that the fact of evolution does not make Christianity impossible. Even the thorny issue of miracle can be handled by the Christian. Either (in an Augustinian fashion) one makes miracle more of a subjective phenomenon—less an actual breaking of the laws of nature and more a matter of meaning—or, believing (in a Thomistic fashion) that miracles are objective breaks in the order of nature, one invokes the traditional distinction between the order of nature and the order of grace. Normally the world works according to law—including evolutionary law—but sometimes, as with the atonement, God breaks with these laws to bring about His ends.

Does the fact of evolution make Christianity unnecessary?
There have certainly been evolutionists—evolutionists that is who were not Darwinians—who were atheists. The eighteenth-century French thinker Denis Diderot was a case in point. Although, note that most pre-Darwinian evolutionists—Erasmus Darwin for one, and his French counterpart Jean Baptiste de Lamarck for a second—were not in fact atheists. They were not Christians but they did believe in an all powerful God. They were deists, denying the Trinity (that Jesus was the son of God), and asserting that God had set things in motion and now no longer interferes with the creation. I am not at all sure that these people were inconsistent or irrational in their theology— God as Unmoved Mover working through law seems to me to be an easy fit with the fact of evolution—so let me broaden my question to understand it as "Does the fact of evolution make belief in a Creator/Designer unnecessary?" If belief in evolution does not make belief in such a being unnecessary, then it does not make belief in the Christian God unnecessary. (Although, of course,

---

[6] Ernest McMullin (ed.), *Evolution and Creation* (Notre Dame: University of Notre Dame Press, 1985).

one might have other reasons—including Darwinian reasons to be discussed shortly—to think that belief in such a God is unnecessary).

Does the fact of evolution make the belief in some kind of Creator/Designer unnecessary? The fact is, as Plato and Aristotle pointed out, there is that about the organic world that calls for explanation over and above unguided, "blind" law. The world functions, it shows adaptations, and these do not come about by chance. Chance leads to things going wrong. Murphy's law: bread always falls on the jammy side down. To turn to the *Phaedo*, Plato's great dialogue about the death of Socrates, consider why it is that a man grows. "I had formerly thought that it was clear to everyone that he grew through eating and drinking; that when, through food, new flesh and bones came into being to supplement the old, and thus in the same way each kind of thing was supplemented by new substances proper to it, only then did the mass which was small become large, and in the same way the small man big" (96d).[7] But then, Plato points out that this kind of explanation unaided will not do. It is not wrong, but it is incomplete. One must address the question of why someone would grow. This is the kind of phenomenon that Aristotle was to label as a situation involving "final cause", or what we today call "teleological". One must (said Plato) bring in a thinking mind, for without this one has no way of relating the growth to the end result, the reason for the growth. "The ordering Mind ordered everything and place each thing severally as it was best that it should be; so that if anyone wanted to discover the cause of anything, how it came into being or perished or existed, he simply needed to discover what kind of existence was *best* for it, or what it was best that it should do or have done to it" (97 b–c).

Now, as is well known, people like David Hume were very critical of this argument—the argument known as the "argument from design" or the "teleological argument" for the existence of God. Hume argued that the world is as much like a vegetable as an object of design, and in any case we have no reason to argue to a powerful or even to a unique god. "If we survey a ship, what an exalted idea must we form of the ingenuity of the carpenter, who framed so complicated, useful, and beautiful a machine? And what surprise must we feel, when we find him a stupid mechanic, who imitated others, and copied an art, which, through a long succession of ages, after multiplied trials, mistakes, corrections, deliberations, and controversies, had been gradually improving?" More generally: "Many worlds might have been botched and bungled, throughout an eternity, ere this system was struck out: much labour lost: many fruitless trials made: and a slow, but continued improvement carried on during infinite ages in the art of world-making. In such subjects, who can determine, where the truth; nay, who can conjecture where the probabil-

---

[7] Plato, *Phaedo*, in: Cooper, J. M. (ed.), *Plato: Complete Works* (Indianapolis: Hackett, 1997).

ity, lies; amidst a great number of hypotheses which may be proposed, and a still greater number which may be imagined."[8]

But even Hume recognized that, for all his arguments, he had not—and could not—do the job completely. There has to be an explanation of contrivance, and blind law will not do. In the absence of an alternative, one must stay with a Creator/Designer God. The argument from design still has some force. The argument may be in bad shape; it is not completely dead. If the proposition before us is that *"the cause or causes of order in the universe probably bear some remote analogy to human intelligence"*, then "what can the most inquisitive, contemplative, and religious man do more than give a plain, philosophical assent to the proposition, as often as it occurs; and believe that the arguments, on which it is established, exceed the objections, which lie against it?"[9]

Technically speaking, what we have here is what philosophers call an "argument to the best explanation."[10] In the absence of alternatives, the appeal to a Creator/Designer is obligatory. In the words of Sherlock Holmes to his friend Dr Watson: "When you have eliminated the impossible, the answer must be that which remains, however improbable."

Does Darwinism make Christianity Unnecessary?

Darwin's natural selection speaks directly to design—at least to the appearance of design in the world. It is the alternative of which Hume was ignorant. After Darwin—and remember, we are assuming his theory to be true and effective—there is no need to make appeal to a god, including the God of the Christians. As British biologist Richard Dawkins has put it bluntly: "After Darwin, it is possible to be an intellectually fulfilled atheist."[11] I am not saying that Christianity is false. I am saying that one can be rational and a non-believer at the same time.

(Obviously my conclusion presupposes positive answers to a host of subsidiary questions, particularly that there are no other compelling reason-based arguments to be a Christian. If you think that the cosmological argument works, or the ontological argument, or even that the Anthropic Principle has force, then you will dispute what I say. Here, let me stay with what I want to talk about and leave these other issues to others. Although, that I not be seen as hiding behind the task at hand, I think that the organic-final-cause problem is by far the strongest card in the hand of the believer who would argue to the existence of his or her God—that is the believer who still practices what is known traditionally as natural theology.)

---

[8] David Hume, *Dialogues Concerning Natural Religion*, ed. N.K. Smith [Indianapolis, IN: Bobbs-Merrill Co., 1947 (1779)] 140.

[9] Ibid., 203 f (his italics).

[10] P. Lipton, *Inference to the Best Explanation* (London: Routledge, 1991).

[11] Richard Dawkins, *The Blind Watchmaker* (New York: Norton, 1986).

Does Darwinism make Christianity Impossible?

Darwinism as such—that is Darwinism considered just as a cause of evolution—does not make Christianity impossible. Because Darwinism makes Christianity unnecessary, it does not follow that one cannot be a Christian. There is no proof that cricket is a better summer sport than baseball, but it does not follow that I cannot be a lover of cricket over baseball. Nevertheless, going beyond Darwinism merely considered as a cause of evolution, Darwinians from Darwin on—very notably, recently, Richard Dawkins—want to argue that Darwinism in particular, especially because of the vile adaptations produced in the struggle for existence, highlights the problem of evil and that hence there can be no Christian God. There can be no being who is all loving and all powerful. (If we do not have the god of the philosophers, then the problem of evil does not necessarily arise, at least not in an extreme form. I am assuming that now that this god is part of what we understand by the Christian God.)

The argument from evil is expressed most clearly in one of Dawkins's recent books: *River Out of Eden: A Darwinian View of Life.* In a chapter entitled "God's Utility Function", he starts by quoting Darwin:

> "I cannot persuade myself", Darwin wrote: "that a beneficent and omnipotent God would have designedly created the Ichneumonidae with the express intention of their feeding within the living bodies of Caterpillars." Actually Darwin's gradual loss of faith, which he downplayed for fear of upsetting his devout wife Emma, had more complex causes. His reference to the Ichneumonidae was aphoristic. The macabre habits to which he referred are shared by their cousins the digger wasps,...A female digger wasp not only lays her egg in a caterpillar (or grasshopper or bee) so that her larva can feed on it but, according to Fabre and others, she carefully guides her sting into each ganglion of the prey's central nervous system, so as to paralyze it *but not kill it.* This way, the meat keeps fresh. It is not known whether the paralysis acts as a general anesthetic, or if it is like curare in just freezing the victim's ability to move. If the latter, the prey might be aware of being eaten alive from inside but unable to move a muscle to do anything about it. This sounds savagely cruel but as we shall see, nature is not cruel, only pitilessly indifferent. This is one of the hardest lessons for humans to learn. We cannot admit that things might be neither good nor evil, neither cruel nor kind but simply callous—indifferent to all suffering, lacking all purpose.[12]

Then, later in the chapter, Dawkins talks about organisms being excellent examples of design-like engineering. If we tried to unpack the engineering principles involved in organisms, the problems of pain and evil come to the fore. Meaning by the notion "utility function" the purpose for which an entity is apparently designed, Dawkins writes as follows:

---

[12] Richard Dawkins, *A River Out of Eden* (New York, NY: Basic Books, 1995) 95f.

Let us return to living bodies and try to extract their utility function. There could be many but, revealingly, it will eventually turn out that they all reduce to one. A good way to dramatize our task is to imagine that living creatures were made by a Divine Engineer and try to work it out, by reverse engineering, what the Engineer was trying to maximize: What was God's Utility Function?

Cheetahs give every indication of being superbly designed for something, and it should be easy enough to reverse-engineer them and work out their utility function. They appear to be well designed to kill antelopes. The teeth, claws, eyes, nose, leg muscles, backbone and brain of a cheetah are all precisely what we should expect if God's purpose in designing cheetahs was to maximize deaths among antelopes. Conversely, if we reverse-engineer an antelope we find equally impressive evidence of design for precisely the opposite end; the survival of antelopes and starvation among cheetahs. It is as though cheetahs had been designed by one deity and antelopes by a rival deity. Alternatively, if there is only one Creator who made the tiger and lamb, the cheetah and the gazelle, what is He playing at? Is He a sadist who enjoys spectator blood sports? Is He trying to avoid overpopulation in the mammals of Africa? Is He maneuvering to maximize David Attenborough's television ratings? These are all intelligible utility functions that might have turned out to be true. In fact, of course, they are all completely wrong. We now understand the single Utility Function of life in great detail, and it is nothing like any of those.[13]

Dawkins's point is that even if God does exist, He is certainly nothing like the Christian God: He is unkind, unfair, totally indifferent.

If Nature were kind, she would at least make the minor concession of anesthetizing caterpillars before they are eaten alive from within. But Nature is neither kind nor unkind. She is neither against suffering nor for it. Nature is not interested one way or the other in suffering, unless it affects the survival of DNA. It is easy to imagine a gene that, say, tranquilizes gazelles when they are about to suffer a killing bite. Would such a gene be favored by natural selection? Not unless the act of tranquilizing a gazelle improved that gene's chances of being propagated into future generations. It is hard to see why this should be so, and we may therefore guess that gazelles suffer horrible pain and fear when they are pursued to the death—as most of them eventually are. The total amount of suffering per year in the natural world us beyond all descent contemplation. During the minute it takes me to compose this sentence, thousands of animals are being eaten alive; others are running for their lives, whimpering with fear; others are being slowly devoured from within by rasping parasites; thousands of all kinds are dying of starvation, thirst and disease. It must be so. If there is ever a time of plenty, this very fact will automatically lead to an increase in population until the natural state of starvation and misery is restored.

Theologians worry away at the "problem of evil" and a related "problem of suffering." On the day I originally wrote this paragraph, the British newspapers all carried a terrible story about a bus full of children from a Roman Catholic school that crashed for no obvious reason, with wholesale loss of life. Not for the first time, clerics were in paroxysms over the theological question that a writer on a London newspaper (*The Sunday Telegraph*) framed this way: "How can you believe in a

[13] Ibid., 104 f.

loving, all-powerful God who allows such a tragedy?" The article went on to quote one priest's reply: "The simple answer is that we do not know why there should be a God who lets these awful things happen. But the horror of the crash, to a Christian, confirms the fact that we live in a world of real values: positive and negative. If the universe was just electrons, there would be no problem of evil or suffering."

On the contrary, if the universe were just electrons and selfish genes, meaningless tragedies like the crashing of this bus are exactly what we should expect, along with equally meaningless *good* fortune. Such a universe would be neither evil nor good in intention. It would manifest no intentions of any kind. In a universe of blind physical forces and genetic replication, some people are going to get hurt, other people are going to get lucky, and you won't find any rhyme or reason in it, nor any justice. The universe we observe has precisely the properties we should expect if there is, at bottom, no design, no purpose, no evil and no good, nothing but blind, pitiless indifference. As that unhappy poet A. E. Houseman put it:

> For Nature, heartless, witless Nature
> Will neither know nor care.

DNA neither knows nor cares. DNA just is. And we dance to its music.[14]

Moral Evil and Physical Evil

My experience of those who work on the science/religion interface, particularly those who work on the Darwinism/Christianity interface, is that they are dreadfully afraid of Richard Dawkins. They fear he might have a point, and so at this stage they usually jettison Darwinism, opting rather for some alternative evolutionary process with a friendly face. We here must not be so cowardly and must take hope from the fact that, despite Dawkins's savage rhetoric, he has never been overburdened with an undue knowledge of philosophy or Christianity. Perhaps things are not quite as cut and dried as he thinks. For a start, let us make the traditional distinction between moral evil — the evil brought about by Hitler — and natural or physical evil — the Lisbon earthquake. Let us note that Christians have traditional answers to both of these issues, and the matter for us must be whether Darwinism — the mechanism of natural selection — destroys one or both of these counter-arguments.

(Again, I am aware that I am jumping over issues, particularly about the effectiveness of these counters. In fact, I myself am not sure that they are truly effective, but again to stay with this discussion I shall presuppose them as well taken in some sense.)

Moral Evil

The Christian response to moral evil is that of Saint Augustine. God gave us free will, that is a great gift for good, and it is better that we have it, even though we will then do evil, than that we do not have free will and do nothing

---

[14] Ibid., 131 ff.

of our own accord. There are two issues here. First, does science as such—and Darwinism is part of science—make free will impossible? Second, is there something in Darwinism itself that makes free will impossible? The answer to the first question is that science and free will can go together, and indeed there are reasons to think that they must go together. David Hume is the authority here.[15] If there are no laws governing human behavior, then we are not free—we are crazy, and do things without cause, without rhyme or reason. The compatibilist argues that the true distinction is not between freedom and law, but between freedom and constraint. The person in chains is not free, nor is the person under hypnosis. It is true that they are subject to law, but so also is the free person not in chains or under hypnosis.

To take up the second question, does not Darwinian science specifically have something about it that puts us all under hypnosis—genetic hypnosis? Or as the critics phrase it, does not Darwinism deny freedom by making us "genetically determined"?[16] We have no freedom, good or ill, because our genes made us do it. Hitler is not to blame. He just had a lousy genotype, and it is natural selection that put that in place. Blame the process not us. Likewise, of course, Mother Teresa is not to be praised. She drew a good genotype.

Fortunately, this argument does not stand up. Some things are surely genetically determined. Ants for instance. They are preprogrammed by the genes, as produced by selection. Daniel Dennett gives a beautiful case of genetic determinism, that (because of its chief player) he call "sphexishness". A wasp (Sphex) digs a hole, finds and brings in a cricket which she stings to paralyze but not to kill, lays her eggs next to this food store, and finally closes off the hole never to return. A wonderful case of thoughtfulness and intention, until something goes wrong and the mechanical nature of the whole process is revealed. "The wasp's routine is to bring the paralyzed cricket to the burrow, leave it on the threshold, go inside to see that all is well, emerge, and then drag the cricket in. If the cricket is moved a few inches away while the wasp is inside making the her preliminary inspection, the wasp, on emerging from the burrow, will bring the cricket back to the threshold, but not inside, and will then repeat the preparatory procedure of entering the burrow to see that everything is all right." This can go on and on indefinitely. "The wasp never thinks of pulling the cricket straight in. On one occasion this procedure was repeated forty times, always with the same result."[17]

But as Dennett (as much a Darwin booster and critic of Christianity as Dawkins) stresses, we humans are not wasps—we are not genetically determined in this way. Our evolution has been such as to give us the power

---

[15] David Hume, *A Treatise of Human Nature* (Oxford: Oxford University Press, 1978).

[16] Richard Lewontin, "Sociobiology–a caricature of Darwinism", in F. Suppe and P. Asquith (ed.), *PSA 1976*, (East Lansing: Philosophy of Science Association, 1977).

[17] Daniel Dennett, *Elbow Room* (Cambridge: M.I.T. Press, 1984), quoting Wooldridge, *The Machinery of the Brain* (New York: McGraw-Hill, 1963).

to make decisions when faced with choices, and to revise and rework when things go wrong. In the language of evolutionists, wasps and ants were produced by "r-selection". They produce lots of offspring, and when something goes wrong they can afford to lose them, because there are more. We humans are "K-selected". We produce just a few offspring and we cannot afford to lose them when things go wrong. Hence, we have the abilities to make decisions, in order to avoid obstacles. That is why we have big brains. (Evolutionists would argue that there has been a feed-back process here. As bigger brains gave us the ability to deal with obstacles, we could invest more in fewer children. And as we invested more, we could provide the energy and time and care needed in the production of bigger brains.)

In a way, ants and wasps are like cheap rockets where many are produced and they cannot change course when once fired. We humans, by contrast, are like expensive rockets where just a few are produced but we can change course even in mid-flight, if the target changes direction or speed or whatever. The expensive rocket has a flexibility—a dimension of freedom—not possessed by the cheaper rocket. Both kinds of rockets are covered by laws, and so are ants, wasps, and humans. We have freedom over and above genetic determinism, and this freedom was put in place by—not despite—natural selection. Hence the argument from evil against free will fails. (Fails in our case, that is.)

Natural or physical evil

This is Dawkins's big argument, and I think one would be insensitive were one not to agree that he does have a point. Darwinism does highlight pain and suffering. But is this a counter to Christianity? The traditional refuting argument is one that is usually associated with the great German philosopher Leibniz. He (as have others) pointed out that being all powerful has never implied the ability to do the impossible. God cannot make 2 + 2 = 5, and no more can God. Having decided to create through law (and surely an Augustinian would think that there may be good theological reasons for this), God cannot make physical evil disappear. Indeed, it may well be that physical evil simply comes as part of a package deal. "For example, what would it entail to alter the natural laws regarding digestion, so that arsenic or other poisons would not negatively affect my constitution? Would not either arsenic or my own physiological composition or both have to be altered such that they would, in effect, be different from the present objects which we now call arsenic or human digestive organs?"[18]

Paradoxically and somewhat amusingly, Dawkins (1983) himself rather aids this line of argument. He has long maintained that the only way in which complex adaptation could be produced by law is through natural selection.

---

[18] Reichenbach, "Natural evils and natural laws: a theodicy for natural evil", International Philosophical Quarterly, 16, 179–196, 1976, 185.

He argues that alternative mechanisms (notably Lamarckism) which produce adaptation are false, and alternative mechanisms (notably evolution by jumps, or saltationism) which do not produce adaptation are inadequate. "If a life-form displays adaptive complexity, it must possess an evolutionary mechanism capable of generating adaptive complexity. However diverse evolutionary mechanisms may be, if there is no other generalization that can be made about life all around the Universe, I am betting that it will always be recognizable as Darwinian life" (423). In short, if God was to create through law, then it had to be through Darwinian law. There was no other choice. (This of course is not to say that, knowing the subsequent pain, God was right to create at all, but that is another matter and none of Darwinism's business.)

In other words, just as the thinking of the arch-Darwinian atheist Dan Dennett can be turned to good account to save Christianity in the face of moral evil, so now the thinking of the arch-Darwinian atheist Richard Dawkins can be turned to good account to save Christianity in the face of physical evil. More than this, of course, today's Christian—painfully aware of the evil in the world, whether in Auschwitz or in the droughts of Africa—emphasizes not just the God of the Greek philosophers, but the God of suffering. The God who died in agony on the cross. In an almost paradoxical way, the God of the Darwinian process is much more in tune with the God of today's theologians—and believers—than was the all-perfect, all-powerful God of old. Perhaps Darwinism does not merely not make Christianity impossible, it speaks positively to the Christian as he or she tried to understand the nature of God.

Conclusions

I have asked four questions and given four answers. Does the fact of evolution make Christianity impossible? No! Does the fact of evolution make Christianity unnecessary? No! Does Darwinism make Christianity unnecessary? Yes! Does Darwinism make Christianity impossible? No! Let me end with the rest of the quotation, given at the beginning, from Darwin's letter to Gray.

> On the other hand I cannot anyhow be contented to view this wonderful universe & especially the nature of man, & to conclude that everything is the result of brute force. I am inclined to look at everything as resulting from designed laws, with the details, whether good or bad, left to the working out of what we may call chance. Not that this notion *at all* satisfies me. I feel most deeply that the whole subject is too profound for the human intellect. A dog might as well speculate on the mind of Newton.—Let each man hope & believe what he can.[19]

Darwin too saw that things are not so simple!

---

[19] Darwin, "Letter to Asa Gray, May 22, 1860".

Nature and Nurture

The Irony of the Sociobiology Debate

James W. Haag

Much of Western philosophy has attempted to bridge a perceived gap between the innate qualities each individual possesses and qualities that are external or experiential. Popular vernacular refers to these qualities as nature (internal) and nurture (external). The interaction between these two notions takes many philosophical forms, such as subject and object, human free will and God's will, or mind and body. While these philosophical formulations remained intellectual fodder for some, discoveries in Twentieth Century biology focused attention on and added weight to internal nature. Such discoveries not only influenced scientific research, but had an impact on philosophical and theological thinking as well. If human life is characterized by selfishness and evil, is this the result of our biology rather than our environment?

In 1953, Francis Crick and James Watson published their paper "A Structure for Deoxyribose Nucleic Acid" in *Nature*.[1] This piece elucidated the structure of DNA, identified as the cellular molecule that is the carrier of heredity. Later, Crick pronounced the entire flow of information in biology, from DNA to RNA to protein, to be the "Central Dogma" of molecular biology.[2] The discovery of the double helix structure of DNA not only changed genetic research, it also provided a new way of dealing with the nature and nurture dichotomy. Since DNA contains the genetic instructions indicating the biological development of cellular life, it is unsurprising that many thinkers have emphasized themes of genetic determination. Watson and Crick's work precipitated increased attention to the importance of genetic inheritance in human nature and behavior. Growing knowledge of DNA intensified concern with the role of the gene.

Among other significant outcomes, this shift in perspective has provided the foundation for the far-reaching scientific and philosophic re-evaluation of human life known as *sociobiology*. Work in sociobiology bears directly on

---

[1] James Watson and Francis Crick, "A Structure for Deoxyribose Nucleic Acid", Nature, 171, 1953, 737f.

[2] Francis Crick, "On Protein Synthesis", in: *Symp. Soc. Exp. Biol. XII*, 1958, 139–163; the model was further elucidated by Crick in 1970, "Central Dogma of Molecular Biology", Nature, 227, 1970, 561ff.

theological anthropology generally, and the theological problem of evolution and evil specifically. This chapter provides an overview of the field of sociobiology with primary focus given to human sociobiology. The purpose of this overview is to provide theologians and philosophers with a base-line understanding of developments in sociobiology that bear on questions of anthropology, evolution, and evil. The first section of the paper begins with a few concepts essential to sociobiology with attention given to the thinkers who developed them. I then move to assess the intriguing work of E. O. Wilson and Richard Lewontin. Their unique approaches spawned an unmatched scientific conflict. It is my contention that these two thinkers, while surely influenced by their history and political inklings, disagreed more due to scientific differences. While this debate is complex, a brief analysis of their specific approaches will provide a beneficial assessment of their differences. Primary attention is given to Wilson's text *Sociobiology*, as well as the critique led by Lewontin and the Sociobiology Study Group. The second section of the paper offers an analysis of one of sociobiology's offspring, evolutionary psychology. Again, some key ideas will be explored. I will conclude by offering a critique of evolutionary psychology's lack of attention to maladaptive behaviors.

Among the questions this chapter provokes is: Why should theologians care about sociobiology? I will try to show that sociobiology has been instrumental in reforming current thinking around several themes of interest to theologians wanting to understand human nature, evolution, and evil: altruism, commitment, cooperation, self-interest, and the like. While a critical stance toward sociobiology may be warranted, theologians and philosophers who completely disavow or ignore developments in sociobiology neglect significant insights that might otherwise inspire more subtle reflections on the nature of the human as an evolutionary animal.

Sociobiology's Background

Sociobiology is a synthetic science that has a complex history, but one of its characteristics is the unique perspective it offers for assessing the nature vs. nurture problem. Sociobiology looks at species' behaviors and inquires to the evolutionary benefit of these behaviors. In this way, biologically inherent (nature) factors are privileged in the explanatory process while environmental (nurture) factors are downplayed. Sociobiologists fully accept Darwin's understanding of natural selection, where the "fittest" traits of an organism are said to survive; thus, existing traits must have an evolutionary advantage.

In 1973, Konrad Lorenz, Nikolaas Tinbergen, and Karl von Frisch received Nobel prizes for their work in animal behavior in the field of ethology. A mere two years later, sociobiology began building upon their work. However, there was a shift in focus to the adaptive value of behavior, rather than the physiological mechanisms of such behavior. In other words, sociobiology was more interested in asking why certain behaviors evolve, instead of asking what motivation brought forth certain behavioral patterns. To accomplish this task, new methods and procedures were produced that quickly reformed much evolutionary thinking about behavior. However, no science begins without certain commitments and connections to past research. Before dealing with sociobiology directly, it is necessary to identify the inherited past it takes seriously.

Gene's-Eye-View

In 1966, George C. Williams published the book, *Adaptation and Natural Selection*, as a critique of the idea that group selection[3] is a means by which natural selection can occur. According to Williams, it is the gene that functions as the fundamental unit of selection because the gene is capable of accurately replicating itself. Consequently, group selection can be more parsimoniously explained by gene selection. Williams' critique of group selection centers on the idea that within groups, certain individuals cheat the system, whereby the cheaters out-compete others in the group. The cheaters increase in numbers and the sacrificial idea of group selection slowly disappears. Williams contends that if one moves from group selection to gene selection, it becomes more plausible to comprehend a gene's representation in the next generation. He writes, "A gene is selected on one basis only, its average effectiveness in producing individuals able to maximize the gene's representation in future generations."[4] Thus, the basic unit of selection is the gene, not the group. In this way, understanding social behaviors is more plausibly accomplished by identifying natural selection as acting between groups, not within groups.[5]

While Williams looks at gene selection, Richard Dawkins thoroughly examines this concept. In *The Selfish Gene*, Dawkins advances the influential notion that evolution is best understood as survival among genes. While evolution appears to promote the group, in reality, it is the survival of the genes which is at stake. Dawkins provocatively refers to genes as "selfish": through its mechanisms of reproduction the gene acts only for itself. Dawkins differentiates between "replicators" and "vehicles" in this process where replicators are "the fundamental units of natural selection, the basic things that survive or fail to survive, that form lineages of identical copies with occasional random

---

[3] See: V.C. Wynne-Edwards, *Animal Dispersion in Relation to Social Behavior* (Edinburgh: Oliver & Boyd, 1962); Elliott Sober and David Sloan Wilson, *Unto Others: The Evolution and Psychology of Unselfish Behavior* (Cambridge, MA: Harvard University Press, 1998).

[4] George C. Williams, *Adaptation and Natural Selection* (Princeton, NJ: Princeton University Press, 1966) 251.

[5] In *Unto Others*, Sober and Wilson make a cogent argument for group selection. They contend that altruistic behavior can evolve within groups if there are variant altruistic individuals within groups and between groups. In short, groups of altruists will be selected for over groups of non-altruists.

mutations."[6] The initial replicator is a particular molecule that forms in the primeval soup that eventually—through the evolutionary process—leads to the most well-known replicator: DNA. This new view, the genes-eye-view, is a key shift in evolutionary theory and a core theme for sociobiology.

Kin Selection

The focus on "selfish genes" seems to make certain behaviors difficult to explain. Here is the problem: Altruistic behavior appears in social behavior. If gene's are selfish, why would an individual sacrifice its own life or reproductive ability for the benefit of another individual? Darwin himself lamented that altruism provides "one special difficulty, which at first appeared to me insuperable, and actually fatal to the whole theory".[7] William Hamilton suggested that the problem of altruism is only apparent. He noted the fact that our genes are not our own—we share them with our relatives. This means, as Michael Ruse puts it, "inasmuch as our genes have been selected precisely because of their ability to cause characteristics which will ensure the genes' replication, it is in our reproductive interests to see that those who share our genes reproduce."[8] This novel idea is known as kin selection or inclusive fitness.

Hamilton studied sterility in worker ants, a problem that also interested Darwin. Darwin argued that since workers operated within colonies of family members, sacrifices made on behalf of other family members perpetuated the lineage to which the sacrificer belonged. Therefore, the sacrificer's lineage out-competes other lineages. Hamilton expanded Darwin's theory by asserting that since relatives share genes, sacrifice by one individual still enables the sacrificer's genes to pass on to the next generation through the relatives' genes. For some individuals who are unable to reproduce, such as worker ants, assisting relatives is their only means for passing their genes to the next generation. Thus, altruism between relatives evolves because it is in the interest of each individual to cooperate with relatives. Furthermore, particularly in ants, cooperation is based on the degree of relatedness. Hamilton clearly explains:

> As a simple but admittedly crude model we may imagine a pair of genes g and G such that G tends to cause some kind of altruistic behavior while g is null. Despite the principle of "survival of the fittest" the ultimate criterion which determines whether G will spread is not whether the behavior is to the benefit of the behaver but whether it is to the benefit of the gene G; and this will be the case if the average

[6] Richard Dawkins, *The Selfish Gene* (Oxford and New York: Oxford University Press, 1976) 254.

[7] Charles Darwin, *The Origin of the Species by Means of Natural Selection, or the Preservation of Favored Races in the Struggle for Life*, 1st ed. reprint (New York: Penguin Books, 1968) 257.

[8] Michael Ruse, *Sociobiology: Sense or Nonsense?* (Boston: D. Reidel Publishing Company, ²1985), 43.

net result of the behavior is to add to the gene-pool a handful of genes containing G in higher concentration than does the gene pool itself. With altruism this will happen only with the affected individual is a relative of the altruist, therefore having an increased chance of carrying the gene, and if the advantage is large enough compared to the personal disadvantage to offset the regression, or "dilution", of the altruist's genotype in the relative in question.[9]

When helping a relative, the helper helps him/her/itself, in that the helper's genes will be passed on through the surviving relative's genes. Hamilton's model of kin selection is based on the "genes-eye-view", since it is the genes of each individual with which one is concerned.

Kin selection received high praise from Robert Trivers, who called it "the most important advance in evolutionary theory since Darwin",[10] while E. O. Wilson regarded it as "the most important idea of all."[11] While it is an important idea, kin selection is powerless to explain the cooperative acts that occur between non-kin organisms.

Reciprocal Altruism

In 1971, Robert Trivers acknowledged kin selection as a powerful theory, but suggested that kin selection cannot explain the apparent cooperative acts that exist between non-relatives. Trivers argued that if non-related individuals interact frequently over a long period of time, then it is possible for them to develop cooperative behavior. Initially, the cooperative behavior is costly for actors and beneficial for recipients, but over time, reciprocity develops. It proves to be more beneficial for both individuals to cooperate than to not cooperate.

In order for reciprocal altruism to evolve, individuals must "keep tabs" on other individuals; otherwise, cheaters emerge and destroy the entire system. If all individuals in a group are concerned for another, one who is concerned for oneself will have an advantage. Therefore, individuals within a group need to identify cheaters for future encounters. If an individual has a history of cheating, it is unlikely that that individual will be the beneficiary of altruistic acts. The distinctive difference between reciprocal altruism and kin selection is that with the latter one does not expect any direct return, but receives an indirect return by having one's genes continue into the next generation. Those participating in reciprocal altruism, however, receive a direct return.

As an example, Trivers describes a certain species of fish that cleans parasites off of another species of fish. For the cleaners, the benefit is gaining a hearty meal. For the cleaned, the benefit is being less susceptible to diseases

[9] William D. Hamilton, "The Evolution of Altruistic Behavior", American Naturalist, 97, 1963, 354f.
[10] Robert Trivers, *Social Evolution* (Menlo Park, CA: Benjamin Cumins, 1985), 47.
[11] Edward O. Wilson, *Naturalist* (Washington, DC: Island Press, 1994), 315.

or sores. The remarkable aspect of this relationship is that the cleaned fish could easily make a satisfying meal out of the cleaners. According to Trivers, this rarely occurs. In fact, the cleaned fish will go out of its way to protect the cleaner fish.[12] Kin selection cannot be at work in this example, since the fish are not related, but reciprocal altruism offers a plausible explanation.[13]

When cooperation or sacrifice occurs between relatives, kin selection is a clear explanation. However, unselfish behavior does not necessarily explain when cooperation occurs between non-kin. Reciprocal altruism allows for trans-kin cooperation to occur, but only between individuals who exhibit reciprocity. Trans-kin altruism, where reciprocity is not a factor, is not accepted as a possible understanding of cooperation within nature.

Evolutionary Game Theory

An additional development important for sociobiology is game theory—created by economists in the 1940s—which predicted people's behavior during times of conflict. In standard game theory, one makes decisions based on a rational choice. In evolutionary game theory, "The various behavioral options simply exist, as if they arose by mutation, and compete against each other in Darwinian fashion."[14] Evolutionary game theory is concerned with evolutionary stable strategies (ESS) which endeavor to prove the inaccuracy of group selection and also make predictions about animal behavior. According to Dawkins, "There is a common misconception that cooperation within a group at a given level of organization must come about through selection between groups...ESS theory provides a more parsimonious alternative."[15] Evolutionary game theory attempts to decipher which behavior leads to the most stable strategy, assuming that this is how it would evolve.

Evolutionary game theory and ESS can best be explicated by presenting a classic example. Imagine a population with two types of birds: hawks and doves. In this population, encounters occur over limited resources. So, when a hawk meets a hawk, there is a struggle in which one hawk will be the victor, while the other will suffer serious injuries. When two doves interact, the struggle will continue until one becomes bored or tired. However, the victor and the loser avoid serious injury. When a hawk and a dove interact, the struggle ends quickly with the hawk victorious and the dove avoiding serious

---

[12] Ibid., 50.

[13] A current example is vampire bats. Vampire bats will roost in social groups. However, due to their high metabolisms and particular diet, feeding is vastly unpredictable. Eventually, most bats will require supplemental feeding from other bats in their group (following the reciprocal altruism model).

[14] Sober and Wilson, *Unto Others*, 79.

[15] Richard Dawkins, "Good Strategy or Evolutionary Stable Strategy?", in: G. W. Barlow and J. Silverberg (ed.), *Sociobiology: Beyond Nature/Nurture?* (Boulder, CO: Westview Press, 1980) 360.

injury. So, it is necessary to identify the ESS. All hawks or all doves in a population will not remain stable because a mutant would quickly be selected. The ESS is a proportion of hawks and doves which is held stable by selection with the proportion dependent on the cost of injuries. Therefore, an ESS will consist of both hawks and doves since "a mutant from Hawk to Dove or *vice versa* would be no better off…In other words, what this model shows is that we could have a population, continuing indefinitely in a stable fashion, where (as in nature) one gets some ritualized non-harmful aggression, and (as in nature) some very real and dangerous aggression."[16]

E. O. Wilson, Richard Lewontin and the Rise of Sociobiology

E. O. Wilson

E. O. Wilson's book *Sociobiology: The New Synthesis* was the catalyst that enabled thinkers to assess behaviors from an evolutionary perspective. The book sets out to compile and analyze existing data on the behavior of social animals, such as ants, monkeys, and birds. However, in the final chapter, Wilson speculated whether human social behavior might be analyzed alongside the behavior of these other animals. The extraordinary accomplishment of the book lies in Wilson's ability to take the insights of Williams, Hamilton, Trivers, and others and integrate them into a single analytic system. He called this system sociobiology and it was the first robust attempt at "the systematic study of the biological basis of all social behavior."[17]

Sociobiology is a thorough treatment of social behavior beginning with simple life forms and moving toward *homo sapiens*. Most scientists agree that *Sociobiology*, up until the last chapter, is a magnificent text with well argued and balanced explanations. For most biologists, the attempt to assess animal behavior in light of evolution is not problematic. However, the inclusion of humans causes concern because it appears to interpret human behavior using data on ant behavior. Some found it troubling that Wilson suggests that human sex role divisions, morality, and religious beliefs can all be accounted for from an evolutionary perspective due to our underlying genetic dispositions. Unfortunately, Wilson neglected to acknowledge this immense jump in social complexity and argued from a disanalogy.

Elliott Sober writes, "Sociobiology is a research program that seeks to use evolutionary theory to account for significant social, psychological, and behavioral characteristics in various species."[18] Had Wilson not included human behavior within the spectrum of his work, he may not have achieved his infamous reputation. Much of the material found in this final chapter is quite

---

[16] Ruse, *Sociobiology: Sense or Nonsense?*, 27 f.
[17] Edward O. Wilson, *Sociobiology: The New Synthesis* (Cambridge, MA: Harvard University Press, 1975) 4.
[18] Elliott Sober, *Philosophy of Biology*, Boulder, CO: Westview Press, [2]2000) 188.

speculative, and some controversial claims are made. One claim, in particular, asserted that sociobiology would achieve explanatory supremacy, so much so that other disciplines would become nonexistent. His later book, *Consilience*, spelled this out more thoroughly when Wilson stated, "Culture and hence the unique qualities of the human species will make complete sense only when linked in causal explanation to the natural sciences."[19] Toward this end, Greg Peterson's assessment seems right on: "While sociobiology has made important contributions to our understanding of the biological world, the attempt at disciplinary reduction and synthesis turns out to have been premature in 1975. It seems to be still premature today."[20]

While sociobiologists, including Wilson, are concerned with human behavior, human beings are not their primary interest. Sociobiologists "want to know the evolved function or purpose of whatever aspect of social behavior they are studying."[21] Where in biology would one place this approach? In *Sociobiology*, Wilson identifies three distinct categories within biology. The first category is integrative neurophysiology, which gains information from cellular biology. The second category is ethology and physiological psychology, which connects the first and third categories. The third category is behavioral ecology and sociobiology, which gain information from population genetics. These divisions are important because they identify what sociobiologists desire to accomplish. The first category is primarily about proximate cause, which "studies how cellular mechanisms and system-operating rules influence behavior."[22] Sociobiology is not explicitly interested in proximate causes. Instead, it focuses on ultimate causes, which deal with "questions about the adaptive (reproductive) value of behaviors."[23] Said differently, sociobiologists are interested in the adaptive value of a specific behavior, such as altruism. Noting this, it is important to recognize that a strict dualism between proximate and ultimate causes is not possible—the two must intertwine. That is, the long-term outcomes combined with short-term variations provides the most complete explanation. As Alcock writes, "No internal proximate mechanism of social behavior exists that cannot be explored in terms of its adaptive value, just as no adaptive behavior occurs whose underlying proximate causes cannot be investigated to good effect."[24] While not desired, it is possible to give attention to only one type of cause. Thus, proximate or immediate causes

---

[19] Edward O. Wilson, *Consilience: The Unity of Knowledge* (New York: Vintage Books, 1998) 292.

[20] Gregory Peterson, "Review of *Sociobiology: The New Synthesis.* 25th Anniversary Edition", Zygon, Vol. 40:1, 2005, 231–234.

[21] Alcock, *The Triumph of Sociobiology*, 10.

[22] Ibid., 12.

[23] Ibid., 12f.

[24] Ibid., 16.

are not of interest to sociobiologists; rather, they sociobiologists focus on ultimate or evolutionary causes.

Interestingly, the negative attention Wilson received from his work in *Sociobiology* did not prevent him from continuing to deal with human behavior. Wilson was convinced that his approach was justifiable and argued that his critics misunderstood his ideas. He suggested that his detractors were political extremists who quoted him out of context in order to perpetuate their agenda of *tabula rasa* (the notion that the mind is a blank slate at birth). In spite of his critics, Wilson wrote his Pulitzer Prize winning book, *On Human Nature*. Wilson's bold statements continued as he argued "that differences in the behavior of men and women reflected past evolutionary events and could only be eradicated at some cost to society."[25]

Did Wilson know his work would cause such controversy? Maynard Smith contends, "It was absolutely obvious to me—I *cannot* believe Wilson didn't know—that this was going to provoke great hostility."[26] It is possible, though, that Wilson really was unaware of the battle ahead of him. He writes,

> [...] it was true. I was unprepared [...] In 1975 I was a political naïf: I knew almost nothing about Marxism as either a political belief or a mode of analysis, I had paid little attention to the dynamism of the activist left, and I had never heard of Science for the People. I was not even an intellectual in the European or New York-Cambridge sense.[27]

This is not to excuse Wilson's claims, which sound similar to the claims made by social Darwinists and members of the eugenics movement. Instead, the approach taken in this chapter assumes that Wilson's primary interest was scientific explanation and not ideological manipulation.

Richard Lewontin
The rise in genetic research led sociobiology to seek explanatory adequacy at the level of the gene. This should not be surprising given the prudent nature of most scientific disciplines. The achievements of the Human Genome Project only perpetuated this way of thinking. After all, an examination of an organism's basic parts would seem to allow us to look directly at the units of inheritance that align with Darwinian theory. For many scientists, genetics was seen as a road toward full explanation of human life. Richard Lewontin disagreed. Lewontin saw this approach as a path of oppressive reductionism. Focusing merely on the gene neglects the complexity of genes and their relation to organisms and environments. Lewontin saw Wilson identifying genes

[25] Kevin N. Laland and Gilliam R. Brown, *Sense & Nonsense: Evolutionary Perspectives on Human Behavior* (Oxford: Oxford University Press, 2002) 90.
[26] Maynard Smith in Ullica Segerstråle, *Defenders of Truth: The Sociobiology Debate* (Oxford: Oxford University Press, 2000) 25.
[27] Wilson, *Naturalist*, 339.

as the "blueprint" for creating each individual which, according to Lewontin, is fallacious because it affirms that only the genotype denotes the phenotype. Lewontin was concerned that the gene would become the "magic bullet" which would explain all of the aspects of being human that have plagued thinkers for millennia. Lewontin wanted to rid biology of the false metaphorical notions that "the organism proposes and the environment disposes. The organism makes conjectures and the environment refutes them."[28] It is not that Lewontin thinks the genes are unimportant, only that they are unable to tell the full story. The complete story involves a complex interaction between genes, organism, and environment. No single factor explains the biological world around us, meaning that any discipline which claims exclusive access in this realm will need to be critiqued.

Unlike sociobiologists, Lewontin gives explanatory power to the environment's role in an organism's development. He writes, "Taken together, the relations of genes, organisms, and environment are reciprocal relations in which all three elements are both causes and effects. Genes and environment are both causes of organisms, which are, in turn, causes of environments, so that genes become causes of environments as mediated by the organisms."[29] Organisms alter and shape their environment as intensely as environments form the organisms.

Lewontin is perhaps most well-known for his work on race, which explains why Lewontin reacted so strongly against Wilson's sociobiology. Lewontin contends that the notion of race is a social construction with no basis in empirical data. This becomes a crucial issue because much of past and present human interaction is seen as related to different races. The lack of food and medical distribution around the world clearly has racial aspects. In the United States, the number of African American men currently in prison is staggering compared with the number of incarcerated white men. Lewontin became concerned that people viewed racial differences as rooted in either biological or environmental causes. In 1775, Johann Friedrich Blumenbach wrote in his book, *On the Natural Varieties of Mankind*, that certain archetypes in our society are for race. He hierarchically organized them as such: Caucasian (white), Asian (Mongoloid, yellow), Americans (Indians, red), Malay (brown), Ethiopian (Negro, black).[30] Lewontin found this history to be unacceptable and without basis.

Lewontin discovered that by analyzing genes (a process called gel electrophoresis) one could identify variation among populations. Using electrical

---

[28] Richard Lewontin, *The Triple Helix: Gene, Organism, and Environment* (Cambridge, MA: Harvard University Press, 2000), 43.

[29] Ibid., 100f.

[30] Johann Friedrich Blumenbach, *On the Natural Varieties of Mankind* (New York: Bergman Publishers, 1969).

current, he separated and analyzed the alleles in human blood. From about 17 proteins and enzymes, he discovered that 70 % of them were constant across all populations. Variation existed in the rest of the genes. In addition, he found that genes restricted to one race were nonexistent. Certain gene variation occurred between populations while others occurred within populations. Surprising many people, Lewontin discovered that differences within populations far exceeded differences between populations.[31] This challenge showed that most of the variation that is present exists primarily within racial groups.

Lewontin's work led him to find minimalist explanations wanting. Wilson's focus on the power of the genes, which Lewontin saw as ammunition for oppression, was one such explanation. While their disagreements have reached mythic status, it is my contention that the root of their problems stemmed from scientific differences and not ideological commitments. This is not to say that either thinker is immune to biases; but, I believe giving primary attention to issues other than their scientific approaches diminishes the nature and importance of their disagreements.

In the Boston-area, a group of professors, students, and researchers, known as the Sociobiology Study Group (SSG), assembled to assess the claims made by Wilson. The first public response from this group was a letter in the *New York Review of Books*. The nature of the letter carried a political tone and was co-signed by Lewontin and Stephen Jay Gould. They were convinced that Wilson's analysis of human behavior amounted to biological determinism. The critics expressed concern that Wilson upheld every *status quo* by seeking genetic justification for oppression and inequalities. Before long, the SSG affiliated with Science for the People (SftP), a group considered to be far-left politically and interested in protesting the misuse of science. SftP included "Marxist and left-wing scholars"[32] who protested against issues dealing with race and IQ. Any genetic explanation for human behavior was rejected as an attempt to justify tyrannical and xenophobic actions as *natural*.[33]

In *Sociobiology*, Wilson employed the mathematical approach of population genetics. Lewontin, a population geneticist, was bound to clash with Wilson. Lewontin had previously published an article criticizing the traditional approaches in population genetics as making inaccurate predictive statements. Ullica Segerstråle writes, "Lewontin's point, especially, was that simple older formulas used for calculations in population genetics were incorrect, because they did not consider recently detected complex interactions between individual genes."[34] Wilson noted Lewontin's critique in *Sociobiology*; never-

---

[31] 85.4 % within; 8.3 % between.
[32] Laland and Brown, *Sense & Nonsense*, 89.
[33] The 1952 UNESCO statement enforced this position: "Any hereditarian explanation of social or cultural characteristics or ability was prone to be classified as racist". Elazar Barkan, *The Retreat of Scientific Racism* (Cambridge: Cambridge University Press, 1992) 342.
[34] Segerstråle, *Defenders of Truth*, 36.

theless, Wilson cited the existing formulas as the best available. Segerstråle
contends that Wilson saw population genetics as a means to an end, whereas
Lewontin saw it as an end in itself. In addition, Wilson thought it worthwhile
to use the existing formulas, while Lewontin believed it necessary to discard
all formulas.[35]

Segerstråle is correct to contend that the differences between Wilson and
Lewontin are based on different understandings of science. From his predecessors at Harvard, "Wilson inherited a particular philosophical style: the
coupling of scientific and moral notions."[36] These interests led Wilson to assert
that the biggest problem for sociobiology is altruism. Beyond this, Segerstråle
argues that Wilson's conservative Christian background led him to emphasize
the genetic contribution to all behavior, in hopes of preventing religion from
having a privileged status when it came to ethics. Segerstråle writes, "In the
notorious passage from *On Human Nature*...where he says that "the genes
hold culture on a leash"—it is really *religion*, not culture *per se* that Wilson is
talking about."[37] In response to the critics, Wilson contended that his impetus
was not political desire to uphold the social order; rather, it was his desire to
resist irrational religious dogmas.

As seen in *Sociobiology*, Wilson emphasized the genetic aspect of social behaviors. Lewontin, a critic of both science and society, found this approach
deficient. His self-claimed Marxist beliefs led him to desire "true" statements
about reality. That is, Wilson favored parsimonious arguments for describing
reality, whereas Lewontin sought more complexity in order to understand the
diversity of reality. This difference is a key reason why Lewontin was skeptical of the Human Genome Project's explanatory achievements. Segerstråle
writes, "While for Wilson the criterion for a good theory was testability, for
Lewontin a theory in addition to being testable has to be a *true* account of
an underlying process in the real world."[38] Methodological and epistemological correctness was Lewontin's concern, which was influenced by his Marxist
notion of a just society. To Lewontin, Wilson's claims promoted an unjust
society with dubious scientific evidence. Segerstråle states,

> The situation could be described as an opposition between a purist, critical, logical
> approach with slightly negative overtones (Lewontin), and a practically oriented, op-
> portunistic, speculative, and generally, "positive" model-building approach, where
> judgment is postponed until later (Wilson). From the protagonists' own perspectives,
> the first approach is "serious science" (Lewontin) or "too safe" (Wilson), while the
> latter one is either "creative and risky" (Wilson) or "not serious" (Lewontin).[39]

---

[35] Ibid., 37.
[36] Ibid.
[37] Ibid., 39.
[38] Ibid., 40.
[39] Ibid., 50.

Lewontin viewed Wilson's approach as fatally flawed. The dangers and inaccuracies of genetic determinism—where all behavior is reduced to the genes' influence—was the critique Lewontin brought against Wilson. In the 1984 book, *Not In our Genes*, Lewontin and others wrote, "Sociobiology is a reductionistic, biological determinist explanation of human existence. Its adherents claim [...] that the details of present and past social arrangements are the inevitable manifestation of the specific action of genes."[40] Ernst Mayr contends that the term "biological" causes some of the confusion because Wilson's use of the term biological in relation to behavior simply means that "genetic disposition makes a *contribution* to social behavior."[41] Wilson's critics believed the reduction to be more complete. A genetic determinist claims that human beings are genetic automata. Since genes do not single-handedly control behavior, the position of genetic determinism is unfounded. In the conflict between Wilson and Lewontin, legitimate scientific critique must receive primary attention.

For evolution by natural selection to be possible, heritable phenotypic variation must occur. For example, the selection of running speed in a certain population of gazelles will increase on average if parents who are faster than average have progeny who are also faster than average. Assuming faster running speed increases the fitness of the gazelle, the correlation between parent and progeny must be recognized. Evolutionary theory affirms that the genetic makeup of parents varies within a population thus producing both faster and slower gazelles. Since the progeny inherit the genes of their parents, faster than average parents tend to have faster than average progeny. In a similar vein, Wilson suggests that xenophobia, indoctrination, and aggression are human traits that evolved because there was selection for them. The problem is whether or not there is a gene or complex of genes for something like xenophobia. Stephen J. Gould writes,

> There is no gene "for" such unambiguous bits of morphology as your left kneecap or your fingernail. Bodies cannot be atomized into parts, each constructed by an individual gene. Hundreds of genes contribute to the building of most body parts and their action is channeled through a kaleidoscopic series of environmental influences: embryonic and postnatal, internal and external.[42]

Gould's comment is a bit misleading since Wilson does not dispute that a combination of hundreds of genes could contribute to the phenotypes they study. The argument is not about the number of genes responsible for a trait

---

[40] Richard C. Lewontin, Stepehn Rose, and Leon J. Kamin (ed.)., *Not In Our Genes: Biology, Ideology, and Human Nature* (New York: Pantheon Books, 1984) 236.

[41] Ernst Mayr, *One Long Argument: Charles Darwin and the Genesis of Modern Evolutionary Thought* (Cambridge, MA: Harvard University Press, 1991) 154.

[42] Stephen Jay Gould, *The Panda's Thumb: More Reflection in Natural History* (New York: W. W. Norton & Company, 1980) 91.

or behavior, but whether genes (singly or in combination) are sufficient to explain a trait or behavior.

We must avoid being too anthropological in our assessment of the difference between sociobiology and its opponents, most specifically Lewontin and Wilson. Both are serious scientists and should be given the benefit that their work is rooted in an honest desire to explain the world as best as possible. This is not to say that either thinker, or any of us, is able to function without certain biases. Rather, I believe that the more interesting story between these two men is lessened if one assumes that their differences were based on an opposition to fundamentalist religion and Marxist inklings. As time has passed, both Wilson and Lewontin have proved to be right and wrong simultaneously. Wilson's focus on the genes provided thinkers with interesting questions to consider. While we must remain cautious when relating genes and behavior, we must also acknowledge the apparent truism that genetic bias is inevitable. Lewontin, with his emphasis on the entanglement between genes and environment, provided interesting ideas. Niche construction is a prime example that the environment and the genes have a reciprocal relationship. The most accurate picture includes both nature and nurture. In different settings, one may be more dominant than the other, but they always remain interdependent.

Evolutionary Psychology

Sociobiology is the precursor to a number of new fields. The most well-known of these fields assesses psychology in the context of evolution. Evolutionary Psychology (EP), while still concerned with the evolution of certain behaviors, is primarily interested in the psychological makeup that allows these behaviors to manifest. For many reasons, the work Wilson completed is altered in the current scientific ethos. The following is a brief analysis of EP that provides a more contemporary view of the problems sociobiology attempted to solve. Like sociobiology, EP is grounded on certain central themes, including its challenge to blank slate theory and its notion environment of evolutionary adaptedness.

Blank Slate Theory
Like most new disciplines, EP developed in opposition to a theory. The basic psychology methods used in the Twentieth Century were EP's antagonist. EP holds that biology is grounded in the theory of evolution and, since brains are biological, it only makes sense to connect biology and psychology. Traditional psychology, in contrast, denies affiliation with biology, instead basing itself on the Standard Social Science Model (SSSM). The SSSM maintains that all ideas derive from sensory impressions. EP challenges this model because SSSM fails "to causally locate their objects of study inside the larger network

of scientific knowledge",[43] and therefore severely constrains physchological outcomes. The methodological basis of this model derives from the view that reason guides human behavior, whereas instinct influences non-human primate behavior. This stance is commonly known as blank slate theory.

Blank slate theory originated in the work of philosopher John Locke, who believed that upon entering the world, the human mind is a *tabula rasa* or a piece of white paper, lacking any writing. The writings or ideas that become scripted onto this paper result from experience. This position builds upon the assumption that all behavior is separable into instinct and learning. Steven Pinker argues, "Locke was taking aim at theories of innate ideas in which people were thought to be born with mathematical ideals, eternal truths, and a notion of God."[44] This understanding became the foundation for most psychology during the Twentieth Century. Leda Cosmides and John Tooby identify blank slate theory as a pitfall for the advancement of psychological theories. Accepting that the human mind is a *tabula rasa* at birth—needing experience to supply its content—merely perpetuates an inaccurate understanding of reality.[45]

Environment of Evolutionary Adaptedness

To what extent do humans adapt to their current environments? EP contends that minds are composed of modular special-purpose capacities.[46] In the production of these modules, evolution works toward satisfaction, not optimiza-

---

[43] John Tooby and Leda Cosmides, "The Psychological Foundations of Culture", in: Jerome H. Barkow, Leda Cosmides, and John Tooby (ed.), *The Adapted Mind: Evolutionary Psychology and the Generation of Culture* (New York and Oxford: Oxford University Press, 1992) 23.

[44] Steven Pinker, *The Blank Slate: The Modern Denial of Human Nature* (New York: Viking, 2002) 5.

[45] The most famous example of the blank slate theory in psychology is called Behaviorism and was founded by John B. Watson. Watson famously argued that he could mold any child into any type of specialist, be it doctor, lawyer, etc. For Watson, "An infant's talents and abilities didn't matter because there was *no such thing* as a talent or an ability". (Pinker, *The Blank Slate*, 19) B.F. Skinner, another behaviorist, adheres to the notion of the blank slate with the findings of the Skinner Box. By rewarding and punishing rats based on their actions toward certain levers, he shaped their behavior. Skinner concludes that all behavior is explained through reinforcement patterns. This harkens back to John Locke's notion that individuals are born with no predisposed behaviors. Watson and Skinner are by no means alone in their assumptions. The great sociologist Emile Durkheim followed a similar path when he asserts, "Individual natures are merely the indeterminate material that the social factor molds and transforms." (Tooby and Cosmides, "The Psychological Foundations of Culture", 24 f.) Anthropologist Clifford Geertz continues this idea with his statement, "Man is the animal most desperately dependent upon such extragenetic, outside-the-skin control mechanisms, such cultural programs, for ordering his behavior". (Pinker, *The Blank Slate*, 25) Cosmides and Tooby argue that the sediment of the blank slate theory is static as evidenced by the language shift to the idea of a general purpose computer.

[46] While there is not room here, it is worth mentioning that this modular view of the brain is contentious. Most attention has been given to Noam Chomsky and his work with language. For more on Chomsky's position, see Chomsky's *Modular Approaches to the Study of the Mind* (San Diego, CA: San Diego State University, 1990). For an opposing approach, see Terrence Deacon,

tion. Natural selection will bias our cognition according to our particular environment. Complicated adaptations, such as language, take longer to evolve than simpler ones. However, the environment that we now inhabit is very different from the environment in which our ancestors evolved.

EP argues that the significant cultural changes occurring over the past 10,000 years progressed at a rate too great for the brain to fully adapt. This resulted in our psychological predispositions evolving in an environment alien to our current, modern world. Cleverly put, "Our modern skulls house a stone age mind".[47] Since our evolved psychological mechanisms for behavior are suited for an environment other than the one we inhabit, it is inaccurate to assume that any modern behavior is adaptive. As Cosmides and Tooby assert, "The fact that we can surf and skateboard are mere by-products of adaptations designed for balancing while walking on two legs."[48]

Since we are not adapted to our current environment, the environment to which we are adapted must be explored. Tooby and Cosmides borrow the phrase Environment of Evolutionary Adaptedness (EEA) from British psychiatrist John Bowlby. The EEA refers to the social, ecological, and technological conditions in which the human psychological mechanisms evolved. The EEA is not a decisive point in time where one locates all psychological adaptations. Instead, the EEA is "a statistical composite of the adaptation-relevant properties of the ancestral environments encountered by members of ancestral populations."[49] Some evolutionary psychologists believe that modern hunter-gatherer societies offer a glimpse into studying this ancestral environment because 99 % of our evolutionary history occurred in hunter-gatherer societies. While evolutionary psychologists firmly contend that the EEA is not an exact time or place, they do imply that the EEA is sometime during the Pleistocene Age (approximately the last 2.5 million years). More specifically, some evolutionary psychologists identify the EEA as prior to the origin of agriculture (10,000 years ago) and the cultural revolution (40,000 years ago).[50] The reason for this identification confirms that "the world to which we are adapted no longer exists."[51] EP argues that identifying the statistical facets of ancestral en-

---

The Symbolic Species: The Co-Evolution of Language and the Brain (New York: W. W. Norton & Company, 1997), esp. ch. 4.

[47] Leda Cosmides and John Tooby, "Evolutionary Psychology: A Primer", 1997, http://www.psych.ucsb.edu/research/cep/primer.html.

[48] Ibid.

[49] John Tooby and Leda Cosmides, "The Past Explains the Present: Emotional Adaptations and the Structure of Ancestral Environments", Ethology and Sociobiology, 11, 1990, 386f.

[50] Cosmides and Tooby avoid an understanding of the EEA as a Pleistocene African Savannah for numerous reasons. Their main point is that any adaptation could not have evolved in any modern environment. However, it is uncertain if they would say whether anything post 10,000 years is modern.

[51] Louise Barrett, Robin Dunbar, and John Lycett, *Human Evolutionary Psychology* (Princeton, NJ: Princeton University Press, 2002) 12.

vironments enhances understanding of the adaptive specializations of modern humans.[52]

A Critique

EP, while distancing itself from sociobiology, is not immune to critique. I want to briefly address one issue that is neglected by evolutionary psychologists.: the disregard for maladaptive traits.

Adaptations play a crucial role in the evolutionary story. If one believes that all traits are adaptive, however, there is a significant aspect of the story missing. Panadaptationism is incomplete and leads thinkers to develop "just so" stories. All of an individual's traits are assumed to "fit" the individual's environment or else natural selection would have selected against them. However, this type of strong adaptationism is somewhat misleading. Natural selection is not a process that selects for the "fittest" traits; the outcome of natural selection is not an environment of perfect individuals. Natural selection is about net results based on costs and benefits. The traits that are best suited to an environment, in comparison to competing traits, get selected. It is not selection of the best of all possible traits. Jerome Barkow notes, "Maladaptation is as much a part of evolution as is adaptation and does not challenge the evolutionary paradigm. Almost every adaptive (fitness-enhancing) trait is likely to carry with it a maladaptive (fitness-reducing) consequence."[53]

An interesting concept is the notion of *niche construction*. The intertwined relationship between genes, organisms, and environments led to the evolved ability of environmental alteration. By modifying our niche—the situation to

---

[52] It is clear that the EEA is a highly controversial issue. Critics have said that it is entirely possible that adaptive outcomes could have been produced in our modern world. They claim that the evidence of the rate of complex adaptations arising is uncertain; thus, it is possible that psychological mechanisms might have evolved since the rise of agriculture 10,000 years ago. See: Robert Boyd and Joan B. Silk, *How Humans Evolved* (New York and London: W.W. Norton & Company, [3]2003); Barret et al., *Human Evolutionary Psychology*, 2002. A second critique states that the EEA resembles modern foraging societies. The critics claim that we know very little about the ecology and behavior of extinct hominids. For example, "Some authorities believe that *homo erectus* and perhaps even earlier *Homo* species were much like contemporary human foragers", while others argue, "*H. erectus* and even the Neanderthals lived completely unlike modern hunter-gatherers." (Boyd and Silk, *How Humans Evolved*, 493). Margo Wilson and Martin Daly combat some of the criticism of the EEA arguing that it has been misconstrued and that most critiques are based on "the evolutionary psychology/human behavioral ecology debate". (Martin Daly and Margo I. Wilson, "Human Evolutionary Psychology and Animal Behavior", Animal Behavior, 57, 1999, 512.) That debate can be briefly described as those who consider traits adaptive if they increase the fitness of those who carry them (human behavioral ecologists) and those who identify selection pressures that have shaped human psychological mechanisms (evolutionary psychology). Judging whether the critiques of the EEA are accurate or misconstrued is beyond the scope of this paper; however, what can be asserted is that the EP notion of the EEA is controversial.

[53] Jerome H. Barkow, *Darwin, Sex and Status: Biological Approaches to Mind and Culture* (Toronto, Canada: University of Toronto Press, 1989) 293.

which you are forced to adapt—an organism can create an evolutionary short circuit, as well as a short circuit in natural selection leading to maladaptive consequences. It creates an artificial selection. Culture, then, may strongly affect what kind of species we are. Terrence Deacon identifies the building of dams by beavers as a great example of niche construction. Beavers build dams creating artificial aquatic environments that lead to the adaptation of beaver bodies. This is a short circuit of evolutionary biology because this behavioral artifact provides novel selection pressures for enhancement of dam construction competence for the new environment. Stone tools and symbolic culture created a similar self-generated niche for humans that masked the selection demands for vegetable food processing. This pressure caused the reduction of large molars and powerful jaws in australopithecines. Like the beaver dam, niche construction puts us in a very specific environment which changed our teeth and our need to cooperate.

The ability to construct our own niche can have maladaptive consequences, as well. Humans develop social structures that influence large groups of individual behaviors. However, occasionally an idea is promoted which is maladaptive, such as birth control. Symbolic thought and communication led to the possibility of actively preventing reproduction, a genetically maladaptive behavior. These symbolic ideas are not simply epiphenomena, but provide strong selection pressure for highly developed symbolic minds.[54]

Barkow analyzes maladaptation from both a coarse and fine grained view. At coarse grain, traits may look adaptive simply because their benefits outweigh their costs. However, a fine grained view may reveal a distinct maladaptive trait. For example, symbolic thought, at a coarse grained view, may be highly adaptive; but, a fine grained view shows the maladaptive trait of reproduction prevention.[55] Barkow cogently argues, "The advantage of the finer grain and the "maladaptive" label is that they force us to pay attention to the consequences for selection of the costs of what are on balance fitness-enhancing traits."[56] It is difficult to contemplate how maladaptive traits persist in an individual's behavior; thus, Barkow's view clarifies how maladaptive traits are passed on.

As shown above, cultural transmission can lead to traits that are genetically maladaptive. Barkow works with a fairly broad understanding of culture, defined as "a pool of at least somewhat organized information, socially transmitted both within and between generations."[57] He argues that four types of processes lead to fitness-reducing consequences. First, environments change

---

[54] See Deacon, *The Symbolic Species*.
[55] Certainly other reasons exist for the practice of birth control, but whatever they may be, they are maladaptive from an evolutionary perspective.
[56] Barkow, *Darwin, Sex and Status*, 294.
[57] Ibid., 295.

and cultural traits that prevent an individual to adapt to these changes are considered maladaptive. Second, costs that are minimal at one point in time can become quite costly over time. Third, mistakes or errors are passed from generation to generation. Fourth, groups are ruled by powerful individuals who can make decisions beneficial to themselves, but costly for others. The maladaptive behavior that these processes produce can be devastating. Even so, we are not simply Dawkins' "lumbering robots;" we have choices to make and these choices can reinforce both adaptive and maladaptive behaviors. Humans must consider that "some human psychological traits may, at least in our current environment, be fitness-reducing."[58]

EP does not take seriously enough this notion of maladaptation. From a coarse grain view, the evolutionary approach appears highly adaptive. From the fine grain view, maladaptive consequences are necessarily a part of the theory. As Barkow argues, "Even when the benefits far outweigh the costs, the latter remain, generating selection pressures."[59] EP's focus on ultimate causes creates a gap between the behavior and its full history; a history filled with maladaptive consequences.

EP is an important field for its attempts to relate human behavior with psychological evolution. While some of their hypotheses are unpopular, this is not reason enough to dismiss them. However, EP errs by making conclusions without robust explanations. Like sociobiology, EP posits questions worthy of consideration. Unfortunately, also like sociobiology, EP does not avoid the hazard of hasty assumptions.

Conclusion

The study of behavior from an evolutionary perspective met its greatest challenge when human behavior was taken up. Siding against the notion that we can understand human social behavior evolutionarily, requires the claim that *homo sapiens* have managed to disentangle ourselves from our evolutionary history. It requires affirmation that our genes have relinquished their power to have an influence on behavior. By denying that genes influence behavior, then one, by default, accepts blank slate theory (in the current context at least; one might believe in karma or Calvinist predestination). One of the greatest and most dangerous accomplishments of sociobiology is its emphasis that genes do play a vital role in social behavior. In reference to the greater topic of this volume, assessing the evolution of evil will always remain incomplete if the relation between genes and behavior is ignored. It so happens that sociobiology is a field of research geared specifically toward

---

[58] Ibid., 296.
[59] Ibid., 319.

this task. Theologians and philosophers who neglect this work do so at their own intellectual peril.[60]

While many reject sociobiology, clearly the breadth of sociobiological thinking has specific impacts. Many scientists with anthropological backgrounds work within the emergent field of *human behavioral ecology*.[61] This field assumes that a great deal of culture is evoked by a range of features of the social and ecological environment, thus exploring the extent to which human behavior is adaptive. A second field, *evolutionary psychology*, emerged out of sociobiology. As stated previously, a primary focus of evolutionary psychology is dismantling the Standard Social Scientific Model which "mischaracterizes important avenues of causation, induces researchers to study complexly chaotic and unordered phenomena, and misdirects study away from areas where rich principled phenomena are to be found."[62] In place of the SSSM, evolutionary psychologists provide the framework of the Integrated Causal Model, which "makes progress possible by accepting and exploiting the natural connections that exist among all branches of science, using them to construct careful analyses of the causal interplay among all the factors that bear on a phenomena."[63] *Behavioral genetics*[64] is a third field to develop, and it seeks to study the relation between genetic mechanisms and behavior. It maintains very close ties with the project of sociobiology. The fields of *human behavioral ecology*, *evolutionary psychology*, and *behavioral genetics* have important differences with sociobiology, but each of these disciplines is indebted to the pioneering work of sociobiologists. The connotations associated with the term sociobiology cause some to avoid its usage in their own work, but it is undeniable that sociobiology gave rise to a wealth of new approaches to the study of human behavior.

George C. Williams writes, "With what other than condemnation is a person with any moral sense to respond to a system in which the ultimate purpose in life is to be better than your neighbor at getting genes into future generations."[65] Unfortunately, some sociobiologists have made certain con-

---

[60] Those interested in a lively exchange between a sociobiologist and a theologian should see William Irons, "Morality, Religion, and Human Evolution", 375–399, and Philip Hefner, "Theological Perspectives on Morality and Human Evolution", 425 f, both in W. Mark Richardson and Wesley J. Wildman (ed.), *Religion and Science: History, Method, Dialogue* (New York & London: Routledge, 1996).

[61] See: B. Winterhalder and E. A. Smith, "Analyzing Adaptive Strategies: Human Behavioral Ecology at Twenty-Five", Evolutionary Anthropology, 9, 2000, 51–72; John R. Krebs and Nicholas B. Davies (ed.), *Behavioral Ecology: An Evolutionary Approach* (Oxford: Blackwell, ⁴1997).

[62] John Tooby and Leda Cosmides, "The Psychological Foundations of Culture", in: Barkow et al. (ed.), *The Adapted Mind*, 23.

[63] Ibid.

[64] See: Robert Plomin, John C. Defries, Ian W. Craig, and Peter McGuffin (ed.), *Behavioral Genetics in the Postgenomic Era* (Washington, DC: American Psychological Association, 2002).

[65] George C. Williams, *The Pony Fish's Glow* (New York, NY: Basic Books, 1996) 154.

clusions which are premature. Sociobiology's interest in ultimate causes, an interest shared with EP, needs to include a strict look at proximate causes. For instance, evolutionary psychologists generate certain hypotheses regarding human behavior. In correlating specific behavior and our evolved history, evolutionary psychologists identify the correlation, or proximate cause, as an evolved device in the brain. While the initial hypothesis may one day prove to be accurate, a full explanation requires the proximate causal story, which, at this point, lacks robust scientific data.

Legitimate and rigorous scientific research exists regarding sociobiology. However, popular reflection on the scientific results also exists. Books like Dawkins' *The Selfish Gene* and Wilson's *On Human Nature* are not specifically works of science, but works about science. Many critics of sociobiology focus on the unfortunate conclusions drawn in a number of these texts and reject the entire field of sociobiology. Like all scientific fields, the meticulous work can be found in journals. The often cited quotes from popular books, such as ethics "is an illusion fobbed off on us by our genes",[66] or "scratch an altruist, watch a hypocrite bleed"[67] only make the task of deciphering sociobiology's promise more difficult. Quality critiques of sociobiology must be heard, but these critiques should strive to strengthen the field and not eliminate it. The question can no longer be posed in such a way that the answer deciphers the percentage split between genes and environment. Ironically, Wilson's nature approach combined with Lewontin's nurture approach is the most promising means for providing a dynamic explanation of sociobiology.

---

[66] Michael Ruse and Edward O. Wilson, "The Evolution of Ethics", in: Michael Ruse (ed.), *Philosophy of Biology*, (Amherst, NY: Prometheus Books, 1998) 316.

[67] Michael T. Ghiselin, *The Economy of Nature and the Evolution of Sex* (Berkeley, CA: University of California Press, 1974) 247.

The Groaning of Creation

Does God Suffer with All Life?[1]

Robert John Russell

> *In a universe of blind physical forces and genetic replication,*
> *some people are going to get hurt, other people are going to get*
> *lucky, and you won't find any rhyme or reason in it, nor any*
> *justice. The universe we observe has precisely the properties we*
> *should expect if there is, at bottom, no design, no purpose, no evil*
> *and no good, nothing but blind, pitiless indifference.*
>
> Richard Dawkins[2]

> *I searched for the origin of evil, but I searched in a flawed way*
> *and did not see the flaw in my very search.*
>
> Augustine[3]

At the outset let me invite Augustine's profound caution, cited above, to govern and circumscribe my attempt to respond to the problem of evil in nature.

Beauty, joy and goodness radiate from the natural world around us and within us, telling us we are beloved creatures of the only eternal reality, the God of Abraham, the Father of Jesus Christ.[4] A spider web glistens with dew

---

[1] This chapter is based in part on "Natural theodicy in an evolutionary context: the need for an eschatology of new creation", in: Bruce Barber and David Neville, *Theodicy and Eschatology, Task of Theology Today, V* (Adelaide: Australian Theological Forum Press; 2005), revised and reprinted in: Robert John Russell, *Cosmology from Alpha to Omega: Theology and Science in Creative Mutual Interaction*, ch. 8 (Philadelphia: Fortress Press, 2007). Some material is drawn from "Entropy and Evil", CTNS Bulletin, 4, Spring, 1984, 1–12, and from Zygon: Journal of Religion and Science, vol. 19, No. 4, December 1984. See also "The Thermodynamics of 'Natural Evil': Response to Polkinghorne's Argument", CTNS Bulletin, 10/2, 1990. Both of these are revised and reprinted in *Cosmology from Alpha to Omega*, ch. 7. I am grateful to the many authors of this volume for their wisdom and insights into this challenge, especially my co-editors Gaymon Bennett, Marty Hewlett, and Ted Peters. I am particularly grateful to Christopher Southgate for his contribution to this volume in delineating the challenge and offering an astute analysis of the potential resources at hand.

[2] Richard Dawkins, *A River Out of Eden: A Darwinian View of Life* (New York: Basic Books, 1995) 133.

[3] Saint Augustine, Bishop of Hippo, *Confessions*, trans. Henry Chadwick (Oxford: Oxford University Press, 1991) 311, 115.

[4] Once again, Augustine is profoundly moving on this point. See for example, Augustine, *Confessions*, 183 (9).

in a dark night. A full moon rises behind flowing clouds at sunset. The satiny warm waters of a luxuriant coral reef teem with life in a Tahitian atoll. Clouds form on the frozen North face of the Matterhorn. The Sarenghetti plain streams with numberless herds of wildebeests. Penguins nest by the thousands in the Antarctic. The melody of a parrot lilts through a tropical Hawaiian jungle. Gorillas emerge from their forest to stop and look upwards at a tremendous waterfall, seeming to experience a moment of sacred space. The blistering heat floods the Australian aboriginal peoples' sacred place, Ulluru ("Ayers Rock"). As the first chapter of Genesis proclaims, all that God creates is good, even very good.

Still there is a "shadow side" to the world without — and within — which we also experience in daily life, and it leads us to cry out to God our Holy Redeemer. The spider web hides the terror of the trapped insect watching the impending jaws of the spider. The full moon rising might cause tidal waves that flood low-lying villages in the Pacific. The brightly-colored coral reef is often the hunt of a reef shark, while the exquisite beauty of the jellyfish distracts us from the poison in its tentacles. Clouds forming on the face of the Matterhorn may actually come from an avalanche taking the lives of climbers. Across the Sarenghetti plain, wildebeests die wrenchingly in the jaws of lions just as Antarctic penguins are sported for and then devoured by killer sharks as they leap an ice shelf into surrounding waters. Indeed, in the food chain that marks the history of life on earth most animals die an agonizing death in the jaws of predation. As Paul's letter to the church at Rome exclaims, "We know that the whole creation has been groaning in travail together until now" (Rom 8:22).[5]

These two views of nature seem at odds, if not mutually incoherent. How then can we proclaim that "the God who creates is the God who saves"? And why does the God who creates allow there to be such suffering, to recall the modern crisis of theodicy brought on by the Enlightenment?

The Bible is striking, compared to the views of its neighboring cultures of Greece and Babylon, in bringing both sides of life together under the single rubric of radical monotheism: God, the creator of the world, is the source of all that is and, ultimately, all that is good (Gen 1:1–2:3), and God, the redeemer of the world, promises that in the New Creation to come (Rev 21–22) such "natural evils" as suffering, disease, and death will be banished.[6] But key

---

[5] These two paragraphs are taken from Robert John Russell, "Natural Sciences", in: Arthur Holder (ed.), *The Blackwell Companion to Christian Spirituality* (Oxford: Blackwell Publishers, 2004) 325–344.

[6] A brief note on terminology: Although there is a great deal of diversity in the details, most scholars make a basic distinction between "moral evil" and "natural evil". They use the term moral evil (or "sin") to refer to acts committed by humanity that are contrary to God's will, acts in which we chose a lesser good instead of God, and thus acts that subvert human flourishing. The term "natural evil" stands for phenomena which are not the result of human agency, such as earth-

to the cogency of this double assertion in the Christian tradition, at least until the Enlightenment, was the understanding, based on Genesis 2–3, that suffering, disease, and death were taken to be the universal consequences of an inestimably tragic but entirely contingent and unnecessary historical event, the Fall.

Today this theological explanation of the two sides of life—as created good and consequentially evil—is severely challenged by the biological history of life on earth (whether or not one accepts the neo-Darwinian explanation for this history, which I do). For here death is integral to multicellular life and extinction is integral to the evolution of species. (See the critique of this claim by Joshua Moritz in this volume.) We now know that death is not the *consequence* of "the Fall" but *constitutive* of life itself. This means that "natural theodicy" as a response to natural evil raises a profound challenge to Christian faith.

This chapter attempts to take on this challenge by focusing on the "underside" of life: how can we believe in the goodness and power of the God who creates life through the very processes of evolution which in turn constitutively involve natural evil? This challenge is one which believers must address as we struggle with our faith in God, as we watch friends turn away from faith because of natural evil, and as we attempt to respond to the atheistic challenge to faith based on natural evil.

On a confessional note at the outset, I want to underscore the apophatic context of theology. What little light we have to shed on theological issues is surrounded by the overwhelming mystery of God which we confess through faith. This is particularly important for the task of theodicy: we should never seek to "solve" the problem of evil. As the Book of Job discloses, our fundamental response to evil must be faith in God and not rational argument or ethical judgment. Karl Rahner writes that the deepest answer to the enormity of suffering is "the incomprehensibility of God in his [sic] freedom and nothing else."[7] This chapter is written with the hope that the kataphatic affirmation that we can know God's ultimate goodness might have a place within the apophatic confession of the mystery of the world as God's creation including its trenchant and stunningly excessive moral and natural evil.

---

quakes, tsunamis, disease, and their consequences including suffering and death, thus phenomena which are in some sense evil but clearly not sinful. A much more detailed set of terms is needed for the careful distinctions one should eventually make in separating out physical evils that can afflict any form of life (human and non-human) but are not the result of agency, such as earthquakes, and biological evils that afflict sentient life (human and non-human) and are the result of non-human processes, such as the suffering of animals during predation. See Christopher Southgate's very helpful chapter in this volume and his previous article, "God and Evolutionary Evil: Theodicy in the Light of Darwinism", Zygon: Journal of Religion and Science, 37:4, December 2002, 803–821.

[7] Karl Rahner, "Why Does God Allow Us to Suffer?", Theological Investigations, Vol. 19, New York: Crossroad, 1983, 206ff.

"Theodicy Lite": Natural Evil Is Not Really Evil

We will first look at two important variations on the view that what we call natural evil is just a normal part of biological evolution and in no way "evil"; consequently "natural theodicy" is a non-issue. I call this view "theodicy lite". Actually theodicy lite represents one of three kinds of views which seek to dissolve the paradox of theodicy, namely the denial (or at least de-escalating) of the reality of evil. (The two other ways are to deny or reinterpret God's goodness or power. I don't treat these here.)

Theodicy Lite 1: Natural Theodicy Is Irrelevant

The most elementary response to natural evil is to view it as theologically irrelevant. Natural evil is "just natural" and it is entirely inappropriate to call it "evil". What we take, erroneously, to be evil is in fact *a constitutive factor of life*; it is no more in need of theological attention than other routine biological features in nature. Pain and suffering go hand in hand with sentience, and the death of organisms and the extinction of species are built into, and necessary for, the processes by which life evolves. In his illuminating article on theodicy, Christopher Southgate calls this response "The Problem Dismissed".[8]

Contrary to the idea that natural evil is just a part of the life process, I do not think that the admittedly constitutive nature of natural evil means that natural evil is theologically irrelevant. The New Testament narratives of the ministry of Jesus combine both physical healing with the forgiveness of sins.[9] In doing so, they link the realm of natural evil (i.e., disease, death) with the realm of moral evil (i.e., sin) and the salvation offered by the ministry of Jesus applies to both realms. It would therefore be impossible from a New Testament perspective to affirm the theological significance of moral evil while dismissing the theological significance of natural evil. Thus while rejecting the Biblical framework in which natural evil is the result of the Fall (and to the extent that this actually is the Biblical, and not just the Pauline / Augustinian interpretative framework) we must not reject the theological questions raised by natural evil in the context of the evolution of all living creatures. The way forward, then, will take us along a more complex path than the outright dismissal of the relevance of natural evil *per se*.

Theodicy Lite 2: Natural Theodicy Is Marginally Relevant

The second argument is that even God had "no choice" but to opt for Darwinian evolution if God is to create life by acting immanently through the processes of nature rather than by intervening in them. This means that adap-

---

[8] Christopher Southgate, "God and Evolutionary Evil", 808f.
[9] Ron Cole-Turner makes a similar point in Ronald Cole-Turner, *The New Genesis: Theology and the Genetic Revolution* (Louisville: Westminster/John Knox Press, 1993).

tation by natural selection, and the resulting "natural evils", are an unavoidable consequence of God's action in creating life which even God could not eliminate. The "no choice" argument aims at lessening the intensity of natural theodicy by letting God "off the hook"—slightly. In an interesting turn of events, Michael Ruse actually offers the "no choice" argument in defense of Christianity against one of its most vocal critics, Richard Dawkins, by citing Dawkins' own reference to it: "Dawkins, however, argues strenuously that selection and only selection can do the job. No one—and presumably this includes God—could have got adaptive complexity without going the route of natural selection."[10]

In response I would suggest that Ruse's "no choice" argument is based on a crucial assumption which he overlooks: namely the assumption that the laws of physics underlying molecular and evolutionary biology are a "given". Admittedly if God were to create life by natural processes *and* if laws of physics which govern these processes are taken for granted, then God may have had "no choice" other than Darwinian evolution, and this then eases the burden of accounting for God's action in evolution somewhat, as Ruse points out. But if we push it one step further, we see that this argument does not really help with theodicy since the question of whether God had a "choice" returns at a more fundamental level in what I will call *cosmic theodicy*:

Since God freely created our universe *ex nihilo*, including the laws of physics and constants of nature, why then did God choose to create *these* laws and constants knowing that they would then make Darwinian evolution possible and with it the sweep of natural evil? (I will return to these issues below.) Thus, the Ruse/Dawkins argument does not on its own rescue God from responsibility, but merely places divine responsibility at a more foundational level. It leads to what we could call a "semi-Manichaen" view of creation: one which is partially evil at its most fundamental, material level, physics. It also leads us to challenge the Leibnizian assertion that this is truly the best of all possible *universes* that God could have created: instead could there be another kind of universe in which life evolved *without natural evil*?[11] For me, "Theodicy Lite" is thus exposed as ultimately a fruitless and unanswerable theodicy, and we must move ahead.

---

[10] Michael Ruse, *Can a Darwinian Be a Christian? The Relationship Between Science and Religion* (Cambridge: Cambridge University Press, 2001) 136. Here Ruse cites Richard Dawkins, "Universal Darwinism", in: D. S. Bendall (ed.), *Molecules to Men* (Cambridge: University of Cambridge Press, 1983) 403–425. In it Ruse gives a very thoughtful and promising account of what he believes is really at stake in the Christianity / evolution controversy. Ruse repeats his "no choice" argument against Dawkins in Ruse's chapter in the present volume.

[11] Robert John Russell, "Physics, Cosmology and the Challenge to Consequentialist Natural Theodicy", in: Nancey Murphy, Robert John Russell and William R. Stoeger S. J. (ed.), *Physics and Cosmology: Scientific Perspectives on Natural Evil* (Vatican City State: Vatican Observatory Publications: Berkeley: Center for Theology and the Natural Sciences, 2007).

"Theodicy Mitigated": Natural Evil May be Overestimated in the Standard neo-Darwinian Scenario

Joshua Moritz offers a very impressive challenge to the central claim of the standard neo-Darwinian scenario, namely that natural selection plays the pivotal role in driving biological evolution. He starts by agreeing with Ruse and Dawkins about the enormity of the pain and suffering that are involved in natural selection and that characterizes the history of life on earth. Nevertheless, drawing on the writings of Jeffrey Schloss, Ian Barbour, Stuart Kauffman, Lynn Margulis, and others Moritz claims that other evolutionary mechanisms, such as symbiogenesis, self-organization, developmental constraints, epigenetics, and generic morphogenic principles, must now be considered by scientists in weighing the relative roles they play, together with natural selection, in the overall evolutionary framework. This in turn challenges us to reconsider the causes and extent of natural evil in the evolution of life, suggesting that the problem of natural evil may be considerably mitigated by this shift away from a unique concentration on natural selection and towards these other mechanisms which suggest elements of natural goodness inherent in evolution. Moritz also takes into account, in a fresh and creative way, the role that animal choice plays in determining the kinds and extent of natural evil, suggesting the term "protomoral" rather than "amoral" for their role in causing natural evil and relating this, in turn, to their need for redemption.[12]

I am greatly persuaded by Moritz's arguments that the central role played by natural selection may be overstated in the literature in theology and science, certainly including in my own writings, and I welcome the participation by him and other biologists in correcting this imbalance. In addition, Moritz's portrayal of the ambiguity of good and evil in the pre-human world opens up a promising connection with what I will describe below in terms of the ambiguous role played by thermodynamics in helping drive evolution and in shaping the phenomena of both natural evil and natural goodness.

Nevertheless, as Moritz clearly acknowledges, the phenomena of suffering and death are real in the pre-human world and are grounded, in part, on the underlying physics of this universe. Because of this the mitigating role played by the alternative mechanisms Moritz describes still leaves intact—tragically—the *in principle* challenge raised by natural evil to faith in the God

---

[12] See Moritz's chapter in this volume as well as his GTU Master's thesis, "Returning to Eden: The Problem of Evil, The Free Will Theodicy, & The Challenge of the Natural Sciences" (December, 2003). See also Barbour's discussion of alternative factors which drive evolution, such as punctuated equilibrium, panadaptionism, neo-Lamarckian effects, self-organization, cooperation and symbiogenesis. As Moritz suggests, these may provide very helpful critiques of the central role accorded to natural selection in neo-Darwinism. Ian G. Barbour, "Five Models of God and Evolution", in: Robert John Russell, William R. Stoeger and Francisco J. Ayala (ed.), *Evolutionary and Molecular Biology: Scientific Perspectives on Divine Action*, (Vatican City State; Berkeley, CA: Vatican Observatory Publications; Center for Theology and the Natural Sciences, 1998) 419–442.

of evolution. I feel that this challenge must therefore still be addressed. In addition, for theological reasons I believe it is unavoidable because the central kerygma of Christian faith is the Resurrection of Jesus and thus the vanquishing of death itself. Hence if "only one sparrow" had died over the past billion years, that fact alone points directly to what the Christian faith in Christ's Resurrection is meant to address, and what theodicy can never achieve: hope that the death which will come to us all in our world is not the end but the beginning of everlasting life.

Robust Theodicies: Two Traditional Forms

If we hope to address natural evil, the first step is to identify criteria which any theodicy must meet. Admittedly I will argue that all theodicies ultimately fail to meet these criteria and for valid theological purposes (hinted at immediately above). Nevertheless, I believe we can make a reasonable attempt at proposing such criteria; in my view there are at least three:

1) it must ward off Manichaen tendencies to "blame God" for creating natural evil or to view nature as unambiguously evil,
2) it must ward off Pelagian tendencies to undercut the universality of moral evil,
3) it must take fully on board Darwinian evolution, and in particular the constitutive character of natural evil to life.

Christian theology includes a variety of theodicies which meet these criteria. For the purposes of this brief chapter I will employ John Hick's analysis of this variety as falling within two broad types—Augustinian and Schleiermachean / Irenaean. The task will be to reformulate these theodicies such that they meet all three criteria and then deploy them in response to the challenge of evolutionary natural theodicy.

The Augustinian Theodicy: The Free-will Defense

Historical Christianity provided a framework which met the first two criteria via the Augustinian theodicy, drawn in large measure from Pauline texts in the New Testament and the dominant context of neo-Platonism. Augustine's theodicy was profoundly influential to Aquinas, Calvin and Luther and such contemporary theologians as Barth and Rahner.

According to Augustine,[13] both moral and natural evil are ultimately the result of free rational beings who sin: they willfully turn from God as the highest good toward a lesser good. Augustine avoids Manichaenism by affirming

---

[13] See for example Saint Augustine, Bishop of Hippo, *Confessions*, trans. Henry Chadwick (Oxford: Oxford University Press, 1991) and St. Augustine, *The City of God*, trans. Henry Bettenson (London: Penguin Books, 1984).

the goodness of all that God creates. Sin began with the premundane, cosmic fall of the angels. It continued with Adam and Eve who, though created "very good" by God, did of their own free will chose creaturely goods over God. The resulting corruption or bondage of the will is transmitted sexually from generation to generation to all humanity from the common human origin in Adam and Eve. On the one hand, then, human beings still have the power of free will, and are thus responsible for, and deserve punishment for, their actions by God. On the other hand, though, in Eden it had been possible not to sin ("*posse non peccare*"), in human history free will is corrupt and without God's grace it is not possible not to sin ("*non posse non peccare*"). Augustine embedded the resulting "free-will defense" in a Neo-Platonic understanding of the plenitude of creation in which evil is a privation of being and in an overarching aesthetic in which God sees all things ultimately as "very good".

Schleiermacher's Theodicy: The Moral Growth Argument

Liberal Protestant theology in the 19th century, and much of Catholic and Protestant theology in the 20th century, have worked within an alternative framework provided by Friedrich Schleiermacher. In the early 19th century, Schleiermacher's *Speeches* and *The Christian Faith*[14] provided a massive reformulation of original perfection and original sin in a developmental / proto-evolutionary framework. Briefly, the *original perfection of the world* according to Schleiermacher consists in the world being such that God's purposes can be achieved in and through natural processes. In particular, the world is such that our experience of our relative dependence on the world leads to our experience of our absolute dependence on God as the source of all that is. The *original righteousness of humankind* consists in our capacity for religious experience both as the personal experience of individuals and as communicated through culture.[15] *Sin* consists in the obstruction of our awareness of God due to our dependence on the world. It is virtually inevitable because we are "sentient animals" embedded in the world as physical and biological creatures, and because in our individual lives our physical character precedes the development of our individual cognitive and spiritual capacities. Yet sin is not necessary, since in Jesus the development of his consciousness of God was unobstructed; he was "sinless". Thus we are still personally responsible for our sins. *Original sin* is both individual and societal in character[16] leading to

---

[14] Friedrich Schleiermacher, *On Religion: Speeches to Its Cultured Despisers*, trans. John Oman (New York: Harper & Row, Torchbooks, 1958); Friedrich Schleiermacher, *The Christian Faith*, ed. H. R. Mackintosh and J. S. Stewart (Edinburgh: T. & T. Clark, 1968); most references can be found in Schleiermacher, *The Christian Faith*, paragraphs 58–89.

[15] Note: "Original" designates a timeless character of the world and of humankind, not a state in the past (Eden) from which we have "fallen": Schleiermacher rejects the Fall unequivocally.

[16] The original sinfulness of the individual (or "congenital sin") is grounded in our developmental phenomenology prior to any specific action or "acts of sin"; we are born this way, and

Schleiermacher's distinctive aphorism, "sin is in each the work of all, and in all the work of each". Finally, *natural evil* does not arise from sin. Still because of our sinfulness we experience natural evils as genuine evil, and for this reason natural evil can be considered a penalty of sin.

It can be argued, then, that Schleiermacher's pivotal reformulation of original perfection and original sin in a time-independent, developmental/proto-evolutionary framework meets our three criteria for an evolutionary natural theodicy, and establishes the terms of such a theodicy decades before Darwin's scientific results were published.

Retrieving and Extending the Augustinian Theodicy to Physics and Cosmology: Insights and Failures

At first glance it might seem clear that Schleiermacher's theodicy would be more compatible with our project of an evolutionary natural theodicy than would Augustine's. The latter is grounded in the framework of the Fall which Schleiermacher in many ways overcame, and Schleiermacher's approach, particularly understood through the lens of John Hick's revisions (as we shall see below) have been highly influential in contemporary theology. However, I believe that there are resources in Augustine's theodicy which should not be overlooked.

Retrieval: Reinhold Niebuhr

The first task is to divest the Augustinian theodicy of its "creation / fall" framework by uncovering its underlying philosophical argument, and then to reinterpret this argument in an evolutionary framework. To do so I have turned, in previous writings, to Reinhold Niebuhr's immensely influential Gifford lectures.[17] Here Niebuhr presented the underlying argument of the Augustinian theodicy stripped of its mythological language. According to Niebuhr, Augustine rejected the Manichaen view which ontologizes evil. Instead he argued that sin has no ontological status and that humans are therefore not sinful because of their created nature. Next Augustine explained why original sin applies to all of humanity through his theory of the biological inheritance of sin and the participation of all people in Adam's sin. Augustine then argued against the Pelagian view that sin could be overcome by human will alone. Instead, redemption is due to God's grace. Finally, against neo-

---

yet we are personally responsible for our specific acts of sin. The original sinfulness of society (or "conditioning sin") is the distorted character of society into which each individual is born, which influences each individual in their lives, and to which each individual contributes by their own acts of sin.

[17] Reinhold Niebuhr, *The Nature and Destiny of Man: I. Human Nature* (New York: Charles Scribner's Sons, 1941 [1964]).

Platonism Augustine located sin within the human will which is corrupted by original sin.

Niebuhr then rendered the underlying logic of the Augustinian theodicy as asserting that sin is *unnecessary but inevitable*.[18] This phrase captures Augustine's argument without tying it to the Fall. It expresses in stark terms what Niebuhr called the "absurd paradox" of the Christian free-will defense. Augustinian theodicy rephrased through Niebuhr's formulation now meets our three criteria for an evolutionary natural theodicy.

Preconditions in Physics That Underlie the Free-will Defense

We are now in a position to think through the free-will defense in the context of an evolutionary history of nature. As a physicist, my approach is to study the underlying laws of physics and the structure of cosmology which play a role, along with many other processes at more complex levels in nature, in making biological evolution possible *and* which contribute to the underlying physical characteristics of evolution which we call natural evil. The challenge is to do so with the reformulated Augustinian / Niebuhrian free-will defense in mind. This means we must search for ways in which the role of physics in evolution, and the subsequent role of evolution in the rise of life, honors the delicate balance Augustine sought to achieve between avoiding the Manichaen move to ground sin in nature and the Pelagian move to ignore the element of original inheritance that makes sin inevitable. Moreover, we must do so without appealing to the contingency of an historical event — the Fall — which offered Augustine a way to achieve that delicate balance.[19] In short, we must search for those aspects and areas of physics and cosmology that satisfy two conditions: they must underlie and make possible biological evolution and they must reflect at the level of physics and cosmology the Niebuhrian reformulation of Augustine's free-will defense of seeing the structure of sin as "unnecessary but inevitable".

Prima facie it is not clear how to undertake such a search, or whether there are in fact aspects and areas of physics and cosmology that satisfy both conditions. An approach which I have explored in previous writings is to start with a second reformulation of Niebuhr's reformulation of the Augustinian concept of sin as unnecessary but inevitable, such that this concept can be more readily discussed at the level of physics. I have suggested that the underlying logical structure of Niebuhr's claim can be described by the term "universal

---

[18] Niebuhr, *The Nature and Destiny of Man: I. Human Nature*, 242. "Original sin, which is by definition an inherited corruption, or at least an inevitable one, is nevertheless not to be regarded as belonging to his essential nature and therefore is not outside the realm of his responsibility. Sin is natural for man in the sense that it is universal but not in the sense that it is necessary."

[19] It is well known that Augustine's account was vehemently debated throughout the subsequent history of Christian thought.

contingent": that which is ontologically contingent and thus not necessary, but that which holds in all cases and thus is inevitable.[20] The task, then, is to search for examples of a "universal contingent" in physics. (Moritz offers a very creative insight into a highly significant "universal contingent", but this time in the domain of evolutionary history. See his chapter in this volume.)

A prime example is found in non-linear, non-equilibrium thermodynamics, with its concepts of entropy and "order out of chaos". As a background, classical thermodynamics through the nineteenth century typically studied closed systems: systems which are isolated from their environment. A measure of the available energy or, equivalently, of the order of such a system is its entropy, S. According to the first law of thermodynamics, the total energy of a closed system is conserved in time while, according to the second law, the entropy S of a closed system increases inevitably to a maximum as time, t, passes according to the simple equation $\Delta S / \Delta t \geq 0$. A simple example is pouring cold milk into a cup of hot tea. It is easy to show that the entropy of the "milk in the tea" system is greater than the "milk and the tea" system before the milk is poured.[21] It is also clear that the "milk in the tea" system is more disordered than the "milk and the tea" system when the tea is uniformly milky.[22]

In the twentieth century, Ilya Prigogine and his colleagues began to study the non-linear, non-equilibrium thermodynamics of open systems: systems contained within larger environments which can exchange energy and matter with their environment.[23] In the process these open systems, by exhausting entropy to the environment, can spontaneously move to greater degrees of order. The total entropy of the environment and its internal, open systems, increases, obeying the second law, but its open subsystems can decrease in entropy and increase in order. Again the tea and milk provide a simple yet elegant example when we consider the milk as the open subsystem within the environment of the tea. If we pour the milk very slowly into the hot tea, beautiful patterns of swirling milk spontaneously appear in the teacup, dynamical structures of immense (probably fractal-like) complexity as heat flows from the surrounding tea into the filaments of cold milk. Nevertheless these pat-

---

[20] Robert John Russell, "The Thermodynamics of 'Natural Evil'", CTNS Bulletin, 10:2, Spring 1990, 20–25.

[21] We define the entropy S in terms of the amount of energy Q transferred between systems at a given temperature T: $\Delta S = \Delta Q / T$. When cold milk is poured into hot tea, an amount of energy ΔQ is transferred from the tea to the milk, bringing them to the same temperature. In the process, $\Delta S = \Delta Q / T_1 - \Delta Q / T_2$ where T_1 is the temperature of the milk and T_2 is the temperature of the tea. Since $T_1 < T_2$, $\Delta Q > 0$ as required by the second law.

[22] After pouring milk into the tea, the milk becomes diffused throughout the tea and our previous knowledge of where it is, in distinction from where the tea is, is lost.

[23] For a technical discussion see Ilya Prigogine, *From Being to Becoming: Time and Complexity in the Physical Sciences* (San Francisco: W.H. Freeman and Company, 1980). For a non-technical introduction see Ilya Prigogine and Isabelle Stengers, *Order Out of Chaos: Man's New Dialogue with Nature* (New York: Bantam Books, 1984) 349.

terns decay in time as the milk becomes evenly dispersed in the tea and both come to the same temperature. In more complicated cases, the spontaneous structures can last much longer, especially if they become embedded in ever greater systems of open, hierarchically-ordered structures. The great spot on Jupiter is a classic example. Better still, the evolution of life on earth, and the complex dynamic web of changing ecological structures, is a large scale example at inter-level hierarchies ranging from physics and molecular biology to organisms, species, and the environment. Ultimately both the complex homeostasis of life on earth at any given moment and the myriad inter-connected processes of biological evolution in which vast increases in biological complexity over time have arisen depend on a thermodynamic "heat exchange" between the sun and the earth. Thus, without thermodynamics, which applies *universally* to all physical and thus all biological systems, the evolution of life on earth would have been impossible.

Yet although thermodynamics applies to all physical systems, we cannot predict whether a given system will remain stable or whether spontaneous fluctuations will drive it towards more complexity: both of these paths are made possible by the laws of non-linear, non-equilibrium thermodynamics, but the details depend on other areas of physics such as kinetic theory. Based on the work of Prigogine and his colleagues, Arthur Peacocke has provided a highly illuminating discussion of this technically complex question.[24] According to Peacocke, we first define the concept of entropy production, P, as the rate at which the entropy S of the system changes in time (i.e., $P = dS/dt$). We next define the excess entropy production E as the variation in the value of P during a fluctuation and due to the fluctuation. Now we are prepared for the following results: If $E > 0$, the system is stable against fluctuations, but if $E < 0$, the system may be either stable or unstable, and a fluctuation might cause the system to move into a more complex state. Thus the advancement to increased complexity in such systems, including biological ones, is *contingent* on factors and processes which lie beyond the thermodynamics of these systems.

The "take-away message" in all this should now be clear: Non-linear, non-equilibrium thermodynamics carries both of the characteristics underlying Augustine's argument about the nature of sin at the level of physics: universality and contingency.

How these preconditions in physics contribute to shaping the ambiguity of "free will" in the Niebuhr / Augustinian Free-will Defense

One of the most profound insights in the Augustinian understanding of sin is that our will is so tainted by sin that we cannot chose not to sin, as Augustine so poignantly emphasized against the Pelagians. Yet since the taint is

---

[24] A. R. Peacocke, An Introduction to the Physical Chemistry of Biological Organization (Oxford: Clarendon Press, 1983) ch. 2, esp. 47.

in our will, the acts of sin are acts for which we are responsible—against the Manichaens. Does thermodynamics have anything to say about this profound ambiguity in the understanding of free will lying at the heart of the "free-will defense"? I believe it does.

In a very interesting way, non-linear, non-equilibrium thermodynamics contributes to the ambiguity of sin, for it shows how thermodynamics underlies the multitude of biological, environmental, personal, social factors entailed by both human virtue and human sin. In essence, thermodynamics provides the physical possibilities for the actions that we consider both virtuous and immoral.

Consider how we find beauty and goodness in the patterns of emergent complexity and creative novelty that characterize the joys of life, while tragedy and sorrow play themselves out in the patterns of dissipation and destruction associated with decay, disease and death. Now thermodynamics underlies and is entailed by all such phenomena. Because of non-linear, non-equilibrium thermodynamics, both emergent complexity and creative novelty on the one hand and dissipation and destruction on the other hand at every level of nature are *possible* physically, although the *causes* for complexity and novelty and for dissipation and destruction are found at *every* level in nature. Thus thermodynamics plays a *dual* role as a physical precondition for the enactment of virtue associated with community celebration, artistic creativity and genuine altruism as well as the enactment of sin associated with family violence, international war, terrorism and human genocide.

One way to frame this complex set of entailments is to suggest that thermodynamics stands in a metaphorical relation with virtue and sin.[25] In previous writings I have followed Paul Ricoeur's understanding of metaphor as including a negative as well as a positive analogy (both an "is" and an "is not"), Ian Barbour's insight that metaphors are extendable to new contexts, and Sallie McFague's development of these resources into what she termed "metaphorical theology".[26] This metaphorical argument then led to a more pointed claim: that thermodynamics is needed if both moral evil (sin) and moral virtue is to be actualized in the world. To recast what I wrote almost two decades ago: since good and evil are realities of human life and history, something like entropy is what one would expect to find at the physical level underlying these realities.[27]

---

[25] Robert John Russell, "Entropy and Evil", Zygon: Journal of Religion and Science, 19:4, December 1984, 449–468. I am grateful for the appreciative inclusion of these insights by Mark Worthing in his book Mark W. Worthing, *God, Creation, and Contemporary Physics, Theology and the Sciences Series* (Minneapolis: Fortress Press, 1996) ch. 4, "The Problem of Evil" and "Summary."

[26] Ian G. Barbour, *Myths, Models, and Paradigms: A Comparative Study in Science & Religion* (New York: Harper & Row, 1974); Sallie McFague, *Metaphorical Theology: Models of God in Religious Language* (Philadelphia: Fortress Press, 1982).

[27] Russell, "Entropy and Evil", 465. I compared Augustine's understanding of evil as privation of being with entropy in physics: Entropy does not refer to something physical (e.g., matter) or

In essence, thermodynamics provides an example at the level of physics of what is needed if the consequences of sinful acts are to be expressed physically, including dissipation and disruption, as well as the consequences of virtuous acts, including acts of beauty and goodness. Natural goodness and natural evil are in some subtle but unavoidable way the indirect consequences of the particular physics of this universe.

Extending the Augustinian/Niebuhrian Free Will Theodicy to Cosmology

If natural goodness and natural evil are the consequences, in part, of physics, does this offer a partial response to natural theodicy and thus God's relation to suffering in nature? Or does it push us far too close to a "semi-Manichaen" view of God's creation? Recall Ruse's response to Dawkins which I characterized as a form of "theodicy lite". According to Ruse's reading of Dawkins, even God had "no choice" but to opt for Darwinian evolution if God is to create life by acting immanently through the processes of nature rather than by intervening in them. But in my response above I pointed out that the question of whether God had a choice actually moves us to a more fundamental level than physics, namely to cosmology and to what I called *cosmic theodicy*: Why did God choose to create *this* universe with *these* laws of physics knowing that they would not only make Darwinian evolution possible but with it the three billion year sweep of natural evil in the biological realm. More than that, because these laws locate the lowest level of the problem of natural evil in physics and not just biology they extend the phenomena of natural evil *throughout the thirteen billion year history of the universe*.[28] In a recent essay I have suggested that no further response to theodicy is possible once one reaches the level of cosmology.[29] We simply cannot answer the question of

---

even a property of something physical (like mass, which is a property of matter). Instead it is a measure of the loss of available energy or the increase in disorder. Hence neither evil nor entropy are "ontological"; both are dependent on being, lacking independent existence. In that paper I compared entropy in physics to evil in Paul Tillich's theology. Tillich describes evil as having "no independent standing in the whole of reality, but…it is dependent on the structure of that in and upon which it acts destructively" and his memorable phrase that the form of evil is the "structure of destruction." Thus evil "aims" at "chaos" and when chaos is attained, "both structure and destruction have vanished." See 457.

[28] With this in mind I have suggested renaming the "anthropic principle" the "thermodynamic anthropic principle" to underscore the irreducible but often overlooked role of thermodynamics in arguments about the anthropic principle in relation to the evolution of moral agents (e.g., the Murphy/Ellis thesis) and to stress its implications for cosmic theodicy. See Nancey Murphy and George F. Ellis, *On the Moral Nature of the Universe: Theology, Cosmology, and Ethics, Theology and the Sciences Series* (Minneapolis, MN: Fortress Press, 1996). See my response in Robert John Russell, "The Theological Consequences of the Thermodynamics of a Moral Universe: An Appreciative Critique and Extension of the Murphy/Ellis Project", CTNS Bulletin, 19.4, Fall 1998, 19–24.

[29] Russell, "Physics, Cosmology and the Challenge to Consequentialist Natural Theodicy".

God's relation to natural evil by searching for a "no choice" solution found in underlying levels of complexity in nature. If vestiges of natural evil, however mute, are found at the level of the physics of this universe, then we are left with the perennial question: Is life, as God's creation in and through the laws of this universe which God chose, worth the price? The only way forward, I will shortly suggest, is to be found in a theology of redemption and not in a theology of creation. God's response to evil is to vanquish it through the life, death and resurrection of Jesus of Nazareth.

Mutual Interaction Model: Implications for Eschatology and for Contemporary Physics

There is, however, one final insight from the Augustinian / Niebuhrian theodicy which invokes a brief analysis here. As I have said, we have found so far that the Augustinian/Niebuhrian theodicy ultimately fails, not because it is tied to a mythical "fall"— which it clearly is not—nor because it views death as a consequence of sin instead of as constitutive of life—which it clearly does not—but because, like "Theodicy Lite" even though it is more complex, it leads to the recognition that underlying moral evil is natural evil that, in an implicitly Manichaen way, characterizes the universe as a whole. I believe that this fundamental problem points at last to the impossibility of articulating an adequate response to theodicy in terms of the universe as it presently exists and thus in the theological context of the doctrine of creation. Instead it forces us to relocate the response to the context of eschatology and its portrayal of the "new creation".

But this failure brings with it an exceptional gift: It gives us a crucial insight into what eschatology must include if it is to address the failure of theodicy to account for natural evil. The insight is that if in the new creation it will be impossible to commit moral evil since we will be liberated from the bondage of the will into true freedom (Augustine: *non posse peccare*), then the new creation will not include natural evil either. This claim could be taken in several ways.

In its most simple form it might mean that the new creation will not include thermodynamics since it contributes to natural evil. In a slightly more complex form it might mean that the new creation will not include thermodynamics to the extent that it produces natural evils, though it might include it to the extent that it produces natural goods.

What is even more interesting is the way this insight works "backwards" from eschatology to the universe as we now know it via the doctrine of creation. It implies that thermodynamics, as a "universal contingent" characterizing this universe, is itself "contingent" since it will not characterize the new creation. This in turn carries *implications for current physics*. One question which has been discussed extensively is whether thermodynamics is a "fundamental" theory comparable to dynamics (e.g., quantum mechanics, quantum field theory, etc.). The implication here is that it is not a fundamental theory since it will not be part of the eschatological destiny of the universe, or at least not a part of it in the way in which it contributes to natural evil. If that is so, it could suggest interesting questions for future research in the foundations of physics regarding the relation of thermodynamics to fundamental physical theories.

Retrieving and Extending Schleiermacher's Theodicy to Evolution

Retrieval: John Hick
The legacy of Schleiermacher's theodicy can be found in part in John Hick's recent and profound treatment.[30] Hick's theodicy, in turn, has been widely influential among scholars in theology and science.

Hick's development of Schleiermacher's theodicy starting in the mid 1960s is "regarded generally as the first clearly defined alternative to the Augustinian-Thomistic perspective".[31] Hick names this type of theodicy after Irenaeus who first brought together themes found in the sub-apostolic Eastern church, such as the distinction between the image and likeness of God in humanity, the understanding of our earthly life as one of gradual spiritual growth from image to likeness, sin as due to weakness and immaturity, and the world as a mingling of good and evil appointed by God for our growth towards perfection.[32] In the 19th century, Schleiermacher was to develop and systematize themes such as these into the rich framework we have just touched on.[33]

Hick's Contribution: Epistemic Distance
Hick develops his own theodicy within the Irenaean context through an extraordinarily careful, detailed, and judicious exploration of multiple problems involving moral and natural evil. In the second edition, he compellingly engages even his most severe critics who raise a variety of issues and objections, offering what I take as relatively persuasive logical responses as to why God does not act to remove or diminish the extent of suffering in nature. These include the impossibility of our doing the "means/end calculation", the limitations on the perspective needed for a "greatest good" argument, the relativity of the "worst evil", etc. Recently, Tom Tracy has explored these in detail.[34]

---

[30] John Hick, *Evil and the God of Love*, Revised Edition (San Francisco: Harper & Row, 1966).

[31] Barry L. Whitney, *What Are They Saying About God and Evil?* (New York: Paulist Press, 1989) 38.

[32] Hick, *Evil*, 211–218.

[33] Hick notes that there is no evidence that Schleiermacher was influenced directly by Irenaeus or the early church, leading Hick to refer to this form of theodicy as a "type", not a "tradition." Hick, *Evil*, 219.

[34] Thomas F. Tracy, "Evolution, Divine Action, and the Problem of Evil", in: Robert John Russell, William R. Stoeger, SJ and Francisco J. Ayala (ed.), *Evolutionary and Molecular Biology:*

The arguments "do not seek to demonstrate that Christianity is true, but that the fact of evil does not show it to be false…"[35] They do not constitute a theodicy as much as they clear the way for one to receive a fair hearing.

Central to Hick's robust theodicy is the argument that "pain and suffering are a necessary feature of a world that is to be the scene of a process of soul-making". Even their "haphazard and unjust distribution" and excess are ultimately beneficial, since "the right must be done for its own sake rather than a reward". Although I will *not* follow Hick to the extent that the "soul-making" theme serves as the basis of his theodicy[36], I do appreciate what is a closely related but still a quite distinct claim, namely that "epistemic distance" is required if humans are to be capable of genuine moral agency. "God must be a hidden deity, veiled by His ⟨sic.⟩ creation" so that, unlike our physical surroundings, God's presence is not coercively imposed on us. The world must be *"etsi deus non daretur"* ("as if there were no God") because in such a world we have the necessary "cognitive freedom" by which faith and moral agency are possible.

Epistemic Distance as the basis for science and for theology-and-science
In my opinion, Hick's idea of "epistemic distance" bears on a three-fold set of questions which do not seem, at first blush, related to the purpose he had in mind, i. e., as a requirement for genuine moral agency.

First, I see epistemic distance as a requirement for *science to be possible*. Science, after all, is based on methodological naturalism[37]: an explanation of the processes of nature which relies solely on natural causes without the explicit introduction of divine causation. Thus, following methodological naturalism, the world must be "as if there were no God" not only because this is necessary for moral freedom (alla Hick *if* you agree with him), *but also because it makes it possible to study the world via scientific methodology.*

Second, this means that when we Christians encounter science and its basis in methodological naturalism, we should not see it as antagonistic to theology (although metaphysical naturalism as a philosophical interpretation of methodological naturalism certainly is) nor try to replace it with a method that includes a "divine designer" *in science* (as Intelligent Design implies since what

---

Scientific Perspectives on Divine Action, (Vatican City State; Berkeley, CA: Vatican Observatory Publications; Center for Theology and the Natural Sciences, 1998) 511–530.

[35] Hick, *Evil*, viii.

[36] Where I part company in particular with Hick is in the implications he draws from this for theodicy: namely that it also goes a long way to accounting for moral evil, since the hiddenness of God makes evil a "virtually inevitable result" of the actions of a free agent. cf. Hick, *Evil*, 281 f, 353. I believe, instead, that the only robust response to moral and natural evil is eschatology and not as their being tied to the necessary conditions for moral agency, as I will suggest shortly.

[37] It shouldn't be necessary to emphasize here that methodological naturalism does not require or logically entail metaphysical naturalism (i. e., atheism, materialism, etc.).

natural agent could have been responsible for evolution?)[38]. Instead we should see science as a legitimate though limited method of knowing the world precisely because it is based on the way God created the world—namely by granting nature a resource of intrinsic causality which does not need continuous divine intervention—and because God's purpose in creating it this way was to make possible faith and moral freedom.

Third, the concept of "epistemic distance" accounts for why it is possible for theists to interpret science as consonant with theology. This is so because epistemic distance is a delicate balance between two extremes: the idea of the world being self-evidently created by God which would make faith unnecessary (naive natural theology, e.g., *Reasons to Believe*, Hugh Ross) and the world being self-evidently self-constituting, which would make faith absurd (naive atheism, e.g., Dawkins, Monod, Sagan). Thus epistemic distance makes the field of "theology and science" possible as a legitimate philosophical interpretation of science and it undercuts the claim by atheists that their interpretation is forced on us.

In short, Hick attempted to construct a Schleiermachian-type natural theodicy based on his view that ours is a "soul making" world, and to be such requires epistemic distance. Even without accepting Hick's "soul making" strategy for responding to natural theodicy, it is clear that epistemic distance is to some extent relevant to the possibility of gaining genuine moral agency. What is striking is that epistemic distance also accounts for why scientific knowledge—as well as moral wisdom—is possible in this world, and in addition why a theological interpretation of science is also possible. What we have learned theologically—and quite unexpectedly—is that in creating this world, God created a world in which both axiology and empirical knowledge can flourish through a gift common to both, a world in which God's presence is hidden behind the veil of creatures—*etsi deus non daretur*—but not sealed irretrievably from view through the eyes of faith.

Hick's Turn to he Crucial Role of Eschatology

The gravest challenge, then, according to Hick, is the excessive violence and its consequent suffering that characterizes the history of life on earth, and here I entirely agree with him.[39] Painful examples of excessive violence litter human history, from the individual violence of mass murderers (e.g., Charles Manson and David Koresh) to organized terrorism and genocide (such as the Nazi Holocaust, the Cambodian killing fields, Rwanda), marring human cul-

---

[38] Although supporters of ID sometimes appeal to "ET" as the non-terrestrial designers of life on earth, this only begs the question of how ET evolved. The only answer that avoids an infinite regress is that they evolved through neo-Darwinian evolution without the assistance of external agency. See Robert John Russell, "Intelligent Design is Not Science and Does Not Qualify to Be Taught in Public School Science Classes", Theology and Science, 3, No. 2, July, 2005, 131f.

[39] Hick, *Evil*, 327–331; 385.

ture as rife with the tragic suffering and senseless death. But long before humanity arrived on the scene, pre-human nature has been plagued with what
might also be called excessive violence. Whether it be individual organisms
(such as Darwin's Ichneumon wasp) or mass extinctions (such as resulted at
the KT event 65 million years ago), excessive violence and suffering seem to
characterize the evolution of life on earth in ways that shake faith in the goodness of creation to its core. If this world of epistemic distance, then, is filled
with such excessive evil as to make the atheist's case invincible, the hopes for
serious faith in God, and not just blind allegiance to God, are shattered.

To his enduring credit, Hick's response is that theodicy can never be fully
addressed by looking to the world as it was in the past and as it is now, for
such an approach is indeed defeated by this world's scars. What then is our
hope, if any, in response to such excessive natural evil? Hick's response is to
turn from the past and look beyond the present to the truest source of hope
that Christians have: eschatology. Only eschatology can provide a context for
addressing the challenge of the excessive suffering of humanity and of nature.
Unfortunately Hick relies on what I would call "eschatology lite": "(W)e
cannot hope to state a Christian theodicy without taking seriously the doctrine of a life beyond the grave."[40] Hick concludes with the "O felix culpa"; it
lies "at the heart of Christian theodicy" and expresses the central paradox that
while present-day evil is really evil, it will eschatologically "be defeated and
made to serve God's good purposes".[41]

*Conclusions: Making Theodicy Work for Us as Establishing Criteria of
Theory Choice for Any Acceptable Eschatology*

> If you are a Darwinian looking for religious meaning, then
> Christianity is a religion which speaks to you. Right at its center
> there is a suffering god, Jesus on the Cross.
>
> Michael Ruse[42]

How then do we respond to the problem of natural theodicy? My response
is to recognize that the problem is generated in part by the fact that natural
evil has been discussed in the context of the theology of creation. I believe,
however, that we *cannot* answer the challenge of theodicy if the framework
is creation—the universe as we know it and the laws that science has discovered, either through an Augustinian/Niebuhrian or an Irenaean/Schleierma-
chian/Hickian approach alone. Given science, we see ever more clearly and
ominously the scale of the problem of natural evil: it extends back before and
down under biology even to the physics of thermodynamics and outwards

[40] Ibid., 339f.
[41] Ibid., 339f; 364.
[42] Ruse, *Can a Darwinian Be a Christian?*, 134.

endlessly to cosmology as the scientific description of the universe as a whole. More ominously, we see that the challenge is immense: we have been forced to recognize "natural evil" as *constitutive of life* and *not just a consequence* of an historical event now taken as mythological.

Hence I propose that the only possibility for an adequate response to natural theodicy will be to relocate the problem of sin and evil beyond the theology of creation into a theology of redemption, and this will involve two theological moves: 1) The suffering of God with humanity through the cross of Christ must be extended to include the suffering of all life on earth, and 2) the eschatological hope for a New Creation that began proleptically at Easter with the bodily resurrection of Jesus must also be extended to include the participation of all life in the New Creation.

1) A number of scholars in theology and science have proposed very promising approaches for extending the redemptive suffering of Christ beyond the domain of humankind to include the history of life on earth. These include authors in this volume such as John Haught, George Murphy, Christopher Southgate, and Ted Peters, as well as Ian Barbour, Celia Deane-Drummond, George Ellis, Jürgen Moltmann, Sallie McFague, Nancey Murphy, Wolfhart Pannenberg, Arthur Peacocke, Holmes Rolston III, Rosemary Radford Ruether, and John Polkinghorne. An assessment of their contributions lies beyond the narrow scope of my chapter.

2) The attempt to extend an eschatology of transformation of the present creation into the New Creation, based on the bodily Resurrection of Jesus, leads to an immense challenge posed by the scientific perspective for the future of the universe. But before considering that, we first need to find a way to ensure that the severe problems posed by natural theodicy are actually addressed by any proffered eschatology. My proposed strategy is to turn the challenges that natural evil poses to eschatology into criteria by which we can assess the plausibility and potential acceptability of any eschatological proposal. In essence the first task is not to construct *an* acceptable eschatology but to decide what types of eschatologies *might* be acceptable. Their acceptability will be based in part, at least, on whether they meet the criteria which been constructed to respond to the challenges raised by natural theodicy. The following is an initial attempt to write down four examples of such criteria for assessing any possible eschatology.

First, it must include not only humanity but all the species in the history of life on earth. The ministry of Jesus includes forgiveness of sins (a strictly human issue) and the healing of disease (a reality we share with all life of earth and in the history of life on earth). An acceptable eschatology must not be limited to the forgiveness of sins and the healing of personal and societal structures, although these are crucially important. It must also include the curing of disease and the overcoming of death. The reality of disease and death is shared by all multi-cellular life on earth. The scope of God's eschatological redemption must therefore be co-terminus with it. Whether it must include not only all species in the history of life on earth but the individual creatures of each species is an open question.[43]

Second, it must include all creatures in terms of their species-specific characteristics. That means it must be related to the concrete details of their own lives and in light of their own capacities, and not as somehow included merely through human redemption as in traditional eschatology. In particular, every moment in evolution, and not just the "end" of time, must be taken up and transformed eschatologically by God into eternal life.

Third, a "greater-good" argument must place this "good" within an eschatological context, for only such a context can offer a goodness sufficient to address the extent of evil in the history of the universe.

Fourth, I believe that eschatology must be structured on a trinitarian doctrine of God. The reason here is self-evident: the trinity is required since the Father who suffers the death of the Son acts anew at Easter to raise Jesus from the dead. In turn, the involuntary suffering of all of nature—each species and each individual creature—must be taken up into the voluntary suffering of Christ on the cross.

To return then to the challenge from science to eschatology very briefly: The standard "freeze or fry" scenarios of scientific cosmology would seem to rule out of bounds any form of robust New Creation eschatology. In addition, the overwhelming conceptual challenge the natural sciences pose to the cogency of Resurrection-based eschatology, even if one meets the initial challenge of the cosmological scenarios, is, in my view, much more severe than the challenge of natural evil to theology. Research in response to these challenges is already underway, but it is in the very initial stages.[44]

---

[43] See Denis Edwards, "Every Sparrow That Falls to the Ground:The Cost of Evolution and the Christ-Event", Ecotheology, 11:1, March 2006, 103–123.

[44] For some initial steps see John C. Polkinghorne, *The Faith of a Physicist: Reflections of a Bottom-up Thinker, Theology and the Sciences Series* (Minneapolis, MN: Fortress, 1994) 211 , John Polkinghorne, *The God of Hope and the End of the World* (New Haven: Yale University Press, 2002), Robert John Russell, "Eschatology and Physical Cosmology: A Preliminary Reflection", in: George F.R. Ellis (ed.), *The Far Future: Eschatology from a Cosmic Perspective* (Philadelphia: Templeton Foundation Press, 2002) 266–315, Robert John Russell, "Bodily Resurrection, Eschatology and Scientific Cosmology: The Mutual Interaction of Christian Theology and Science", in: Ted Peters, Robert John Russell and Michael Welker (ed.), *Resurrection: Theological and Scientific Assessments* (Grand Rapids: Eerdmans Publishing Company, 2002) 3–30.

II. Evolution and God:
Theodicy

Evolutionary Evil and Dawkins' Black Box

Changing the Parameters of the Problem

Joshua Moritz

> *Nature does not abhor evil; she embraces it...Death, destruc-*
> *tion and fury do not disturb the Mother of our world; they are*
> *merely parts of her plan...For we are casualties of Nature's cal-*
> *lous indifference to life, pawns who suffer and die to live out her*
> *schemes.*
>
> Harold Bloom, The Lucifer Principle[1]

> *DNA neither knows nor cares. DNA just is. And we dance to*
> *its music.*
>
> Richard Dawkins, River Out of Eden

> *The wolf also shall dwell with the lamb, and the leopard shall*
> *lie down with the kid; and the calf and the young lion and the*
> *yearling together; and a little child shall lead them. And the cow*
> *shall feed with the bear; their young ones shall lie down togeth-*
> *er: and the lion shall eat straw like the ox. And the infant shall*
> *play near the hole of the cobra, and the young child shall put his*
> *hand into the viper's nest. They shall not hurt nor destroy all on*
> *my holy mountain: for the earth shall be full of the knowledge of*
> *the Lord, as the waters cover the sea.*
>
> Isaiah 11:6–9

Meditating upon the "brutal inefficiency" of evolution by natural selection, Charles Darwin lamented to his friend Joseph Hooker, "What a book a devil's chaplain might write on the clumsy, wasteful, blundering, low and horribly cruel works of Nature!"[2] Yet, many contemporary theologians of nature exclaim that evolution is the very way God creates life.[3] If God is directly active

---

[1] Harold Bloom, *The Lucifer Principle: A Scientific Expedition into the Forces of History* (New York: Atlantic Monthly Press, 1997) 3.

[2] Charles Darwin quoted in Jerry A. Coyne, "Gould and God, Review of *A Devil's Chaplain* by Richard Dawkins", Nature, 422, April 24, 2003, 813.

[3] See for example Robert John Russell, "Special Providence and Genetic Mutation: A New Defense of Theistic Evolution", in: Robert John Russell, William R. Stoeger, SJ and Francisco J. Ayala (ed.), *Evolutionary and Molecular Biology: Scientific Perspectives on Divine Action* (Vatican City State; Berkeley, CA: Vatican Observatory Publications; Center for Theology and the Natural Sciences, 1998) 194; and William Hasker, "Theism and Evolutionary Biology", in: Philip L. Quinn

in natural selection, however, a troubling dilemma would appear to emerge, namely, one can easily equate the word "Nature" in Darwin's quote above with "God". The question of Darwinian evolution thus becomes a question of God's malevolence, and at its very core, the story of creation's evolution through natural selection is twisted into a dysteleological tale of competition, struggle, selfishness, suffering, and existential futility. "There is no getting away from this", says philosopher of biology Michael Ruse, because "pain and suffering are right there at the heart of" natural selection, and "are intimately involved in the adaptive process".[4] When, as Richard Dawkins explains, "the ultimate rationale for our existence" is the action and preservation of selfish replicators whose only interest is to make it into the next generation, one should expect nothing less than nature and her creative processes to be "wasteful, cruel, and low".[5]

In this chapter I agree with Ruse and Dawkins. I do not question the pain, suffering, and associated processes inherent in nature's creation of life through natural selection. Rather, in view of the idea that creation has inherited its propensity for evil I intend to investigate which factors specifically generate the problem of theodicy in a Neo-Darwinian evolutionary view of nature. Then, I will examine, unmask, and ultimately reject several foundational assumptions underlying the challenge of evolutionary theodicy in its current state.

The first fundamental premise that I will examine is found in the work of those who build on the genic selectionist position of Richard Dawkins. I intend to demonstrate that the theoretical biological foundation of Dawkins' challenge from "evolutionary evil" to the creator God's goodness is brittle because the "selfish-gene" of Dawkins is essentially a "black box" which was historically constructed through the bracketing-off of questions concerning the complexity of organismal ontogeny, or development.[6] This black box of Dawkins does not contain one-way causal arrows connecting our phenotypes—the biological level at which the question of the cruelty of nature emerges—to the essence of life, encoded on self-replicating, self-causing "immortal coils" of DNA. Rather, it contains a complex, networked series of relationships which show that the flow of genetic information is multidirectional. To show the origin and nature of Dawkins' conceptual confusion, I will trace the concept of the evolutionary gene through its historical emergence, and subsequently

and Charles Taliaferro (ed.), *A Companion to Philosophy of Religion*, (Malden, MA: Blackwell Publishers, 1999) 427.

[4] Michael Ruse, *Can a Darwinian Be a Christian?: The Relationship Between Science and Religion* (Cambridge: Cambridge University Press, 2001) 131.

[5] Richard Dawkins, *The Selfish Gene* (Oxford: Oxford University Press, 1976,1989) 21. and Richard Dawkins, *A Devil's Chaplain: Reflections on Hope, Lies, Science, and Love* (New York: Houghton Mifflin, 2003) 11.

[6] For a detailed discussion on the current status of the problem of "evolutionary evil" and the usage of the term see Christopher Southgate, "God and Evolutionary Evil: Theodicy in Light of Darwinism", Zygon: Journal of Religion and Science, 37:4, December 2002, 807.

bring it into dialogue with the concept of the gene which has emerged from the discoveries of developmental and molecular biology. From this dialogue it will be clear that Dawkins' world of selfish replicators violently vying for existence is a house built on sand, because the classical gene or evolutionary gene concept on which it rests is incommensurable with the picture of the gene that has been empirically elucidated by contemporary research.

Taking into consideration Dawkins' and Classical Darwinism's mistaken understanding of the gene concept, I will then examine the central role of natural selection *itself* as a creative mechanism, and question its significance and centrality in light of viable alternative interpretations of evolution. I will show how the geno-centric view of biological evolution—and the priority and sufficiency of natural selection alone—is less than fully persuasive; alternative research programs have generated several viable alternatives to Classical Darwinian natural selection. Given the centrality of natural selection as the creative mechanism in Classical Darwinism, the problem of evolutionary evil may seem almost insurmountable from within a *scientific* framework. My chapter responds directly to this challenge. Specifically, I will discuss the role of symbiogenesis, self-organization, developmental constraints, epigenetics, and generic morphogenetic principles in evolution and will explore how these alternative evolutionary mechanisms—where natural selection is not the driving force—may shift the parameters of the evolutionary theodicy problem and possibly offer a way forward for a viable theodicy of nature.

Lastly, I will embark on this possible way forward by enumerating precisely what a viable biological "free-process defense" might consist of. To do this I propose what I have named the *Free Creatures Extension* to the free-process defense. In light of recent research on the active role of an animal's behavior and choices in their own niche construction and evolution, I suggest that *animal choice* also plays a considerable role in determining the types and degrees of violence and victimage in nature. Animals have an active rather than passive part in their own evolution, and their choices, though not as self-conscious or culpable as those of humans, are theologically significant insofar as they influence the degree and specific types of evolutionary suffering in both ecospace and time. In light of the empirical reality of interspecific continuity between human and non-human animals in mental, emotional, and social life, I will suggest that non-human animals should be seen as *protomoral* rather than amoral, and as such animals both need and partake in redemption and ultimate eschatological transformation.

The Problem of Evil in Creation's Evolution

Historically, a marked anthropocentrism has dominated the theodicy question.[7] The vast majority of work done has focused on moral evil, and where

---

[7] See Christopher Southgate, "God and Evolutionary Evil", 807.

natural evil *has been* discussed it has been in the context of how such natural evil affects *humans*.[8] Much less has been written on the problem of evil and suffering in the non-human world. This is not because it is a new problem, but rather, I believe, because it is such a difficult problem. The ancients were certainly aware that all is not perfect in the realm of nature. Heraclitus ex-claimed that "struggle is the father of everything",[9] and Aristotle observed the place of fierce competition between animals in nature.[10] It wasn't until Charles Darwin, however, that the problem of evolutionary evil came into full focus. In discussing the evolutionary origin of species, Darwin writes:

> How do those groups of species, which constitute what are called distinct genera, and which differ from each other more than do the species of the same genus, arise? *All these results...follow from the struggle for life.* Owing to this struggle, variations, however slight and from whatever cause proceeding, if they be in any degree profit-able to the individuals of a species...will tend to the preservation of such individu-als, and will generally be inherited by the offspring.
>
> I have called this principle, by which each slight variation, if useful, is preserved, by the term Natural Selection...but the expression often used by Mr. Herbert Spen-cer of the Survival of the Fittest is more accurate.[11]

Darwin continues a few lines later,

> *All organic beings are exposed to severe competition. Nothing is easier than to admit in words the truth of the universal struggle for life...*We behold the face of nature bright with gladness, we often see superabundance of food; we do not see or we forget, that the birds which are idly singing round us mostly live on insects or seeds, and are thus constantly destroying life; or we forget how largely these songsters, or their eggs, or their nestlings, are destroyed by birds and beasts of prey.[12]

The bottom line as Darwin conveys it is that, "All nature is at war, one or-ganism with another, or with external nature". Suffering, says Darwin, "is quite compatible with the belief in Natural Selection which is not perfect in its action".[13]

---

[8] See for example, Peter van Inwagen, "The Magnitude, Duration, and Distribution of Evil", 200; and David R. Griffin, "Creation Out of Chaos and the Problem of Evil", in: Stephen T. Davis (ed.), *Encountering Evil: Live Options in Theodicy*, (Edinburgh: T & T Clark, 1981) 111.

[9] Heraclitus of Ephesus (ca. 500 BCE), quoted in *The Fragments of the Work of Heraclitus of Ephesus on Nature,* trans. from the Greek text of Ingram Bywater by G. T. W. Patrick (Baltimore: N. Murray, 1889) fragment #62.

[10] Aristotle, *The History of Animals* in *The Basic Works of Aristotle*, ed. Richard McKeon (New York: Random House, 1941), see pages 637 ff or Book IX, paragraphs 608b–609b.

[11] Charles Robert Darwin, *The Origin of Species or The Preservation of Favoured Races in the Struggle for Life* (London: John Murray, ⁶1872) 48 f, emphasis added.

[12] Charles Robert Darwin, *The Origin of Species or The Preservation of Favoured Races in the Struggle for Life,* vol. XI, The Harvard Classics (New York: P. F. Collier & Son, 1909–1914); Bartleby.com, 2001 www.bartleby.com/11/ [May 1, 2003] ch. 3, "The Struggle for Existence", em-phasis mine.

[13] Ibid.

In Darwinian evolution by natural selection, pain, self interest and competition are not just contingencies which may be "readily explained away". On the contrary, they are entailed in the *very process* by which organisms were created.[14] As Arthur Peacocke points out, this means that "the development of pain and suffering, as well as decay, death, and indeed extinction…are necessary concomitants of the evolutionary process".[15] Competition is a key and the unyielding struggle to survive is an evil inherent to the system. "Organic nature is savage; life preys on life" and "struggle is the dark side of creativity". As Holmes Rolston III puts it, the mechanism of natural selection, "from the perspective of the individual, is [indeed] built on competition and premature death".[16] The cornerstone of the "stupendous edifice of evolution"[17] is a trillion bloody corpses of the slain competitors whose genes were not fit enough to survive in the ruthless and unending battle of nature.

But what exactly is the dilemma at hand? So nature destroys nature — why is that God's problem? It is God's problem insofar as God is the benevolent creator of life. Affirming that God works in and through nature, we must "identify God's [creative] action with the processes themselves, as they are revealed by the physical and biological sciences".[18] Consequently, this is not just an issue of *why* God would permit such suffering, but *why* God would use this *very suffering* to create organic life in the first place. Given the *fact* of evolution,[19] why would God use the *mechanism* of natural selection to create, when there is so much suffering inherent to the process? Darwin, having wandered far from the Palean vision of a cheerful natural world which he was nursed on, continuously struggled with this question. He laments to his friend Asa Gray: "There seems to me too much misery in the world. I cannot persuade myself that a beneficent and omnipotent God would have designedly created the [ichneumon wasp] with the express intention of their feeding within the living bodies of caterpillars, or that the cat should play with mice."[20]

Richard Dawkins puts this image into sharper relief by pointing out that the wasp mentioned above, "carefully guides her sting into each ganglion of the prey's central nervous system, so as to paralyze it but not kill it." Thus,

---

[14] Ruse, *Can A Darwinian Be a Christian?*, 131.

[15] Arthur Peacocke quoted in, Southgate, et al., *God, Humanity and The Cosmos*, 274; also see Arthur Peacocke, "The Cost of New Life", in: John Polkinghorne (ed.), *The Work of Love: Creation as Kenosis* (Grand Rapids: Eerdmans, 2001).

[16] Holmes Rolston III, "Naturalizing and Systematizing Evil", in: Willem B. Drees (ed.), *Is Nature Ever Evil?: Religion, Science, and Value* (London: Routledge, 2003), 78 f.

[17] Jacques Monod, *Chance and Necessity* (New York: Vintage Books, 1972), 112 f.

[18] Arthur Peacocke, *God and the New Biology*, 95.

[19] For a discussion on the difference between the fact and the mechanism of evolution see Michael Ruse, "Darwinism and Christianity: Does Evil Spoil a Beautiful Friendship?" in this volume.

[20] Darwin quoted in Phillip R. Sloan, "The Question of Natural Purpose", in: Ernan McMullin (ed.), *Evolution and Creation* (Notre Dame, IN: University of Notre Dame Press, 1985), 139.

"the prey might be aware of being eaten alive from the inside but unable to move a muscle to do anything about it." This "sounds savagely cruel", says Dawkins, but "nature is not cruel, only pitilessly indifferent".[21] To insist that the creator God is responsible for this behavior would be to accuse God of utmost cruelty.

In another example, Dawkins unabashedly throws down the gauntlet. Goading the would-be theodicist, he observes:

> Cheetahs give every indication of being superbly designed for something, and it should be easy enough to reverse-engineer them and work out their utility function. They appear to be well designed to kill antelopes. The teeth, claws, eyes, nose, leg muscles, backbone, and brain of a cheetah are precisely what we should expect if God's purpose in designing cheetahs was to maximize deaths among antelopes… If there is only one creator who made the tiger and the lamb, the cheetah and the gazelle, what is he playing at? *Is he a sadist who enjoys spectator blood sports?*[22]

If so, it would seem the story of life's creation is more akin to the gruesome struggle in the Babylonian creation epic where life results directly from the blood of the slaughtered, than the Genesis account of a "very good" creation tenderly spoken into existence by and through God's Word.[23]

Over and above the evidence for the ruthless struggle inherent to evolving nature, we find the disturbing phenomenon of mass extinctions. For instance, the Permian extinction—the most severe mass extinction—was an event 250 million years ago that annihilated 90–95 percent of species on Earth.[24] Furthermore, many cases of extinction are a direct result of predator-prey dynamics and thus are an evil intrinsic to the system. An example of this can be seen in recent studies of sea otter populations that are in abrupt decline in large areas of western Alaska. Investigators believe that increased killer whale predation is the primary reason for the dramatically increased mortality rates observed.[25] While it reeks of horrible waste and has the appearance of cruelty on a global scale, extinction is just part of the evolutionary process. As a major force of selection in nature, it is would appear to be a necessary condition for the creation of life.

---

[21] Richard Dawkins, *River Out of Eden: A Darwinian View of Life* (New York: Basic Books, 1995), 95.

[22] Ibid., 105, emphasis mine.

[23] Besides the Babylonian *Enuma Elish*, the motif of creation from dismemberment of a primordial victim is also present in the *Rig Veda* of the Hindu tradition, in Norse Creation accounts, and others. See David and Margaret Leeming, *A Dictionary of Creation Myths* (New York: Oxford University Press, 1994) 26–29, 60.

[24] D. H. Erwin, "The Permo-Triassic Extinction", Nature, 367: 6460, January 20, 1994, 231–236; and Y. G. Jin, Y. Wang, W. Wang, Q. H. Shang, C. Q. Cao, and D. H. Erwin, "Pattern of Marine Mass Extinction Near the Permian-Triassic Boundary in South China", Science, 289: 5478, July 21, 2000, 432–436.

[25] J. A. Estes, M. T. Tinker, T. M. Williams, and D. F. Doak, "Killer Whale Predation on Sea Otters Linking Oceanic and Nearshore Ecosystems", Science, 282: 5388, October 16, 1998, 473–476.

The font of creativity and variation is likewise aesthetically poisoned by the vile reality of chance mutations, which are most often maladaptive and frequently the cause of much pain and suffering. "For every mutation which brings benefit", says Ruse, "there are hundreds which spell doom and disaster". But these very mutations are "absolutely central to the Darwinian evolutionary process". Random genetic mutations are the crux of Darwinian novelty, and struggle for existence depends on these "to create selection and consequent adaptation".[26] Theodosius Dobzhansky agrees. "Evolutionary plasticity", he says, "can be purchased only at the ruthlessly dear price of continuously sacrificing some individuals to death from unfavorable mutations".[27]

To make matters worse, many biologists and theologians of nature would agree with Dawkins' fundamental premise that the relentless battle for life goes all the way down. This is because in Dawkins' understanding the key players in life's evolution are selfish genes "driven by an impersonal physical necessity to secure their immortality…even if it means invading innocent organisms and exploiting these in devious and destructive ways".[28] No cost in the evolutionary suffering of organisms is too high for these selfish replicators to exact as they violently strive to secure their genetic legacies in the bodies of future generations. "So long as DNA is passed on", declares Dawkins, "it does not matter who or what gets hurt in the process…Gene's don't care about suffering, because they don't care about anything."[29]

So if natural selection is the way God creates, Dawkins' question remains. Is the Creator God a sadist? Would an almighty and loving God have "laid the foundations" "determined the measurements", and "set the cornerstone" of a creative system "whose law is a ruthless struggle for existence in an over-crowded world?"[30] Could the all-knowing, all-powerful, and all-benevolent Father of Jesus have "devised such a cold-blooded competition" of gene with gene, "beast with beast, beast with man, man with man, [and] species with species", in which only "the clever, the cunning and the cruel survive?"[31]

---

[26] Ruse, "Can a Darwinian Be a Christian?", 131.

[27] Theodosius Dobzhansky, *Genetics and The Origin of Species* (New York: Columbia University Press, 1982) 127.

[28] John Haught, *God After Darwin: A Theology of Evolution* (Boulder, CO: Westview Press, 2000) 13.

[29] Richard Dawkins quoted in Haught *God After Darwin*, 9.

[30] Job 38:1 and Haught, *God After Darwin*, 21.

[31] Haught, *God After Darwin*, 21. Niels Henrik Gregersen asks a similar question, "Indeed, if God's way of maintaining and developing the world of creation happens through the means of natural selection, how can the Christian belief in the mercy of God be consonant with the ruthlessness of evolutionary processes?" in "The Cross of Christ in an Evolutionary World", Dialog: A Journal of Theology, 40:3, Fall 2001, 192. For another formulation of this objection see Thomas Tracy, "Evolution, Divine Action, and the Problem of Evil", in: Robert John Russell, William R. Stoeger, SJ and Francisco J. Ayala (ed.), *Evolutionary and Molecular Biology: Scientific Perspectives*

Responding to the Problem of Evolutionary Evil

Some, like Michael Ruse, have sought to respond to Dawkins' challenge by invoking Dawkins' own assertions as a way out of the evolutionary theodicy dilemma which he himself poses. If Darwinian natural selection is the "only way in which complex adaptation could be produced by law", God essentially had his hands tied when creating biological life.[32] Consequently, maintains Ruse, there is a ready-made theodicy inherent in the necessity of natural selection to produce adaptively complex life. "Physical evil exists", says Ruse, "and Darwinism explains why God had no choice but to allow it to occur."[33] Were Darwinism an ontological imperative in God's creation of the cosmos, Ruse's theodicy might be adequate. As it stands, however, this line of argument is ultimately not helpful because it begs the question of why God, creating the universe *ex nihilo*, would choose such callously indifferent and bloodthirsty bio-physical laws in the first place.[34]

At this point, the problem of evolutionary evil may seem almost insurmountable from within a *scientific* framework. There are, however, two fundamentally problematic scientific presuppositions underlying Dawkins' theodical challenge which Ruse does not consider: Firstly, that the "selfish genes" interpretation of evolution is fundamentally correct, and secondly that the *mechanism* of natural selection is the *only* viable way to understand the *fact* of life's evolution. In the remainder of this chapter I will critically examine each of these foundational assumptions and will argue—in light of current empirical investigations—that they are ultimately mistaken. Challenging basic scientific assumptions under girding Dawkins' (and others) position, will allow us to explore alternative evolution theories that pose much less of a problem to the belief in the benevolence of a God who creates through evolution.

The Historical Construction of Dawkins' Black Box

From Mendel to Morgan
As I have noted, Dawkins' challenge requires a bracketing of certain developmental questions. This bracketing has, in fact, been present to the modern study of genetics since its inception. It is only in recent years that serious conceptual and experimental problems associated with this bracketing have become fully evident. In preparation for my constructive response to Dawkins I will review the history of how Dawkins' black box was constructed.

The field of classical genetics began in 1856 in the experimental garden of the Augustinian monastery school of Saint Thomas at Brünn in Moravia,

---

on Divine Action (Vatican City State; Berkeley, CA: Vatican Observatory Publications; Center for Theology and the Natural Sciences, 1998) 523.

   [32] See Ruse this volume 19.
   [33] Ruse, *Can A Darwinian be a Christian?*, 136 f.
   [34] See also Robert J. Russell, "Is Evil Evolving?", 311.

with a monk and natural history teacher named Gregor Mendel. Possessing a background in physics and mathematics, and mindful of the concerns of his fellow countrymen, Mendel was searching for laws governing developmental invariance which might prove useful for the agricultural breeding of intraspecific hybrids.[35] Mendel presumed correctly that "unit characters"—or traits which demonstrate constancy of type—behave independently, and working with this assumption he cultivated and tested over 28,000 garden pea plants between 1856 and 1863.[36] Analyzing his data, which revealed numerous characteristics that were passed on and expressed through several generations without blending, Mendel believed he observed evidence supporting the notion that characters, or traits, were inherited independently as discreet units, or as he called them, "factors". The 1865 paper he published on his pea hybridization experiments, *Versuche über Pflanzen-Hybriden*, illustrates Mendel's concept of these developmentally stable factors which "can be brought together in hybrids and separated again without any effect on their capacity to act as factors."[37] Mendel conceived of the independence of his factors in an atomistic way and believed that such hereditary factors were *material entities* located within the components of the germ cells. Furthermore Mendel held that the hidden heritable factors, transmitted faithfully throughout the generations, acted as *preformed* traits so that the unseen factors need not be conceptually distinguished from the visible traits which they gave rise to.[38] *By holding the preformed unit-factors as alone responsible for determining the expression of characteristics, Mendel was able to circumvent issues involving developmental interactions which were both outside the scope of his interest and immaterial to the practical applications of his research.*[39]

Though he had done his research as a contemporary of Darwin[40], Mendel's work on heredity, in contrast to his contemporary, remained in relative obscurity for almost four decades. In the early years of the 20th century his work was "rediscovered" and verified through the research of three botanists—Hugo de Vries, Karl Correns, and Erich von Tschermak—each independently citing Mendel's 1866 paper.[41] These three championed the explanatory power of

---

[35] Lenny Moss, *What Genes Can't Do* (Cambridge, MA: The MIT Press, 2003) 24.

[36] Robert C. Olby, "The Emergence of Genetics", in Robert C. Olby, G. N. Cantor, J. R. R. Christie and M. J. S. Hodge (ed.), *Companion to the History of Modern Science* (London: Routledge, 1996) 527.

[37] James Griesemer, "Reproduction and the Reduction of Genetics", in: Peter Beurton, Raphael Falk, and Hans-Jörg Rheinberger (ed.), *The Concept of the Gene in Development and Evolution: Historical and Epistemological Perspectives* (Cambridge: Cambridge University Press, 2000) 266.

[38] Olby, "The Emergence of Genetics", 527 f.

[39] Moss, *What Genes Can't Do*, 25.

[40] Mendel was familiar with Darwins work, having read a German translation of the second edition of Darwin's *Origin of Species* in 1862.

[41] The extent to which these three botanists independently "rediscovered" Mendel's segregation ratios is a matter of some debate. See Robert Olby, *Origins of Mendelism* (Chicago: University of

the Mendelian "unit-character" and, along with William Bateson—who translated Mendel's paper into English—and Wilhelm Johannsen—who coined the
word "gene" to describe Mendel's "factors"—they employed Mendel's work
as a critical resource in shifting the parameters of biological thought on heredity and evolution. De Vries and Bateson appropriated the Mendelian heu-
ristic to bolster their own particular interpretations of Darwin's theory, and
they used Mendel's notion of unit-characters to demonstrate how variation
between different species and populations could be discreet rather than continuous.[42] Under this new breed of Evolutionary Mendelians "the scope and
ambitions of Mendel's exemplar with its rhetorical resources became greatly
expanded" and the implicit particulate preformationism in Mendel's work became unequivocal as de Vries, Bateson, and others "sought to ground a discontinuous model of heritable variation in a theory of encapsulized, developmentally preformed units of hereditary transmission."[43]

From Morgan to the Modern Synthesis
The hegemony of the Mendelian framework became particularly decisive under the tutelage of Thomas Hunt Morgan. Conducting breeding experiments
using the fruit fly *Drosophila*, Morgan and his lab at Columbia University
developed a highly successful research program founded on the principles of
Mendelian genetics. Morgan inherited Wilhelm Johannsen's *theoretical* pos-
ture of separating traits from genes and distinguishing between genotypes
and phenotypes. In theory, observable characters or traits were to be used
as merely "*markers* for the hereditary entities", and Morgan never maintained that "a science of the genotype was tantamount to a science of the
phenotype."[44] When it came to *practical* matters of research, however, Morgan bracketed out any developmental mechanisms that might be required to
generate or actualize traits at the visible level of the organism. Morgan argued
that it would be pragmatic "*for the present at least*", to keep apart "questions concerned with the distribution of the genes in succeeding generations
from questions concerned with the physiological action of the genetic factors

---

Chicago Press, [2]1985). There seems to be a general consensus, however, that each of them, in varying degrees, were enabled to understand the significance of their own experimental results only in
the light of Mendel's previous work. For our purposes here, it need only be said that the fundamental significance of Mendel's work was acknowledged at this time and as a result his notion of
developmentally invariant 'factors' came to dominate the discussion on heredity. See Olby, "The
Emergence of Genetics", 529f.

[42] David Depew and Marjorie Grene, *The Philosophy of Biology: An Episodic History* (Cambridge: Cambridge University Press, 2004) 239.

[43] Moss, *What Genes Can't Do,* 25 and 27, For a discussion of DeVries and Bateson's appropriation of Mendel see Raphael Falk, "The Rise and Fall of Dominance", Biology and Philosophy,
16: 285–323, 2001.

[44] Moss, *What Genes Can't Do,* 36.

during development."[45] In doing this Morgan intended to "establish the acquisition of genes and genotypes as the *definition* of what counts as heredity, that is to separate by definitional fiat the inheritance of genes from the developmental context and mechanism which allow heritable traits to appear."[46] Consequently, Morgan could declare in 1926: "Except for the rare cases of plastid inheritance all known characters can be sufficiently accounted for by the presence of genes in the chromosomes. In a word the cytoplasm may be ignored genetically."[47] Gene expression and questions of development were relegated to a "black box" to be set aside until it could be opened at some undisclosed future time.

As Morgan's practical or instrumental reductionism was bequeathed to succeeding generations of geneticists, the conceptual rather than methodological construal of *genes as determinants of characters* began to gain theoretical momentum. Consequently the expression "genes for" became a standard component of the scientific vocabulary and part of the received wisdom concerning the nature of heredity. The geneticists that followed Morgan all retained "this basic assumption of the direct quantitative relationship between the gene and its product",[48] and the black box became a family heirloom.

Following on the heels of Morgan, the framers of the Neo-Darwinian Modern Evolutionary Synthesis adopted this conception of the gene as causal agent or statistically invariant determiner of traits. While Mendelian genetics and Darwinian evolutionary gradualism originally existed as two separate—and even at times conflicting—scientific traditions, in the first three decades of the 20th century scientists from both camps began to reconcile the two theories through the development of statistical Darwinism and population genetics. Key among the early synthesizers was evolutionary biologist, geneticist, and statistician Ronald A. Fisher. Fisher's 1918 paper *The Correlation Between Relatives on the Supposition of Mendelian Inheritance*, in which he redefined evolution as changes in gene frequencies over time, is often considered the beginning of the Modern Evolutionary Synthesis.[49] While previous Darwinians, such as those influenced by the biometrics program of Francis Galton, argued that inherited characters or traits must be continuously variable rather than discreet in order for natural selection to occur, Fisher demonstrated in his 1918 paper that if one thinks in terms of populations then heredity can be understood as discontinuous or discrete, and can be measured in the heritable units of genes. To address the problem—at least for Mendelians—of the phenotypic continuity of characteristics, Fisher assumed that continuous traits

---

[45] Morgan quoted in Raphael Falk, "The Rise and Fall of Dominance", *Biology and Philosophy*, 16, 2001, 301.

[46] Moss, *What Genes Can't Do*, 36.

[47] Thomas Hunt Morgan quoted in Moss, *What Genes Can't Do*, 36.

[48] Falk, "The Rise and Fall of Dominance", 301.

[49] See Alan Grafen, "Fisher the Evolutionary Biologist", The Statistician, 2003, 52:3, 319–329.

were "determined by a large number of Mendelian factors", each acting independently in an additive and particulate manner to produce a cumulative phenotypic result.[50] This conception of the particulate and additive inheritance of
genes became *the* focus of Fisher and the earliest neo-Darwinists.[51] Given this
foundational theoretical assumption regarding genes, Fisher could ask rhetorically "Is *all* inheritance particulate?" and answer "The Mendelian theory
is alone competent…"[52] By assuming a nearly infinite number of particulate
factors, or atom-like genes—each with a negligible effect and acting autonomously—the Modern Synthesizers following Fisher could, as a consequence,
ignore the details of the *action* of Mendelian genes or alleles and treat them
as preformed traits which are directly accountable to the selective forces of
nature.[53] Furthermore, when the Modern Synthesis re-defined evolution as a
change of gene frequencies in the gene pool of a population, genes—now considered as developmental invariants in reproduction, solely obeying the Mendelian laws in their transmission from one generation to the next—supplied
"a kind of inertia principle against which the effects of both developmental
(epistasis, inhibition, position effects etc.) and evolutionary factors (selection,
mutation, recombination etc.) could be measured with utmost accuracy."[54]

Schrödinger's Code-Script

By the end of the 1930s the success of the neo-Darwinian synthesis in elucidating the gene's role in evolution had become proverbial, as had the amazing
ability of Mendelian genes to represent traits faithfully throughout multiple
generations. Intrigued by the stability of genes and their capacity to resist the
destructive forces of entropy, the well-known physicist Erwin Schrödinger
wondered what sort of object the gene might be to reproduce itself with "a
durability or permanence that borders upon the miraculous."[55]

    In his monograph *What is Life?* Schrödinger suggested a possible solution
to this riddle. Inspired by the physicist-turned-molecular biologist Max Del-
brück and presupposing a constitutive genetic preformationism which was
the common intellectual currency of the genetics of his time, Schrödinger
speculated on what he thought a peek inside the "black box" might reveal.

---

[50] R. A. Fisher, quoted in Sahotra Sarkar, *Genetics and Reductionism* (Cambridge: Cambridge
University Press, 1998), 107.
    [51] See R. A. Fisher, *The Genetical Theory of Natural Selection* (Oxford: Oxford University
Press, 1930).
    [52] R. A. Fischer quoted in Daida, J. M. et al., "Of Metaphors and Darwinism: Deconstructing
Genetic Programming's Chimera", in: *Proceedings on the 1999 Congress on Evolutionary Compu-
tation*, Vol. 1, 1999, 463.
    [53] Sahotra Sarkar, *Genetics and Reductionism*, 108.
    [54] Hans-Jörg Rheinberger and Staffan Müller-Wille, "Gene" in: *The Stanford Encyclopedia of
Philosophy* (Stanford, CA: Stanford University, 2004). http://www.seop.leeds.ac.uk/index.html.
    [55] Quoted in Evelyn Fox Keller, *The Century of the Gene* (Cambridge, MA: Harvard Univer-
sity Press, 2001) 21.

He argued that the only thing which could stand as a bulwark of order against the disintegrating forces of chaos is a type of molecule which had remarkable stability and duration, sufficient length, and a sufficient heterogeneity in its composition to be "the putative bearer of coded information which allows for the sustenance and reproduction of organized life-forms."[56] An aperiodic crystal or solid,[57] maintained Schrödinger, could serve as such a template for the "hereditary code-script" of life. Such genetic code-scripts would be self-executing and causally "instrumental in bringing about the development which they foreshadow." As Schrödinger remarked of these information-encrypted genes he envisioned, "they are *law-code* and *executive power*—or, to use another simile, they are *architect's plan* and *builder's craft*—in one."[58] Schrödinger's metaphorical framework collapsed the distinction between genotype and phenotype, and here the phenotypic pattern emerges as merely an expression of the genes which "code for" it.

Schrödinger's metaphor of the gene as a hereditary code-script provided the vision for the future of genetics research and inspired countless physicists and chemists to join the ranks of biology in an endeavor to discover the "essence of life". Among those in this new generation of researchers enticed by Schrödinger's tempting trope were two young men—James Watson and Francis Crick.[59] Working off of the research of Avery, MacLeod and McCarty; and Hershey and Chase—which established that DNA was the carrier of the genetic material—Crick and Watson uncovered the structure of the DNA molecule and, in language reminiscent of Schrödinger's monograph, announced to the world, "Today we have discovered the secret of life!"[60] With the discovery of Watson and Crick, it appeared that the prophetic words of Schrödinger had been fulfilled and that the material reality of the gene was secured. As a result, his metaphor of the gene as a self-executing hereditary code-script became the idea that fueled the intellectual fires of the research in molecular biology which would immediately follow. In light of Schrödinger's metaphor and the preformationist presuppositions surrounding the gene concept inherited from the previous generations of geneticists, Crick in 1957 formulated his "central dogma of molecular biology": *genetic information* flows one way only—from DNA to RNA to proteins to phenotype.

> [The central dogma] states that once "information" has passed into protein *it cannot get out again*. In more detail, the transfer of information from nucleic acid to nucleic acid, or from nucleic acid to protein may be possible, but transfer from protein to

---

[56] Moss, *What Genes Can't Do,* 59.
[57] An aperiodic solid is one that does not oscillate or have periodic vibrations.
[58] Schrödinger, *What is Life?*, 21.
[59] Moss, *What Genes Can't Do,* 53, Fox Keller, 23.
[60] Francis Crick quoted in Brian Hayes, "The Invention of the Genetic Code", American Scientist, Vol. 86:1, January–February, 1998, 8.

protein, or from protein to nucleic acid is impossible. Information means here the precise determination of sequence, either of bases in the nucleic acid or of amino acid residues in the protein.[61]

In other words, "DNA makes RNA, RNA makes proteins, and proteins make us."[62]

With the Central Dogma in the back of their minds and a devout zeal in their hearts to decipher "the secret of life", molecular biologists began the race to "decode" the DNA. Code-breakers fresh from the fronts of World War II and cryptologists from deep within the secret caverns of government intelligence organizations all flocked to the scene. The Navy's Bureau of Ordnance, which had cracked the Japanese code, was even recruited as lists of amino acids and DNA bases were entered into its deciphering computer.[63] Schrödinger's metaphor was being considered with utmost earnestness and the metaphors of the gene as blueprint, computer program, text, instructions, and plan were born.[64]

Evolutionary biologists and behavioral geneticists, for the most part, had watched these momentous events from the sidelines because by this point in time molecular biology and evolutionary biology had begun to wander their separate methodological ways.[65] From the perspective of the evolutionary biologists, though, the work of the previous generation on the Modern Synthesis seemed to be vindicated as the material reality and atom-like nature of the gene received a substantial amount of empirical corroboration. Furthermore, the essential gene rhetoric was in place for the next generation of evolutionary biologists to do their work.

Williams and Units of Selection

Preeminent in this next generation of neo-Darwinian evolutionary biologists was George C. Williams. Working off of the received understanding of the gene as both causal agent and information, Williams endeavored to conceptually clarify the Modern Synthesis and clear up any confusion which remained concerning the *targets* and *units* of natural selection. Williams pointed out that while individual organisms and their traits and behaviors were clearly *targets* of selection, these are too transient to serve as *units* of natural selection. The "only entities that have sufficient temporal staying power" to act as units of selection, argued Williams, "are genes, conceived (in post Watson-

---

[61] Francis Crick, "On protein synthesis", in: *Symposium of the Society of Experimental Biology,* 12, 1958, 152 f.

[62] Keller, 54. The position has been referred to as "Molecular Weismannism" see Peter Godfrey-Smith "On the Theoretical Role of 'Genetic Coding'", Philosophy of Science, 67, 2000, 39.

[63] Moss, *What Genes Can't Do,* 64 f.

[64] Rheinberger, "Gene".

[65] Depew and Grene, 280.

Crick fashion) as chunks of DNA that survive repeated meiotic divisions."[66] Genes, for Williams, are stable "sections of DNA that code for proteins" and they are essentially informational. "In evolutionary theory", explained Williams, "a gene could be defined as any *hereditary information* for which there is a favorable or unfavorable selection bias equal to several or many times the rate of endogenous change."[67]

The genes of evolution are "DNA segments for which there is 'a statistical bias in the relative rates of survival of alternatives.'"[68] Like atoms in physics, genes, according to Williams, are the most basic units of selection. Likewise, evolution through the process of differential conservation of genes over time occurs only because "the phenotypes they code for (through the production of amino acids and then proteins, followed by the folding up of proteins into tissues) are better able than other phenotypes to deal successfully enough with their environments to leave, on the average, more offspring."[69] It is thus not organisms, but essentially "genes that compete and are selected for", and the resulting "change in gene frequencies" is "the heart of the process of evolution."[70]

Williams' view above has been referred to as "genic selectionism" and his way of reformulating the Modern Synthesis permitted one truly to say, "organisms exist for the sake of genes."[71] His "genes-eye-view" reconstruction of Darwinism also helped settle one of the most vexing conundrums within evolutionary theory—namely the pervasive phenomenon of cooperation and even self-sacrificial altruism among members of the same species. Taking up the thought of William D. Hamilton before him, Williams suggested that fitness "is measured by the extent to which [an allele] contributes genes to later generations of the population of which it is a member."[72] This is the notion of "inclusive fitness" and it means that the fitness of an organism's genes depends not only on the reproductive success of the primary organism which the genes directly code for, but also on the success of the organism's kin to the extent that these kin carry copies of the primary organism's genes. J. B. S. Hal-

---

[66] Depew and Grene, 268.

[67] Williams 1966, 25 quoted in Stephen M. Downes, "Heredity and Heritability", in: *The Stanford Encyclopedia of Philosophy* (Stanford, CA: Stanford University, 2004). http://www.seop.leeds.ac.uk/index.html.

[68] G. C. Williams, *Adaptation and Natural Selection*, (Princeton: Princeton University Press, 1966) 22. See also Robin D. Knight and Paul E. Griffiths, "Selfish Genes—The Eunuchs of Selection", Paper delivered at the International Society for History, Philosophy and Social Studies of Biology in July 1997. www.usyd.edu.au/hps/preprints/preprint1/Knight.pdf.

[69] Depew and Grene, 268.

[70] Williams 1966 quoted in Paul E. Griffiths and Russell D. Gray, "Darwinism and Developmental Systems", in: S. Oyama, P.E. Griffiths, R.D. Gray (ed.), *Cycles of Contingency: Developmental Systems and Evolution* (Cambridge, MA: MIT Press, 2001), 215.

[71] Depew and Grene, 269.

[72] Quoted in Depew and Grene, 269.

dane, one of the founding fathers of the Modern Synthesis, expressed the idea
of "kin selection" this way: "I will die for two brothers or eight cousins."[73]
From the gene's point of view, the body that contains it matters not. In fact,
its *only* care is to get itself into the succeeding generation.

Dawkins' Selfish Genes

Williams and Hamilton's interpretation of the Modern Synthesis—and the
concept of the gene entailed therein—did not fall onto barren soil, and their
gene-centered understanding of biological reality found a passionate propo-
nent in the person of Richard Dawkins. Dawkins regards himself as heir to the
mantle of the Neo-Darwinian tradition before him, and, given that, he desires
in *The Selfish Gene* to "reassert the fundamental principles of Fisher, Haldane, and Wright, the founding fathers of Neo-Darwinism in the 1930s."[74]

At the core of the Modern Synthesis, for Dawkins, is the idea that the fitness value of each gene or allele is context independent, and that the "gold-
standard of evolution" is "gene survival."[75] Agreeing with Williams that the
gene is the "unit of heredity", Dawkins declares that the "fundamental unit
of selection, and therefore of self-interest, is not the species, nor the group,
nor even strictly, the individual. It is the gene."[76] Like Williams, Dawkins
argues that groups of organisms and "individuals are not stable things" but
fleeting phenomenon "like clouds in the sky or dust storms in the desert."[77]
Only genes—as "replicators with high copying-fidelity"—are forever, and
this is precisely why these "immortal coils" of DNA may serve as the basic
units of selection.[78] Organisms with all their characteristics and behaviors are
merely artifacts of the primal nature of these undying replicators, which of
course consists of nothing more than an inherent tendency to replicate. Here
Dawkins agrees with the crux of Williams' aforementioned argument: the
phenotype, or the organism considered as a sum of distinct traits, "exists for
the sake of getting the genes that code for phenotypic adaptations maximally
represented in the next generation."[79]

Because it is only concerned with its own replication, "the gene is the basic
unit of selfishness."[80] These "selfish genes" compete "directly with their alleles for survival, since their alleles in the gene pool are rivals for their slot on
the chromosome of future generations."[81] The way in which they compete,

---

[73] Quoted in Depew and Grene, 269.
[74] Dawkins, *The Selfish Gene*, 273.
[75] Ibid., xi and 124.
[76] Ibid., 11.
[77] Ibid., 34 f.
[78] Ibid., 28.
[79] Depew and Grene, 270,
[80] Dawkins, *The Selfish Gene*, 36.
[81] Ibid.

though, is through the medium of the phenotypes which they create. All living beings—bodies and minds—are survival machines, or vehicles, created by genes and "their preservation is the ultimate rationale for our existence."[82] Waxing philosophical on this last point, Dawkins writes:

> Darwin made it possible for us to give a sensible answer to the curious child whose question heads this chapter. ['Why are people?'] We no longer have to resort to superstition when faced with the deep problems; Is there meaning to life? What are we for? What is Man?…The argument of this book is that we, and all other animals, are machines created by our genes.[83]

Combining the received notion of genes as both causal agents and hereditary code-scripts, Dawkins makes *explicit* what is *implicit* in the earlier concept of the evolutionary gene—the selfish genes of natural selection have an active and direct role as a "causal force in creating and preserving the phenotypes that shelter them."[84] In other words, there is no relevant degree of mediation between genotype and phenotype. For example, explains Dawkins, "there is a causal arrow going from gene to bird, but none in the opposite direction."[85] Genes "control the manufacturing of bodies, and the influence is strictly one way: acquired characteristics are not inherited…A body is the gene's way of preserving genes unaltered."[86] With Dawkins the developmental details, bracketed generations earlier by T. H. Morgan, are now whited-out and a direct causal arrow is inserted in their place. Generations come and go and the mysterious black box resting on the mantelpiece remains unnoticed.

This is the same black box that allows Dawkins to build his argument from evolutionary evil, his argument questioning the goodness of any God who would create through evolution. But how persuasive is the theoretical-biological foundations upon which Dawkins and others build their theodical challenges if the black box is opened and its contents attended to? In the pages that follow, I will demonstrate that Dawkins' arguments only remain persuasive to the extent that the black box remains ignored. This black box—containing the cluster of experimental and conceptual problems first bracketed in Mendel's garden—has allowed Dawkins, Ruse, and others, to construct conceptual Towers of Babel. And just like in the biblical story, the consequence rendered has been a world of conceptual confusion.[87] To understand the nature of this confusion, though, we must peer into Dawkins' black box and examine what its mysterious contents reveal.

---

[82] Ibid., 20.
[83] Ibid., 1 f.
[84] Depew and Grene, 271.
[85] Richard Dawkins, *The Extended Phenotype* (Oxford: Oxford University Press, 1981), 98.
[86] Dawkins, *The Selfish Gene*, 23
[87] See Moss, *What Genes Can't Do*, 37.

Inside the Black Box

The originator of the black box, Thomas Hunt Morgan, began his scientific career in embryology and he concluded it in genetics. His switchover from the one field to the other has been described as a "conversion" because Morgan's research in "embryology did not culminate in genetics". Instead, "Morgan converted to the practice of the new discipline, leaving the unresolved problematics of embryology to fare for themselves."[88] Morgan's conversion from developmental biology might well serve as a symbol of the greater exodus in his generation to questions of ontogeny from those of phylogeny. About the same time that the Modern Darwinian Revolution was occurring in the 1930s, similar far-ranging developments were taking place in the field of developmental biology.[89] While the Modern Synthesizers were working out equations concerning the statistically abstracted gene, and bracketing off the questions of the gene's role in development, developmental biologists were painstakingly trying to tease apart the intricate sets of complex relationships that associate genotype to phenotype.[90] Over time developmental biology and developmental genetics would form close methodological ties with molecular biology as it emerged in the middle of the 20th century, but even then –and this is a source of Dawkins' conceptual trouble—its questions would remain distinct from those of evolutionary biology and behavioral genetics. The result of this historical divide between evolutionary biology and developmental biology has been the emergence of two distinct concepts of the gene. Each of these two concepts, cellular biologist and philosopher of science Lenny Moss explains, "can be seen as an heir to one of the two major historical trends in explaining the source of biological order: preformationism and epigenesis."[91]

By now we should already be fairly familiar with the evolutionary concept of the gene or, as Moss names it, "Gene P". The evolutionary gene (Gene-P) is a particulate preformationist conceptualization of the gene that regards the gene as an abstract, invariant unit which predicts phenotypes—but only as an instrumental basis. For statistical purposes, Gene P is understood as "that which is responsible for a trait."[92] Thus Gene-P is "defined by its relationship to a phenotype, albeit with no requirements as regards specific molecular sequence nor with respect to the biology involved in producing the phenotype."[93] In this way the evolutionary gene concept ignores devel-

---

[88] Ibid., 30 f.

[89] Scott Gilbert, *Developmental Biology*, (Sinauer, Sunderland MA, [5]1997), 38 f.

[90] James R. Griesemer, "Reproduction and the Reduction of Genetics", in: Peter Beurton, Raphael Falk and Hans-Jörg Rheinberger (ed.), *The Concept of the Gene in Development and Evolution: Historical and Epistemological Perspectives* (Cambridge: Cambridge University Press, 2000) 277.

[91] Moss, *What Genes Can't Do*, xiv.

[92] Ibid., 2.

[93] Moss, "Deconstructing the Gene", 87.

opmental processes for pragmatic reasons related to mathematical analysis. "[T]he mechanisms accounting for genetic change (mutation, recombination) were unexplained" but, "given the abstract, mathematical nature of the gene, none of this mattered. The gene could be anything that had the properties of transmittal with infrequent change."[94] Identical to the gene defined by Williams and Dawkins, Gene P is "that which segregates and recombines with appreciable frequency."[95]

Genes in this evolutionary sense are spoken of *as if* the gene directly causes the phenotype—as with Dawkins' genetic causal arrows. We speak of a gene *for* blue eyes even though there is no definite molecular sequence which specifies blue eyes (rather blue eyes are related to the deficiency of such a sequence-based resource). As a Gene P, a "gene for blue eyes" need not contain "any knowledge of the developmental pathway that leads to blue eyes (to which the "gene for blue eyes" makes a negligible contribution at most)", but it matters only that this gene may be tracked as a generationally transmitted predictor of blue eyes. At this point "Gene-P sounds purely classical, that is, Mendelian as opposed to molecular". However, elaborates Moss,

> [...] a molecular entity can be treated as a Gene-P as well. BRCA1, the gene for breast cancer, is a Gene-P, as is the gene for cystic fibrosis, even though in both cases phenotypic probabilities based upon pedigrees have become supplanted by probabilities based upon molecular probes. What these molecular probes do is to verify that some normal DNA sequence is absent, by confirming the presence of one, out of many possible, deviations from that normal sequence that has been shown to be correlated (to a greater or lesser extent) with some phenotypic abnormality. To satisfy the conditions of being a gene for breast cancer, or a gene for cystic fibrosis, does not entail knowledge about the biology of healthy breasts nor of healthy pulmonary function, nor is it contingent upon an ability to track the causal pathway from the absence of the normal sequence resource to the complex phenomenology of these diseases. The explanatory "game" played by Gene-P is thus not confined to purely classical methods, which unfortunately has made it all the easier to conflate this meaning of the "gene" with the one I will refer to as Gene-D.[96]

The Gene-D which Moss mentions here is the Gene concept which has emerged from developmental biology and developmental genetics. In contrast to Gene-P—which is defined according to its *instrumental utility* in predicting a phenotype outcome—the developmental gene (Gene-D) is defined by its *specific molecular sequence*. This gene is essentially a developmental *resource* rather than an indicator of the *absence* of some normal sequence, and

---

[94] Scott Gilbert, "Genes Classical and Genes Developmental: The different use of genes in evolutionary syntheses", in: Peter Beurton, Raphael Falk and Hans-Jörg Rheinberger (ed.), *The Concept of the Gene in Development and Evolution: Historical and Epistemological Perspectives* (Cambridge: Cambridge University Press, 2000) 178.

[95] Robin D. Knight and Paul E. Griffiths, "Selfish Genes—The Eunuchs of Selection".

[96] Moss, "Deconstructing the Gene", 87f.

by itself—or divorced from its ontogenic context—Gene D is *indeterminate* with regard to ultimate organismal phenotypic outcomes. The developmental gene is the gene of epigenesis, understood to be only one type of resource and one kind of molecule among many. As such it is not causally privileged, or even the first cause among equals. Moss provides a detailed example of why this is so:

> To be a Gene-D is to be a transcriptional unit (extending from start to stop codons) within which are contained molecular template resources. These templates typically serve as resources in the production of various "gene-products"—directly in the synthesis of RNA, and indirectly in the synthesis of a host of related polypeptides.
>
>   To be a gene for N-CAM, the so-called "neural cell adhesion molecule", for example, is to contain the specific nucleic acid sequences from which any of a hundred potentially different isoforms of the NCAM protein may ultimately be derived… Studies have shown that NCAM molecules are (despite the name) expressed in many tissues, at different developmental stages, and in many different forms. The phenotypes of which N-CAM molecules are co-constitutive are thus highly variable, contingent upon the larger context, and not germane to the status of N-CAM as a Gene-D. The expression of an embryonic form (highly sialylated) in the mature organism is associated with neural plasticity in the adult brain…but could well have pathological consequences if expressed in other tissues—yet it would not affect the identity of the N-CAM sequence as a Gene-D.[97]

In addition to this, molecular and developmental biology have discovered that specific nucleotide sequences or Gene-Ds are often "edited" midstream enroute to translation and the content of the sequence is thereby altered. Where DNA-RNA transcription is concerned, "overlapping reading frames have been found on one and the same strand of DNA, and protein coding stretches have been found to derive from both strands of the double helix in an overlapping fashion."[98] After transcription, the picture has become similarly complex. We now know that DNA transcripts such as transfer RNA and ribosomal RNA have "to be trimmed and matured in a complex enzymatic manner to become functional molecules", and that eukaryotic messenger RNAs undergo "extensive posttranscriptional modification both at their 5'-ends (capping) and their 3'-ends (polyadenylation) before they are ready to go into the translation machinery."[99] Thanks to developmental and molecular biology, we are also aware that eukaryotic genes are made up of modules, and that, "after transcription, *introns* are cut out and *exons* spliced together in order to yield a functional message". The resulting "spliced messenger" is often much less "verbose" than the original bearer of the message and may sometimes "comprise a fraction as little as ten percent or less of the primary

---

[97] Moss, "Deconstructing the Gene", 88.
[98] Hans-Jörg Rheinberger, "Gene".
[99] Ibid.

transcript."[100] On the level of the RNA transcript another phenomenon un-nerving to the evolutionary gene coneptualizers has been found, called *mes-senger RNA editing. During RNA messenger editing,*

> the original transcript is not only cut and pasted, but its nucleotide sequence is sys-tematically altered after transcription. The nucleotide replacement happens before translation starts, and is mediated by various guide RNAs and enzymes that excise old and insert new nucleotides in a variety of ways to yield a product that is no longer complementary to the DNA stretch from which it was originally derived, and a protein that is no longer co-linear with the DNA sequence in the classical molecular biological definition.[101]

To make matters worse for the evolutionary gene, there is also a process known as "chromatin marking" whereby gene activity is contextually modu-lated by direct chemical modification.[102] The DNA modification which oc-curs during chromatin marking is accomplished by DNA methylation—the enzyme-mediated addition of methyl groups ($CH3$), to individual bases of DNA. Besides its influence on transcriptional activation, the methylation state of DNA "is also found to affect the susceptibility of DNA toward muta-tion, translocation, and meiotic recombination."[103] Such chromatin marking likewise occurs in "context-dependent modulation of genome activity...dur-ing the gametogenesis of mammalian eggs and sperm" differentially predis-posing the "genes of the mammalian zygote [...] to activation or inactivation depending on the parent of origin."[104] With chromatin marking and DNA methylation, not only has Crick's Central Dogma been violated, but the age-old Weismannian Barrier separating somatic cell influences from germ line cells has been crossed.[105]

At this point one may now surmise that the developmental gene is radi-cally different from the evolutionary gene espoused by the descendents of the Modern Synthesis. One may even be persuaded that Gene-D should be understood, as the leading molecular developmental biologist Scott Gil-bert argues, to be "the exact counterpart to the gene of the evolutionary synthesis."[106] From the perspective of developmental biology, the evolution-ary gene concept and the genic selectionsim it entails "is based on mistaken views about the roles of genes in development and evolution". In light of this fact, developmental biologists argue that "the following claims are all either seriously misleading or false:"

---

[100] Ibid.
[101] Ibid.
[102] Eva Jablonka and M.J. Lamb, *Epigenetic Inheritance and Evolution: The Lamarckian Di-mension* (Oxford: Oxford University Press, 1995).
[103] Moss, *What Genes Can't Do*, 111.
[104] Ibid., 112.
[105] Ibid., 194.
[106] Scott Gilbert, "Genes Classical and Genes Developmental", 178–192.

1. genes code for phenotypic traits
2. genes replicate themselves,
3. genes are all that is inherited,
4. genic selectionism is the most general way of representing evolution.[107]

The strength of the developmental critique of the Neo-Darwinist evolutionary gene and the selfish gene of Dawkins has not gone unnoticed, and "something of a consensus has formed among philosophers of biology against genic selectionism…as a general formulation of genetic Darwinism."[108] Some researchers and philosophers of biology have remarked that "molecular biology…has made a caricature of this kind of evolutionary gene"[109] and others have declared that this Dawkinsian concept of the gene "must be held empirically accountable."[110] On this last point Moss minces no words:

> Dawkins's selfish replicator constitutes the quintessence of conflationary confusion. His viewpoint does not build on the advancing elucidation of molecular biology but rather depends on an enforced ignorance of it. His biology is built of ontotheology.[111]

In view of developmental and molecular biology's devasting critique of the genetic assumptions made by the Modern Synthesis, it appears that Dawkins' black box has become a time-bomb. As Raphael Falk expresses, "In retrospect we see that the triumph of the concept of the gene as the material unit of inheritance was also the crucial step of its downfall."[112] Consequently, the edifice of Dawkins' theodical challenge from evolutionary evil is a "house built on sand"[113] and philosophical theologians would be well advised to either keep away from this unstable structure entirely, or, at the very least, exercise extreme caution when entering into it. A new evolutionary synthesis is in the making, however, and this time around, Dawkins' black box is nowehere to be found.[114] In this new synthesis the evolutionary mechanism of natural selection, likewise plays a much-mediated role.

With the new evolutionary synthesis already dawning on the scientific horizon we find ourselves in a scenario which not only offers an opportunity

---

[107] Russell D. Gray, *Selfish genes or developmental systems?*

[108] Depew, 273.

[109] Hans-Jörg Rheinberger, "Gene".

[110] Moss *What Genes Can't Do*, xviii and Thomas Fogle, "The Dissolution of Protein Coding Genes in Molecular Biology", in: Peter Beurton, Raphael Falk, and Hans-Jörg Rheinberger (ed.), *The Concept of the Gene in Development and Evolution: Historical and Epistemological Perspectives* (Cambridge: Cambridge University Press, 2000).

[111] Moss, *What Genes Can't Do*, 194.

[112] Raphael Falk, "The Gene—A Concept in Tension", in: Peter Beurton, Raphael Falk, and Hans-Jörg Rheinberger (ed.), *The Concept of the Gene in Development and Evolution: Historical and Epistemological Perspectives* (Cambridge: Cambridge University Press, 2000) 343.

[113] Saunders.

[114] Scott F. Gilbert, J.M. Opitz, R.A. Raff, "Resynthesizing Evolutionary and Developmental Biology", Developmental Biology, 173:2, Febrary, 1996, 357–372.

for a further *scientific* critique of how the evolutionary theodicy problem is presently framed, but also points to a constructive way forward—and possibly out of the *structural dimension* of the evolutionary theodicy dilemma altogether. Biologist Jeffrey Schloss has spoken of the possibility of such a scientific critique of the problem of evolutionary evil. Schloss observes, "Where competition is the engine of evolutionary change, death is the requisite fuel for the fire—but this is only in accounts where natural selection is the driving force in evolution."[115] In principle, however, says Schloss, "evolution does not require death, and competition does not have to be the driving force". Ian Barbour likewise calls attention to the existence of alternative evolutionary mechanisms and mentions that "Darwin himself stressed the struggle and competition for survival, but more recent interpretations point to a larger role for cooperation and symbiosis."[116] Instead of the competitive displacement of natural selection, we may thus ask how a theory where evolution proceeds through cooperative synergism would change the parameters of the evolutionary theodicy problem. In the following pages I will discuss one such theory, and will then go on to describe other evolutionary mechanisms as well—all of which elude the intractable problem of having evolutionary pain, suffering, and evil as inherent aspects of their creative process.

Evolutionary Alternatives to Evolutionary Evil

Symbiogenesis

Molecular and cellular biologist Lynn Margulis provides us with a theory of evolution through cooperation and mutualism. Margulis and her colleagues criticize the efficacy of natural selection on several fronts. She reviews studies conducted on gene frequencies over time, the most prominent and extensive being Peter and Rosemary Grant's thirty-year investigation of Darwin's Galapagos finches.[117] While this and other studies have recorded significant morphological changes, Margulis points out that no cases of speciation have been documented in such investigations. There is "no evidence whatsoever", she says, that Darwinian natural selection "is leading to speciation."[118] In fact, it remains to be empirically demonstrated that "this process does more than change gene frequencies in populations."[119] Since selection operating on "intraspecific variation never seems to lead, by itself, to new species", she under-

---

[115] Jeffrey Schloss, in a class presentation on February 18, 2003 in ST5095 (Theodicy, Evolution, and Genocide) at the Graduate Theological Union, Berkeley, CA.

[116] Barbour, "Five Models of God and Evolution", 421.

[117] Peter R. Grant, *Ecology and Evolution of Darwin's Finches* (Princeton: Princeton University Press, 1986); and Peter R. Grant, *Evolutionary Dynamics of a Natural Population: The Large Cactus Finch of the Galapagos* (Chicago: University of Chicago Press, 1989).

[118] Margulis and Sagan, *Acquiring Genomes*, 31.

[119] Ibid., 82.

stands natural selection to play a peripheral role in the actual origin of species, and regards Darwin's mechanism to be "a strictly subtractive process."[120] Margulis argues that "because it is nothing more than differential survival, natural selection perpetuates but it cannot create."[121] She and others likewise argue that "random mutation, a small part of the evolutionary saga, has been dogmatically overemphasized."[122]

The school of thought which Margulis represents sees Neo-Darwinian gradualism as inadequate for explaining life's overall history and trends. In particular, Margulis and her frequent co-author, Dorian Sagan, appeal to Stephen Jay Gould and Niles Eldredge's criticism of phyletic gradualism. Pointing to the punctuated nature of the fossil record and failed attempts to find gradual transitions from species to species, Margulis and Sagan argue for "genuine gaps" in the evolutionary history of life.[123] The Neo-Darwinian understanding of natural selection is thus seen as having little historical explanatory power when it comes to how complex life on earth emerged.

Margulis' own understanding of evolution, which focuses on cooperation rather than competition, has grown out of her widely accepted early work.[124] This foundational research demonstrates how the complex inner components of eukaryotic cells—such as chloroplasts, mitochondria, the nuclear envelope, and endoplasmic reticulum, evolved as infoldings of the cell membrane thus allowing for the separate packaging of cellular processes.[125] She suggested that mitochondria and chloroplasts originated as free-living organisms, and that modern eukaryotic cells are essentially communities of different cell types living cooperatively. The association between host and endosymbiont becomes so intimate over time, Margulis argued, that formerly independent organisms eventually achieve total reliance on each other for their survival and reproduction, and effectively become a single organism.[126] Such *endosymbiosis* or

---

[120] Ibid., 68.

[121] Ibid., 75.

[122] Ibid., 15.

[123] Ibid., 83.

[124] Lynn Margulis, *Origin of Eukaryotic Cells* (New Haven, CT: Yale University Press, 1970). Even Dawkins, who vehemently disagrees with Margulis's overall thrust, calling her the "high priestess of symbiosis", accepts the importance of this work. See Richard Dawkins, *Unweaving the Rainbow: Science, Delusion, and the Appetite for Wonder* (New York: Houghton Mifflin, 1998), 225.

[125] Lynn Margulis and D. Bermudes, "Symbiosis as a Mechanism of Evolution: Status of Cell Symbiosis theory", Symbiosis, 1, 1985, 101–124.

[126] Lynn Margulis, *Symbiosis in Cell Evolution: Life and its Environment on the Early Earth* (San Francisco: WH Freeman, 1981); Lynn Margulis, Michael F. Dolan, and Ricardo Guerrero, "The Chimeric Eukaryote: Origin of the nucleus from the Karyomastigont in Amitochondriate Protests", Proceedings of the National Academy of Sciences, 97 (June 2000): 6954–6959; and Lynda J. Goff, "Symbiosis, Interspecific Gene Transfer, and the Evolution of New Species: A Case Study in the Parasitic Red Algae", in: Lynn Margulis and René Fester (ed.), *Symbiosis as a Source of Evolutionary Innovation: Speciation and Morphogenesis* (Cambridge, MA: MIT Press, 1991).

"living together inside", has since then been found to be quite common in nature.[127] The discovery that mitochondrial DNA is distinct from nuclear DNA gives especially strong testimony to the evolutionary efficacy of this process.[128] The endosymbiotic mechanism for evolutionary novelty has likewise been verified in the lab. For example, in an experiment done in the laboratory of Kwang W. Jeon at the University of Tennessee, a possible species change was witnessed as "new bacterial symbionts became integrated in the host amoeba such that the hosts became dependent on the symbionts within a few years". Furthermore, says Jeon, "the presence of endosymbionts has caused changes in several phenotypic characters of the host cells."[129]

Symbiogenesis, coined by the Russian biologist Konstantine Merezhkovsky (1855–1921), is the term used to describe the process like the one above whereby new morphologies and physiologies evolutionarily emerge by symbiosis.[130] Interestingly, this concept has been a dominant paradigm in Russian evolutionary biology since before the Neo-Darwinian synthesis, and it still exerts a substantial influence in Russian biological thought today.[131] Margulis defines symbiogenesis as "the evolutionary origin of new morphologies and physiologies by symbiosis",[132] and offers it as an alternative mechanism of evolution which addresses the problem of generative novelty. Symbiogenesis involves the wholesale acquisition of new genomes and, unlike natural selection, is an irreversible process.[133] While the Neo-Darwinian understanding of descent with modification entails that evolutionary novelty arises "vertically", by mutations in parental genes which are subsequently inherited by offspring, symbiogenesis, by contrast, involves the "horizontal" transfer of genes, where a single descendant inherits the combined genetic material of disparate organisms.[134]

Unlike mutation in the Neo-Darwinian model, the rapid acquisition of novel, highly refined traits by acquirement and integration of former genetic strangers "confers immediate selective advantages on protoctist, plant or ani-

---

[127] For example, see G.I. McFadden, P.R. Gilson, and S.E. Douglas, "The photosynthetic endosymbiont in cryptomonad cells produces both chloroplast and cytoplasmic-type ribosomes", Journal of Cell Science, 107, Febrary 1994, 649–657. See also footnote 36.
[128] Michael W. Gray, W.F. Doolittle, "Has the Endosymbiont Hypothesis been Proven?" Microbiological Reviews, 46:1, 1982, 1–42.
[129] Kwang W. Jeon, "Amoeba and x-Bacteria: Symbiont Acquisition and Possible Species Change", in: Lynn Margulis and René Fester (ed.), *Symbiosis as a Source of Evolutionary Innovation: Speciation and Morphogenesis*, (Cambridge, MA: MIT Press, 1991), 118.
[130] Lynn Margulis, *Symbiotic Planet: A New Look at Evolution* (New York: Basic Books, 1998), 33.
[131] Lynn Margulis, "Symbiogenesis and Symbioticism", in: Lynn Margulis and René Fester (ed.), *Symbiosis as a Source of Evolutionary Innovation: Speciation and Morphogenesis* (Cambridge, MA: The MIT Press, 1991) 1. One should also note that the understanding of evolution as proceeding through cooperation was preferred by A.R. Wallace over competition.
[132] Ibid.
[133] Margulis and Sagan, *Acquiring Genomes*, 72.
[134] See Margulis and Sagan, *Acquiring Genomes*, 41.

mal captors."[135] Often the association begins as predatory. One organism attempts to ingest and digest the other, which resists. The acquiescent prey or undigested bacterium subsequently gives rise to a trapped cellular population. The inheritance of trapped populations, especially in the form of microbial genomes, creates novel evolutionary lineages.[136] In this way, "dramatic new traits may be acquired in a single lifetime through adoption and subsequent integration of genomes."[137]

Margulis's understanding of the biological world requires a slight shift of perspective from that which is evident to the naked eye. She points out that for most of life's history on earth, bacteria were the sole inhabitants of the planet and that even today the main biological dividing line is not between plants and animals but prokaryotes and eukaryotes.[138] Long before plants or animals even emerged from the primeval oceans, prokaryotes had "invented all of life's essential, miniaturized chemical systems—achievements that humanity has so far not approached."[139] There is an astonishing diversity represented among present and ancient microorganisms, and all the processes that are needed for the sustenance and thriving of life are found beneath the horizon of human vision. Indeed, at the macrolevel, we lose sight that humans are largely assemblages of communities of microorganisms, and a full ten percent of our dry body weight is made up of *free-living* symbiotic organisms, that perform a myriad of tasks so that we may live, and live abundantly.[140] Like all of animal life, our bodies "contain a veritable history of life on Earth". Our cells maintain "an environment that is carbon- and hydrogen-rich, like that of the earth when life began". The human cellular menagerie lives, says Margulis, "in a medium of water and salts like the composition of the early seas."[141] Humans, like all "higher" life-forms are interactive communities of cells. As such communities of cells grew and complexified over evolutionary time, new properties emerged. As distinct genotypes merged, novel phenotypes were born and with them "new beings at higher levels of organization."[142]

To reiterate her position, Margulis believes that speciation through cooperative synergism, or symbiogenesis, has been the major driving force throughout the entire evolutionary history of life. Heralding what she sees as the future biological paradigm, she exclaims, "the view of evolution as chronic bloody competition among individuals and species, a popular distortion of

---

[135] Ibid., 72.
[136] Ibid.
[137] Ibid., 73.
[138] Lynn Margulis and Dorian Sagan, *Microcosmos: Four Billion Years of Microbial Evolution* (Berkeley, CA: University of California Press, 1986), 29.
[139] Ibid.
[140] Ibid., 33.
[141] Ibid., 32 ff.
[142] Ibid., 246.

Darwin's "survival of the fittest", dissolves before a new view of continual co-operation, strong interaction, and mutual dependence among life forms. Life did not take over the globe by combat, but by networking."[143]

In symbiogenesis, relationality rather than struggle is the axis of creativity, and extreme parasitism and vicious predation ultimately have no evolutionary future.[144] Genetic selfishness is not rewarded for its own sake. Death and extinction, while still present, are no longer central to the creative mechanism itself. In my opinion, this understanding of evolution seems to pose much less of a problem for evolutionary theodicy than the neo-Darwinian view.[145] It offers a view of creation, and life in general, as a mutual indwelling that is reminiscent of the theological concept of perichoresis. Margulis's perspective stresses the image of organisms as one body with many parts working together, rather than dwelling on the hyper-individualistic language of selfish genes at war. More complex forms of life emerge through a greater circle of genetic "trust" whereby formerly independent organisms "shed most of their tools of self-sufficiency."[146] In higher organisms it was not the best competitors which survived, but the best cooperators—those cells which had the greatest regard for their neighbors, in terms of both structural place and function.[147] There is a future thrust towards greater relationships of mutuality in this view of life, and a vision of evolutionary creativity as the triumph of intimacy over struggle.[148]

Self-Organization and Complexity

A second alternative understanding of evolution comes from the work of Stuart Kauffman, a developmental geneticist and theoretical biologist who is most well-known for his Santa Fe Institute work in applying complexity and non-linear dynamics to biological systems. Kauffman sees his program as "beyond Darwinism",[149] and argues for an expanded evolutionary theory which transcends the confines of natural selection's operation on random mutations.[150]

Kauffman, like Margulis, is skeptical about natural selection's capacity to generate novel forms of complex life. "Darwinism, and certainly Neo-Dar-

---

[143] Ibid., 28.

[144] Ibid., 130.

[145] Jacobus J. De Vries, "Cooperation or Competition: Comments on Rolston", in: Willem B. Drees (ed.), *Ever Evil?: Religion, Science, and Value*, (London: Routledge, 2003), 88.

[146] Margulis and Sagan, *Microcosmos*, 134.

[147] Ibid., 148. Margulis says that the behavior of cancer cells is essentially a rejection of such cellular alliances and an assertion of independent tendencies which she sees as an evolutionary regression.

[148] This vision holds on Earth at least. The future of the universe as a whole and the eschatological "freeze or fry" scenario is a different problem for biological life.

[149] Barbour, "Five Models", 424; and Ian G. Barbour, *Nature, Human Nature, and God* (Minneapolis: Fortress Press, 2002), 16.

[150] Stuart A. Kauffman, "Prolegomenon to a General Biology", Annals of the New York Academy of Sciences, 935, 2001, 18.

winism", says Kauffman, "grew as a concept of natural selection acting on heritable variations to weed out the less fit, culling for further amplification of the more adapted phenotypes". He continues, "nowhere in the core of Darwinism, and certainly not in Neo-Darwinism, is the issue of how forms happen to come into existence addressed."[151] For Kauffman, the concept of natural selection does "not answer the question of how forms, morphologies, phenotypes, and behaviors arise in the first place."[152]

Kauffman is also skeptical about the evolutionary adequacy of chance genetic mutations.[153] He argues that arbitrary, unconstrained mutations of genes can only result in regulatory chaos that will inevitably be deleterious to an organism.[154] Rather than seeing life as resulting from random mutations and the struggle for existence, Kauffman argues that "there is a natural, spontaneous, law-like source of order beyond that provided by natural selection."[155] Drawing from theories of complexity and his work on Random Boolean Networks, he insists that "self-organization is a natural property of complex genetic systems". "There is 'order for free' out there", says Kauffman, "a spontaneous crystallization of generic order out of complex systems, with no need for natural selection or any other external force."[156]

Kauffman argues that biological evolution is primarily the product of these self-organizing tendencies, and he maintains that dynamical systems can achieve new ordered states without any external selective pressures. Only after such order emerges does natural selection subsequently come into play. This means that natural selection is highly constrained by the emergent phenomenon of self-organization.[157]

As mentioned above, much of Kauffman's theoretical work has been done with the aid of Boolean networks, which are simulations that operate by simple logical rules and allow one to study the behavior and interconnectivity of various nodes or elements. In these networks, N represents the number of nodes and K the average number of interactions or inputs to operators. Using

---

[151] Stuart A. Kauffman, "Darwinism, Neodarwinism, and an Autocatalytic Model of Cultural Evolution", Psycology, 10 , 1999, 22.

[152] Ibid.

[153] See Stuart A. Kauffman, "Self-Organization, Selective Adaptation and its Limits: A New Pattern of Inference in Evolution and Development", in David J. Depew and Bruce H. Weber (ed.), *Evolution at the Crossroads: The New Biology and the New Philosophy of Science,* (Cambridge, MA: MIT Press, 1985).

[154] Kauffman, *At Home in the Universe: The Search for the Laws of Self-Organization and Complexity* (New York: Oxford University Press, 1995), 183.

[155] David Depew and Bruce Weber, *Darwinism Evolving: Systems Dynamics and the Genealogy of Natural Selection* (Cambridge, MA: MIT Press, 1995), 431.

[156] Stuart Kauffman, quoted in Depew and Weber, *Darwinism Evolving,* 431.

[157] Stuart A. Kauffman, "Origins of Order in Evolution: Self-Organization and Selection", in: Brian Goodwin and Peter Saunders (ed.), *Theoretical Biology: Epigenetic and Evolutionary Order from Complex Systems* (Baltimore: Johns Hopkins University Press, 1992), 67–88.

such networks in his early work, Kauffman discovered that random networks often generate a set of states that are continually repeated.[158] In other words, he found that Boolean networks may become spontaneously ordered. They achieve this, furthermore, in ways that are surprisingly resilient to perturbations. These recurrent loops or patterns, called *state cycles,* are emergent properties of computational systems in which sets of local rules give rise to global order.[159] The most interesting phenomena for Kauffman were those hovering at the "edge of chaos."[160] These states were the most resistant to perturbations and occasionally when disturbed would instantly jump to an entirely new and different state of repeated order.

Keeping this research in mind, Kauffman decided to investigate developmental constraints in organisms. With the aid of Boolean Networks again, Kauffman developed a model based on François Jacob and Jacques Monod's discovery of regulatory proteins (or repressors) that turn structural genes on and off, and he found the same types of patterns.[161] Applying this research to human ontogeny, Kauffman endeavored to see if his model could elucidate "why the approximately 100,000 genes of *Homo sapiens sapiens* direct the development of only 250 or so cell types, when 10^{30000} activity patterns are mathematically possible."[162] Setting N as 100,000 in his model with K = 2, he found that $N^{0.5}$ (or square root of N) equaled 317, which is roughly the number of cell types in humans. This result likewise allowed him to view cell types as state cycles or *attractors.*

The above result led Kauffman to the conclusion that perhaps this "range of cell types had been determined not by natural selection, or even by the properties of particular materials that cells are made from, but from the inherent mathematical properties of systems with a large array of elements and connections among them."[163] Kauffman also found that there is a critical point at which the complexity of the regulatory connectivity undergoes a "phase transition". This happens when the model becomes large enough to prevent selection from overriding the emergence of a "generic complex pattern."[164] These results have persuaded Kauffman that in actual genetic regulatory programs, there can be basic features that were never selected for. In fact, "they are there in spite of selection."[165]

---

[158] Ibid., 192 ff. See also Depew and Weber, *Darwinism Evolving,* 431.

[159] Kauffman, *At Home in the Universe,* 77.

[160] Ibid., 86.

[161] Ibid., 96.

[162] Depew and Weber, *Darwinism Evolving,* 432. See Figure 2 for the relationship between humans and other organisms.

[163] Ibid.

[164] Kauffman, "Self-Organization, Selective Adaptation and its Limits", 184 f; and Depew and Weber, *Darwinism Evolving,* 446.

[165] See Kauffman, "Origins of Order", 16; Depew and Weber, *Darwinism Evolving,* 446.

Recent estimates on the number of human genes, given by the Human Genome Project, range from about 30,000-48,000 genes.[166] Substituting these new numbers into Kauffman's original equations, one finds that the derived figure (~219) comes even closer to the actual number of human cell types (~250) than his initial number (317). Regardless of the precise number, though, when one considers that there are about 10^{30000} mathematically possible cell types, all of the above figures fall within an acceptable range. This data, showing an approximate correlation between calculated and observed number of cell types, thus appears to give credence to the sort of developmental constraints and emergent order in ontogeny which Kauffman's work suggests.[167]

Kauffman's research also elucidates how these genetic regulatory networks may influence the process of speciation in evolution. If cell types are seen as attractors, then one can visualize certain ontogenetically stable areas in NK space which will be sought out early on during the developmental trajectory. One may then "reconceive the process of speciation as a shift in attractors acting late in the developmental trajectory."[168] As we have seen above, such attractors, being "near the edge of chaos", exhibit a certain developmental plasticity. When this fact is combined with the "tendency of complex systems to restabilize", one can see how relatively few genetic mutations in a developmental program might "come under the influence of another attractor that could produce an emergent evolutionary novelty" within a rather short period of time.[169]

The basics of this process, detailed in Kauffman's work, have indeed received a fair amount of empirical support. For example, in an experiment conducted by the lab of John Doebley at the University of Minnesota it was found that only five genes control up to 80 % of morphological expression in corn. These same genes were shown to adequately account for the rapid evolutionary transformation of Teosinte grass into corn.[170] Other research in evolutionary developmental biology involving genetic manipulations in animals such as butterflies, nematodes, and cavefish has substantiated these findings.[171]

To summarize Kauffman's position, then, he holds that "the emerging sciences of complexity suggest that the order is not all accidental, that vast veins of spontaneous order lie at hand."[172] The underlying principles and laws of

---

[166] Ornl.gov, www.ornl.gov/TechResources/Human_Genome/faq/genenumber.html [May 1, 2003] "How Many Genes Are in the Human Genome?" See also Jean-Michel Claverie, "Gene number. What if there are only 30,000 human genes?" *Science*, 291, 5507, February, 2001, 1255 ff.

[167] See Richard Sole and Brian Goodwin, *Signs of Life: How Complexity Pervades Biology* (New York: Basic Books, 2000) 75.

[168] Depew and Weber, *Darwinism Evolving*, 450.

[169] Ibid.

[170] Elizabeth Culotta, "How Many Genes Had to Change to Produce Corn?" Science, 252, 5014, June 28, 1991, 1793.

[171] Elizabeth Pennisi, "Evo-Devo Enthusiasts Get Down to Details", Science, 298, 5595, November 18, 2002, 953–955.

[172] Kauffman, *At Home in the Universe*, 8.

complexity, says Kauffman, "spontaneously generate much of the order of the natural world."[173] Only after such complex morphologies and behaviors emerge does natural selection come into play, as it acts to further mold and refine life. Kauffman remarks that many biologists see the order in ontogeny and phylogeny as due to "the grinding away of a molecular Rube-Goldberg machine, slapped together piece by piece by evolution". Kauffman proposes a counter thesis: "the beautiful order seen" in these evolutionary processes "is spontaneous, a natural expression of the stunning self-organization that abounds in very complex regulatory networks."[174]

Developmental Systems Theory
Others coming from various sub-disciplines in biology have supplemented Margulis and Kauffman's work to provide a third alternative to the narrow Neo-Darwinian notion of evolution via nature's selection of selfish genes. Coming from a Developmental Systems Theory (DST) perspective, Susan Oyama and her colleagues critique the archonic or gene-centered view of biological reality which is inherent in Dawkins' and the Modern Synthetic understanding of evolution. They comment on how prevailing biological thought entertains the notion that the nature and form of a being is *already present* in its genome and that development merely reveals or "expresses" what is already innate in the "genetic plan". This assumption is evident in the popular "blue print" and "program" metaphors which are often used to describe genomic material.[175] Oyama believes such metaphors and the assumptions they reveal are not only mistaken but scientifically indefensible since "the genome represents only a part of the entire developmental ensemble" and "cannot by itself contain or cause the form that results."[176] The same genetic "message" can be read in a variety of ways and it is only the entire developmental context or system which decides which reading is to be preferred. Genes do not contain or transmit organismic form but rather form is *constructed* in highly environmentally-contextualized developmental processes, and is a function of the total input of a series of nested systems in which the genome is one component among many.[177] Furthermore, this entire developmental complex, and not just the DNA, is passed on or inherited in reproduction.[178] Thus, if an organism, though well suited to its living conditions, "fails to assemble for

---

[173] Ibid.
[174] Ibid., 25.
[175] See Susan Oyama, Paul E. Griffiths, and Russell D. Gray (ed.), *Cycles of Contingency: Developmental Systems and Evolution* (Cambridge, MA: MIT Press, 2001) 5; and also Susan Oyama, *The Ontogeny of Information: Developmental Systems and Evolution*, (Duke University Press, ²2000) 55.
[176] Oyama, Griffiths and Gray, 5; and Oyama, *The Ontogeny of Information*, 23.
[177] Oyama, *The Ontogeny of Information*, 26.
[178] Ibid., 206.

its offspring the developmental system that formed it, it may pass on its genes but its phenotype will not be produced". As a result, both ontongeny (individual development) and phylogeny (evolutionary development) "depend on ecologically embedded developmental systems."[179]

Having rejected the evolutionary gene concept (or Gene P) of the Modern Synthesis, Developmental Systems theorists seek to redefine the evolutionary process according to the inheritance and generative transformation of the entire developmental ensemble — "a mobile set of interacting influences and entities" including "all influences on development, at all levels of analysis", consisting of the molecular, cellular, organismal, ecological, and biogeographical.[180] The evolution of developmental systems is the evolution not only of organisms and populations but also "of the features of the extraorganismic environment that influence development."[181] "Just as there are no preexisting representations or instructions that shape organisms from within", DST argues that, "there are no preexisting niches or environmental problems that shape organisms from without". Change in evolutionary time is the consequence "of interactions in which outcomes are co-determined or co-constructed, by populations and environments with their own, often intricately interrelated, histories and characteristics". The upshot of this perspective is that "it is no longer possible to think of evolution as the shaping of the organism to fit an environmental niche."[182] DST acknowledges a variety of viable evolutionary mechanisms — including symbiogenesis, self-organization, generative entrenchment, epigenesis, change through behavioral and ecological inheritance, niche construction, process structural morphogenesis and natural selection — and it seeks to integrate them into a unified evolutionary framework by both expanding the notion of inheritance beyond mere genetics and by recognizing the fact that each of these various evolutionary mechanisms has explanatory value for elucidating life's evolution. As we have seen previously many of these alternative mechanisms function independently and even in spite of natural selection.

To summarize, Oyama and her colleagues in Developmental Systems Theory point out that "the life cycle of an organism is developmentally constructed, not programmed or preformed". Such life cycles come "into being through interactions between the organism and its surroundings as well as interactions within the organism."[183] Their view is a "thoroughly epigenetic account of development" which flies in the face of the central dogma of molecular biolo-

---

[179] Ibid., 182.
[180] Oyama, *The Ontogeny of Information*, 72 and see Jason Scott Robert, "Developmental Systems and Animal Behaviour", Biology and Philosophy, 18, 2003, 477–489.
[181] Oyama, *The Ontogeny of Information*, 82.
[182] Oyama, Griffiths and Gray, 6.
[183] See Oyama, Griffiths and Gray, 4.

gy.[184] This and other epigenetic accounts of development and evolution "challenge the metaphysics and epistemology of a gene-centric viewpoint" and "involve an ontological reversal implying a priority of dynamic interactions over static states."[185] By first challenging and then providing an alternative to the Modern Synthetic understanding of evolution, DST also mediates the problem of evolution and evil. Recognizing the crucial role of evolutionary mechanisms which are not fueled by struggle, competition and death, DST offers yet another way forward for a theodicy of nature.

Developmental Constraints, Process Structualism, and Morphogenetic Law
A fourth evolutionary alternative is found in the work of Brian Goodwin and many of his colleagues researching in the area of developmental-evolutionary biology. Goodwin and others perceive a problem within the current Neo-Darwinian model of evolutionary development because of its "theoretical inadequacy" in "identifying correlative factors with sufficient causes of organismic morphology" and this model's inability to account "in causal terms for observed differences of form in organisms by the identification of differences in heredity factors."[186] They point to a growing body of empirical evidence which, on the one hand, demonstrates "that genes do not generate form", and, on the other hand, provides "evidence of regularity in, and constraint on, biological form."[187] Rather than taking the Neo-Darwinian *historical* approach to the problem of biological form, Goodwin takes a *structuralist* approach which perceives an "invariant relational order in organisms" that "underlies reproduction and results in the regularities observed in development and evolution."[188] In other words, Goodwin and his colleagues maintain that biological form in both ontogeny and evolution is constrained not so much by historical con-

[184] For similar views which stress the roles of developmental contingency, and of epigenetic inheritance and evolution see Lenny Moss, "From Representational Preformationism to the Epigenesis of Openness to the World?: Reflections on a New Vision of the Organism", Annals of the New York Academy of Sciences, 981 2002, 219–230; E. Jablonka, M. Lachmann and M.J. Lamb, "Evidence, mechanisms and models for the inheritance of acquired characteristics", J. Theoret. Biol., 158, 1992, 245–268; and Richard Von Sternberg, "Genomes and Form: The Case for Teleomorphic Recursivity?" Annals of the New York Academy of Sciences, 901, 2000, 224–236.
[185] Gertrudis Van De Vijver, Linda Van Speybroeck, and Dani De Waele, "Epigenetics: A Challenge for Genetics, Evolution, and Development?" Annals of the New York Academy of Sciences, 981, 2002, 4.
[186] Brian C. Goodwin, "A relational or field theory of reproduction and its evolutionary implications", in: Mae-Wan Ho and Peter T. Saunders (ed.), *Beyond Neo-Darwinism: An Introduction to the New Evolutionary Paradigm*, (London: Academic Press, 1984.); for a similar critique see Stuart A. Kauffman, "Self-Organization, Selective Adaptation and its Limits: A New Pattern of Inference in Evolution and Development", in: David J. Depew and Bruce H. Weber (ed.), *Evolution at the Crossroads: The New Biology and the New Philosophy of Science* (Cambridge, MA: MIT Press, 1985) and Stuart A. Kauffman, *At Home in the Universe*.
[187] Goodwin, "A Relational or Field Theory", 220.
[188] Ibid., 221.

tingencies and pathways as by relational laws which govern development and morphological structure. This means, in contradiction to the Neo-Darwinian view, that certain morphological forms are possible while others are not.[189] Here organisms are described as generic states or forms which are "high-probability, robust, or natural states of the developmental-evolutionary dynamic", and consequently evolution is seen as "the exploration of the potential set of such forms as defined by morphogenetic principles."[190] Such morphological states may be mathematically described as "highly discrete, well-defined attractors" and the biological properties which produce them — whether ontogenetic or phylogenetic — emerge as fields of relational order.

Goodwin argues that such morphogenic fields are the "source of developmental and evolutionary potential."[191] Within developmental biology it has been shown many times over that such fields are able to generate "a great diversity of forms which belong to a general type or class of structure", and many experiments have explored the range of morphologies that result in systematic perturbations of these fields. In the development of limbs, for example, it has been shown that a limb morphogenetic field of a single species (or genotype) "is capable of generating a variety of basic skeletal patterns...which is greater than that observed in the full range of tetrapod limbs."[192] The observed diversity of limb forms arises from the "existence of a large number of solutions of the limb field equations" which defines "the potential or possible set of forms which can be generated". The specific solutions to the morphogenetic field which are selected and stabilized are a product of the "initial and boundary conditions which act on the field, specifying relevant parameter values."[193] This type of field behavior characterizes regenerative processes as well.

According to Goodwin, such fields play a crucial role in evolution or, as Goodwin calls it, "generative transformation". During an organism's development there are a number of distributed morphological potentials which define the morphogenetic field. Because every morphogenetic field is described by equations which have a number of solutions that are each expressed as a different morphological form, each individual organism "carries within it the potential of creating a great variety of forms."[194] The actualization of any one

[189] Brian C. Goodwin, "The Evolution of Generic Form", in: J. Maynard Smith and G. Vida (ed.), *Organizational constraints on the dynamics of evolution* (Manchester and New York: Manchester University Press, 1990) 107. See also Paul Griffiths, "The Philosophy of Molecular and Developmental Biology", in: Peter K. Machamer and Micheal Silberstein (ed.), *The Blackwell Guide to the Philosophy of Science* (Malden, MA: Blackwell Publishers, 2002).

[190] Ibid., 116.

[191] Ibid., 113.

[192] Brian C. Goodwin, "Changing from an evolutionary to a generative paradigm in biology.", in: Jeffrey W. Pollard (ed.), *Evolutionary Theory: Paths Into the Future,* (Chichester: John Wiley & Sons, 1984) 114.

[193] Ibid.

[194] Ibid., 118.

specific morphological form or pattern depends on "the action of particular genes and environments on the space-time order of the developing organism described by the laws of organization of the living state."[195] This same series of events constitutes the occasion for speciation or "the biological process of creation". Thus evolution is the process in which the potential set of morphological forms defined by these relational-organization laws—those of the morphogenetic or phylogenetic field—is explored through internal (genetic) variations or changes, and changes in the external environment (parametric variation).[196]

The implication of this understanding of evolution is that the speciation process entails "the generation of separate and distinct forms *ab initio* so that species are natural kinds."[197] The result is a quantization of biology where intermediate levels are ruled out. An additional implication of this position is that biological species "do not arise as a result of natural selection operating on a continuum of forms to give speciation", but "come into existence by virtue of the spectral (quantized) nature of the morphological stability domains of the generative process."[198]

Programs comparable to Goodwin's have been carried out in other areas of the biological sciences as well, and many have reached similar conclusions.[199] In the area of paleontology, for example, Simon Conway Morris investigates instances of the evolutionary convergence of biological form which range from the camera-eye, found in both humans and advanced cephalopods,[200] to echolocation in birds, dolphins, and bats.[201] Morris shows how countless different historical evolutionary trajectories, which began from radically dissimilar starting places, have arrived at the same morphological destination. This for Morris seems to reveal a deeper structure within life's evolution, and indicates that the pathways which evolution takes are most likely *highly constrained*. Morris believes that these constraints on evolution and "the ubiquity of convergence make the emergence of something like ourselves a

---

[195] Ibid.

[196] Brian C. Goodwin, "Evolution and the Generative Order", in: Brian C. Goodwin and Peter Saunders (ed.), *Theoretical Biology: Epigenetic And Evolutionary Order From Complex Systems* (Baltimore: Johns Hopkins University Press, 1992) 96; and see Goodwin, "Changing from an evolutionary to a generative paradigm", 118.

[197] Goodwin, "Changing from an evolutionary to a generative paradigm", 114.

[198] Ibid.

[199] See for example Scott F. Gilbert, John M. Opitz and Rudolf A. Raff, "Resynthesizing Evolutionary and Developmental Biology", Developmental Biology, 173:2, February 1996, 357–372. and John Maynard Smith, and G. Vida (ed.), *Organizational constraints on the dynamics of evolution.* (Manchester and New York: Manchester University Press, 1990).

[200] Simon Conway Morris, *Life's Solution: Inevitable Humans in a Lonely Universe* (Cambridge: Cambridge University Press, 2004) 151.

[201] Morris, 181.

near-inevitability". Indeed, declares Morris, "the contingencies of biological history will make no long-term difference to the outcome."[202]

With the alternative evolutionary mechanisms of Goodwin and Morris, we have come full circle. Here waste, suffering, bloodshed, death, competition, and contingency are no longer understood to be par for the evolutionary course. Indeed these disquieting behaviors and phenomena are seen to have no necessary or essential role in how or why evolutionary complexification proceeds. Generative transformation would occur with or without such troubling occurrences and in this view the multifarious forms in which life is embodied owe little or nothing to historical accident, coincidence, or chance because the morphological structure and generative principles giving rise to such evolutionary incarnations are written in the laws of nature. In this account evolutionary evils are not entailed in the *very process* by which organisms were created, and life's evolutionary creation comes without the intrinsic cost of pain and suffering.

Fleshing Out the Free Process Defense
From the examples above we have seen that natural selection was not God's only option in creating complex life. Indeed when the creator God declared, "Let the earth bring forth living creatures", it appears that God mediated life's creation through a variety of creative processes. The empirical reality and efficacy of alternative evolutionary mechanisms reveals to us that when "God invoked the powers of generativity latent in the earth by his own creative action", God may have chosen to use natural selection to very limited degree, or even not at all.[203] The future of empirical research in evolutionary biology will reveal whether or not this is so, but for our purposes here, let us assume that these alternative evolutionary research programs will continue to be fruitful, and will indeed show us that natural selection does not play *the* major role in life's evolution. The *philosophical-theoretical* necessity of evolutionary evil would be gone from the font of life's creativity, but we would still be faced with the *fact* of much pain and suffering within nature.

Confronted with the universal *fact* of evolutionary evils without any *systemic necessity* for them, we are borne back to Epicurus' and Augustine's perennial question: *Unde Malum*—from where or what source does evil arise? Stemming from Augustine's initial response, a traditional solution to the moral and human aspect of this dilemma has centered on some form of the free will defense or theodicy.[204] John Polkinghorne has suggested a similar ap-

---

[202] Morris, 328.

[203] Lawson G. Stone, "The Soul: Possession, Part, or Person? The Genesis of Human Nature in Genesis 2:7", in: Joel Green (ed.), *What About the Soul?: Neuroscience and Christian Anthropology* (Nashville: Abingdon Press, 1999) 51.

[204] Alvin Plantinga, *God, Freedom, and Evil* (Grand Rapids, MI: Eerdmans, 1974).

proach to the question of "natural evil" in what he has called "the free-process defense."[205] In God's "great act of creation", explains Polkinghorne, "God allows the physical world to be itself, not in Manichean opposition to him, but in that independence which is Love's gift of freedom to the one beloved."[206] Both the free will and free process theodicies seek to ground their theological logic in the existence of a type of "universal contingent", described by Robert John Russell as events or circumstances, which while not necessary in themselves, give rise to conditions which are presently unavoidable.[207] Accordingly, the open and flexible processes of the cosmos provide "the means by which the universe explores its own potentiality, humankind exercises its will, and God interacts with his creation. The first, through its limitation and frustration, gives rise to physical evil. The second through its sinfulness gives rise to moral evil."[208] Non-human animal suffering and other *evolutionary* evils are not directly addressed in this treatment, however.[209] In light of this deficiency I would like to suggest a third universal contingent by which many evolutionary evils may enter into a world declared "very good". This third universal contingent is the reality of active *animal choice* as a crucial factor in determining and directing which of the various evolutionary trajectories are followed throughout biotic history. In the following paragraphs I will elaborate on the character of animal choice in nature and, in light of its actuality and significance throughout evolutionary history, propose the *Free Creatures Extension* to the free-process defense.

Polkinghorne points out that God is not the puppet-master of either matter or of men, and I would like to point out that God is not the puppet-master of non-human animals either. The view that God directs the behaviors of animals was the common fare of pre-Darwinian natural theology. Theologically understood, such "innate behavior" was any "behavior that cannot be explained by an animal's use of reason."[210] To the natural theologians, innate behaviors or "complex instincts" demonstrated the "hand of divine providence, equipping the organism in advance for the challenges that it will face when it is born". As the Darwinian tradition inherited and modified natural theology's concept of innateness, "natural selection [took] the place of God in explaining how organisms can manifest behavior that is adaptive when they

[205] John Polkinghorne, *Science and Providence: God's Interaction with the World* (Boston: New Science Library, 1989), 65f.
[206] Polkinghorne, *Science and Providence*, 66.
[207] Robert John Russell, "The Thermodynamics of Natural Evil", CTNS Bulletin, 10:2, Spring 1990, 20–25.
[208] Polkinghorne, *Science and Providence*, 67.
[209] Southgate also makes this point. "See God and Evolutionary Evil", 809.
[210] Paul E. Griffiths, in press: "The Fearless Vampire Conservator: Philip Kitcher on Genetic Determinism", in: C. Rehmann-Sutter and E.M. Neumann-Held (ed.), *Genes in Development* (Durham, NC: Duke University Press).

have had no opportunity to learn that behavior". Furthermore, the existence
of such "complex, instinctive behaviors" was seen as providing "evidences
of evolution."[211] The founders of ethology, and Konrad Lorenz in particular,
continued to promote such an understanding of innateness, and when the genetic revolution transpired innate traits were redefined as "genetic traits" or
"traits that are the product of genetic information."[212] The behaviors of animals were consequently described as being genetically determined or "genetically hardwired". This understanding has continued to hold sway to this day,
especially in evolutionary psychology and behavioral genetics circles.[213]

Genes are not the puppet-masters of animals either, though, because
Lorenz's genetic "concept of innateness is irretrievably confused."[214] Molecular developmental biology has revealed the notion of innateness to be "as an-
tiquated a theoretical construct as instinct and equally peripheral to any actual
account of gene regulation or morphogenesis."[215] To date, no one has been
able to demonstrate that the "notion of genetic coding" can be "legitimately
applied to the mapping between genes and phenotypes in general". Lacking
any feasible "account of the general notion of genetic information, identifying
innateness with the genetic coding of phenotypes is trading one confused notion for another and is therefore no progress at all."[216]

The genetic innateness paradigm in biology visualizes animals as passive
objects whose behaviors were and are sculpted by the blind and fumbling
hand of natural selection. In a similar manner the classical understanding of
Darwinian adaptation regards evolution as a "process by which natural selection, stemming from an external environment, gradually molds organisms to
be well suited to their environments."[217] It appears, though, that the converse
is largely true. Whereas Neo-Darwinism treats "the environment as a source
of fixed problems which every organism must solve or die", much empirical
investigation has shown that "organisms and their ecological niches are co-
constructing and co-defining".[218] Through active decision-making, "organisms both physically shape their environments and determine which factors
in the external environment are relevant to their evolution, thus assembling

---

[211] Ibid.

[212] Konrad Lorenz, *Evolution and the Modification of Behavior* (London: Eyre and Methuen, 1966) 37.

[213] For examples of this see Mateo Mameli and Patrick Bateson, "Innatness and the Sciences", Biology and Philosophy, (Forthcoming).

[214] Paul E. Griffiths, "What is Innateness?", The Monist, 85:1, 2002, 70.

[215] Paul E. Griffiths, "What is Innateness?", 70 f.

[216] Mameli and Bateson, "Innatness and the Sciences".

[217] Rachel L. Day, Kevin N. Laland and John Odling-Smee, "Rethinking Adaptation: The Niche-Construction Perspective", Perspectives in Biology and Medicine, 46:1 81.

[218] Paul E. Griffiths and Russell D. Gray, "Darwinism and Developmental Systems", in: Susan Oyama; Paul E. Griffiths; and Russell D. Gray (ed.), *Cycles of Contingency: Developmental Systems and Evolution,* (Cambridge, MA: MIT Press, 2001) 203.

such factors into what biologists describe as a niche. Organisms are adapted to their ways of life because organisms and their way of life were made for (and by) each other."[219] Animals are not merely the passive objects of evolution but rather the active executive subjects who significantly determine the paths which their own—and their descendents—evolution will take.

This phenomenon whereby animals select and shape their own habitats and environments is called "niche construction", and the taxonomic breadth of such "species that modify their selective environment to a significant degree is astonishing."[220] In fact, "all living creatures, through their metabolism, their activities, and their choices, partly create and partly destroy their own niches, on scales ranging from the extremely local to the global". To different degrees, organisms from every major group select habitats, resources, and foods; "construct aspects of their environments, such as nests, holes, burrows, webs, pupal cases, and a chemical milieu, and destroy other components; and frequently choose, protect, and provision nursery environments for their offspring."[221] Through active niche construction, non-human animals "not only shape the nature of their world, but also in part determine the selection pressures to which they and their descendants are exposed". In this way the behavioral decisions, environmental alterations—whether physical, social, or nutritional—and subjective choices of animals "play a major role in introducing evolutionary change."[222] Patrick Bateson elaborates specifically on how such evolutionary change takes place:

> If a population of animals should change their habits (no doubt often on account of changes in their surroundings such as food supply, breeding sites, etc. but also sometimes due to their exploratory curiosity discovering new ways of life, such as new sources of food or new methods of exploitation) then, sooner or later, variations in the gene complex will turn up in the population to produce small alterations in the animal's structure which will make them more efficient in relation to their new behavioral pattern.[223]

Recent mathematical investigations using population genetics models have substantiated this picture of evolution revealing that "feedback from niche construction can make a considerable difference to the evolutionary process and can generate unusual evolutionary dynamics". Because of the estimated evolutionary impact of the niche constructing activities of animals some biol-

---

[219] Griffiths and Gray, "Darwinism and Developmental Systems", 204.

[220] Day, Laland, and Odling-Smee, "Rethinking Adaptation", 84.

[221] John Oding-Smee, K. Laland, and M. Feldman, *Niche Construction: The Neglected Process in Evolution*, (Princeton: Princeton University Press, 2003) 1. and Day, Laland, and Odling-Smee, "Rethinking Adaptation: Rethinking", 81.

[222] Patrick Bateson, "The Active Role of Behavior in Evolution", in: M. W. Ho, S. W. Fox (ed.), *Evolutionary Processes and Metaphors* 191 (London: John Wiley and Sons, 1988) 192–207 and "The Active Role of Behavior in Evolution", Biology and Philosophy, 19, 2004, 283–298.

[223] Bateson, "The Active Role of Behavior in Evolution", in: *EvolutionaryProcesses*, 196.

ogists have even called for a complete "overhaul in evolutionary thinking."[224]
Once niche construction is taken into account we are confronted with a "sub-
stantially revised model" of the evolutionary process in which the causal relationships between organism and organism, and organism and environment
are significantly redefined.[225] Animals and their behaviors become much more
than just mere "utility functions" of their environment, and consequently the
"reverse-engineering" exercises of Dawkins and others are exposed as profoundly misdirected.

It appears, then, that the behaviors and choices of animals serve as a significant universal contingent in evolutionary history and I suggest that these
same choices are theologically relevant insofar as they create instances of evolutionary suffering. Such animal choices affect the actual occurrence of evolutionary evils by playing a central role in determining the specific forms in
which such evolutionary evils are historically embodied. A few examples will
aid us in making the further connection between animal choices and evolutionary evils.

Rape, as violently forced "copulation resisted to the best of the victim's
ability" is a universal phenomenon within human cultures, and within all cultures rape is judged to be an unmediated evil.[226] Even those who argue that
rape is an evolutionary adaptation, which allows males on the fringes of society without resources to have a chance at successfully mating, acknowledge
the pain, suffering, and associated evils caused by this brutal act.[227] The human
species is not alone, however, in exhibiting this aggressive "alternative mating
strategy". In fact, rape as defined above is found among a wide spectrum of
animals including insects, birds, fishes, reptiles, amphibians, marine mammals,
land mammals, and non-human primates. The last four decades of research in
animal behavior have revealed that "physical force, harassment, and intimida-
tion are used widely by males across animal species, including the great apes,
to obtain mates."[228] Biologist John Alcock describes one example of rape in
non-human animals:

> I have on occasion seen a male of the desert beetle *Tegodera aloga* run to a female
> and wrestle violently with her in an attempt to throw her on her side. If successful,
> the male probes the female's genital opening with his everted aedeagus (the entomo-
> logical label for "penis") and he sometimes is able to achieve insertion of the same,
> despite the female's attempts to break free. What makes this behavior so striking is
> that the male *Tegodera aloga* are perfectly capable of courting potential partners in a

---

[224] Day, Laland, and Odling-Smee, "Rethinking Adaptation", 82.

[225] Griffiths and Gray, "Darwinism and Developmental Systems", 204.

[226] R. Thornhill, C.T. Palmer and M. Wilson, *A Natural History of Rape: Biological Bases of Sexual Coercion* (Cambridge, MA: MIT Press, 2000) 1. and John Alcock, *The Triumph of Sociobiology* (Oxford: Oxford University Press, 2001) 209.

[227] Thornhill, Palmer, and Wilson, *A Natural History of Rape,* 67, 85 ff.

[228] Thornhill, Palmer, and Wilson, *A Natural History of Rape,* 144.

decorous manner. In these nonviolent interactions, a male cautiously moves in front of a female, often one that is feeding...and he uses his antennae to sweep her antennae into two groves in the front of his head. The two may stand facing one another for many minutes while the female feeds and the male strokes her antennae over and over again...[Through this ritual] courting males communicate their capacity to provide their mates with a nuptial gift. If a female perceives her suitor to be in possession of valuable resources that she will receive, she may eventually permit him to mount and copulate sedately. If not she pulls her antennae free and walks away.[229]

Many other such examples of "rape" in nature are available but this one will suffice.[230] Here the animal in question is confronted with two choices—one, which through coercion and violence, causes unwanted pain and suffering to the victim, and one, which through tenderness and mutual trust, provides an image of inter-relationality and something akin to love in the pre-human animal world. The decision, however, resides solely with the animal, and its choice has the potential to "initiate and direct lines of evolution" for the future of its own descendents and its species.[231] In scenarios like this, the theater of nature is the arena of decision and evolution's future lies in the balance.

The world of non-human animals is teeming with examples of these types of historically contingent choices which must be made every day. Even Darwin's parasitic wasps and Dawkins' cheetah have made such choices in their evolutionary history and still must make them today. Though the cheetah of Dawkins prefers to eat Thomson's Gazelle, as I might prefer to eat veal, both of us also eat fruits and vegetables and cheetahs have been observed enjoying watermelon in the wild.[232] When the evolutionary predecessors of the present-day cheetah chose in the remote past to pursue gazelles as their preferred food, they initiated an evolutionary trajectory which would eventually result in the amazing ability of today's cheetahs to efficiently hunt down their prey of choice. In a similar manner the evolutionary predecessors of Darwin's Ichneumonidae or parasitic wasps had their larvae feed on the tissue of plants, mushrooms and fruits, rather than the living tissue of other organisms.[233] Somewhere along the evolutionary way, however, the ancestors of

---

[229] Alcock, *The Triumph of Sociobiology*, 209.

[230] Thornhill, Palmer, and Wilson, *A Natural History of Rape,* 143 ff.

[231] Bateson, "The Active Role of Behavior in Evolution", in: *EvolutionaryProcesses*, 192.

[232] See for example www.indianchild.com/cheetah.htm, http://www.ttgps.sa.edu.au/TTGPS/Student_Page/67w_web/Nicole_H/web/webpage.html, http://www.shrewsbury-ma.gov/schools/District/Technology/SummerEnrichment/Malavika/page1.html. For other examples of variation in carnivore diet see TM Caro and C. Stoner, "The potential for interspecific competition among African carnivores", Biological Conservation, 110:1, 2003, 67–75.

[233] J.B. Whitfield, "Phylogeny and Evolution of Host-Parasitoid Interactions in Hymenoptera", Annual Review of Entomology, Vol. 43, January 1998, 129–151; Miodrag Grbić and Michael R. Strand, "Shifts in the Life History of Parasitic wasps Correlate with Pronounced Alterations in Early Development", Proceedings of the National Academy of Sciences, Vol. 95:3, February 3,

the parasitic wasps decided that fresh meat was superior to fresh mushrooms, fruits, and vegetation.[234]

Patricia Williams makes clear in her chapter in this volume, that evolutionary evil only really surfaces with the emergence of sentient life. "As life grew more complex and evolved more capacities, the greater capacities brought more evil into the world."[235] I would like to also point out that evolutionary evils among sentient beings are proportional to the organism's capacity to choose different courses of action which in turn may affect the future of evolutionary suffering. The death of stars and the erosion of mountains are not instances in themselves of subjective pain and suffering and thus do not qualify as evolutionary evils. As a result the "free-creatures extension" of the free process defense need not be expanded beyond the point where sentient life emerges. In other words the metaphysical framework here need not be the panexperientialism of Process thought. Atoms and stars need not have the capacity for qualia in order for a viable free process defense to hold. On the other hand, where non-human animals are concerned, "it is important not to be a cognitive or a moral speciesist."[236]

In considering the possibilities for extending the free process defense, Christopher Southgate has argued that a necessary condition for such an extension would be to demonstrate that "something akin to human experience and subjectivity is present throughout the [animal] creation". If this can be established, he says, "then perhaps the free-will defense can be extended after all". In response I maintain there is sufficient empirical evidence to warrant the notion that "animals have minds and rich cognitive lives."[237] Darwin's understanding of nature revealed to us the amazing degree of evolutionary continuity between humans and other animals, and now we know that "behavioral, cognitive, and emotional variations among different species are differences in *degree* rather than differences in *kind*."[238] Over a century of research has substantiated Darwin's initial insight that human nature and nature are a continuum, and many biologists today even recognize "morality…as a naturally developing phenomenon that is not confined to human beings and does not

---

1998, 1097–1101; Fredrik Ronquist, and Johan Liljeblad, "Evolution of the Gall Wasp–Host Plant Association", Evolution, Vol. 55:12, 2503–2522.

[234] W. T. Wcislo, "Behavioral Environments and Evolutionary Change", Annual Review of Ecology and Systematics, Vol. 20, November, 1989, 137–169.

[235] Patricia Williams, "How Evil Entered the World: An Exploration Through Deep Time", in this volume.

[236] Marc Bekoff, "Social Play Behavior: Cooperation, Fairness, Trust, and the Evolution of Morality", Journal of Consciousness Studies, Vol. 8:2, 2001, 82.

[237] Southgate, "God and Evolutionary Evil", 812; Colin Allen and Marc Bekoff, *Species of Mind: The Philosophy and Biology of Cognitive Ethology* (Cambridge, MA: MIT Press, 1997). See also Marc Bekoff, Colin Allen, and Gordon Burghardt (ed.), *The Cognitive Animal: Empirical and Theoretical Perspectives on Animal Cognition* (Cambridge, MA: MIT Press, 2002).

[238] Marc Bekoff, "Social Play Behavior", 81.

require higher-level rational reflective processes."[239] With this in mind I would like to suggest that non-human animals in their activities and choices should be understood not as *amoral* but rather as *protomoral.* While humans, as fully moral beings, are maximally conscious and thus maximally culpable for their actions, non-human animals, according to their various kinds, are culpable only to the degree which their capacity for sentience allows. From its Latin origin *moralis, morality* is concerned with the proper inter-relationships of entities within a society. In addition to this horizontal aspect concerning relationships with each other, morality also contains a vertical dimension—how creatures exist in relation to their Creator. It is clear from Scripture that God's intention is for relationships in Creation's Kingdom to be peaceful and without bloodshed. Having given creation the gift of freedom, in Genesis 1:29–30 God prescribes the dietary limits necessary for a creation without carnage.

> And God said, "Behold, I have given you every plant yielding seed which is upon the face of the earth, and every tree with seed in its fruit; you shall have them for food. And to every beast of the earth, and to every flying creature of the air, and to everything that creeps on the earth, everything that has the breath of life, I have given every green plant for food."

The above passage reveals that the early Hebrews "were deeply convicted of the view that violence between humans and animals, and indeed between animal species themselves, was not God's original will for creation."[240] The temptation to eat that which has not been given by God for consumption, however, is primal, and both human and non-human animals discovered against God's intentions that other things are also "good for food". Both animals and humans are tempted "to suppose that [their] own good is *the good* sought by God in creation."[241] Remember that in Genesis it is the serpent, as the most worldly-wise representative of the non-human animals, who seduces humans with the idea of eating forbidden food. As the Genesis story unfolds we see that God holds "all flesh" accountable—at least to some degree—for the actions whereby it strays from God's primeval purposes for a peaceable creation. God judges both humans and animals for their bloodthirsty behavior.

> Now the earth was corrupt in God's sight, and the earth was filled with violence. And God saw the earth, and behold, it was corrupt; for all animals and humans had corrupted their way upon the earth. And God said to Noah, "I have determined to make an end to all humans and animals; for the earth is filled with violence through them."[242]

---

[239] Bruce Waller, "What Rationality Adds to Animal Morality", Biology and Philosophy, 12, 1997, 341.

[240] Andrew Linzey, *Animal Theology* (Chicago: University of Illinois Press, 1995) 126.

[241] Tracy, "Evolution, Divine Action, and the Problem of Evil", 520.

[242] Genesis 6:11–14, the Hebrew word RXb (Basar) refers to all living things besides plants, i. e., animals and humans.

In the Free-Creatures model, God is dynamically present "in, with, and un-der" creation, and is intimately involved in the lives and choices of non-hu-man animals. The Creator shows concern for and cares for all creatures (see Psalm 84:3; 104:27–28) and God beckons each living thing towards a harmo-nious existence with others, even while drawing them into their own indi-vidual fulfillments. The Lord who gives life "is present with every creature in the universe as its faithful companion, accompanying it with love, valuing it, bringing it into an interrelated world of creatures, holding it creatively in the dynamic life of the divine Communion."[243] Possessing various degrees of au-tonomy—though constrained somewhat by the behavioral choices and phylo-genetic contingencies handed down from previous generations—creatures are free to respond to God's will for their existence. Nevertheless, animals—and humans—often choose the good for themselves, rather than allowing their Creator to determine the good for them. Such expressions of self-interest, such as "killing for gastronomic pleasure" introduce discord into the harmo-ny of creation and generate a multitude of evolutionary evils.[244]

Because of these protomoral choices which cause much suffering and ev-olutionary evil, animals are in need of redemption and transformation. The first-fruits of their redemption is already present in the cross and resurrection of Christ as he reconciled *all things* in both heaven and earth to Himself, hav-ing made peace through his blood (Colossians 1:20). In this way the death and resurrection of Jesus is a "promise, not only for human beings, but for other living creatures as well."[245] Final redemption, and the ultimate completion and transformation of creation, however, cannot be accomplished by the contin-ued process of evolution alone. Though the Spirit of the Living God holds every creature in "redemptive love, and is in some way", even now "draw-ing each into an unforeseeable eschatological future in the divine life", the ultimate redemption and "new creation of all created things can be expected only from *the coming of Christ* in glory."[246] The *telos* or perfection of creation can only result from a radical *eschatological* act of intervention by God the Creator on behalf of a groaning and suffering creation. At that point "crea-tion itself also will be set free from its slavery to corruption into the glorious freedom of the children of God", "the glory of the LORD shall be revealed, and *all* living things shall see it together." (Romans 8:21 and Isaiah 40:5).

---

[243] Denis Edwards, "Every Sparrow that Falls to the Ground: The Cost of Evolution and the Christ-Event", unpublished paper, 11 f.

[244] See Andrew Linzey, *Animal Theology*, 125. Southgate describes the possibility of a similar position developed within the framework of Process Metaphysics, but ultimately rejects it on ac-count of its panexperientialism and apparent lack of scientific support. "God and Evolutionary Evil", 812. The "Free-Creatures Extension" avoids both of these dilemmas.

[245] Denis Edwards, "Every Sparrow that Falls to the Ground", 12.

[246] Jürgen Moltmann, *The Way of Jesus Christ: Christology in Messianic Dimensions* (Minne-apolis, MN: Fortress Press, 1993) 34.

Conclusion

In this chapter I have strived to overcome the marked anthropocentrism which has long dominated the theodicy discussion. I have acknowledged the historical reality of animal suffering and the acuteness of evolutionary evil, and we have made clear the necessity of such evils within a Neo-Darwinian framework. We have seen that the problem of evolutionary evil is especially pronounced within the gene-selectionist evolutionary scenario offered by Dawkins because there selfishness and the relentless struggle for existence are as basic as the basic units of life themselves—selfish replicators. Dawkins' theoretical biological premise has not gone unchallenged, however. From the discoveries of developmental biology and the last fifty years of molecular biology it is clear that the gene-centered view of biological reality offered by Dawkins, his successors, and his Neo-Darwinian forebears is no longer empirically warranted, and thus no longer an adequate account of the complex and mysterious evolutionary world in which we live. The selfish-genes view of biological life may now be recognized as conceptually unwarranted and as such it should no longer be permitted to orient the discourse on evolutionary theodicy.

In addition to this we have seen, contra Dawkins and Ruse's theodical appropriation of him, that God's hands were not tied with regard to evolutionary mechanisms capable of creating adaptively complex life. We have shown that other viable evolutionary mechanisms are available and that these alternative mechanisms—where natural selection is not the driving force—significantly shift the parameters of the evolutionary theodicy problem and offer a possible way forward for a viable theodicy of nature. These "alternatives to evolutionary evil" present an elegant view of life, and of the place of life in the cosmos. Several even suggest that life is not "unexpected, and orphaned in the spellbinding vastness of space" but indeed anticipated and written into the very mathematics of complex organic dynamics.[247] Removing the harsh overtones of contingency and happenstance from the evolutionary tale, these mechanisms—to varying degrees—eliminate the *structural necessity* of the most severe evolutionary evils and intimate that life is "truly at home in the universe."[248] Nevertheless, we have seen that even if these alternative evolutionary mechanisms were entirely efficacious in their construction of complex life we would still be left with the *fact* of particular evolutionary evils.

To address these particular instances of suffering and evil observed in nature I proposed the *Free Creatures Extension* to the free-process defense. This model assigns a theological interpretation to a large amount of recent research which suggests that animal behavior and choice not only play an active role

---

[247] Kauffman, *At Home in the Universe*, 98.
[248] Ibid., 20.

in an animal's own niche construction and evolution, but also play a considerable role in determining the types and degrees of evil in nature. Animals are active subjective participants in their own evolution, and their choices, though not as self-conscious or culpable as those of humans, are theologically significant and may even be called *protomoral*. As it stands, the world of human and non-human animals abounds with ample evidence of both evil and good, and in this way it seems to be a universe profoundly balanced on the edge of moral—and protomoral—decisions.[249] Such a balance is precisely that required if God's creatures are to freely respond to their creator in obedience, faith, and love. Evil may be the unfortunate result of some of these free decisions, and for now fear may exist as the creeping shadow of faith. The ultimate purpose of both evolutionary and moral evil is indeed still deeply shrouded in mystery. God's ways will always transcend those of humanity and nature, and for now we must content ourselves with seeing through a glass darkly.

---

[249] For an account of how cosmology points to this aspect of the universe, see Nancey Murphy and George Ellis, *On the Moral Nature of the Universe: Theology, Cosmology, and Ethics* (Minneapolis: Fortress Press, 1996), 206–210.

Evolution and The Suffering of Sentient Life

Theodicy After Darwin

John F. Haught

Among the countless features of life that now seem to find an adequate explanation in Darwinian biology is the fact of suffering.[1] Suffering, if you are a Darwinian, is simply an adaptation without which complex organisms could not survive and reproduce. Without the irritation of pain, certain kinds of organisms, including humans, could not respond to threatening circumstances and thus place themselves out of danger. Darwin himself said that "all sentient beings have been formed so as to enjoy, as a general rule, happiness", but pain or suffering is "well adapted to make a creature guard against any great or sudden evil."[2] If life's internal warning systems tend at times to be hyper-sensitive and excessive in the torment they permit, then this tragic augmentation is still consistent with a purely natural explanation of suffering.

If you are one of today's Darwinians you will more than likely account for the suffering of sentient life in terms of the striving of genes to get themselves passed off into future generations. Genes, over the course of time, have somehow discovered that they will not survive in very complex organisms unless they create for themselves "vehicles" that are able to realize when they are in danger. The genes that assembled various species of life eventually manufactured sensitive nervous systems that have served well the cause of gene-survival.

It is nothing short of remarkable that the life-process, however one explains it, has gradually woven more and more delicate nervous systems into organisms. But, at least for some sensitive scientists, the specter is as disturbing as it is remarkable. Consider, for example, Sir Charles Sherrington, who in his 1940 Gifford Lectures *Man On His Nature* gave us this poignant portrayal of how the lowly fluke-worm secures its existence at the expense of excessive suffering in higher organisms:

> There is a small worm (Redia) in our ponds. With its tongue-head it bores into the
> lung of the water-snail. There it turns into a bag and grows at the expense of the

---

[1] Although some writers do not attribute "suffering" to nonhuman forms of life, reserving for the latter only the term "pain", I consider the distinction arbitrary and unnecessarily anthropocentric and Cartesian, as the following reflections will try to make clear.

[2] Nora Barlow (ed.), *The Autobiography of Charles Darwin* (New York: Harcourt, 1958) 88f.

snail's blood. The cyst in the snail's lung is full of Redia. They bore their way out and wander about the body of the snail. They live on the body of the snail, on its less vital parts for so it lasts the longer; to kill it would cut their sojourn short before they could breed. They breed and reproduce. The young wander within the sick snail. After a time they bore their way out of the dying snail and make their way to the wet grass at the pond-edge. There amid the green leaves they encyst themselves and wait. A browsing sheep or ox comes cropping the moist grass. The cyst is eaten. The stomach of the sheep dissolves the cyst and sets free the fluke-worms within it. The worm is now within the body of its second prey. It swims from the stomach to the liver. There it sucks blood and grows, causing the disease called "sheeprot".

The worms then produce eggs that travel down the sheep's liver duct and finally exit into the wet pasture. "Thence as free larvae they reach the meadow-pond to look for another water snail. So the implacable cycle rebegins."

What does all of this mean? To Sherrington:

> it is a story of securing existence to a worm at cost of lives superior to it in the scale of life as humanly reckoned. Life's prize is given to the aggressive and inferior of life, destructive of other lives at the expense of suffering in them, and, sad as it may seem to us, suffering in proportion as they are lives high in life's scale. The example taken is a fair sample of almost countless many.[3]

Even if there is a fascinating ingenuity to such phenomena, it is not easy to attribute them to beneficent divine design. Darwin himself was led to reject the idea of divine design in specific forms of life after learning about such indecorous curiosities as ichneumon wasps laying their eggs inside living caterpillars so that their larvae will have fresh, rather than decaying, flesh upon which to nourish themselves. Those of us who take the idea of a good and powerful Creator seriously must wonder what could possibly be going on in these scenarios that we might account for theologically. What holy message can we wrest from the book of nature as we read about fluke worms and ichneumon wasps?

Here is the message that Richard Dawkins sees there: "So long as DNA is passed on, it does not matter who or what gets hurt in the process. It is better for the genes of Darwin's ichneumon wasp that the caterpillar should be alive, and therefore fresh, when it is eaten, no matter what the cost in suffering. Genes don't care about suffering, because they don't care about anything."[4] And if genes are so uncaring about suffering, then may we not conclude that the universe that sponsors evolution "has precisely the properties we should expect if there is, at bottom, no design, no purpose, no evil and no good, nothing but blind, pitiless indifference"?[5]

---

[3] Charles Sherrington, *Man on His Nature* (Cambridge: Cambridge University Press, 1951) 266.

[4] Richard Dawkins, *River Out of Eden* (New York: Basic Books, 1995), 131.

[5] Dawkins, *River Out of Eden*, 133.

For centuries, however, religions and theologies have been explaining suffering without the benefit of Darwinian expertise. Religions have appealed to people not only because their sacred stories seemed to account quite satisfactorily for the existence of suffering, but also because they gave hope of release from it. Religious salvation, though it means more than permanent release from suffering, means at least that much. Religions generally encourage us to hope that, in the end, all tears will be wiped away. Pain and death will be no more. But, now that evolutionary biology has graced us with an elegant "naturalistic" answer to the question of why suffering occurs in sentient life, what are we to do with all the convoluted but apparently healing perspectives of our religions? After Darwin can religious myths about the origin and end of suffering any longer be said to have either explanatory power or salvific efficacy? Now that evolutionary science can plausibly account for suffering as a purely natural adaptation, what possible meaning or truth could religious myths about the origin and end of suffering still claim to have?

Likewise, what standing could theodicy have after Darwin? Theodicy is the theoretical attempt to "justify" the existence of God in the face of evil and suffering. If God is all-good and all-powerful, then surely God would be both able and willing to prevent life's suffering. Yet such suffering exists, and, according to evolutionary accounts, much more abundantly than we ever used to think. Evolution, at least for many who have looked closely at it, has made the existence of God more questionable than ever.[6] Theodicy after Darwin would have to try to explain how the (undeserved) suffering of most of life could be compatible with the existence of an all-good and all-powerful God. Many people seriously doubt that it can succeed.

Today a good number of Darwinians consider both religion and theodicy to be cognitively vacuous. Nevertheless, they cannot help observing that religions and theodicies still persist.[7] So why do they persist? A typically Darwinian reply might be that the religious myths of suffering, along with the theodicies that defend them, also have a purely adaptive function.[8] Recently a few Darwinian psychologists have admitted that religious ideas are not necessarily adaptive *per se*, but that the cerebral modules upon which religious ideas are "parasitic" (such as the brain's Pleistocene hyper-active "predator

---

[6] For a fuller discussion see my book *God After Darwin* (Boulder, CO: Westview Press, 2000).

[7] See Robert Hinde, Why *Gods Persist: A Scientific Approach to Religions* (New York: Routledge, 1999); Walter Burkert, *Creation of the Sacred: Tracks of Biology in Early Religions;* Pascal Boyer, *Religion Explained: The Evolutionary Origins of Religious Thought* (New York: Basic Books, 2001).

[8] See, for example, E.O. Wilson, *Consilience: The Unity of Knowledge* (New York: Knopf, 1998); and Loyal Rue, *By the Grace of Guile: The Role of Deception in Natural History and Human Affairs* (New York: Oxford University Press, 1994), 82–107.

detection" system) are the primary evolutionary adaptations.[9] In almost all cases, however, the assumption of the Darwinian anthropologists is that religious myths and theodicies, lacking our modern scientific criteria of truth, may be dismissed as illusory. After all, why should we look upon them as bearers of truthful cognitive content if their existence can be explained far more simply in terms of survival value?[10] Hasn't Darwin permitted us, at long last, to comprehend the real truth about religions, namely, that they possess no truth, but only functionality? Today an increasingly vocal group of Darwinian naturalists, especially those influenced by E. O. Wilson and who hold to a materialist philosophical world view, are claiming not only that sentient life and suffering can be *fully* accounted for in Darwinian terms, but that human religious responses to suffering, including our most elaborate theodicies, can also be explained *ultimately* in evolutionary terms.[11]

In the following, therefore, I shall address this evolutionist naturalism by asking three interrelated questions: (1) Just how deep can Darwinism (or neo-Darwinism) take us in our attempts to understand the suffering of sentient life? (2) Can contemporary Darwinism, at least in principle, give us an adequate or "ultimate" explanation of religion and theodicy? And (3) what can theodicy possibly mean after Darwin?

Darwinism and the Suffering of Sentient Life

Even though science does not yet have a clear understanding of the origin of life itself, evolutionary biology claims at least to have a powerful explanation for the existence of *sentient* life. Apparently life gradually became sentient because the capacity to have feelings endowed complex organisms with a delicate informational apparatus. Informational adroitness gave complex forms of life a survival value that they could not have had if they did not feel anything at all.

But does the notion of survival value really get us to the bottom of what is involved in the naked fact of sentience as such, let alone suffering? Sentience, after all, entails *subjectivity*, that is, the existence of centers where feeling is registered and adaptive responses initiated. Sentience is an empty notion apart from subjectivity. The need for informational capacity alone, moreover, is not enough to account for sentient subjectivity.[12] As we know from physics and

---

[9] See the illuminating online article by Professors Scott Atran and Ara Norenzayan, "Religion's Evolutionary Landscape: Counterintuition, Commitment, Compassion, Communion", at: http://jeanNicod.ccsd.cnrs.fr/documents/disk0/00/00/02/56/index.html.

[10] Holmes Rolston III, calls this *non sequitur* the "if functional, therefore untrue fallacy". *Genes, Genesis and God: Values and Their Origins in Natural and Human History* (New York: Cambridge University Press, 1999) 347.

[11] See, for example, L. A. Kirkpatrick, "Toward an Evolutionary Psychology of Religion and Personality", Journal of Personality, 1999, 67, 921–952.

[12] The transmission of information alone does not require sentience. Negative feedback mechanisms abound in nature and human machines without sentience (and suffering) being present.

engineering, the mere transmission of information does not require a capacity to feel. Hence, our question comes down, in part at least, to that of whether science in general, and evolutionary theory in particular, can explain fully just why and how subjectivity *as such* entered into the universe. Whiteheadians of course would insist that the physical universe was *never* devoid of subjectivity, even prior to life. Apart from subjects, as A. N. Whitehead insists, there is "bare nothingness."[13] But let us, at least for now, take subjectivity here to mean—in a more conventional sense—the capacity of sentient organisms to feel and respond. Darwinism may help us understand the gradual *intensification* of sentience as a consequence of the gradual complexification of nervous tissue over the course of time. But can it give us a fully satisfying account of the existence of subjectivity as such?[14]

In addition to possessing subjectivity, moreover, sentient forms of life also have the capacity to *strive*, and therefore to achieve or fail. We humans can identify living beings and distinguish them from inanimate ones only because, as Michael Polanyi rightly notes, we personally intuit in them a striving and struggling, as well as a capacity to suffer, at least to some degree, the way we do ourselves. Only sentient *subjects* can strive, achieve, fail and suffer.[15] Striving is a quality that we do not attribute to inanimate things like rocks, liquids or chemical reactions. We do not speak except poetically of a river, mountain or thunderstorm *straining* to accomplish some goal, whereas we do speak quite literally of sentient animals *grubbing* for food or *trying* to avoid predators, and therefore of their *succeeding* or *failing* in such exertions. Striving is no less fundamental to sentient living beings than is subjectivity. Furthermore, sentience itself already entails an exploratory striving, an active reaching out to gather in the world. Without this inner dynamic of striving we may ask whether there would ever have been either sentience or suffering.

Because of its capacity for striving, therefore, sentient life—and perhaps to some degree all of life—conforms to what Michael Polanyi calls the "logic of achievement."[16] Only a subjective kind of being would be able to strive, and only a striving being would have the capacity to succeed or fail—or to suffer. Moreover, it is only because we humans, including scientists, are centered (personal) striving beings, able to achieve and fail in our own endeavors, that we can recognize certain other beings and species as also being instances of aliveness. It is especially our own experience of subjective striving that allows

---

[13] Alfred North Whitehead, *Process and Reality,* Corrected Edition, edited by David Ray Griffin and Donald W. Sherburne (New York: The Free Press, 1968) 254: "[A]part from the experiences of subjects there is nothing, nothing, nothing, bare nothingness".

[14] We could also ask whether the neo-Darwinian notion of adaptation has *fully* explained why life has had a tendency to *complexify* at all, especially since simple forms of life, like bacteria, have proven to be quite adaptive without being as complex as sentient life.

[15] Michael Polanyi, *Personal Knowledge* (New York: Harper Torchbooks) 327 ff.

[16] Ibid.

us to distinguish the rich realm of life from its inanimate background, and to establish the field of biology as distinct from those of chemistry or physics.[17] Science as such does not deal with subjectivity, but only with what can be objectified; and so, the elements of subjectivity and striving that accompany sentient life and are able to register suffering, remain, at least formally, outside the range of natural science.

Nevertheless, Darwinians apparently *presuppose* the facts of subjectivity and striving as essential categories in the evolutionary understanding of life.[18] Since only striving, sentient subjects are capable of suffering at all, in order to account *fully* for the fact of suffering, Darwinism would first have had to account fully for the facts of subjectivity and striving. Instead, however, Darwinian explanation simply takes both of these for granted. It is not its business formally to ground or explain their existence. And yet, try as they might to exorcize subjectivity from their models of nature, Darwinians cannot prevent the tabooed dimension of striving subjectivity from popping back up in one way or another as a foundational, presupposed, and hence unilluminated, category in their explanatory schemes. In some highly influential contemporary versions of Darwinism, for example, the gene itself is pictured as a centered subject, *striving* to get into the next generation. In *The Red Queen* science writer Matt Ridley reveals, perhaps unwittingly, just how difficult it is for the new gene-centered evolutionary thinking to explain life without tacitly appealing to the logic of achievement in which striving subjects (rather than passive objects) are the primary actors. He points out that:

> [...] in the last few years the revolution begun by [George] Williams, [William] Hamilton, and others has caused more and more biologists to think of genes as analogous to *active and cunning individuals*. Not that genes are conscious or driven by future goals—no serious biologist believes that—but the extraordinary purely logical fact is that evolution works by natural selection, and natural selection means the enhanced survival of genes *that enhance their own survival*. Therefore, a gene is by definition the descendant of a gene that was *good at getting into future generations*. A gene that *does things* that enhance its own survival may be said, *teleologically*, to be doing them because they enhance its survival. *Cooperating* to build a body is as effective a *survival strategy* for genes as cooperating to run a town is a successful social strategy for human beings.[19]

---

[17] Ibid.

[18] So disturbing is this fact to some scientists and eliminative materialists that, astoundingly, they even deny that subjectivity has any real existence at all. See, for example, Paul Churchland, *The Engine of Reason, The Seat of the Soul* (Cambridge, MA: Bradford Books, 1995) and Daniel Dennett, *Consciousness Explained* (New York: Little, Brown, 1991). For a critical discussion Alan Wallace, *The Taboo of Subjectivity: Toward a New Science of Consciousness* (New York: Oxford University Press, 2000).

[19] Matt Ridley, *The Red Queen: Sex and the Evolution of Human Nature* (New York: Penguin Books, 1993), 92f. [Emphasis added.]

A generation ago, as Ridley realizes, biologists avoided such personalizing language when speaking about genes, but today their discourse is loaded with terms that pertain to the logic of achievement. In the above quote, for instance, I have italicized those terms and phrases that attribute to genes an intentionality and purposiveness that can make sense only where there is centered (subjective) striving, open to success and failure. Genes are pictured here as entities able to "cooperate" and thus realize their main objective, which is "survival". "A gene has only one criterion by which posterity judges it: whether it becomes an ancestor of other genes. To a large extent it must *achieve* that", Ridley continues, "at the expense of other genes."[20] Genes, he says, devise *strategies* to avoid their demise at the hand of parasites.[21] Some genes (or arrays of genes) succeed and others fail in this endeavor.

In a similar way, evolutionary psychologists now write as though in the remote past our ancestors' genes deliberately devised game plans to build into human organisms linguistic, ethical and even religious instincts that would help the genes *succeed* in satisfying their inherent aim toward immortality. Stephen Pinker, for example, claims that language acquisition is "an *attempt* by the genome" to get our culture-acquiring apparatus on-line.[22] Notice once again the motif of striving. Other Darwinians view morality as a concoction of human genes that make humans cooperate with one another so that the genes may attain a figurative sort of immortality.[23] And Pascal Boyer attributes our puzzling tendency to believe in God or gods ultimately to Pleistocene genetic strategies that fashioned brains capable of predator-detection, a propensity that still inclines us to look for unseen agents such as deities.[24]

But if genes can strive or "strategize" in order to perpetuate themselves, then mindless segments of DNA all of a sudden turn out in the new biology to be operating in accordance with the logic of achievement. They are treated as sensitive striving subjects. But since natural science does not deal formally with subjectivity or intentional striving, one can only conclude that our evolutionists have strayed beyond the accepted boundaries of science. What is even more fascinating is that in the new biology subjective striving is subtracted from human and other sentient organisms, and the latter are now understood as passive mechanisms or "vehicles" governed by a more veiled kind

---

[20] Ibid., 94. [Emphasis added.]
[21] Ibid., passim.
[22] Stephen Pinker, *The Blank Slate: The Modern Denial of Human Nature* (New York: Viking, 2002) 63. [Emphasis added.]
[23] Michael Ruse and Edward O. Wilson, "The Evolution of Ethics", in: James Huchingson (ed.), *Religion and the Natural Sciences* (New York: Harcourt Brace Jovanovich, 1993) 308–311.
[24] Pascal Boyer, *Religion Explained: The Evolutionary Origins of Religious Thought* (New York: Basic Books, 2001) 145.

of striving, that of genes.[25] The irony here is that subjectivity has not been destroyed, but merely transplanted from one location to another. Subjectivity has disappeared from organic centers of feeling and initiative, but it now shows up in the domain of DNA.

My point here is simply that even the most sweeping brand of ultra-Darwinism available today *presupposes* rather than truly explaining the slippery and irreducible reality of sentient, striving subjectivity in the universe. Hence it is also unable to account in an absolutely foundational way for the *feeling* or *experience* of suffering. Even after Darwin there is still plenty of room, I believe, for theology to add even deeper levels of understanding to the Darwinian explanation of the great mystery of suffering.

Darwinism and Religion

Darwinism, of course, can bring intelligibility to suffering in terms of the notion of evolutionary adaptation, but it cannot account either for the bald fact of subjectivity in the universe or for the striving that underlies living, centered subjectivity in such a way that they are able to experience the frustration of suffering. Instead of *explaining* the subjectivity and purposive striving that make suffering possible, Darwinism simply presupposes them. In fact, subjectivity and striving, both formally ignored by scientific method itself, show up as foundational notions either at the periphery of Darwinian discourse or, as in the case of genes-eye Darwinism, at its very center.

The displacement of scientifically tabooed subjectivity onto the domain of genes may seem innocent enough until it becomes clear that, in order to provide a purely naturalist account of religion, some Darwinians apparently consider it necessary to divest religion itself of the aspect of striving that is essential also to that peculiarly human venture. Whatever else religions may be, after all, they are instances of *life* striving to achieve something, not least the surmounting of suffering. Social scientists would never have been able to identify religious activity as markedly "religious" without a tacit recognition that religions manifest themselves to us as intensely vivid instances of the same logic of achievement that frames the existence of all sentient beings. Religious people struggle, journey, hope and aspire in many diverse ways to overcome what John Bowker calls the "compound of limitations" that perpetually ob-

---

[25] See Richard Dawkins, *The Selfish Gene* (New York: Oxford University Press, 1989) and *The Extended Phenotype: The Long Reach of the Gene* (New York: Oxford University Press, 1999). Dawkins occasionally qualifies his anthropomorphism with statements such as: "Neither individuals nor genes really strive to maximize anything. Or rather, individuals may strive for something, but it will be a morsel of food, an attractive female, or a desirable territory, not inclusive fitness". But then he adds: "To the extent that it is useful for us to think of individuals working as if to maximize fitness, we may, with precisely the same licence, think of genes as if they were striving to maximize their survival". (*The Extended Phenotype,* 189).

structs the continuation of human life. Religious symbols, rites, teachings, ethical activity and institutions are all consequences of life—intelligent life, in this case—endeavoring, and therefore risking failure, in quest of the extension of human life beyond the limits of suffering, death, fate, guilt and the threat of meaninglessness.[26]

Its quality of striving, therefore, places religion in a line of inheritance that stretches across the epochs of evolution, all the way back even to the earliest instances of sentient life. The striving of intelligent living persons and groups to carve out religious pathways through the most intransigent blockades, especially suffering and death, is continuous with the striving characteristic of all sentient life. As Bowker puts it, religious endeavor is a kind of "route-finding."[27] In diverse ways religious persons *aim* toward an ultimate liberation and fulfillment. Although after Darwin one may be tempted to view religions as mere adaptations, the fact remains that religions at root consist of living, sentient *subjects* engaging in the most serious and intense kind of centered striving imaginable.[28] And, to repeat my point, striving—since it arises from the irreducibly mysterious realm of subjectivity—is not something that science, including Darwinian biology, can ever fully excavate. Hence we may confidently conclude that Darwinism has not, and logically cannot, fathom the full depth of suffering or religion either.

Further, the debunking Darwinians end up not eliminating, but only relocating, the reality of subjective striving, projecting it (fictitiously, they would be compelled by their own objectivism to confess) onto the impersonal domain of DNA. Although they are *striving* to avoid the embarrassing use of anthropomorphic projections characteristic of religious naivete, gene-centered Darwinians themselves typically project fictitious subjectivity onto mindless chemical processes. They attribute to insentient strands of DNA the very same sentient, striving subjectivity that they first deleted from *religious persons* in order to account for religion "objectively" or "naturalistically."[29]

---

[26] John Bowker, *Is Anybody Out There?* (Westminster, MD: Christian Classics, Inc., 1988), 9–18; 112–143.

[27] Bowker, 9–18; 112–143.

[28] We need not enter here into the theological question of whether by its own efforts our religious striving can ever be successful. In fact, religious striving by itself risks the greatest of failures, and according to some interpreters of religion it is in moments of failure that the religious personality is finally in a position to surrender to "grace".

[29] In *subjectifying* our genes the scientists have put themselves in the ironic situation where *objective* knowledge of both genes and religion is inaccessible after all. After all, if genes are centered *subjects*, capable of striving, then the inevitably objectifying method of science cannot come near to grasping their *essential* reality. For a fuller discussion see my book *Deeper Than Darwin* (Boulder, CO: Westview Press, 2003).

Theodicy after Darwin

The issue I have been exploring so far is that of whether the Darwinian notion of adaptation or reproductive success alone can get us to the ultimate depths of what suffering is all about. I have argued that sentient life entails the existence of subjects able to strive. Striving beings, moreover, may sometimes fail to achieve their objectives and thus experience frustration in a way that can be registered only by living, striving subjects, nonhuman as well as human.[30] I have contended that since Darwinism cannot tell us exactly what subjectivity and striving are really all about, let alone why subjective, striving centers ever came into the cosmos at all,[31] it cannot give us a truly *fundamental* explanation of suffering. Suffering at one level may be adaptive in an evolutionary sense, but the sense of failure or frustration and the specific affective content involved in suffering are no more reducible to adaptation than the words on this page are reducible to ink and paper. Second, I have proposed that the Darwinian interpretation of religious responses to suffering, as just one more instance of evolutionary adaptation, also fails to tell us what religion, at bottom, is really all about either.

The third issue I wish to probe (all too briefly here) is the status of theodicy after Darwin. The term theodicy, as I mentioned above, formally means the attempt to justify God's existence given the fact of evil, a notion that includes suffering. In the process of trying to "justify" rationally the existence of a powerful and benevolent God who permits suffering, theodicies typically also offer general proposals as to how and why the evil of suffering entered into the world in the first place, as well as how it can be conquered. Today many thoughtful people have abandoned theodicy as arrogant and futile, especially in light of life's innocent suffering. And yet the whole laborious enterprise of theodicy, regardless of its plausibility, is at the very least another instance of living beings striving (in often elaborately theoretical ways) to get beyond the limits that suffering and evil impose upon life. Theodicy, at root, is a thoroughly religious kind of striving, however unsuccessful it may turn out to be as far as conceptual rigor is concerned. This point is often overlooked by those who criticize theodicy as useless and even evil.[32]

Nevertheless, it seems to me that theodicy cannot go on making the same arguments after Darwin as it did prior to the discovery of evolution. In the first place, the millions of years of life's suffering prior to human emergence in evolution demand that theodicy become less anthropocentric than ever before: it must now turn its attention to the tragic, innocent suffering of all

---

[30] The Latin for suffering is *passio*, from which we get the words "passion" and "passivity".

[31] Negative feedback can occur in machines, as I noted earlier, without having to be registered in a subjective center of experience.

[32] See, for example, Terrence Tilley, *The Evils of Theodicy* (Washington, DC: Georgetown University Press, 1991).

the non-human forms of life that preceded and prepared for our own recent emergence in evolution. And in the second place, theodicy henceforth needs to take into account the evolutionary fact that the universe is a still unfinished creation, a status that makes all the difference in the world as far as the interpretation of evil and suffering in the world is concerned.

As theodicy emerged in the biblical context, it generally focused on how to justify God's existence in the face of *human* suffering. Nonhuman suffering has been virtually ignored, even by the most sophisticated theodicies.[33] Theodicy in the classical sense (unlike Buddhist religious thought, for example) has concentrated almost exclusively on human (rather than nonhuman) suffering, and it has generally understood this suffering to be the consequence of sin and guilt.[34] In order to safeguard the ideas of divine power and goodness, theodicy has virtually denied that innocent suffering could ever exist at all, for if it did, God would have to be either powerless or unjust.[35] Hence nonhuman animals, as has often been thought or implied, do not *really* suffer, at least in any significant way. And even if they do, this too must have something to do with the impact of human guilt. In any case, the existence of suffering has been understood by classical theodicies to be *deserved* in one way or another. To preserve the idea of divine justice our theodicies, generally speaking, have assumed that suffering simply cannot be innocent—except in the case of Christ's suffering and death.

The belief that suffering is essentially punishment or penalty may be called the "expiatory vision". In spite of protests by the book of Job and other innocents that suffering is often unjustified, the theme that suffering is essentially punishment for guilt has persisted into our own times. Here I wish to distinguish between the doctrine of atonement and the archaic demand for expiation, even though some theologians fail to do so. Etymylogically the term "at-one-ment" has the connotation of reconciliation, and as such it does not have to entail substitutionary satisfaction in the sense of God's demanding suffering proportionate to guilt.

Nevertheless, the punitive sense of expiation unfortunately still deeply penetrates our psychic and social dynamics—even where its originally religious setting has been renounced. We feel the weight of the expiatory view of suffering, for example, whenever we assume that a price must be paid for any good fortune that comes our way. The idea that a price in punishment or misfortune must be paid to satisfy divine justice has even shaped one of the

---

[33] A very recent example of a theodicy that ignores nonhuman suffering is John Thiel's otherwise insightful book *God, Evil, and Innocent Suffering: A Theological Reflection* (New York: Crossroad, 2002).

[34] Thiel's discussion of theodicy scarcely even mentions evolution, an oversight still shared by most Christian theologians.

[35] Thiel, 1–31.

dominant interpretations of soteriology in Christianity, that of Christ's substitutionary satisfaction for the dishonoring of God's glory by human sin.[36]

The expiatory understanding of suffering had for ages prior to Christianity
wormed its way into myths about the origin of evil, many of which tell about
the spoiling of an original cosmic perfection by angelic, human or godly acts
of rebellion. In the biblical world the Adamic myth, as Paul Ricoeur names
it, expresses the conjecture that it is mostly due to human fault that we have
been sentenced to a life of struggle and suffering.[37] And it is also because of
the influence of expiatory interpretations of suffering that those persons and
communities who may tacitly suspect that they are not themselves responsible for suffering, often look around for a culprit or culprits upon whom to
cast blame.[38] It has thereby at times supported the human habit of scapegoating violence and victimization that has left so wide a trail of misery and death
in human history.[39] The ethical instincts of large portions of humanity still
abide by the assumption that a price in suffering must be paid for the befoul-
ing of an original purity of being. This view of things has only exacerbated the
suffering of human life and, indirectly, much nonhuman life as well.

In 1933 Teilhard de Chardin wrote:

> In spite of the subtle distinctions of the theologians, it is a matter *of fact* that Chris-
> tianity has developed under the over-riding impression that all the evil round us was
> born from an initial transgression. So far as dogma is concerned we are still living in
> the atmosphere of a universe in which what matters most is reparation and expia-
> tion. The vital problem, both for Christ and us, is to get rid of a stain. This accounts
> for the importance, at least in theory, of the idea of sacrifice, and for the interpreta-
> tion almost exclusively in terms of purification. It explains, too, the pre-eminence in
> Christology of the idea of redemption and the shedding of blood.[40]

In order to dramatize the rupture imagined to have been caused by an hy-
pothesized primordial offense, the expiatory vision must first emphasize the
pristine perfection of God's original creation. Accounts of how suffering
came into existence through primordial acts of human willfulness or rebellion
are placed in a setting that, by way of contrast, underscores the magnitude of
the supposed original fault. Myths of origins provide this contrast by posit-
ing a state of pre-existing paradisal perfection that preceded the original fault.
Without such a setting of the stage there could be no truly dramatic narrative
of how suffering came about and why we should be so upset about it. Nor
would there be any great need for expiation, or for scapegoating, since noth-

---

[36] Ibid., 150–156.

[37] Paul Ricoeur, *The Symbolism of Evil,* Trans Emerson Buchanan (Boston: Beacon Press,
1967).

[38] Pierre Teilhard de Chardin, *Christianity and Evolution,* trans. René Hague (New York: Harcourt Brace & Co., 1969) 81.

[39] Ibid.

[40] Ibid.

ing significant would have been lost. After all, it is only a sense of the *enormity* of what has been forfeited that allows remorse to swell, resentment to fester, and vengefulness to be unleashed. If the original breach had been one of only minor consequence, the felt loss would not be so momentous, and the need to look for culprits and victims would be proportionately abated. But myths that paint vivid pictures of original cosmic perfection render the sense of loss too earth-shattering to be ignored.

Thus the expiatory vision fastens its teeth most zealously into those myths that solemnize a supposed primordial paradise. Or is it perhaps just as accurate to say instead that the expiatory vision is the quiet social and psychic infrastructure that gives rise to projections of perfection into a paradisal past in the first place? In any case what would be the consequences for theodicy if, as evolutionary science implies, there never was an originating state of complete cosmic perfection? What would happen to the expiatory vision, in other words, if we really began to take seriously the evolutionary understanding of life and the universe. That is, what if we understood the cosmos as having relatively modest beginnings and then evolving over time only gradually toward fuller modes of being, rather than straying degenerately from a primordial plenitude? By disallowing a cosmic state of initial completeness, could not evolution in principle contribute to the dismantling of theodicies built around the theme of punitive expiation? This would in no way mean that there is no longer any room for a sense of sin, of genuine remorse for human misdeeds, or of the need for "at-one-ment" in the literal sense of "reconciliation" made possible by our human solidarity with the crucified and risen Christ. But what it could mean is that at least the traditional *cosmological* underpinnings of the expiatory vision would be challenged. At any rate, it seems to me that theodicy—if it is to survive at all after Darwin and contemporary cosmology—must take advantage of the new conceptual and cultural setting in which the universe, rather than having been completed *ab initio,* is pictured as still emerging into being.

Of course, it would be an act of violence on the part of a theology of evolution to wrest from human hearts their native tendency to conjure up an idealized state of perfection. Human vitality requires the pursuit of such an ideal. However, we need not picture the perfection to which our hearts aspire as though it were something that once was and has now been lost or besmirched. It will in no way detract from our idealism or the doctrine of atonement to picture perfection as a state that has never yet been actualized but that we may hope will come into being in the future.[41] One of the great implications of evolution for theodicy is that it allows for just such a transpositioning of the ideal of perfection.

---

[41] Not just our own future, but also that of God and the entire universe. Here too we have to be careful not to over-idealize our own visions of the future, the forced implementation of which can wreak untold violence.

It seems to me that the biblical accounts of creation and God's promises are struggling to bring about just such a radical redirecting of the human longing for perfection. The Biblical narratives of a promising God, a God who opens up a new future whenever dead ends appear, encourage us to move beyond our nostalgic obsession with a lost Eden, and into an open history that relocates the essential domain of perfection into the unimaginable "up-ahead", in the direction of a creation yet to come. Atonement does not mean simply paying the price for sin, but the bringing of an unfinished creation to an unprecedented fulfillment. The Bible's eschatological intonation animates hope for a radically new future, even as it deflects our nostalgic pining for a paradisal past. In other words, evolution suggests that the doctrine of redemption must converge increasingly with that of creation.[42]

A religious consciousness dominated by the longing for a lost Atlantis can easily become the breeding ground for resentment and expiatory violence. Hope for an ideal that has not yet been fulfilled, on the other hand, undercuts resentment and the impulse for revenge. Instead of looking for culprits and scapegoats, or indulging in interminable acts of expiation, hope seeks fellow travelers into the uncertain future. By our participating in a "great hope held in common"[43] the roots of violence are numbed, and human energy cooperatively directed toward the horizon of a new creation. The age of expiation, as the Letter to the Hebrews implies, is now completely a thing of the past.[44]

In my view, therefore, one of the implications of evolution for theodicy is that it curtails the longing to restore any imagined primal perfection, since there never could have been such a state of things in the history of creation. There never has been any point in past cosmic history when the universe was pristinely perfect. Accordingly, even though the notions of "Original Sin" and "Fall" still rightly remind us of the radicality of our need for redemption, we need not take this to mean a literal ancestral transition from a past cosmic paradise into the state of imperfection. Imperfection would have been there from the start, as the shadow side of an unfinished universe.[45] Hence, it would follow from this that there can be no cosmological substructure for expiatory self-punishment, resentment and victimization, since no loss of primordial perfection has ever occurred that could justify our resentment at such an imagined loss. There is no reason either to indulge in endless acts of expiation or to look for culprits whom we could justifiably blame for the miseries of our condition. Scapegoating violence would make no sense in a universe whose

[42] Following St. Paul, evolution allows us to interpet redemption and atonement as "new creation".

[43] Pierre Teilhard de Chardin, *The Future of Man*, trans. Norman Denny (New York: Harper Colophon Books, 1964) 83.

[44] Gerd Theissen, *The Open Door*, trans. by John Bowden (Minneapolis: Fortress Press, 1991) 161–167.

[45] Teilhard, *Christianity and Evolution*, 40.

essential or ideal status has yet to be brought about in the promised new creation in Christ.

Unfortunately, however, the story of human religiosity has been more one of nostalgia for an imagined past perfection than the eschatological anticipation of new creation. Even in religions descended from the biblical environment a longing to restore or recover some idyllic past has often suppressed the spirit of Abrahamic adventure into the unknown future opened up by a God of promise. To repeat my question, therefore, what would be the implications of situating the longed for realm of perfection in the not-yet-future instead of in a remote cosmic *Urzeit*, or in a Platonic realm of present perfection hovering eternally above the flow of time? What if perfection is not-yet because the world is in some sense not-yet?

I believe that one of the consequences of a serious encounter between theodicy and evolutionary science would be to relativize and perhaps even demolish, at least in principle, what I have been calling the expiatory interpretation of suffering. Moreover, a vivid awareness of evolution would no longer permit our theodicies to ignore the fact that a great portion of life's suffering has been tragic and innocent, having nothing at all to do with guilt. Sentient forms of life have been subjects of striving and failure for many millions of years prior to human emergence. After Darwin a sense of our human solidarity with the suffering of all sentient life, therefore, can no longer permit our interpreting suffering, even our own suffering, as primarily punishment. Rather, suffering is essentially the tragic consequence of the fact that life, including our own, is still emerging in an unfinished universe. Therefore, going far deeper than the Darwinian understanding of suffering in terms of adaptation, theology may emphasize that the meaning of suffering is—at the very least—that of turning the face of life, especially in its recent mode of human sensitivity and striving, irreversibly toward a new future, one in which pain will be healed and all tears wiped away.

Consequently, the task of theodicy henceforth should not be to fit the fact of suffering onto the grid of guilt and punishment. Instead, if it hopes to get closer to the truly absorbing issue, it might ask why an all-good and all-powerful God would create an *unfinished, imperfect, evolutionary* universe in the first place rather than one that is complete and perfect from the beginning. Could it be that a truly good and deeply powerful God has no choice? This, however, is material for another essay.

How Evil Entered the World

An Exploration Through Deep Time

Patricia A. Williams

Traditional theism believes God exists and is omniscient, omnipotent, omnibenevolent, and creator of the world. The logical conclusion to these beliefs is that the world ought to be entirely good; it should contain no evil. Yet most people think the world does contain evil, for they see around them things commonly considered evil: death and physical and mental suffering and all their causes, from natural disasters to bad character.

One way to resolve this disagreement between logic and experience is to change the concept of God. Perhaps God is not good, or did not foresee the advent of evil, or does not have the power to stop it. However, traditional theism has been unwilling to weaken its concept of God and, so, has tried other ways to solve the problem. These attempts are known as *theodicy*. This essay is an attempt at theodicy. For simplification, it is limited to answering the question of how pain and death came into the world. The existence of pain and death are central to the problem of evil. The other things usually considered evil—vicious character, diseases, and natural disasters—are normally deemed evil because they cause pain and death.

The two best classical answers to the problem of evil assume the world is unchanging and God created everything almost concurrently. Augustine's answer depends on the Genesis creation stories as he interpreted them and rests on Adam and Eve's having had free will. Although scientifically educated people reject the Adam and Eve story as history, Augustine's basic insight that evil is here because people have free will is still interesting and useful. It accounts for some evils. However, it neglects the pain and death of most other organisms and is unable to account for the apparently huge amount of evil in the world.

Irenaeus's answer, recently popularized by John Hick and Richard Swinburne,[1] is that evil is necessary for soul making, that is, as we encounter evil, we learn charity, compassion, cooperation, courage, self-control, and forgiveness. Because we are better people with such traits than without them, evil ultimately makes the world a better place than it would be without evil.

---

[1] John Hick, *Evil and the God of Love* (New York: Harper and Row, 1978) and Richard Swinburne, *The Existence of God* (Oxford: Clarendon Press, 1979).

This explanation, too, is interesting and useful, but it also neglects most animal pain and death and does not account for evils that destroy the soul.

My answer is different. It looks through deep time and sees an evolving universe. It says that good and evil are inextricably intertwined. As good capacities enter the world, evil capacities enter with them. My outlook is hopeful, however: for every several goods that enter the world, only a small amount of evil enters, so that the good in the world far outweighs the evil. I begin my exploration of this process at the beginning of deep time, with the development of the cosmos.[2]

The Development of the Cosmos

Science says the cosmos began about 13.7 billion years ago in a hot, violent event, the big bang. Right after the big bang, chaotic radiation filled the universe. Then, as the cosmos expanded and cooled, the first elements formed, hydrogen and helium. They are the simplest elements in the universe and are still the most prevalent. Hydrogen, a component of organic molecules, is necessary for life. One sign of the unity of the universe is that the very first atoms created in it sustain our lives today.

As the first elements formed, the first laws manifested themselves as the strong and weak nuclear forces binding atoms together. Atoms have mass and, so, another law became manifest at the same time: gravity. Gravity slowly counteracted the expansion begun by the big bang and pulled the elements together. Eventually the elements coalesced, creating stars and galaxies. As elements in the stars fused and the stars exploded, elements that are more complex formed. Stars are creative furnaces, making carbon, nitrogen, oxygen, magnesium, iron—almost a hundred elements.

After bursting stars spewed the heavier elements across galaxies, gravity gathered the elements together again, solar systems formed, and our planet came into existence. Thus, from a plain and simple beginning, after 10 billion years or so, the cosmos filled with complexity, structure, and variety—the elements, planets, moons, myriad types of stars, numerous kinds of galaxies, and even super-galaxies. There is no sign that God intervened externally in this development.[3] The laws and the nature of matter were sufficient to bring order out of chaos. Apparently, God created a cosmos that could develop autonomously. Is the cosmos as it developed until this time good or evil?

---

[2] The best general reference is still Joseph Silk, *The Big Bang* (New York: Freeman, 1989). The ideas expressed here about cosmic development were influenced by Lee Smolin, *The Life of the Cosmos* (New York: Oxford University Press, 1997). Smolin is an atheist.

[3] If there were any sign that God intervened externally in cosmic development, then science would cease at that point, for science seeks to explain material events by material causes without reference to spirits, whether gods or demons.

Cosmic Good Precedes Cosmic Evil

If existence is better than non-existence, as most philosophers and, indeed, most ordinary people suppose, the cosmos is good, just by existing.[4] Moreover, it is creative, and we usually consider creativity good. However, its creativity works through destruction, by recycling. Hydrogen and helium fuse into other elements and cease to exist as hydrogen and helium. Stars explode and die while creating more elements. These, in their turn, coalesce into different types of stars, moons, and planets, all of which will eventually be destroyed. However, neither physical nor mental suffering occurs, for in this lifeless cosmos nothing exists that is sentient—nothing that is capable of suffering—so by the classic definition of evil, this cosmos contains no evil. Therefore, evil has not appeared in 10 billion years of cosmic activity, but good arrived at the beginning of cosmic existence and continued to increase as the universe changed. So far, the cosmos is good, without any admixture of evil.

Because this is an essay on theodicy, one of its assumptions is that God created the cosmos. The exploration of God's creation thus far suggests that it develops from simple to complex. It began very simply, with chaotic radiation. After 10 billion years of creative development, however, the cosmos became extremely complicated, filled with variety and structure. Apparently, God wants a universe that increasingly creates complexity, variety, and structure. God's method of creation seems to be law-like recycling that is autonomous from God's external intervention. As life evolves, this development continues through a similar method of recycling, and a new law manifests itself: natural selection.

Because we know life only on our own planet, the investigation of the evolution of life is necessarily limited. I have also exercised the philosophers' prerogative and greatly simplified the story while presenting it in an order that is more logical than historical, although it has historical verisimilitude. The following five sections explore the evolution of life before the advent of primates, seeking to identify the moment when evil entered the world.

The Evolution of Life

Perhaps as early as 3.8 billion years ago, life appeared on Earth. For another two billion years or so, it stayed very simple, remaining single-celled. Many of these cells moved about. In those that survived to replicate, approach-avoidance mechanisms evolved, enabling them to find food and flee danger. The approach-avoidance mechanisms were simple chemical systems that I will call

---

[4] Exactly where lines are drawn—whether the universe is good just by existing or how valuable the lives of non-human animals are—is fascinating to discuss, but does not change the overall argument, which rests on developing capacities and the good and evil they bring to the world.

mechanical. The reason to call them mechanical is to emphasize that these simple creatures were not sentient. They knew neither pain nor pleasure.

This is the stance of science. Science holds that attributes such as the feeling of pain must have a material substrate. Thus, science says that creatures without eyes cannot see; those without ears cannot hear; those lacking echolocation devices cannot echolocate. It follows scientifically that organisms lacking nervous systems and pain receptors cannot feel pain or pleasure. And although some of these organisms ate others, this was a mechanical process, too. No sentience is involved. Advocates of panpsychism disagree; they believe that even non-living entities and living ones lacking neurological equipment may be sentient. However, as outlined briefly above, the scientific evidence is against this viewpoint. Because this chapter seeks to follow science, it will ignore panpsychism.

Whether these simple organisms died is an interesting question. They reproduced by division and, in that sense, they were immortal. However, no doubt billions of interesting genetic combinations were destroyed and billions mutated, for a new law had become manifest, the law of natural selection, which requires that more organisms are produced than survive to propagate. Creativity through recycling assumed a new form. The elimination of certain gene combinations and the retention of others enabled change to continue. If life is better than non-life, of course, the elimination of living organisms was a kind of evil, but at the very same time it also was a good, for the organisms' elimination provided nutrients for others and allowed the creativity of natural selection to continue. Their elimination maintained the universal recycling process. Moreover, while some view this process as wasteful, others interpret it as a variety of cornucopia. Whether evil has entered the world yet is ambiguous.

With the evolution of multicellular plants, life became more complex, more structured, and more varied. Plants thrived on radiation from the sun and, being motionless, the evolution of pain would have been detrimental, so pain, if ever evolved in them, disappeared. So far, evil had not entered the world. Assuming, still, that only asexual reproduction has evolved, the plants are also immortal in principle, although, again, some are eliminated. As in the world of single cells, whether evil has entered the world yet is ambiguous.

Once plants existed, herbivores could evolve. Because they moved, they required approach-avoidance systems to find food and flee danger. As herbivores became more structured and complex, neurologically based pleasure-pain systems evolved, enabling those who had them to survive better than those whose systems were mechanical. Sentience appeared in the world. The sentient organisms needed both pain and pleasure—pain to get them to flee from danger and harm and pleasure to help them find safety and nourishment. In evolutionary terms, pain and pleasure turned out to be very successful approach-avoidance systems. Scientists know this because an enormous variety of organisms and species retain pleasure-pain systems from the time the systems evolved until the present day. Because these systems help organisms avoid harm and find the necessities for living, they are good.

Yet, they may carry evil with them. Certainly, our first reaction to the evolution of pain is to say, "Pain hurts! Therefore pain is evil. Evil has now entered the world." However, the fact that pain saves organisms from harm elicits the opposite response, namely, "Pain saves creatures from harm. Pain is good. Evil has not yet entered the world." Thus, pain seems to be both good and evil. To discover whether evil has entered the world, it is necessary to reexamine the definition of evil.

The Definition of Evil

Evil is defined as death and physical and/or mental suffering. Is feeling pain the same as physical suffering? The classical answer has been no, because suffering involves the self. These herbivores had no self, no "I". We have little idea what it is like to feel pain without pain affecting our selves.

The problem of how to assess others' pain is an old and deep philosophical conundrum, usually discussed under the heading of *other minds.* We do not feel other people's pain, not to mention the pain of other animals. We feel only our own. Yet recently science has discovered that we have *mirror neurons* that fire as if we were experiencing what others experience. When we see another human being writhing and screaming, grasping her twisted arm with its protruding bone, we assess the situation rationally by analogy, and also, through the excitation of our mirror neurons, experience some anguish like hers.

Such a response requires that we have a *theory of mind*. Having a theory of mind means knowing our own minds, assuming by analogy that other human beings' minds are like our own, and understanding their situation both intellectually and emotionally. Most human beings have a theory of mind, but it is not robust. Autistic persons seem to lack one entirely, and high-functioning autistics have one that is noticeably inaccurate. For example, Temple Grandin, a high-functioning autistic who designs cattle handling equipment, seems able to assess cows' feelings adequately, but not the feelings or needs or reactions of other human beings. A less-functional autistic, Donna Williams, failed the "self" test that even chimpanzees pass, the test of recognizing the figure in the mirror as oneself. For many years, Williams thought the person she saw in the mirror, who mimicked her every move, was another human being, a friend behind the mirror.[5]

---

[5] Temple Grandin and Donna Williams have written autobiographies about being autistic. See Temple Grandin and Margaret M. Scariano, *Emergence: Labeled Autistic* (Novato, CA: Warner Books, 1986) and Donna Williams, *Nobody Nowhere: The Extraordinary Autobiography of an Autistic* (New York: Bard Books, 1992) and *Somebody Somewhere: Breaking Free from the World of Autism* (New York: Times Books, 1994).

Moreover, recent work in psychology has disclosed significant differences between the minds of men and women.[6] Even with all the power of communication symbolic language gives us, we have trouble understanding the minds of the opposite sex.

So our powers of understanding others minds are rather fragile and easily led astray because we know only our own minds (and those imperfectly), and other human beings' minds may be—indeed, often are—different from our own, although we are the same species. For animals very close to us on the phylogenetic bush, we may have some inkling of what is going on in their minds, but we might not. In addition, they cannot tell us. Even chimpanzees that we have diligently taught "language"—a very limited manipulation of symbols—cannot tell us about their own minds. They are insufficiently self-reflective to do so.

Therefore, I think we need humility and skepticism when we speak of what other animals feel, especially if they are distant from us on the phylogenetic bush, like earthworms. At this point in the evolutionary story I am telling, the animals are distant from us. We know their pain hurts them, for they move away from and/or avoid what is painful. But we do not know what their pain feels like to them.

However, I can keep the problem of other animals' pain salient by labeling pain felt by organisms without selves *incipient evil,* the entrance of a source of evil into the world. Because incipient evil is evil, evil entered the world when sentience did. However, even when the evil of pain that hurts a creature's self enters the world, pain will retain its good role, for it will continue to save lives.

A similar problem haunts death. These herbivores are sentient organisms, so they have experiences that cease at death. The loss of their pleasurable experiences is probably an evil—but, if so, the loss of their painful ones must be a good, creating a balance of good and evil. Moreover, if there is no "I" to have the experiences, who has them? And what dies? Not "I". An organism that is the subject of experiences dies, but it does not know what death is, or that it will die. It cannot fear death. At most, then, death for it is another incipient evil, the beginning of the entrance of evil into the world. Again, incipient evil is evil. With death as with pain, evil entered the world along with sentience.

Thus far in our exploration through deep time, many types of organisms have evolved. Earth now contains an enormous variety of complex, sessile and mobile organisms. The mobile ones needed the sensations they had: hunger, thirst, and hurt—painful sensations—but they also experienced pleasurable ones like satiety and coolness and warmth. They died, but did not know they would and so, did not fear death. They even had interests, the decrease of pain and the increase of pleasure. Evil has arrived, but it rode in on the back of

---

[6] David M. Buss, *The Evolution of Desire: Strategies of Human Mating* (New York: Basic Books, 1994).

a powerful good, sentience, with its concomitant goods, the pleasures. Much good entered the world, bringing with it some evil. The interplay of good and evil has begun, with good far in the lead—existence, life, sentience, pleasures, all are good. Furthermore, death enables the universal recycling process to continue. This, perhaps, was paradise. Maybe the creation should have ended here, before more evil entered the world. Instead, natural selection's most creative agent evolved: sex.

The Evolution of Sex

With the evolution of two different sexes and the recombination of genes sex makes possible, variety increased enormously. New structures became possible. Moreover, the pressure for the evolution of intelligence intensified, for mobile sexually reproducing creatures must find, woo, and copulate with members of the opposite sex. Only those sexually reproducing, mobile creatures capable of accomplishing these complex tasks produced offspring and passed their genes for completing these tasks on to future generations.

In many birds and some mammals, the evolution of sex entailed the evolution of parental care. *Care* is ambiguous here. It could mean a mechanical taking care of, doing the acts necessary to raise dependent offspring to maturity. However, at some time, as with approach-avoidance systems, mechanical systems for taking care of offspring proved inadequate for getting the job done. Then caring, in the sense of having warm emotions between parent and offspring, evolved. The capacity for something like human love evolved.

The evolution of sex also required good judgment, for the creatures needed to know whether the mate they found was close kin to avoid inbreeding depression and whether it had good genes to produce offspring that would also survive to reproduce successfully. Sex drove the evolution of greater intelligence in mobile organisms and, with it, the evolution of more complexity, variety, and structure. The evolution of sex made more laws manifest, laws governing sexually reproducing species and genetic recombination. The evolution of sex brought many goods with it, goods congruent with cosmic development of increasingly complexity.

However, the evolution of sex also added evil to the world. It set the stage for the evolution of deception. If the limiting resource (usually the female) would not mate without the male's bringing her a gift—a nuptial tax, so to speak—as is the case with many insects, the male who could deceive her about the quality or quantity of the gift passed copies of his genes on to the next generation without forfeiting the tax. Deception paid.

The evolution of sex also meant the evolution of direct competition. Up to this point, organisms might be said, rather metaphorically, to compete for resources, but the usual case of competition might simply be the failure of one organism to find enough water for itself. Genuine contests were usually not necessary. With the evolution of sex, males competed directly against each other for females (again, the limiting resource) and females competed to some extent for males. Certainly, competition increased.

With the evolution of the capacity for emotions accompanying caring, concomitant painful emotions also evolved. Jealousy arose as fear over losing out; grief accompanied loss. New pleasures and new pains appeared. The new pains were novel, too, in being psychological, although still without a developed "I" to feel them. Nonetheless, additional evils had evolved. The evolution of jealousy and grief brought more evil into the world.

Sex also brought death into the world in a new way. Asexual organisms reproduce by division and are therefore in principle immortal, although they can be destroyed. But sexually reproducing organisms are all mortal, in principle; they die; only copies of their genes continue to exist. Mobile sexually reproducing organisms are largely sentient, so death means the end of any pleasure they may feel. It is a harm to them. More evil entered the world.

In summary, with the evolution of sex, the world became a wonderfully richer place, with enhanced choices, interests, and emotions. Much good entered the world when sex evolved. However, the evolution of sex also enhanced evil. The evolution of sex entailed the evolution of deception; the evolution of direct competition entailed pain and, sometimes, death; the evolution of emotion resulted in psychological suffering; and individual organisms died. With the evolution of sex, the world is richer in both good and evil. It is a more complex, structured, varied, and interesting world. It becomes even more so with the evolution of carnivores.

The Evolution of Carnivores

If sex drove the evolution of intelligence, so did the evolution of carnivores, animals that eat other animals to survive. (A few carnivorous plants evolved as well.) Compared to herbivores, carnivores eat their protein in compact packages. They also hunt for it. In their different ways, both these characteristics eventually enhanced intelligence. The compact packages of protein could feed bigger brains, organs that consume large quantities of energy. The compact packages required less gut than herbivores needed, and less gut used less energy, freeing even more energy to enhance brainpower. Hunting required new intellectual capacities for knowledge of the behavior of prey animals. With the evolution of carnivores, variety, complexity, structure, and intelligence increased. Creatures that are more intelligent see more options and thus have more choices. It may be that they began to develop incipient selves to handle them. Again, new goods entered the world.

Yet, the evolution of carnivores was a mixed blessing. For the first time on Earth, immediate, living agents caused pain and death. They did not do so deliberately, of course. They were not empathetic; they did not know they caused pain. However, because they did not know, they often ate their screaming prey

alive. Moreover, their evolution brought about the evolution of the new psychological pains of fear and nervous vigilance, for the prey animals that felt
them fled from their predators and, so, survived to reproduce. Nonetheless,
the universe as it evolved to this point was still a morally thin place.

A Morally Thin Universe

The entire organic world on Earth has now evolved up to the evolution of
primates. Evils have also evolved, but they have evolved because they helped
organisms survive to reproduce and enabled natural selection to continue its
creative work. Meanwhile, natural selection has brought increased goodness
into the world. It has added enormously more complexity, variety, and structure, and has manifested more laws. It has enhanced intelligence and choices,
bringing animals to the edge of evolving a new feature that God apparently
values: autonomy.

Despite this enormous increase in variety, the universe has maintained its
integrity. All the organisms are related, as we know from comparing their
DNA; most even share central DNA complexes like the homeobox that han-
dles the development of bodily symmetry. All their cells contain the salt water
of the primordial seas where evolution began, and that water contains the
oxygen starry furnaces fused into being and the hydrogen formed just after
the big bang. The universe is truly what the term claims it to be: a unity.

All these evolved creatures have intrinsically valuable lives, but they do not
have individual biographies. All are born, eat, drink, sleep, mate, perhaps take
care of young and learn a few species-specific behaviors, and die. Other than
these activities, they accomplished little.

If this process had been completely meandering, it seems almost pointless.
However, it flows like cosmic development does. It, too, adds variety, structure, and complexity to the world. Moreover, like the cosmos, it creates these
through recycling. Unlike the cosmos, it adds choice and intelligence, pleasure and pain, to the world. Good predominates over evil. Still, the world is
very thin, morally. Is this still paradise? Perhaps God should have finished
creation here, when evil had evolved but not proliferated.

God did not end it. A new species evolved: *Homo sapiens.*

The Evolution of Homo Sapiens

Homo sapiens: Genus, *Homo;* Family *Hominidae;* Order, *Primates* evolved
about 200,000 years ago in east Africa as the climate there changed from rain
forest to open woodland to savanna.[7] We, of course, are *Homo sapiens:* we

---

[7] A good introduction to human evolution is Roger Lewin, *Principles of Human Evolution:
A Core Textbook* (Oxford: Blackwell, 1998). No one else I know of has published similar ideas
about human capacities being responsible for evil. Mine were first published in chapter 10 of my

the people, humanity. Other members of our genus went extinct, but many primates survive today.

To discuss which characteristics are uniquely ours and which are incipient in the other primates would be of interest, even moral interest, but it would require a lengthy, complex discussion impossible here. Suffice it to say that our species, when viewed against other species, is unique—and so is every other species. Our species also has many characteristics, for good and evil, found incipiently in other animals, especially the other primates. Here I must simplify, so I will examine four human capacities that make a moral difference and that also, in part, make us who we are. Because I am discussing neither the other primates nor human hunter-gatherers, these capacities will seem to have evolved much more suddenly than they actually did.

First, we have a fully realized self. All organisms need to distinguish self from other. Many do so in a manner similar to our immune system—silently, mechanically, without sentience or consciousness. Chimpanzees, our closest relatives, recognize that the figure they see reflected in a mirror is their own. Monkeys, dogs, and cats do not recognize themselves. So chimpanzees are, in some sense, self-conscious.

We are self-conscious, too, and, in addition, we can self-reflect and even reflect on our reflections. This capacity underlies our moral capability.[8] Having a fully realized self also allows us to develop a theory of mind.

Traditional theology says God is good and God makes laws. Insofar as we are moral creatures, we are like God, in God's image. We, too, can be good, and we can and do make laws, some of them distinctly moral. Having a fully realized self is very valuable, morally. With our evolution, the world is a morally richer place.

Our moral capability has one very interesting ramification. We seem inherently disposed to think of pain as morally deserved punishment and pleasure as morally deserved reward. Thus, when harmed, even by non-agents such as natural disasters, we cry, "What did I do to deserve this?" even in societies that know the causes of natural events scientifically. When beset by illness, many of us, even when we know the scientific causes, cry, "But I followed the rules!"—the rules of morality and health. Non-scientific societies say explicitly that afflictions are punishments, as happens throughout the Bible. In the

---

book *Doing without Adam and Eve: Sociobiology and Original Sin* (Minneapolis: Fortress, 2001), 159–179.

[8] As Francisco J. Ayala has argued in "So Human an Animal: Evolution and Ethics" in Ted Peters (ed.), *Science and Theology: The New Consonance* (Boulder, CO: Westview Press, 1998) 121–136; our moral capability also requires that we be able to anticipate the consequences of our actions, make value judgments, and choose among courses of action. He does not discuss the self, but having a fully realized self either enables or greatly enhances our ability to do the things he mentions.

Bible, God is the ultimate cause, punishing individuals and entire peoples—once the whole of humanity except Noah and his family. This human disposition to think of pain and death as punishments by a righteous agent calls forth works on theodicy—topic, perhaps, for another day.

However, knowing that we tend to think of pain and death as punishments serves here as a warning: pain and death are not punishments. They are products of evolution. They are natural and necessary. Pain is good, helping creatures survive. Death is good, a part of the universal recycling process. Evil is only their shadow, the harm that accompanies the goods they bring.

Having a realized self casts its evil shadow, too. Because we have fully realized selves, we can center our interest on ourselves as no other creature can. We are capable of great selfishness, of a stark rejection of the claims of others.

Self-awareness and self-reflection entail fear of death, whether we think of death as annihilation or continuation into the unknown. Without our fear of death, death would be far less of an evil than we feel it to be.

With selves, we suffer. When we hurt, the self hurts. Part of the difficulty of assessing whether the pain of other animals is evil, or how much evil it might be, is that we have very little idea what it is like to feel pain without a self-reflective "I" to feel it. No doubt other animals' pain hurts them: it would fail in its mission of making them flee harm if it did not. Their capacity for pain is both good and evil. Probably our capacity for suffering is also.

Like bodies, selves can sicken. Having a self means the possibility of having a sick self, of suffering mental disorders. Other very complex animals probably have some sorts of mental disorders, but none experiences dissociative disorders that afflict the self, like schizophrenia and multiple personality.

This wonderful, even god-like capacity, the self, that makes us moral creatures and legislators of law, then, brings much evil with it—the evils of selfishness, fear of death, and mental illness. Moreover, having a self heightens, and perhaps makes qualitatively more awful than they are for other animals, every bodily and psychological pain. The only way to rid ourselves of these evils is to remove the self, which probably means committing suicide.

Second, we have the capacity to envision a future for ourselves and strive to realize it. This capacity enables us to envision a future self freed from the evils attached to it and to try to bring that self about. It also enables us to envision a future society in which pleasure is enhanced, pain diminished, and death delayed. It allows us to imagine a world where everyone has full human rights, where our lifestyles are ecologically sustainable, and everyone has adequate food, clothing, shelter, and health care. It enables us to work toward these things.

However, the capacity to envision a future for ourselves also brings evil with it. It leads us to fear death, and this in two respects. Because we can envision a future, we make plans, we begin projects, and we scrimp and save today so tomorrow we may flourish. Death wrecks our projects and renders today's sacrifices hollow. Best to eat, drink, and be merry today, for tomorrow will never come. Death makes today's decisions difficult.

Moreover, in envisioning the future, we try to peer beyond death's veil, and our imaginings frighten us. Which circle in the inferno is ours? Eternally? If some of our theologians are correct, we can do nothing to save ourselves, and because all are totally depraved, none better in God's sight than another and all our works dung, God can only save arbitrarily. If these theologians are correct, best to eat, drink, and be merry, for tomorrow is heaven or hell no matter what we do here.

Worse yet, the ability to envision a future means the capacity to plan others' destruction, to design torture and murder and war, to envision taking another nation's buildings, waterways, and farms, and enslaving and/or massacring all the former inhabitants.

This unique capacity, the capacity to envision a future for ourselves and others, brings with it many evils. To destroy these evils, we must destroy a capacity that contributes crucially to making us human.

Third, we are a uniquely creative species. We have created culture, literature, art, science, and technology. For the first time in history we know the cosmic story; we know how Earth came to be; we also know our own origins from a common ancestor with the apes in east Africa through an amazing number of species that walked upright, to us, who decorated our bodies, clothes, pottery, and weapons and told tales of our origins. Then, 40,000 or 50,000 years ago, some of us left Africa and traveled north to paint the caves of Europe and turn thin-lipped and pale under a dim northern sun. Others crossed into Asia, and with the change of climate, their skin and features also changed. Thus, we know to some extent how those superficial differences once called *racial* came to be.

All this knowledge brings many of us great satisfaction. It demonstrates a unity in humanity that idealists once could only imagine. However, it also divides us, for scientific knowledge frightens and angers those who cling to the origin stories their religion provides. Scientific knowledge has undermined their world, and some are willing to kill to stabilize the foundations they feel slipping away.

To kill, they turn to the science they reject and despise—an irony worthy of laughter and tears. To kill, they may use scientifically developed technologies of mass destruction so powerful and so awful that most of us avoid thinking about them most of the time.

Meanwhile, satellite technology enables us to communicate with homes around the world. Most massively communicated are pornography, superficial soap operas, and advertisements that play on fear. Our remarkable creativity has a dark, evil side. Many think the world would be a better place without it.

Fourth, we are an extraordinarily cooperative species. We form bands, tribes, and nations based on real or fictive ethnicity, and we create states founded on ideals and/or constitutions. We also organize corporations, civic groups, professional societies, dance troupes, sports teams, religious assemblies, and a dizzying variety of clubs.

However, we often cooperate for nefarious ends. The Nazis cooperated to organize mass rallies to stir up ethnic hatred. They cooperated to organize the railroads to ship Jews to death camps. They cooperated to organize armies to invade other countries and murder or enslave the populations. In addition, every nation during World War II with sufficient money and scientific knowledge cooperated to organize physicists and their adjuncts to invent weapons of mass destruction. Our ability to cooperate has enabled us to go to war, commit genocide, foment a holocaust, and devise weapons that may destroy life on Earth. If we could not cooperate with one another successfully, wars would cease.

One conclusion to draw from this examination of four of our capacities and the evil accompanying them is that the world would be a better place without us, and the only moral act is to commit mass suicide. If we departed, most evil on Earth would go with us. Yet, so would most good.

Good Capacities Enhance Cosmic Good

A different conclusion is that, in themselves, our capacities are so good having them far outweighs the capability for evil they entail. Moreover, our capacities also bring about great good. When seen from a cosmic perspective, they complement cosmic development. They add complexity, structure, and variety to the world. Moreover, they enable us to harmonize with the law-likeness of the world by creating new laws. In addition, they increase autonomy fantastically, for we make choices no other animal can imagine. We choose clothing, coiffures, cars, and crimes. We decide to pursue art, arcane knowledge, asceticism, affluence, and augury. We indulge in lust, licentiousness, lasciviousness, lewdness, lechery, and selfless love.

Furthermore, for the first time in evolutionary history on Earth, our activities themselves add complexity, structure, and variety to the world. We have biographies. We have countless, vastly varied accomplishments, accomplishments like writing books, raising food, weaving tapestries, cross-breeding flowers, inventing airplanes, and creating governments. Because we have so many purposes, we bring purposefulness to the world.

Thus, we enhance those attributes in the world that have increased since the big bang, and we add new ones, making the world a richer place. Furthermore, we are one with the first simple elements, one with the complex elements fused in the stars, one with the primordial seas, and one with other organisms. Evidently, we belong here; we are neither exiles nor aliens, as so much Christian theology suggests. Moreover, we bring morality to a largely amoral universe and add purposefulness to it.

That recycling drives cosmic development and organic evolution hints that our selves do not dissolve at bodily death. Just as nature recycles our bodies as food for other organisms, and our atoms continue to exist, so our selves may be recycled, either through reincarnation or continued existence on another plane. Since reincarnation destroys the old self rather thoroughly, because it destroys memories, continued existence on another plane seems a richer way of recycling the self. Perhaps it is God's way.

In conclusion, when we explore the universe through deep time, we discover a world that is self-creating — famously, God makes a universe that makes itself. God as creator of this universe must be fully invested in it. In Christian theological terms, we might think of the universe, from the beginning, as consubstantiated, pervaded with the divine. Because more good than evil arises with increased capacities, we might also think of the universe as self-redeeming, with God fully invested in it and, therefore, in its redemption.

The world of deep time needs no redemption by an external source, whether the source be an eschatological event that God imposes on the world from without, sometime in the future, or yesterday's cruciform suffering that appeases God's wrath over sin (sin for which God as creator of this universe is ultimately responsible, the miscreant biblical couple never having existed in it). Indeed, in the world of deep time, suffering seems not so much to redeem as to require redemption. In such a universe, redemption occurs continuously as cosmic violence and destruction are redeemed by the construction of structure, complexity, and novelty, and the shadows of organic death and pain are redeemed by the evolution of marvelous capacities. Because good and evil are conjoined, evil is redeemed as it arises. Our own capacities permit us to devise atrocities, yet also empower us to create magnificent goods. As the free-will solution to the problem of evil suggests, we have a choice. Making the right one is likely to be soul-building.

Making the Task of Theodicy Impossible?

Intelligent Design and the Problem of Evil

William A. Dembski

Intelligent design—the idea that a designing intelligence plays a substantive and empirically significant role in the natural world—no longer sits easily in our intellectual environment. Science rejects it for invoking an unnecessary teleology. Philosophy rejects it for committing an argument from ignorance. And theology rejects it for, as Edward Oakes contends, making the task of theodicy impossible.[1] I want in this essay to address all these concerns but especially the last. For many thinkers, particularly religious believers, intelligent design exacerbates the problem of natural evil—intelligent design makes natural evil not an accident of natural history or a price exacted by evolution or a necessary consequence of creation's freedom but an outcome fully intended by a sadistic designer. Or, as Robert Russell put it to me on the PBS program *Uncommon Knowledge*, "The notion of intelligent design is incoherent because it's either a natural cause, in which case you don't go anywhere, or it's a divine cause, in which case you don't have the biblical God."[2] The biblical God, presumably, would not design the rabies virus, the bubonic plague bacterium, or the mosquito.

The Task of Theodicy

I want in this essay to address Russell's concern, sketching why intelligent design does not too brutally violate the current intellectual environment and can indeed be squared with a specifically Christian theodicy. My foil throughout the ensuing discussion will be Edward Oakes. Oakes, a Catholic theologian, is a trenchant critic of intelligent design. According to Oakes, intelligent design attempts to foist a crude interventionist conception of divine action on Christian theology and, to boot, call it science. Intelligent design advocates, according to him, "claim that both the universe and biological systems have been intelligently designed (by God presumably, although some authors are

---

[1] Edward T. Oakes, "Edward T. Oakes and His Critics: An Exchange", First Things, 112, April 2001, 11.

[2] Transcript of program available at http://www.uncommonknowledge.org/01–02/635.html (last accessed 26 February 2003).

annoyingly coy about saying so)."[3] "Advocates of Intelligent Design share the metaphysical presuppositions of their [Darwinian] opponents."[4] "One should not seek to refute the (admittedly improper) extrapolations of evolutionary theory in the work of such Darwinian bulldogs as Richard Dawkins and Daniel Dennett by using the same tiresome and jejune positivism they use, for then the argument descends to fossil dating or how flagella got attached to bacteria and the like. This is the mistake of the advocates of Intelligent Design."[5] Intelligent design advocates start out by urging "the blatantly obvious truth, which no one has ever denied, that contraptions require assembly. But then…comes the whopper: and *therefore* God is the Artificer of the universal artifact".[6]

"If God was supposed to have intervened so directly 3.5 billion years ago to construct a well-designed cell, and if He is needed to design new *Baupläne* at irregular intervals, why does He not intervene when a fire breaks out in the cockpit of an airplane flying over the Atlantic? Or when stray radiation from the sun affects the sequence of a DNA molecule, later causing birth defects?"[7] To identify the Designer as the Logos of God in John's Gospel "force[s] us to claim that the Logos of God *directly* attached the flagellum to the first bacterium, that the Second Person of the Trinity *explicitly* toggled a complex molecule to bring about the first act of self-replication, and that the Deity *immediately* altered the architecture of one species, say a tiger, to lead to another conspicuously different species. For each and every one of these hypotheses (when they are not downright preposterous) the scientific evidence is exactly zero, the logic fallacious, and the theological implications grotesque."[8] Intelligent design makes "the task of theodicy impossible."[9]

"Paley did far more damage to nineteenth-century Christianity than Friedrich Nietzsche ever managed to do to twentieth-century religion. Design is the founding axiom of Deist religion; and as Darwin's own life attests, nothing more rapidly congeals into atheism (or agnosticism) than Deism."[10] Intelligent Design is "either Creation "Science" on the installment plan, or (more likely) Deism put under a stroboscope. If one *must* conceive of the universe as an artifact (and how odd that materialist Darwinians and Intelligent Designers both hold that life is a mechanical artifact), then the idea of a Clockmaker

---

[3] Edward T. Oakes, Commentary 115:3, March 2003, 21. Letter in response to David Berlinski's article "Has Darwin Met His Match?" Commentary, 114:5, December 2002, 31–41.

[4] Oakes, "Oakes and His Critics", 12.

[5] Edward T. Oakes, First Things, 132, April 2003, 14. Reply to letter in response to book review by Oakes of Robert Pennock's book *Intelligent Design Creationism and Its Critics: Philosophical, Theological, and Scientific Perspectives* (Cambridge, MA: MIT Press, 2001).

[6] Oakes, "Oakes and His Critics", 12f.

[7] Ibid., 12.

[8] Ibid., 8.

[9] Ibid., 11.

[10] Ibid., 9.

God who winds it all up and then departs the scene has a certain plausibility."[11] The God of Intelligent Design is "one who, with disconcerting inconsistency, intervenes *every now and again*. As I say, Deism under a stroboscope."[12] "The design argument will only end up becoming a breeding ground for atheism, a fetid terrarium for a whole new brood of Richard Dawkinses (not a pleasant thought, that)."[13]

These quotes by Edward Oakes, culled from his writings in *First Things* and *Commentary*, sum up and state forcefully the most common theological objections to intelligent design. If his characterization of intelligent design is correct, then intelligent design is theologically hopeless and does indeed render the task of theodicy impossible. But Oakes's characterization of intelligent design is deeply flawed, indeed so much so that his concerns about intelligent design undermining the task of theodicy in the end prove groundless.

According to Oakes, the task of a Christian theodicy is to "show that an omnipotent and benevolent God can coexist with evil in His finite creation."[14] The key to resolving the theodicy problem for Oakes is Augustine's insight that God would not allow evil to exist unless God could bring good out of evil.[15] Nevertheless, to speak of God bringing good out of evil could just be a fancy way of dressing up a consequentialism in which the means justifies the end. To avoid this charge, Oakes requires that the world be viewed "both as a totality and under the aegis of eschatology."[16] Accordingly, God-bringing-good-out-of-evil must be judged not on the basis of isolated happenings but on the basis of the totality of happenings as they relate to God's ultimate purposes for the world. All of this is sound Christian theodicy as far as it goes. I'm going to argue that intelligent design, rightly understood, is companionable with such a theodicy.

Interventionism

Let's begin with Oakes's concern that intelligent design is an interventionist theory. For intelligent design the crucial question is not how organisms emerged (for example, by gradual evolution or sudden special creation) but whether a designing intelligence made a discernible difference regardless how they emerged. For a designing intelligence to make a discernible difference

---

[11] Ibid., 11.
[12] Ibid.
[13] Ibid.
[14] Ibid., 12.
[15] Oakes will frequently cite the following quote by Aquinas (who in turn is quoting Augustine): "As Augustine says, since God is the highest good, He would not allow any evil to exist in His works unless His omnipotence and goodness were such as to bring good even out of evil. This is part of the infinite goodness of God, that He should allow evil to exist, and out of it produce good". *Summa Theologiae*, I.2.3.
[16] Oakes, "Oakes and His Critics", 12.

in the emergence of some organism, however, seems to require that an intelligence intervened at specific times and places to bring about that organism and thus seems to require some form of intervention. This in turn raises the question: How often and at what places and in what manner did a designing intelligence intervene? According to Oakes, intelligent design draws an unreasonable distinction between primary and secondary causation; it claims that secondary causation is fine most of the time but then on rare (or perhaps not so rare) occasions a designing intelligence (God) needs to act directly to get over some hump that secondary causes can't quite manage ("deism under the stroboscope", as Oakes puts it).

This criticism is misconceived. The proper question is not how often or at what places or in what manner a designing intelligence intervenes but rather at what points do signs of intelligence first become evident. To understand the difference, imagine a computer program that outputs alphanumeric characters on a computer screen. The program runs for a long time and throughout that time outputs what look like random characters. Then abruptly the output changes and the program outputs sublime poetry. Now, at what point did a designing intelligence intervene in the output of the program? Clearly, this question misses the mark because the program is deterministic and simply outputs whatever the program dictates.

There was no intervention at all that changed the output of the program from random gibberish to sublime poetry. And yet, the point at which the program starts to output sublime poetry is the point at which we realize that the output is designed and not random. Moreover, it is at that point that we realize that the program itself is designed. But when, where, and how was design introduced into the program? Although these are interesting questions, they are ultimately irrelevant to the more fundamental question whether there was design in the program and its output in the first place. Similarly in biology there will be clear times and locations where we can say that design first became evident. But the precise activity of a designing intelligence at those points will require further investigation and may indeed not be answerable. As the computer analogy just given indicates, the place and time at which design first becomes evident need have no connection with the place and time at which design was actually introduced.

Intelligent design is not a theory about the frequency or locality or modality by which a designing intelligence intervenes in the material world. It is not an interventionist theory at all. Indeed, intelligent design is perfectly compatible with all the design in the world coming to expression by the ordinary means of secondary causes over the course of natural history, much as a computer program's output comes to expression simply by running the program (and thus without monkeying with the program's operation). In fact, one way to think of the secondary causes responsible for biological evolution is as intelligently designed programs whose computational environment is the universe and whose operating system is the laws of physics and chemistry. This actually is an old idea, and one that Charles Babbage, the inventor of the digital computer, explored in the 1830s in his *Ninth Bridgewater Treatise* (thus predating Darwin's *Origin of Species* by twenty years).[17]

Of course, there are other ways to think about secondary causes that leave room for genuine teleology in nature. Programming is one option, but it implies a highly mechanical or algorithmic view of secondary causation. Augustine, by contrast, thought of design in the world as coming to expression through seeds planted by God at creation.[18] Here we have an organismic rather than algorithmic view of secondary causation. Physical necessity can also be the carrier of teleology through laws of form that channel evolution along certain preset paths. Late nineteenth and early twentieth century orthogenesis is an example. More recently Michael Denton has been exploring laws of form in the context of protein folding.[19] And then there are the more frankly vitalistic options, like Aristotelian entelechy, the Stoic world-soul, and more recently morphogenetic fields (as in the work of Rupert Sheldrake).[20] Now all these options, and others as well, are compatible with intelligent design. Intelligent design's only concern is that secondary causes leave room for teleology and that this teleology be empirically detectable.

Material Mechanisms

Nevertheless, a design-theoretic view of evolution would be very different from evolution as it is now conceived. Evolution, as currently presented in biology textbooks, operates not just by secondary causes but by material mechanisms. And while material mechanisms are perfectly acceptable secondary causes, secondary causes need not be material mechanisms. It is a huge and unwarranted assumption to identify the two. And yet many scientists and philosophers make this identification. The reason is easy to see. Material mechanisms allow for a reductive science in which the complex can always be explained in terms of the simple. This is convenient as far as it goes. The problem is that it doesn't go very far, at least not in evolutionary biology.

Lord Kelvin summed up the attraction of material mechanisms thus: "I never satisfy myself until I can make a mechanical model of a thing. If I can make a mechanical model I can understand it. As long as I cannot make a me-

---

[17] Charles Babbage, *The Ninth Bridgewater Treatise* (London: Murray, 1836).

[18] Augustine, *The Literal Meaning of Genesis*, 2 vol., J. H. Taylor, transl. (New York: Newman Press, 1982), V:4.9–11, V:23.45, VI:11.19, VI:14.24, X:20.35.

[19] M. J. Denton and J. C. Marshall, "The Laws of Form Revisited", Nature, 410, 2001, 411 and M. J. Denton, J. C. Marshall, and M. Legge, "The Protein Folds as Platonic Forms: New Support for the Pre-Darwinian Conception of Evolution by Natural Law", Journal of Theoretical Biology, 219, 2002, 325–342.

[20] Rupert Sheldrake, *A New Science of Life: The Hypothesis of Morphic Resonance* (Rochester, VT: Park Street Press, 1995).

chanical model all the way through, I cannot understand."[21] This mechanistic approach to science, which last was appropriate to the physics of the nineteenth century, has become *de rigueur* for many contemporary evolutionary thinkers. Thus Richard Dawkins will write, "The one thing that makes evolution such a neat theory is that it explains how organized complexity can arise out of primeval simplicity."[22] To this Daniel Dennett adds that any scientific explanation that moves from simple to complex is "question-begging."[23] Dawkins explicitly equates proper scientific explanation with what he calls "hierarchical reductionism", according to which "a complex entity at any particular level in the hierarchy of organization" must properly be explained "in terms of entities only one level down the hierarchy."[24]

A mechanism is a well-defined process where each step of the process leads predictably to the next. A mechanism can be deterministic, in which case one step leads with certainty to the next. Or it can be stochastic, in which case one step leads with a given probability to the next. Mechanisms are often embodied in objects but need not be. Hilbert's program for "mechanizing" mathematics attempted to show that all mathematical truths could be proven by mechanically applying logical rules of inference to manageable sets of axioms (manageable sets being those that are "recursive" as defined by mathematical logic). Hilbert's program failed (at the hands of Kurt Gödel), but the point I wish to stress here is that the program's underlying mechanism was a consequence relation on an abstract class of symbol strings, and thus not located in any material object but rather in an abstract computational space.[25]

The mechanism in Hilbert's program was deterministic. Other mechanisms are stochastic. Preeminent among stochastic mechanisms is, of course, the Darwinian mechanism of natural selection and random variation. The Darwinian mechanism is supposed to make it possible to get from anywhere in biological configuration space to anywhere else provided one can take small steps. How small? Small enough that they are reasonably probable. But what guarantee is there that a sequence of baby-steps connects any two points in configuration space? There is none.

The problem gets worse. For the Darwinian selection mechanism to connect point A to point B in configuration space, it is not enough that there merely exist a sequence of baby-steps connecting the two. In addition, each

---

[21] Lord Kelvin, *Baltimore Lectures* (Baltimore: Publication Agency of Johns Hopkins University, 1904), 270.

[22] Dawkins, *The Blind Watchmaker: Why the Evidence of Evolution Reveals a Universe without Design* (New York: Norton, 1986), 316.

[23] Daniel Dennett, *Darwin's Dangerous Idea* (New York: Simon & Schuster, 1995), 153.

[24] Dawkins, *The Blind Watchmaker*, 13.

[25] For a summary of Hilbert's program and Gödel's demolition of it, see Roger Penrose, *The Emperor's New Mind: Concerning Computers, Minds, and the Laws of Physics* (Oxford: Oxford University Press, 1989), ch. 4.

baby-step needs in some sense to be "successful". In biological terms, each step requires an increase in fitness as measured in terms of survival and reproduction. Natural selection, after all, is the motive force behind each baby-step, and selection only selects what is advantageous to the organism. Thus, for the Darwinian mechanism to connect two organisms, there must be a sequence of successful baby-steps connecting the two.

Richard Dawkins compares the emergence of biological complexity through the steady improvement of fitness to climbing a mountain—Mount Improbable, as he calls it.[26] He calls it Mount Improbable because if you had to get all the way to the top in one fell swoop (that is, achieve a massive increase in biological complexity all at once), it would be highly improbable. But Mount Improbable does not have to be scaled in one leap. Darwinism purports to show how Mount Improbable can be scaled in small incremental steps. Thus, according to Dawkins, Mount Improbable always has a gradual serpentine path leading to the top that can be traversed in baby-steps. But such a claim requires verification. It might be a fact about nature that Mount Improbable is sheer on all sides and getting to the top from the bottom via baby-steps is effectively impossible. A gap like that would reside in nature herself and not in our knowledge of nature (it would not, in other words, constitute a god-of-the-gaps).

Consequently, it is not enough merely to presuppose that a fitness-increasing sequence of baby-steps connects two biological systems—it must be demonstrated. For instance, it is not enough to point out that some genes for the bacterial flagellum are the same as those for a type III secretory system (a type of pump) and then handwave that one was co-opted from the other.[27] Anybody can arrange complex systems in a series. But such series do nothing to establish whether the end evolved in a Darwinian fashion from the beginning unless each step in the series can be specified, the probability of each step can be quantified, the probability at each step turns out to be reasonably large, and each step constitutes an advantage to the organism (in particular, viability of the whole organism must at all times be preserved). Only then do we have a mechanistic explanation (in Darwinian terms) of how one system arose from another.

Convinced that the Darwinian mechanism must be capable of doing such evolutionary design work, evolutionary biologists rarely ask whether such a sequence of successful baby-steps even exists; much less do they attempt to quantify the probabilities involved. I attempt that in chapter 5 of my book *No*

---

[26] Richard Dawkins, *Climbing Mount Improbable* (New York: Norton, 1996).

[27] For an example of such handwaving, see Kenneth Miller's article "The Flagellum Unspun: The Collapse of 'Irreducible Complexity'", available online at http://www.millerandlevine.com/km/evol/design2/article.html. For my response, see http://www.designinference.com/documents/2003.02.Miller_Response.htm. Both articles last accessed 27 March 2003.

Free Lunch.[28] There I lay out techniques for assessing the probabilistic hurdles that the Darwinian mechanism faces in trying to account for complex biological structures like the bacterial flagellum. The probabilities I calculate—and I try to be conservative—are horrendous and render natural selection entirely implausible as a mechanism for generating the flagellum and structures like it.

A Gödelian Argument Against Darwinism

According to intelligent design, Darwin's theory fails for essentially the same reason that Hilbert's program failed. Hilbert's program for mechanizing mathematics failed because Gödel was able to demonstrate that logical rules of inference could not connect all mathematical truths back to a reasonable set of starting points (that is, a recursive set of axioms). Likewise Darwin's program for mechanizing biological evolution fails because it can be demonstrated that the Darwinian mechanism lacks the capacity to connect biological organisms exhibiting certain types of complex biological structures (for example, irreducibly complex or complex specified structures) to evolutionary precursors lacking those structures.

Note that to attribute such an incapacity to the Darwinian mechanism isn't to say that it's logically impossible for the Darwinian mechanism to attain such structures. It's logically possible for just about anything to attain anything else via a vastly improbable or fortuitous event. For instance, it's logically possible that with my very limited chess ability I might defeat the reigning world champion, Vladimir Kramnik, in ten straight games. But if I do so, it will be despite my limited chess ability and not because of it. Likewise, if the Darwinian mechanism is the conduit by which a Darwinian pathway leads to an irreducibly complex biochemical system, then it is despite the intrinsic properties or capacities of that mechanism. Thus, in saying that irreducibly complex biochemical structures are inaccessible to Darwinian pathways, design proponents are saying that the Darwinian mechanism has no intrinsic capacity for generating such structures except as vastly improbable or fortuitous events. Accordingly, to attribute irreducible complexity to a direct Darwinian pathway is like attributing Mount Rushmore to wind and erosion. There's a sheer possibility that wind and erosion could sculpt Mount Rushmore but not a realistic one.

Gödel's demonstration of the failure of Hilbert's program was strictly deductive. Intelligent design's demonstration of the failure of Darwin's program is a combination of empirical and theoretical arguments. In both cases, however, the issue is one of connectivity—can the mechanism in question supply a step-by-step path connecting two otherwise disparate elements (distinct

---

[28] William A. Dembski, *No Free Lunch: Why Specified Complexity Cannot Be Purchased without Intelligence* (Lanham, MD: Rowman and Littlefield, 2002).

mathematical propositions in the Hilbert-Gödel case, distinct organisms in the Darwinian case). Of course, while Gödel's anti-mechanistic argument for mathematics is entirely uncontroversial, intelligent design's anti-mechanistic argument for evolutionary biology has yet to win the day. I've argued in a number of my writings that the logic underlying this argument is sound.[29] Whether it is, however, is not the issue here. Our concern in this lecture is whether intelligent design smuggles in dubious theological assumptions that are inimical to the task of theodicy.

Mechanism as Process and Function

According to Edward Oakes, intelligent design smuggles in at least one dubious theological assumption. Thus he charges intelligent design with presupposing the same positivism and mechanistic metaphysics that drives Darwinian naturalism. But the only way to make this charge stick is by arguing that both intelligent design and Darwinian naturalism entail the same mechanistic view of causality. Oakes argues that they do by casting intelligent design as an interventionist theory of divine action in which mechanism rules the day except for the sporadic poke of a divine finger here and there. Although Oakes may be correct that some proponents of intelligent design have interpreted it this way, it hardly follows that intelligent design must be interpreted this way. Intelligent design makes few demands on theology. It is committed to an ontological claim and an epistemological claim. The ontological claim: Material mechanisms are incomplete—they are not coextensive with secondary causes. The epistemological claim: Design is empirically detectable. Note that intelligent design does not merely assert these claims but attempts to justify them.

But if intelligent design is theologically undemanding and eschews a mechanistic metaphysics, why does it continually emphasize mechanism? Why is it constantly looking to molecular machines and focusing on the mechanical aspects of life? If intelligent design treats living things as machines, then isn't intelligent design effectively committed to a mechanistic metaphysics however much it might want to distance itself from that metaphysics otherwise? Such questions confuse two senses of the term "mechanism". Michael Polanyi noted the confusion back in the 1960s: "Up to this day one speaks of the mechanistic conception of life both to designate an explanation of life in terms of physics and chemistry [what I've been calling "material mechanisms"], and an explanation of living functions as machineries—though the latter excludes the former. The term "mechanistic" is in fact so well established for referring to these two mutually exclusive conceptions, that I am at a loss to find two dif-

---

[29] See my book *No Free Lunch* as well as my article "The Logical Underpinnings of Intelligent Design", in: W. Dembski and M. Ruse (ed.), *Debating Design: From Darwin to DNA* (Cambridge: Cambridge University Press, forthcoming 2004).

ferent words that will distinguish between them."[30] In his arguments against reductionism, Polanyi argues that mechanisms, conceived as causal processes operating in nature, could not account for the origin of mechanisms, conceived as "machines or machinelike features of organisms."[31]

In focusing on the machinelike features of organisms, intelligent design is not advocating a mechanistic conception of life. To attribute such a conception of life to intelligent design is to commit a fallacy of composition. Just because a house is made of bricks doesn't mean that the house itself is a brick. Likewise just because certain biological structures can properly be described as machines doesn't mean that an organism that includes those structures is a machine. Intelligent design focuses on the machinelike aspects of life because those aspects are scientifically tractable and precisely the ones that opponents of design purport to explain by material mechanisms. Intelligent design proponents build on and extend Polayni's arguments. In a way similar to Polayni's arguments against the explanatory adequacy of reductionism, intelligent design proponents argue that material mechanisms (like the Darwinian mechanism of natural selection and random variation) have no inherent capacity to bring about the machinelike aspects of life. This is for now where much of the debate is focused. I look forward to the day when intelligent design moves beyond the machinelike aspects of life and, as a discipline, starts to focus explicitly on the higher-level design features of living systems such as elegance and beauty.[32]

Kant's Framing of the Theodicy Problem

I've now addressed Edward Oakes's main criticisms against intelligent design. In particular, I've shown that intelligent design is compatible with the Augustinian theodicy sketched by Oakes, which permits evil because of the good that God ultimately brings out of it. Mere compatibility with an existing theodicy (albeit the one I find most persuasive) is, however, not all that exciting. I therefore want to switch gears and examine next what positive contribution intel-

---

[30] Michael Polanyi, "Life Transcending Physics and Chemistry", Chemical and Engineering News, 45, August 1967, 65.

[31] Ibid., 55.

[32] I fully admit, and regard it as unfortunate, that the aesthetic dimension of intelligent design has till now received short shrift. When I helped organize the Nature of Nature conference at Baylor University in the spring of 2000, I attempted to enlist John Updike as the keynote speaker. Design has been a long-standing theme in Updike's writings, with his emphasis being not on functionality but on aesthetics. He declined my offer not for lack of interest in the conference or topic but for not feeling sufficiently expert to address the question of design before an audience of scientists and philosophers. That was too bad because precisely that audience needed to hear Updike's insights into the aesthetics of intelligent design. For details of the Nature of Nature conference, go to http://www.designinference.com/documents/2000.04.nature_of_nature.htm (last accessed 26 March 2003).

ligent design makes to the theodicy problem. The positive contribution, I take it, is this: Intelligent design restores to nature the artistic wisdom that Darwin banished from it and that Kant regarded as necessary to any theodicy.

Kant's discussion of theodicy occurs in a hard-to-find essay titled "On the Failure of All Attempted Philosophical Theodicies."[33] Kant wrote this essay in 1791, ten years after the first edition of his *Critique of Pure Reason* and four years after the second edition of that work. His essay on the failure of philosophical theodicies therefore represents the thought of a mature Kant. As he saw it, for a philosophical theodicy to succeed, it must prove one of three things:

Either that what one deems contrary to the purposefulness in the world is not so; or that while it is indeed contrary to purposefulness it must be considered not as a positive fact but as an inevitable consequence of the nature of things; or finally that, while a positive fact, it is not the work of the supreme Creator of things, but of some other responsible being, such as man or superior spirits, good or evil.[34]

Kant imagines that a defense attorney must plead "God's cause" and that "to win the case, the so-called advocate of God must prove one of [these] three things."[35]

The operative word here is "prove". Kant requires of a philosophical theodicy that it provide apodeictic certainty. But that seems to be precisely the one thing that no theodicy can provide. The problem is that theodicies by definition attempt to correlate the evil in the world, which is known by experience, with the moral wisdom of God. But, as Kant remarks, "The proof of the moral wisdom of God is completely a priori and cannot at all be based upon experience of what happens in the world."[36] After playing the role of defense attorney and trying to plead God's cause in each of the three ways just described, Kant concludes: "The result of the trial before the tribunal of philosophy is that no theodicy proposed so far has kept its promise; none has managed to justify the moral wisdom at work in the government of the world against the doubts which arise out of our experience of the world."[37]

In the current intellectual environment, God is guilty until proven innocent. Hence the failure of philosophical theodicies shows that God, if there is a God, cannot be a good God. And since, as Kant rightly observes, "the concept of God must be the concept of a moral being"[38]—by which he means

---

[33] Immanuel Kant, "On the Failure of All Attempted Philosophical Theodicies", M. Despland, transl., originally published 1791, in: Michel Despland, *Kant on History and Religion*, 283–297 (Montreal: McGill-Queen's University Press, 1973).

[34] Ibid., 283.

[35] Ibid.

[36] Ibid., 284n1.

[37] Ibid., 290.

[38] Ibid., 284n1.

a holy, good, and just being[39] — from the failure of philosophical theodicies it follows that there is no God at all. Given a presumption of guilt, the *modus tollens* here is conclusive. In my view, this anti-theodicy, more than any other, justifies atheism within the current intellectual environment.[40]

Nevertheless, for Kant God was not guilty until proven innocent. For one thing, Kant allowed that some philosophical theodicy might still achieve apodeictic certainty. The title of his essay after all was "On the Failure of All Attempted Philosophical Theodicies". Kant didn't think that he had necessarily attempted or exhausted all possible philosophical theodicies. As Kant remarked:

Will it be possible in time to find better grounds of justification so that the supreme wisdom under attack will not be simply absolved on lack of evidence but will be positively vindicated? This question remains undecided, since we cannot demonstrate with certainty that reason is completely powerless when it comes to determining the *relationship between this world, as we know it through experience, and the supreme wisdom*.[41]

Yet even without a successful philosophical theodicy to quell the doubts that experience urges against the moral wisdom of God, Kant saw no basis for a successful philosophical anti-theodicy. As he put it, "It is also true, I must add, that, in the light of the limits of our reason, these doubts cannot disprove such moral wisdom either."[42] To which he added, "We are capable at least of a negative wisdom. We can understand the necessary limits of our reflections on the subjects which are beyond our reach. This can easily be demonstrated and will put an end *once and for all* to the trial [that is, the trial of God before the tribunal of reason]."[43]

Even so, the question remains, What are we to make of our doubts that experience urges against the moral wisdom of God? Do we give up on all theodicy and embrace either fideism (if we are religious believers) or atheism (if we are inclined the other way)? Having shown the failure of philosophical theodicies, Kant does not give up on theodicies as such. Theodicies still have their place. According to Kant, "All theodicy must be an interpretation of nature and must show how God manifests the intentions of his will through it."[44] To illustrate this view of theodicy, Kant examines the case of Job. De-

---

[39] Ibid., 285.

[40] This anti-theodicy is especially popular in Darwinian circles where natural biological evil is widely cited as evidence against God's involvement in the world and thus as evidence for the absence of God from the world altogether. For an entire book devoted to this topic see Cornelius Hunter, *Darwin's God: Evolution and the Problem of Evil* (Grand Rapids, MI: Brazos Press, 2001).

[41] Kant, "Failure of All Theodicies", 290. Emphasis in original.

[42] Ibid.

[43] Ibid.

[44] Ibid., 291.

spite all his trials, Job in the end accepts the moral wisdom of God—that God is holy, good, and just. Why?

Crucial here, according to Kant, was God's artistic wisdom displayed in nature. Kant writes:

When art shows itself capable of achievements the possibility of which lie beyond all human reason, for instance, when ends and means bring each other out reciprocally, like in organic bodies, this divine art may not without reason be also called wisdom. Nevertheless, to avoid confusion we shall call this kind of wisdom the Creator's artistic wisdom, to keep it distinct from his moral wisdom. Teleology (physical theology) finds in experience abundant proof of [God's artistic wisdom].[45]

It's not widely advertised these days that Kant was quite sympathetic to teleology in nature and even in biology. Kant even admitted the legitimacy of natural (or physical) theology: "We have in fact a concept of an *artistic wisdom* manifested in the arrangement of the world. The objective reality of this knowledge is adequate and our speculative reason can develop a physical theology."[46] In fact, Kant's criticism of the teleological proof for the existence of God was simply that it tried to accomplish too much. In his first critique, Kant wrote: "The utmost, therefore, that the [teleological] argument can prove is an architect of the world who is always very much hampered by the adaptability of the material in which he works, not a creator of the world to whose idea everything is subject."[47] The point to appreciate is that Kant found the teleological argument, and in particular its conclusion of an architect or designer, compelling. Moreover, he saw no difficulty assigning to this architect, who for Kant was God, an artistic wisdom based not on a priori principles but on experience of nature, a wisdom remarkably illustrated in the reciprocal adaptation of means to ends in organisms.

Restoring Artistic Wisdom to Nature

For Kant any successful theodicy required that nature exhibit God's artistic wisdom. Kant illustrated the role of such wisdom in theodicy with his analysis of the book of Job. What convinced Job of God's holiness, goodness, and justice (that is, of God's moral wisdom) was a reflection on nature. When God finally appeared to Job, God did not defend himself or try to rationalize Job's sorrows. Instead, God asked Job to consider the wonders of creation. Kant writes:

God honored Job by showing him the wisdom of his creation and its unfathomable nature. He let him see the beautiful side of creation, where man can

---

[45] Ibid., 284n1.
[46] Ibid., 291.
[47] Immanuel Kant, *Critique of Pure Reason*, N. K. Smith, transl. (1787; reprinted New York: St. Martin's, 1929), 522.

see in an indubitable light (and understand) the purposes of the Creator and his wise providence. But he also showed the horrible side, by naming the products of his might, among which there are harmful and terrible things. These things by themselves can serve some purpose but in relationship to other beings and especially to man, they are destructive, run against all purposes, and do not seem to agree with the idea of a plan established with wisdom and goodness. Even through these things, God showed to Job an ordering of the whole which manifests a wise Creator, although his ways remain inscrutable for us, already in the physical ordering of things but even more in the connection between this order and the moral one (which is even more unfathomable to our reason). The conclusion is this: Job confessed not that he had spoken sacrilegiously, for he was sure of his good faith, but only that he had spoken unwisely about things that were above his reach and which he did not understand.[48]

Kant offers here a richer understanding and vision of theodicy than either William Paley or Charles Darwin. For Paley, the natural world was a happy place in which organisms frolicked and lived in delicate harmony and balance.[49] Only such a world could sustain a successful theodicy for Paley. For Darwin, on the other hand, the natural world was a cruel or indifferent place in which organisms took part in, as he put it, "the great battle of life."[50] Such a world led Darwin to despair of the possibility of any successful theodicy. For Kant the beauty and horror of creation coexist and still allow a successful theodicy (as in the case of Job). Nevertheless, it is a theodicy that depends fundamentally on there being an artistic wisdom manifest in creation, one we cannot fathom entirely but one we cannot discount either. Paley's understanding of God's artistic wisdom in nature was shallow and incomplete. Darwin, by contrast, in propounding his theory, banished artistic wisdom from nature.

From the vantage of Darwinian evolutionary theory, the emergence of biological complexity and diversity is as much to be expected as the emergence of twenty heads in a row among a crowd of a million coin tossers (imagine each person in the crowd tosses a coin and keeps standing so long as he or she tosses heads but must sit down otherwise). The science of coin tossing (probability theory) tells us that out of a million coin-tossers one person will on average be left standing who has tossed twenty heads in a row. So too the science of Darwinian evolution tells us that the cumulative effect of natural selection and random variation over several billion years is likely to produce the degree of biological complexity and diversity we observe now. Just as the

---

[48] Kant, "Failure of All Theodicies", 292 f.

[49] See especially the second to the last chapter in Paley's Natural Theology titled "The Goodness of the Deity". William Paley, *Natural Theology; Or Evidences of the Existence and Attributes of the Deity Collected from the Appearances of Nature* (1802; reprinted Boston: Gould and Lincoln, 1852).

[50] Charles Darwin, *On the Origin of Species*, facsimile 1st ed. (1859; reprinted Cambridge, MA: Harvard University Press, 1964), 76.

science of coin tossing does not justify attributing to the person who tossed twenty heads in a row any special skill or wisdom at coin tossing, so too the science of Darwinian evolution does not justify attributing to the evolutionary process any special skill or wisdom at generating biological complexity and diversity. In each case the outcome is properly regarded as expected or predictable and not, as Kant put it, an artistic achievement "the possibility of which lie[s] beyond all human reason."[51]

For Kant one such achievement that lay beyond all human reason was the reciprocal adaptation of means to ends in organisms. He referred to this achievement as an instance of "divine art" that "may not without reason be also called wisdom."[52] He then identified this wisdom with God's artistic wisdom: "We shall call this kind of wisdom the Creator's artistic wisdom."[53] What's more, for Kant this wisdom was exhibited in nature and provided a sound basis for teleology: "Teleology (physical theology) finds in experience abundant proof of [God's artistic wisdom]."[54] Elsewhere in his essay on theodicy Kant calls this wisdom "unfathomable."[55]

Unfathomable. Beyond all human reason. A source of wonder and awe. Darwin's theory evacuates biology of all of these. Within Darwinism the reciprocal adaptation of means to ends in organisms (which Kant found so conclusive as signaling God's artistic wisdom) is eminently fathomable — Darwin's theory purports to provide a complete accounting. Richard Dawkins even wrote a book to stress this point and palliate the loss of wonder that Darwin's theory entails. It was titled *Unweaving the Rainbow*. Note the subtitle: *Science, Delusion, and the Appetite for Wonder*.[56] Whereas for Kant wonder sprung from discerning God's artistic wisdom in creation, for Dawkins wonder is an appetite that becomes delusory as soon as it seeks fulfillment in God. What makes it delusory? As Francisco Ayala put it, Darwin showed us how organisms could arise "without any need to resort to a Creator or other external agent."[57] Ayala hit the nail on the head. A creator God might resort to creating life by means of the Darwinian mechanism, but the Darwinian mechanism need not resort to a creator God to bring about the diversity of life. It follows that the Darwinian mechanism does not function to make manifest the artistic wisdom of God in creation. Granted, that wisdom might still be there, but it is not there to be discerned.

---

[51] Kant, "Failure of All Theodicies", 284n1.

[52] Ibid.

[53] Ibid.

[54] Ibid.

[55] Ibid., 292.

[56] Richard Dawkins, *Unweaving the Rainbow: Science, Delusion, and the Appetite for Wonder* (New York: Houghton Mifflin, 1998).

[57] Francisco J. Ayala, "Darwin's Revolution", in: J. H. Campbell and J. W. Schopf (ed.), *Creative Evolution?!*, (Boston: Jones and Bartlett, 1994), 4. The subsection from which this quote is taken is titled "Darwin's Discovery: Design without Designer".

Intelligent design, by finding clear signs of intelligence in nature, makes plausible that an artistic wisdom underlies nature. Ayala's remark therefore needs to be contrasted with the following by Thomas Aquinas: "By his natural reason man is able to arrive at some knowledge of God. For seeing that natural things run their course according to a fixed order, and since there cannot be order without a cause of order, men, for the most part, perceive that there is one who orders the things that we see. But who or of what kind this cause of order may be, or whether there be but one, cannot be gathered from this general consideration."[58] Aquinas here was not doing first philosophy or metaphysics. He was simply noting that our natural reason readily infers some sort of "orderer" behind nature. Similarly, intelligent design argues that natural reason readily infers some sort of designer. Whereas Darwinism short-circuits this inference, intelligent design restores and clarifies it. Indeed, the various aspects of nature to which God drew Job's attention and which helped convince Job of God's artistic wisdom—and therewith of God's goodness—would continue to convince Job in light of intelligent design. Not so for Darwinism. As with Aquinas's orderer, intelligent design cannot, without drawing on philosophy and theology, specify who or what the designer is. But whatever else this who or what may be, whatever its ultimate nature, it is at least a designer, and demonstrably so. The unique contribution of intelligent design to current theodicy discussions is restoring artistic wisdom to nature.

---

[58] Thomas Aquinas, "Summa Contra Gentiles", in: A. C. Pegis (ed.), *Introduction to St. Thomas Aquinas* (New York: Modern Library, 1948), 454 f.

Evolution, Suffering, and the God of Hope in Roman Catholic Thought after Darwin

Peter M. J. Hess

Nineteenth century Roman Catholics recognized the problem of suffering and death as a theological mystery embedded deeply within the Judeo-Christian tradition. They were quite familiar with the profound treatment of the problem in a monotheistic context in the Hebrew book of *Job*. But theologians had not always been content simply to allow evil to remain a raw mystery; they wanted to explain it, to assign it a cause, to give it a place in an ordered universe. Suffering was linked in *Genesis* to Adam's disobedience: "cursed is the ground because of you; in toil you shall eat of it all the days of your life; thorns and thistles it shall bring forth to you; and you shall eat the plants of the field." (Gen 3:17–18). And although Saint Paul's nuanced treatment of evil included such sophisticated articulations as the doctrine that the whole of creation is groaning in travail (Rom 8:20–23),[1] he also tied mortality directly sin: "For the wages of sin is death, but the free gift of God is eternal life in Christ Jesus our Lord." (Rom 6:23) Augustine coupled death specifically with Adam's sin.[2]

The idea of a connection between sin, death, and suffering would be further elaborated in succeeding centuries of Christian theology, edging out the more subtle Pauline integration of human misery into the cosmic drama of salvation. The idea of suffering and death as the penalty of the Adamic Fall from grace in the Garden of Eden became a stock-in-trade of moral theologies and homiletical traditions for seventeen centuries, and was formalized in the decrees of the Council of Trent.[3] But this long-standing theological *topos*

---

[1] "For the creation was subjected to futility, not of its own will but by the will of him who subjected it in hope; because the creation itself will be set free from its bondage to decay and obtain the glorious liberty of the children of God. We know that the whole creation has been groaning in travail together until now; and not only the creation, but we ourselves."

[2] Augustine, *The Literal Meaning of Genesis*, trans. John Taylor, SJ vol. 2. (New York: Newman Press, 1982), 80 ff.

[3] *Canons of the Council of Trent*, ed. H. J. Schroeder, O. P. (B. Herder, 1941), 21. Fifth Session, "Decree Concerning Original Sin", par. 1: "If any one does not confess that the first man, Adam, when he had transgressed the commandment of God in Paradise, immediately lost the holiness and justice in which he had been constituted, [and] incurred [...] together with death, captivity under his power who thenceforth had the empire of death, that is to say, the devil, and the entire Adam, through that offence of prevarication, was changed, in body and soul, for the worse; let him be anathema."

would be challenged as ideas emerged from the Scientific Revolution and the Enlightenment which began to unravel the connection between creaturely misery and moral guilt. Voltaire ridiculed in *Candide* the idea that the Lisbon earthquake of 1755 could in any intelligible way be interpreted as a just judgment of God,[4] and eighteenth-century geology and paleontology began to sketch the outlines of a "deep history of time", in which Earth was far older than the biblical chronology allowed, and prehistory was populated with animals engaging for eons in voracious and painful predation.[5]

The publication of Darwin's *On the Origin of Species* in 1859 shifted the dynamics of this traditional conversation even more. Although the idea of evolution was hardly novel in 1859,[6] Darwin placed a cogent theory of descent with modification on the solid foundations of detailed observation. The prospect of a parade of species passing into and out of existence over countless millennia constituted a threat of major proportions to received wisdom about the fixity of all living kinds. A dynamic universe challenged the intelligibility of traditional doctrines about scriptural veracity, about divine design and the love of God, about the problem of evil, and about the very purpose and meaning of human life.

This chapter sketches some stages in the Catholic reception of Darwin's evolutionary theory, and in particular the treatment of the problem of suffering. The Catholic assimilation of evolution reflects as it were a sort of "punctuated equilibrium": (1) an initial period (1859–ca. 1900) which saw (variously) either vehement rejection or enthusiastic endorsement of evolution or some more neutral response; (2) a second phase (Teilhard de Chardin to the 1970s) that witnessed more critical assessment of evolution; and (3) the current generation of scholarship in which some visionary thinkers are attempting to integrate Christian theology and a comprehensive evolutionary worldview. A review of this history provokes a number of fascinating questions. Why did some Catholic theologians accept Darwin's theory so readily, while others rejected, modified, or otherwise resisted it? At what point in the assimilation of evolution did Catholics recognize that the eons of pain and death entailed by evolution merited theological consideration? How did those who accepted it reconcile a brutal and implacable process with the Christian God of hope? These are indeed important questions, for at stake is the integrity and coher-

---

[4] Voltaire, *Candide*. John Rogers (1712–1789) likewise suggested that earthquakes "are not properly miraculous or preternatural", and that the Catholic victims of the 1755 Lisbon quake were no greater sinners than the survivors, or than their American Protestant contemporaries. *The Terribleness, and the Moral Cause of Earthquakes* (Boston: S. Kneeland, 1756).

[5] Martin J.S. Rudwick, in: *Scenes from Deep Time: Early Pictorial Representations of the Prehistoric World* (Chicago: 1992) traces significant influences – including religious ones – on the development of the 18th–19th century iconographic tradition of depicting deep geological time.

[6] See Peter J. Bowler, *Evolution: The History of an Idea* (Berkeley: University of California Press, 1984).

ence of the claims of any religious world view that dares to take evolutionary science seriously.

Darwin's Challenge to Theology

The reception of Darwinism has been misleadingly characterized as an epic struggle between science and religion, or between courageous free-thinkers and the narrow dogmas of the past. But critical historiography has long demonstrated the need for a more nuanced perspective on reactions to Darwin's theory of descent. Hunter Dupree showed that among Protestants there were scientists and theologians on both sides of the issues: some naturalists opposed Darwin on scientific grounds, and some divines appropriated his theory as being compatible with theology.[7] Moreover, Darwin himself matured in a Christian cultural context and had early training in divinity. John Brooke has inferred that Darwin's gradual loss of traditional faith had as much to do with his emotional response to the tragic death of his daughter Annie as it did with his developing perspective on natural selection.[8] Although the theory of evolution was in some respects consonant with his agnosticism, it was not necessarily causative of it.

Nevertheless, the appearance of *The Origin of Species* did provoke a wide range of reactions to the idea of evolution.[9] Ingenious though Darwin's theory of descent with modification and differential rates of survival was, for decades it remained no more than an intriguing idea in search of a cogent mechanism of operation. Only with the integration of Mendelian genetics into the neo-Darwinian synthesis in the twentieth century could evolution be established as a solid and coherent framework for explaining biological diversity.[10] Evolution's theoretical strength has been borne out by the gradual accumulation of evidence that natural selection, working upon genetic variation, can account for the evolution of complex systems and structures.

---

[7] A. Hunter Dupree, "Christianity and the Scientific Community in the Age of Darwin", in: David C. Lindberg and Ronald L. Numbers (ed.), *God and Nature: Historical Essays on the Encounter between Christianity and Science* (Berkeley: University of California Press, 1986) 351–368.

[8] John H. Brooke, "Revisiting Darwin on Order and Design", in: Niels Gregersen and Ulf Gorman (ed.), *Design and Disorder: Perspectives from Science and Theology*, (London: T & T Clark, 2002), 31–52.

[9] John H. Brooke, *Science and Religion: Some Historical Perspectives* (Cambridge University Press, 1991), 275–320. See Thomas F. Glick, *The Comparative Reception of Darwinism* (Austin: The University of Texas, 1972).

[10] For an excellent summary of the modern synthesis see Ted Peters and Martinez Hewlett, *Evolution from Creation to New Creation: Conflict, Conversation, and Convergence* (Nashville: Abingdon Press, 2003), ch. 2, "Darwin, Darwinism, and the Neo-Darwinian Synthesis, 35–50; see also Edward J. Larson, *Evolution: The Remarkable History of a Scientific Theory* (New York: Modern Library, 2004), 219–243. For a reference from a specifically scientific text see Bernard Campbell, *Human Evolution: An Introduction to Man's Adaptations* (Piscataway, NJ: Aldine Transaction, ⁴1998).

Even before the discovery and application of Mendel's idea of genes as transmitters of variation, the responses to Darwin's theory within Roman Catholicism were surprisingly varied. The thorough-going evolutionary theism of Pierre Teilhard de Chardin in the 20th century sprang from a context of long discussion among Catholic theologians dating almost from the publication of *The Origin of Species*. The halting assimilation of evolutionary ideas, with its episodes of rejection and adaptation, was determined by a variety of factors, ranging from the ecclesio-political issues surrounding the controversy over "modernism", to philosophical and theological commitments, to cultural attitudes toward science, to the baffling personal predilections of individual thinkers.[11]

The Phase of Reaction: the Range of Catholic Responses to Darwin

Any theologian who considered appropriating the theory of biological evolution had to deal with a variety of challenges it posed to traditional belief. These included the nature of biblical inspiration, the relative importance of the literal as opposed to figurative or other interpretations of the text, and the difficulty of the short historical time frame demanded by such a reading of *Genesis*. For Catholic theologians, a major challenge was the problem of theodicy: why would God have incorporated suffering and death into the world from the moment of creation of life? Evolution shifted the frame of reference from an anthropocentric context – in which human affliction had often been neatly fit into a theological framework of general or special providence – to the global context of life on earth. Some theologians, eager to adapt theology to the new scientific theory, dealt only with the issue of its congruence with the *Genesis* story. Others glossed over the problem of suffering, either by minimizing animal pain or by justifying it theologically on the grounds that animals lack conscious anticipation.[12] In the twentieth century, in fits and starts beginning with Teilhard, Catholic thinkers began to confront these issues directly.

Catholicism and Science before the Origin of Species: Cardinal Newman

In the intellectual ferment of the nineteenth century, biology was rapidly gaining status as a profession, and its concepts carried increasing cultural weight.[13] How might a progressive Catholic theologian have regarded science in such

[11] R. Scott Appleby offers a lucid exposition in "Exposing Darwin's 'hidden agenda'": Roman Catholic responses to evolution, 1875–1925, in: Ronald L. Numbers and John Stenhouse (ed.), *Disseminating Darwinism: the Role of Place, Race, Religion, and Gender* (Cambridge University Press, 1999), 173–207.

[12] As apparently does J. C. Munday in "Animal pain: beyond the threshold?", in: Keith B. Miller (ed.), *Perspectives on an Evolving Creation* (Grand Rapids: Eerdmans Publishing, 2003), 435–468.

[13] J. W. Burrow, *The Crisis of Reason: European Thought, 1848–1914* (Yale University Press, 2000), 42–52.

a context? A few years before Darwin's *The Origin of Species* appeared, John
Henry Newman offered in *The Idea of a University* some intriguing Catholic perspectives on the proper relationship between theology and science. Or
rather, he offered a perspective that allows interpretation in at least two ways:
on the one hand, Newman seems to have articulated a two languages position,
in that since theology is the "philosophy of the supernatural world" and science the "philosophy of the natural",

> Theology and Science, whether in their respective ideas, or again in their own actual
> fields, on the whole, are incommunicable, incapable of collision, and needing, at
> most to be connected, never to be reconciled.[14]

On the other hand, Newman remained serenely confident that Truth is one,
even if known through different modalities, and that the theologian has no
reason to become nervous that discoveries arrived at by means of any scientific method other than theology can truly contradict formal religious dogma.
In fact, Newman argued, theology is the one science which from its "sovereign and unassailable position" can remain epistemologically unperturbed:

> He is sure, and nothing shall make him doubt, that, if anything seems to be proved
> by astronomer, or geologist, or chronologist, or antiquarian, or ethnologist, in con-
> tradiction to the dogmas of faith, that point will eventually turn out, first, *not* to be
> proved, or, secondly, not *contradictory*, or thirdly, not contradictory to any thing
> *really revealed*, but to something which has been confused with revelation.[15]

Newman cautioned both scientists and theologians to observe the integrity of
their respective disciplines and to avoid trespassing into intellectual territory
outside their competence. He scolded contemporary theologians

> [...] who, from a nervous impatience lest Scripture should for one moment seem
> inconsistent with the results of some speculation of the hour, are ever proposing
> geological or ethnological comments upon it, which they have to alter or obliterate
> before the ink is well dry, from changes in the progressive science, which they have
> so officiously brought to its aid.[16]

This position clearly reflects a commitment to theology in dialogue with scientific culture, not hermetically sealed off from it. Moreover, though we cannot
either impute or deny to Newman a specific endorsement of human evolution,
he was one of the first theologians to accept the scientific principle of the mutation of species.[17] As a friend of the English biologist Mivart, Newman endorsed

---

[14] John Henry Newman, *The Idea of a University Defined and Illustrated*, ch. 7, "Christianity
and Physical Science" (New York, Bombay, and Calcutta: Longmans, Green, and Co., 1907), 431.

[15] Ibid., 466 f.

[16] Ibid., 472. Galileo ought rather "to have held hold his doctrine of the motion of the earth as a
scientific conclusion, leaving it to those whom it really concerned to compare it with Scripture".

[17] Gregory P. Elder, Chronic *Vigour: Darwin, Anglicans, Catholics, and the Development of a
Doctrine of Providential Evolution* (New York: University Press of America, 1996), 74.

the latter's ideas, and he speculated in a letter to E. B. Pusey (1870) that Darwin's views about human bodily descent did not contradict scripture.[18] However, Newman's assent came with reservations: no more than most Catholics of the time could he countenance the evolution of the human soul.

Endorsement of a Modified Darwinism: St. George Jackson Mivart

One of the early significant endorsements of the theory of evolution from a solidly theistic perspective came from the English anatomist and convert to Catholicism, St. George Jackson Mivart (1827–1900). In his *On the Genesis of Species* (1871), he expounded arguments important enough for Darwin to pay serious attention to in subsequent editions of the *Origin of Species*. Mivart had taught himself zoology, developing a specialization in the anatomy of newts and monkeys. With the sponsorship of Thomas Huxley, he became a Fellow of the Royal Society and made the acquaintance of Darwin.[19]

In support of his view that Christian doctrine and the theory of evolution were compatible, Mivart appealed to patristic and medieval articulations of an unfolding universe. For example, he cited Augustine's "derivative sense in which God's creation of organic form is to be understood", namely the conferral on the world of the power to evolve from *logikoi spermatikoi*, or "word empowered seeds."[20] Mivart declared that creation was in fact part of revelation, and this led him to a natural theology in which the intelligent acceptance of theistic evolution on purely rational grounds served to prepare the way for acceptance of the reasonableness of revelation.[21] Darwin and Spencer, he argued, had created straw person characterizations of teleology or "ultimate cause". Since the claims of theism are made entirely in analogical language, theists confess at the outset that their conceptions of God are utterly inadequate, and therefore scientists who ridicule belief in God as Creator on the grounds of lack of physical evidence are guilty of what might today be termed "scientism."[22]

As a defense against the perceived threat of a thoroughly naturalistic evolution, Mivart constructed protective zones around doctrine at two points. The first was to safeguard the Christian dogma of "absolute or primary creation", which stands completely outside the purview of physical science. While "derivative creation"—or the action of evolution upon the animate word to provide a diversity of species—lay within the realm of the natural, primary creation could only be a purely supernatural act. Mivart believed that care-

---

[18] Ibid., 75 f.

[19] The relationship soured after Mivart's publication of his own book and worsened following the appearance of Darwin's *Descent of Man*, not so much on account of Mivart's opposition to elements of Darwin's theory as because of the personal nature of his attacks upon the latter.

[20] Mivart, *On the Genesis of Species*, 281.

[21] Ibid., 261.

[22] Ibid., 264; 272 f.

ful distinction between these categorically different sorts of creation not only could dispel theological reluctance to accept evolution, but might obviate a simplistic rejection by scientists of the theological doctrine of creation. Unable to countenance the derivation of the human spirit from the dust of the earth, Mivart constructed a second protective zone around the creation of the human soul. As a strategy for integrating biological evolution with theological anthropology, this would be echoed by Catholic theologians up to Popes Pius XII and John Paul II. It would be more than a century before the idea of the soul as an "emergent property" of evolving matter would be developed as a coherent alternative to this "special creationism."

One of the least satisfactory aspects of Mivart's enterprise of merging evolutionary theory into a perspective of providentialist theology was his treatment of the problem of evolutionary suffering. He tried to minimize animal pain, suggesting that

> only during consciousness does it exist, and only in the most highly organized men does it reach its acme. The author has been assured that lower races of men appear less keenly sensitive to physical pain than do more cultivated and refined human beings. Thus only in man can there really be any intense degree of suffering, because only in him is there that intellectual recollection of past moments and that anticipation of future ones, which constitute in great part the bitterness of suffering.[23]

Today this view would be judged not only to be racist and classist, but also to entail a cavalier dismissal of the reality of pre-human sentient experience. However much truth there may be in the differentiation between physical and psychological pain, Mivart's minimization of the former was not a sufficiently convincing refutation of Darwin's recognition that the process of natural selection had involved countless conscious beings in a systematic web of predatory suffering. Mivart's metaphysics of design predisposed him to an inevitably beneficial reading of evolution: "The natural universe has resulted in the development of an unmistakable harmony and beauty, and in a decided preponderance of good and happiness over their opposites."[24] This reads uncomfortably and unconvincingly like a utilitarian justification of suffering, or anthropomorphically like William Paley's cheerful vicarage garden with its millions of joyously buzzing insects. Scholars and other observers of nature in subsequent generations would be compelled to take the problem of animal suffering far more seriously.

Rome and Evolution: A Pregnant Ambiguity

We cannot think in terms of a monolithic reaction from Rome on the part of either the papacy or the curia or the bishops. Instead, various forces within

---

[23] Ibid., 277.
[24] Ibid., 278.

Catholicism would serve to retard or deflect the trajectory of its gradual acceptance of the theory of evolution. Modifying centuries of established tradition was no mean task, as exemplified by the earliest official statement by the ecclesiastical hierarchy. In 1860, at a provincial Council of Cologne, during deliberations about principles of Christian anthropology, the council declared as contrary to scripture and faith both the opinion that the human body was derived from the spontaneous transformation of an inferior nature, and the view that the entire human race had not descended from Adam.[25] The discussion of faith and reason at the First Vatican Council, convened in 1868 by Pope Pius IX, includes a thinly veiled attack on evolution:

> Hence all faithful Christians are forbidden to defend as the legitimate conclusions of science those opinions which are known to be contrary to the doctrine of faith, particularly if they have been condemned by the Church; and furthermore they are absolutely bound to hold them to be errors which wear the deceptive appearance of truth.[26]

But the *Dogmatic Constitution* does not explicitly name developmental biology, and the declaration that "faith and reason [can] never be at odds with one another but mutually support each other" leaves considerable room for interpretation. The Church does not forbid the sciences to employ their own proper principles and method, although

> While she admits this just freedom, she takes particular care that they do not become infected with errors by conflicting with divine teaching, or, by going beyond their proper limits, intrude upon what belongs to faith and engender confusion.[27]

Beyond the official pronouncement there was no substantial campaign of enforcement or repression. When Mivart taught that God could infuse a soul into a body prepared by a preceding process of evolution, he was strongly criticized by some Catholic authors, but the authorities did not intervene; in fact, in 1876 Pope Pius IX conferred upon him the degree or doctor of philosophy. In 1891 Cardinal Zeferino Gonzáles corrected the theory of Mivart that evolution could prepare the body by introducing the idea of a "special action" by God to render the body capable of receiving a spiritual soul, which he thought necessary to preserve human dignity and distinction from the beasts.[28]

---

[25] *Collectio Lacensis*, 5, 292; cited in Zoltán Alszeghy, S.J., "Development in the doctrinal formulation of the Church concerning the theory of evolution", in: Johannes Metz (ed.), *The Evolving World and Theology*, Concilium, vol. 26 (New York: Paulist Press, 1967), 25.

[26] *Dogmatic Constitution on the Catholic Faith* (April 1870), ch. 4, par. 9. The council was convened to deal with, *inter alia*, the problem of "modernism".

[27] Pope Pius IX, *Dogmatic Constitution on the Church* (1870), par. 10.

[28] Owen Garrigan, *Man's Intervention in Nature* (New York: Hawthorn Books, 1967), 84. Even Mivart's dispute with Church authority near the end of his life (1900) was not about the question of evolution.

Pope Leo XIII declared in *Providentissimus Deus* (1893) that the science is "admirably adapted to show forth the glory of the Great Creator, provided it be taught as it should be", but that if it be "perversely imparted to the youthful intelligence" it can prove most fatal by destroying the principles of true philosophy and corrupting morality. Science thus serves a protective role, assisting in detecting attacks on the Sacred Books, and in refuting them. In fact,

> There can never, indeed, be any real discrepancy between the theologian and the physicist, as long as each confines himself within his own lines, and both are careful, as St. Augustine warns us, "not to make rash assertions, or to assert what is not known as known.[29]

In fact, Pope Leo appealed to the rule of St. Augustine that in cases of conflict, it was the Church's right and responsibility to enforce an interpretation of scientific evidence consonant with scripture:

> Whatever they can really demonstrate to be true of physical nature, we must show to be capable of reconciliation with our Scriptures; and whatever they assert in their treatises which is contrary to these Scriptures of ours, that is to Catholic faith, we must either prove it as well as we can to be entirely false, or at all events we must, without the smallest hesitation, believe it to be false.[30]

Again, here was an ambiguity pregnant with possibility. Almost in echo of Bellarmine's quip that the scriptures teach us how to go to heaven, not how the heavens go, Pope Leo XIII declared that we must bear in mind that the sacred writers, "or to speak more accurately, the Holy Ghost Who spoke by them, did not intend to teach men these things (that is to say, the essential nature of the things of the visible universe), things in no way profitable unto salvation". That is, biblical writers had not written as scientists in quest of the secrets of nature, but rather described and dealt with their subject in figurative language, or in terms which were commonly used at the time.

Enthusiastic Appropriation: John Augustine Zahm

The foremost American Catholic apologist for the harmonization of evolutionary theory with Catholic dogma during this early period was John Augustine Zahm (1851–1921). Ordained a priest in the Holy Cross order in 1875, he was a professor of physics and chemistry at the University of Notre Dame. In the year of publication of his book *Evolution and Dogma* Zahm was transferred to Rome as procurator general for the Holy Cross Community, which some opponents incorrectly interpreted as censure for his dubious views. Nevertheless, the appearance of the French and Italian editions of

---

[29] Leo XIII, *Providentissimus Deus*: Encyclical of Pope Leo XIII on the Study of Holy Scripture, Given at St. Peter's, at Rome, the 18th day of November, 1893, the eighteenth year of Our Pontificate, Paragraph 18.

[30] Loc. sit.

Evolution and Dogma inevitably led to intensified debate about the issues for a year, until the Sacred Congregation of the Index issued an injunction against its further publication and distribution in 1876, an injunction that appears never to have been enforced.[31]

Zahm demonstrated a sophisticated understanding of evolutionary theory, noting that Darwinism "is not evolution, as is so often imagined, but only one of numerous attempts which have been made to explain the *modus operandi* of evolution."[32] He was also well aware of the baggage that Darwinian evolution carried in its being associated with atheism, contesting Canadian geologist William Dawson's claim that "the doctrine of evolution carried out to its logical consequences excludes creation and Theism."[33] Zahm was current with European controversies, citing the French Dominican theologian M. D. Leroy in support of his argument that evolution in fact made the doctrine of divine creation more elegant:

> Far from compromising the orthodox belief in the creative action of God [evolution] reduces this action to a small number of transcendent acts, more in conformity with the unity of the Divine plan and the infinite wisdom of the Almighty, who knows how to employ secondary causes to attain his ends.[34]

Zahm recognized the paucity of transitional forms, referring to Darwin's own concession that our knowledge of the geological record is incomplete.[35] He was convinced that although we do not at present understand the production of variations (not for some time would Mendelian genetics be incorporated into the neo-Darwinian synthesis) we would eventually arrive at this understanding. And he critically reviewed the evidence on both sides of the controversy about Lamarckian transmission of acquired characteristics, weighing Darwinian and non-Darwinian approaches, and judiciously concluded that a true, all-embracing theory of evolution still awaits us.[36]

What is most remarkable is Zahm's serene confidence in the ultimate consonance between progressive science and revealed theology. In discussing Mivart's exclusion of the human soul from evolution, he judged that whatever science ultimately concluded about the evolution of the human body, it could not contradict Catholic dogma. Even if future research in paleontology, anthropology, and biology, were to demonstrate conclusively that humans are genetically related to lower animals, we would have no ground to assume that "the conclusions of science are hopelessly at variance with the declarations of

---

[31] John Zahm, *Evolution and Dogma* (Chicago: D.H. McBride and Co., 1896; rpt. ed., New York: Arno Press, 1978), introduction.

[32] Ibid., 207.

[33] Ibid., 209.

[34] Ibid., 212. M.D. Leroy, *L'évolution restreinte aux espèces organiques* (Paris/Lyons, 1891).

[35] Ibid., 161, 173

[36] Ibid., 195–202.

the sacred text, or the authorized teachings of the Church of Christ" Indeed, in the event of an indisputably proven evolutionary descent of humanity,

> We should be obliged to revise the interpretation that has usually been given to the words of scripture which refer to the formation of Adam's body, and read these words in the sense which evolution demands, a sense which, as we have seen, may be attributed to the words of the inspired record, without either distorting the meaning of terms or in any way doing violence to the text.[37]

Thus Zahm's favorable early response to theory of evolution reflects a maturing historical-critical hermeneutic: the book of God's Word must be read in light of the book of God's Works, the paleontological record. *Evolution and Dogma* represents a sort of preliminary assessment of Darwinism, and one only wonders whether, had his work not been suppressed, he would have ventured further with a consideration of the darker implications of natural selection throughout geological history.

Studied Rejection of Darwinism: Martin S. Brennan

Not all American Catholics, by any means, were proponents of evolution. Clergy of modest education serving the church on a rapidly expanding frontier had pastoral concerns more pressing than assessing arcane intellectual arguments.[38] But there were clear antipathies that ran deeper than this, even among those who had leisure for and relished the life of the mind. Orestes Brownson, an opinionated Unitarian convert to Catholicism, categorically rejected evolution on the grounds that it "denies the doctrine of the creation and immutability of species, as taught in Genesis."[39]

A much more carefully considered rebuttal came from a St. Louis seminary science professor, Martin Brennan. Two years after the appearance of Zahm's book, Brennan published his lengthy *The Science of the Bible* (1898), which offered a comprehensive assessment of the contemporary sciences in light of scripture. He was clearly conversant with recent theories in physics, chemistry, biology and earth sciences, including the geological "deep history of time". Still, his careful review led him ineluctably to the conclusion that Darwinism was simply incorrect.

The weakest link in Darwin's chain of reasoning, in Brennan's view, was his confounding of "variety" with "species".[40] But Brennan also saw geology and the incompleteness of the fossil record – which might hide missing links and

---

[37] Ibid., 364 f.

[38] Appleby, op. cit., 178.

[39] Orestes Brownson, "Review of *Darwin's Descent of Man*", Brownson's Quarterly Review, July, 1873.

[40] Martin S. Brennan *The Science of the Bible* (St. Louis: B. Herder, 1898), 282. Some Intelligent Design creationists make essentially the same claim when allowing micro- but not macro-mutation.

connections – as nemeses of the Darwinian hypothesis. Accepting the later-disproven argument of Sir William Thompson, Lord Kelvin, concerning the thirty-million year life of the sun, he reckoned that solar physics offers solid evidence to believe that far too little time has elapsed to accomplish all the changes demanded by natural selection.[41] Brennan concluded that

> [Darwin's] hypothesis, like all novelties and sensations in the scientific world, however popular and successful at first, is being tested in the crucible of facts and is declared a failure because it cannot satisfactorily answer the difficulties pressed against it.[42]

Thus, for Brennan a special creative act was required at the origin of each species. Quoting Joseph Le Conte, Asa Gray, and Louis Agassiz to deny the transmutation of species, he contended that the creator established a definite number of species in the beginning which endure even today. Moreover, regarding human evolution

> Genesis tells us that God created man to his own image;...Evolutionists rely upon biology and anthropology to establish their theories. But both biology and anthropology very plainly and positively favor the statement of Moses...showing that it is absolutely impossible for man to have been evolved by transmutation from any inferior species, but must have come by a special creative act of the almighty as the great Hebrew prophet records."[43]

Brennan's critical discussion of the Darwinian and other positions regarding evolution led him to conclude that biology and anthropology confirm rather than contradict the Mosaic record: "God called man into being by a special creative act. The whole human family belongs to the one same species, and man's Simian desent must be abandoned."[44] Brennan's position illustrates the subtlety of theological distinctions at this time: although he came out against biological evolution, he was by no means an unswerving biblical literalist. While on the one hand he calculated human antiquity on earth at between 8,000 and 10,000 years, on the other hand his review of biogeographical, linguistic, and other evidence led him to maintain that the Noachian deluge had been a strictly local flood.[45]

It is not easy to explain why two such scholars such as John Zahm and Martin Brennan – both priests teaching in Catholic institutions in the American Midwest and publishing within two years of each other – could arrive at such opposite conclusions regarding Darwin's theory.

---

[41] Ibid., 282, 286, 292.
[42] Ibid., 294.
[43] Ibid., 314 f.
[44] Ibid., 356.
[45] Ibid., 385 f.

A Progressive View from the Magisterium: John L. Spalding

Catholic thinking about the natural sciences underwent a gradual transformation in the twentieth century. This is prefigured in important ways by the though of John L. Spalding, Bishop of Peoria, Illinois, in his book *Religion, Agnosticism, and Education* (1902). Spalding began with an assumption of the fundamental intelligibility of the world: "We find that thoughts and things are co-ordinate. Ideas have their counterparts in facts. Everywhere there is law and order." The fact that every aspect of animate nature unfolds by an inner drive testifies to a divine planning:

> In the minute cell there is the potency which creates the most perfect form. And, if it could be proven that the infinite variety of nature is but the result of the manifold evolution of a single elementary substance, we should still inevitably see the work of reason in it all.[46]

Regarding the world as an effect, in other words, necessarily leads us to a knowing and wise cause, "though the knowledge and wisdom of the Infinite are doubtless something inconceivably higher than what these terms can mean for us". As a bishop in the American hierarchy – and therefore a member of the teaching magisterium of the church – Spalding made a passionate plea for liberty of speculation:

> To forbid men to think along whatever line, is to place oneself in opposition to the deepest and most invincible tendency of the civilized world. Were it possible to compel obedience from Catholics in matters of this kind, the result would be a hardening and sinking of our whole religious life. We should more and more drift away from the vital movements of the age, and find ourselves at last immured in a spiritual ghetto, where no man can breathe pure air, or be joyful or strong or free.[47]

But Spalding was certainly not naive about the dangers of scientific materialism, warning that a reductionistic world-view has led to an exclusive emphasis on heredity and environment at the expense of all other explanatory factors:

> The opinion tends to prevail that the mind and character of man, like his body, like the whole organic world, is the product of evolution, working through fatal laws, wherewith human purpose and free will – the possibility of which is denied – cannot interfere in any real way.[48]

Spalding asserted that no educator could accept this position without losing conviction in the ultimate and transcendent value of his work. But he noted with confidence that "fortunately, one may admit the general prevalence of the law of evolution without ceasing to believe in God, in the soul, and in

---

[46] John L. Spalding, *Religion, Agnosticism, and Education* (Chicago, A.C. McClurg & Co., 1902), ch. 2. "Agnosticism".
[47] Spalding, ch. 5. "Education and the Future of Religion".
[48] Ch. VI. "Progress in Education".

freedom". In the same way as Zahm and Brennan, Spalding represented an important point along the spectrum of opinion about evolution in late-nineteenth-century America.

The Phase of Critical Assessment: Evolution and Suffering in Catholic Thought, 1900–1955

In the twentieth century, the theory of evolution would continue its slow and halting process of being assimilated into the framework of theological and religious thought. Writing in 1928, Père de Sinéty, S.J. summarized the range of Catholic views on evolution as including "those who reject evolution as theologically erroneous, those who consider Catholics absolutely free to accept transformism, and the great number who take a middle position."[49] For some, like French theologian Henry de Dorlodot, the answer came easily: "the teaching of the fathers is very favorable to the theory of absolute natural evolution."[50] But the Thomist influence on seminary education cannot be underestimated, and to Thomists Darwinism seemed philosophically absurd, deriving the more perfect from the less perfect, drawing being from nothing, postulating an effect without a cause.[51] Others proffered a qualified acceptance, such as German scholar Hermann Muckermann who, weighing in favor of vitalism, wrote that an explanation of life "must ultimately be sought in a creative act of God, who endowed matter with a force *sui generis* that directed the material energies toward the formation and development of the first organisms."[52] And William Hauber nicely demonstrated the fluidity of concepts in this discussion: on the one hand, he noted that "although St. Thomas had no reason to be an evolutionist, his theory of the tendency of matter to move toward greater and greater perfection in form was entirely compatible with biological evolution";[53] on the other hand he wrote approvingly of ornithologist Richard Goldschmidt's claim that it is consistent with the evidence to suppose that nature could produce "in one generation a full-fledged bird, ready for flight, and fit to survive in a hostile environment."[54]

---

[49] *Dictionnaire apologétique de la foi catholiques* [Paris, G. Beauchesne, 1911–1922 (i.e. 1928)], "Transformism".

[50] Henry de Dorlodot, Canon, *Darwinism and Catholic thought*, trans. Rev Ernest Messenter [London: Burns, Oates and Washbourne, 1922. vol. 10 (no more published)], 169.

[51] Harry W. Paul, *The Edge of Contingency: French Catholic Reaction to Scientific Change from Darwin to Duhem* (Gainesville: University Presses of Florida, 1979), 62.

[52] Hermann Muckermann, "Biogenesis and Abiogenesis", in: *The Catholic Encyclopedia* (New York: Robert Appleton Company, 1907), quoted in: W.A. Hauber, "Evolution and Catholic Thought", American Ecclesiastical Review, 106, 1942, 173.

[53] Hauber, 169, quoting Henri de Dorlodot, *Darwinism and Catholic Thought* (London, 1922).

[54] Hauber, 162. Richard Goldschmidt, *The Material Basis of Evolution* (Yale: Yale University Press, 1940).

Evolution as Cosmogenesis: Pierre Teilhard de Chardin

With evolution gaining a comfortable foothold in the scientific community,[55] Catholic theologians (like Protestant theologians) were obliged to begin a critical assessment of its implications. For some thinkers, evolution was acceptable so long as humanity was exempt from its processes, and the problem of suffering was rendered less complicated. In his classic *Natural Theology*, Dominican philosopher Bernard Boedder drew two corollaries from the doctrine of Providence: first, "God does not intend the final well-being of any individual living creature of this world except man", and second, "man himself is to be perfectly happy, not here on earth, but hereafter". Boedder regarded it as perfectly consistent with Catholic teaching to maintain that

> It is therefore quite intelligible, that God should allow millions of irrational creatures to be sacrificed for the sake of man, to serve his eternal welfare remotely or proximately. No less reconcilable is it with Divine Providence, that under certain conditions mortal men should be wasted by contagious diseases, emaciated by famine, or fall in the flower of their age on the battlefield. In a word: God cares more for one immortal soul that does not resist Him, than for the whole of the material universe.[56]

Such a traditional Thomist position would enjoy strength well into the twentieth century. Nevertheless, the seeds of doubt about the suffering of prehistoric sentient life had already been sown, and they found fertile ground in the thought of evolution's most famous Catholic apologist, the brilliant and controversial Jesuit Pierre Teilhard de Chardin.

Early in his assimilation of Darwin's ideas into a Christian theological framework, Teilhard recognized that the theory of biological evolution carried profound implications for the doctrines of sin, suffering and death. Early on he rejected the myth of a paradisal state:

> We often represent God to ourselves as being able to draw from non-being a world without sorrows, faults, dangers – a world in which there is no damage, no breakage. This is a conceptual fantasy, and makes it impossible to solve the problem of evil. Our being must, indeed, be precious for God to continue to seek it through so many obstacles.[57]

In Teilhard's view, identifying "original sin" with some initial transgression was a static solution to the problem of evil. He suggested that evil is neither

---

[55] Edward Larson asserts that evolution was widely accepted within the scientific community by 1880. *Evolution*, 143.

[56] Bernard Boedder, S.J., *Natural Theology*, (New York: Longmans, Green, and Co., ²1902), ch. 2, "Divine Providence and its Relation to Existing Evil", 226.

[57] Pierre Teilhard de Chardin, "Note on the modes of Divine action in the universe", (unpublished essay, 1920), in: *Christianity and Evolution*, trans. René Hague (New York: Harcourt Brace Jovanovich, 1971), 33.

bound up with human generation, nor even specific to the earth; it is simply the inevitable result of an open creation: "Original sin is the essential reaction of the finite to the creative act…It is the *reverse side* of all creation."[58] Moreover, suffering and death seem to have been present from the beginning: "As far as the mind can reach, looking backwards, we find the world dominated by physical evil, impregnated with moral evil…we find it in a state of original sin."[59] Evil is not an "unforeseen accident" but rather "a shadow that God inevitably produces simply by virtue of the fact that God decides on creation."[60] This new perspective carried profound implications for Christology as well, as the death of Christ ceased to be primarily about expiation of sin through suffering, and became instead the suffering of God with a world struggling to evolve.

Teilhard continued to develop his ideas about suffering in the context of evolution. Although acknowledging that in his *The Phenomenon of Man* (completed in 1940) he had focused upon the grand tapestry of evolution, he anticipated the criticism that nowhere had he mentioned physical suffering or moral wrong. His justification for this omission was that his "purpose has been solely fixed on isolating the *positive essence* of the biological process of hominization". Acutely aware of the problem of suffering, he asked "is it not precisely evil in its many forms that invincibly wells up through every pore, every joint, every articulation of the system within which I place myself?"[61] He identified four categories of evil: 1. Evil in the form of disorder and failure. "On the material level, there is the simple physical lack of arrangement, or disorder, but soon, suffering encrusted in sensitive flesh; and higher still, the wickedness or torture of the mind's self-analysis and choosing." 2. Evil of decomposition: "For the living being, dying has become the regular and indispensable condition for the replacement of one individual by another along the same phylum. Death is the essential cog in the mechanism and rise of life." 3. Evil in the form of solitude and anguish, identified by the consciousness of living in a universe we still do not understand very well. 4. Evil in the form of growth (the least tragic form): all progress toward more unity requires work and effort.

But even accepting natural evil within the rubric of evolution, Teilhard recognized that the extent of suffering spread throughout the world was simply too great not to compel us to think in the direction of some "catastrophe or

---

[58] Teilhard, "Fall redemption and geocentrism" (unpublished essay, 1920), in: *Christianity and Evolution*, 40.

[59] Teilhard, "Note on some possible historical representations of original sin" (before 1922), in: *Christianity and Evolution*, 47.

[60] Teilhard, "Christology and Evolution" (1933), in: *Christianity and Evolution*, 84 f.

[61] Pierre Teilhard de Chardin, *The Phenomenon of Man* [1955], trans. and ed. Sarah Appleton-Weber (Brighton: Sussex Academic Press, 1999), 224 f. Appendix: "Some comments on the place and role of evil in an evolving world."

primordial deviation" above and beyond the normal consequences of evolution. As a non-theologian he disqualified himself from further speculation, except to insist that "In one way or another, even in the eyes of a mere biologist, it is still true that nothing resembles the way of the Cross so much as the human epic."[62] For Teilhard evolution offered the unique opportunity of reinterpreting the cross of Christ at the heart of the Christian kerygma. Shifting the focus from the purely expiatory or redemptive character of the crucifixion, he reinterpreted it by placing the cross squarely within the structure of biological evolution with all the eons of death it entailed, by "organic senescence, genetic substation, and metamorphosis". This is the vision of "Cosmogenesis": the cross of the Christ of evolution "finally attains its fullness, which is to become the dynamic and complete symbol of a universe in a state of personalizing evolution."[63]

The Phase of Integration: the Task of the New Millennium

Catholic theology in the second half of the twentieth century was compelled to come to terms with a strengthening neo-Darwinism. In 1950 Pope Pius XII marked a cautious but important milestone in the official recognition of evolution as a valid scientific theory with his encyclical letter *Humani generis*. This permitted Catholic thinkers to engage in scientific discussion of the evolution of the human body from animal nature, but reiterated the exclusion of the human soul from any such research and debate.[64] Nor did *Humani generis* deal with the wider theological implications of evolution. Although Teilhard had broached in significant ways the relationship between evolutionary suffering and Christian soteriology, his works languished inaccessible during his lifetime, under censorship from the Church. Even today, as Catholic theology begins to take evolution seriously, not all theologians seem cognizant of the problem of animal pain.[65]

---

[62] Ibid., 226.

[63] Teilhard, "A generalizing and a deepening of the meaning of the Cross", in: *Christianity and Evolution*, 218 ff.

[64] Pius XII, *Humani Generis* (August 12, 1950), par. 36. "The Teaching Authority of the Church does not forbid that, in conformity with the present state of human sciences and sacred theology, research and discussions, on the part of men experienced in both fields, take place with regard to the doctrine of evolution, in as far as it inquires into the origin of the human body as coming from pre-existent and living matter – for the Catholic faith obliges us to hold that souls are immediately created by God."

[65] For instance, John E. Thiel, *God, Evil, and Innocent Suffering: a Theological Reflection* (New York: Crossroad, 2002), 31, n. 22: "We may speak of the innocent suffering of animals, and some people do. I suggest, though, that such talk is either an anthropomorphic rhetoric or a way of speaking of human guilt, when human actions cause such suffering." (I am indebted to John Haught for this reference.)

From Hominization to Incarnation: Karl Rahner

Karl Rahner stands out among Catholic theologians in the generation after *Humani generis* in recognizing the autonomy of science, and in taking the conclusions of biology seriously. Not only did he readily accept the evolution of humanity in its physical aspect from prehuman ancestors, but he declined to draw the protective zone around the human soul or spirit that had been a *sine qua non* of almost every Catholic response to evolution from John Zahm to Pope Pius XII. Rahner noted that since "the old ontology recognized an *eductio e potentia materiae* for living animal matter", there should be no ontological problem in accepting the emergence of consciousness from below.[66] In fact, Rahner noted, the teaching tradition of the Church "did not always clearly enunciate an immediate creation of the individual human soul". There should be no prohibition, therefore, on science placing the evolution of the human – body and soul – in an evolutionary context, so long as science eschews the claim to an exclusive right to interpret human nature, and recognizes an essential distinction between animal and human.[67] Rahner's theology assumed a traditional anthropocentrism in concluding that humans are ontologically different from animals. Nevertheless he acknowledge that the human carries the entire inheritance of biological pre-history into his present and future existence, however different we now appear to be from other animals. "Because now his biological, spiritual and divine elements are present in him, they are also quite plainly and simply to be affirmed of the beginning."[68]

It is possible to piece together the elements of a Rahnerian position on the problem of suffering from his treatment of the doctrine of original sin. Since paleontology amply demonstrates that death and predation were integral to biological nature long before the evolution of humankind, we can no longer interpret sin theologically as the cause of death. Assuming therefore the naturalness of death, Rahner proposed, as alternative models, (a) original sin as "a profound social and cultural upheaval which inaugurated a whole new sinful situation of humanity", and (b) original sin as a conscious rejection by emergent humanity of a "supernatural relationship to God in grace."[69] Although the relationship of suffering to divine grace remains a mystery, Rahner insisted on the ultimate goodness of created nature: "In a world of evolution of this kind matter cannot be conceived as a mere launching pad which is left behind…" Suffering and death are accordingly fully understandable only in light of the incarnation:

---

[66] Karl Rahner, *Theological Investigations*, vol. XXI, *Science and Christian Faith*, trans. Hugh M. Riley (New York: Crossroad, 1988) 40.

[67] Ibid., 46.

[68] Karl Rahner, *Hominization: the Evolutionary Origin of Man as a Theological Problem* (Freiburg: Herder, 1958; London: Burns & Oates, 1965), 108 f.

[69] Ibid., 46 f.

In our context it is especially worthy of note that the point at which God in a final self-communication irrevocably and definitively lays hold on the totality of the reality created by him is characterized not as spirit but as flesh. It is this which authorizes the Christian to integrate the history of salvation into the history of the cosmos, even when myriad questions remain unanswered.[70]

For Rahner, the suffering of sentient life in an evolving universe was meaningful because human beings "who are nature, endure nature, and pursue the study of nature, are called to that salvation which is the incomprehensible God himself."

Evolutionary Theodicy: John F. Haught

Among contemporary Catholic theologians who have addressed the problem of suffering and evil in an evolutionary context, a notable example is John F. Haught.[71] Welcoming theological engagement with science, Haught suggests that evolutionary biology is Darwin's gift to theology, in that it allows theology "to enlarge its sense of God's creativity by extending it over countless eons of time". Evolutionary history "also gives comparable magnitude to our sense of the divine participation in life's long and often tormented journey."[72] Science after Darwin shows us the "cruciform" visage of nature, and forces us to depart from classic notions of an impassive God untouched by the world's suffering. If the essence of God is compassionate love, then every instance of suffering in evolutionary history is enfolded in God's care:

> A vulnerable God, as the Trinitarian character of Christian theism requires, could not fail to feel intimately and to remember everlastingly all of the sufferings, struggles, and achievements in the *entire story* of cosmic and biological evolution.[73]

Haught regards this understanding of God as immanent to suffering as both faithful to religious tradition and explanatory of the natural world. In *Deeper than Darwin* he underscores the idea that the contingencies of nature and the apparent randomness of evolution are reflective not of the traditionally assumed divine omnipotence, but rather

> [...] of a God caring and self-effacing enough to wait for the genuine emergence of what is truly other than God, with all the risk, tragedy, and adventure this patience

---

[70] Ibid., 55.

[71] Although I am focusing on Haught's contributions to the contemporary discussion, other Roman Catholic thinkers have also produced significant work on this topic. As such, I do not mean to suggest that Haught's work represents a unique culmination of modern Catholic thought on the problem of theodicy and evolution. Other contemporary Roman Catholic thinkers who have dealt with this problem include, Martinez Hewlett (see his contribution to this volume) and, not least, John Paul II (see, for example, his "Evolution and the Living God", in: Ted Peters (ed.), *Science and Theology: The New Consonance* (Boulder: Westview Press, 1998), 149–152).

[72] John F. Haught, *God after Darwin: a Theology of Evolution* (Boulder, CO: 2000) 46.

[73] Ibid., 56.

entails…Such a God is also vulnerable enough to suffer along with life in its occasion of failure, struggle and loss.[74]

As we have seen in our review of earlier thinkers, neither dismissing animal suffering and death as non-problematic, nor linking human suffering and death to sin, are theologically constructive. Haught has recently suggested ways in which the texture of theology would change if theologians were to take suffering seriously. Cautioning against a wholesale dismissal of scriptural myths of the origins of evil, he notes that none of these myths – any more than their ancient near eastern counterparts – had anything to say about evolution.[75] All anthropocentric theodicies, in Haught's view, have to be radically restructured in light of Darwinian evolution. At the very least, he seems to argue that theodicy must become decoupled from the idea of suffering as expiation for guilt, and the consequence will be of profound value for theology:

> What if theologians really began to take seriously the evolutionary understanding of life and the universe? What if they realized that the cosmos, earth and humanity, rather than having wandered away from an original plenitude of perfection, are even now, in spite of all failures, tragedies and dead ends, invited to fuller modes of being?[76]

Conclusions

Roman Catholic responses to Darwin's theory of evolution through natural selection were far from being homogeneous. In the century and a half following the publication of Darwin's *On the Origin of Species*, Catholic theologians assumed almost every conceivable position on the question, from outright rejection to critical adoption, in a pattern of assimilation less like a steady progression than like Steven Jay Gould's model of "punctuated equilibrium."

To the first thesis question posed at the beginning of this chapter, "Why did some Catholic theologians accept Darwin's theory so readily, while others rejected it?", there is no single or clear-cut answer. Factors range from ecclesiopolitical issues, to matters of cultural independence, to the personalities of theologians and their degree of exposure to science, to controversies within the biological community itself. In the several generations of debate from 1859 to Teilhard's adoption of the theory, the focus of the initial Catholic reaction appears to have been on two fronts: (1) assessing the scientific plausibility of the theory and the extent of its supporting evidence (and here they mirrored to some extent the debate between contemporary scientists), and (2) deliberating about the compatibility of evolution with the doctrine

---

[74] John F. Haught, *Deeper than Darwin: the Prospect for Religion in the Age of Evolution* (Boulder, CO: Westview Press, 2003), 80.

[75] John F. Haught, "What if theologians took suffering seriously?", New Theology Review, 13:4, 2005, 12.

[76] Ibid., 8.

of creation as it was portrayed in the book of *Genesis*. It is certainly true that some churchmen rejected evolution and that others enthusiastically endorsed it, but perhaps the majority modified their understanding either of evolution or of creation (or of both) as needed in order to craft a coherent position.

In answer to our second question, it took at least a half century of scholarly assimilation of evolution on the part of Catholics before the matter of pain and death entailed by millions of years of natural selection was recognized as meriting theological attention. In the second phase, the period of critical assessment (1900–1955), Catholic thinkers reflected increasing awareness that evolutionary ideas were by now solidly entrenched within the scientific community. Beginning with Pierre Teilhard de Chardin, their emphasis shifted from challenging the science of evolution and debating matters of biblical exegesis to elaborating a non-reductionistic Darwinism compatible with an authentic theology of creation. This included careful consideration of the problem of the suffering of sentient life.

The answer to our third question can never be truly complete: "How did those who accepted an evolutionary explanation for biological diversity reconcile its brutal and implacable processes with the God of Christian hope?" Historically, dogma has not developed in isolation from philosophical, scientific, and other currents of thought. It is essential that Christian theologians reexamine doctrinal questions in soteriology, Christology, theodicy, and eschatology and articulate responses that are at once faithful to the kerygma and ring true to a dynamic and evolutionary cosmology. Teilhard openly confessed that he did not have an answer to the problem of suffering, and John Haught has noted that no Christian anthropology or theology of nature can claim to be adequate that refuses to address the problem.

Evolutionary biology has fundamentally altered our approach to the problem of evil: we can no longer retreat to the comfort and safety of an old anthropocentric citadel. Suffering can never again be linked primarily with an imagined Edenic "original sin", or with deserved personal chastisement. Henceforth a credible Christian theodicy must be must be embedded within a theology of creation that is cosmocentric. We inhabit a dynamic and open universe, whose life-giving potential has unfolded over billions of years. When life emerges on a planet, as it did on Earth, it appears to evolve steadily until it fills every conceivable niche. Morbidity and senescence are structural features of life, and when predation and competition for the planet's finite resources are factored in, the result is incalculable suffering and death. For a non-theist this is not a problem, merely a brute fact. For a theist it is a problem, and one which remains ultimately a raw mystery. Is suffering the necessary consequence of an open universe, a cosmos designed to invite an uncoerced response to God on the part of self-reflective creatures? However we answer this, or any other formulation of the question, it is a matter warranting earnest and prayerful theological discussion.

III. Evolution and the Human:
Anthropodicy

"What A Piece of Work Is Man!"

The Impact of Modern Biology
on Philosophical and Theological Anthropology

Martinez J. Hewlett

> *What a piece of work is man! How noble in reason! How infi-
> nite in faculties! In form and moving, how express and admi-
> rable! In action how like an angel! In apprehension, how like a
> god! The beauty of the world! The paragon of animals! And yet,
> to me, what is this quintessence of dust?*
> William Shakespeare, Hamlet, Act II, Scene 2

> *"Memento, homo, quia pulvis es, et in pulverem reverteris."*
> Roman Catholic Ash Wednesday service

Who are we that we can create such wonders and, at the same time, wreak
such havoc in our world? Shakespeare's Hamlet, in these oft-quoted lines, sar-
castically considers one of the questions that rests at the heart of this volume.
Indeed, we soar to the heights because of our reason and, some would argue,
because of our God-given spirit. Yet these same "infinite faculties" have led to
some of the most outrageous horrors we can imagine; we stand on the brink
of degrading the very planet upon which we live. And, as Hamlet continues,
we are the "quintessence of dust". Everything about our evolutionary history
tells us that we share with all other life on Earth the same origin story…we
are made from the very elements upon which we walk, from which we take
our sustenance, and of which everything else is made. On Ash Wednesday, the
Roman Catholic rites reinforce this by recalling to each person, as the ashes
are imposed, the Genesis words of God upon expelling Adam and Eve from
the garden: "you are dust and to dust you shall return". The Latin rendition
of the rite uses the word *homo*, translated as "man" and, more recently, "human". I particularly like this text because it uses a part of our biological name
in this important reminder, almost as though it could read "*Memento, Homo
sapiens…*"

Who are we, then? Let's begin with the obvious. It is our common experience that we are both self-conscious and self-reflective. We recognize our
own image in the mirror and we think about who that is. And because every
human does this, our cultures have constructed stories about who we are and
from where we came. My task in this chapter is to consider the impact of the

most modern of these stories in the western culture—the scientific story of humans—on the other stories, both metascientific and spiritual.

I want to focus on three stories about us as humans, each of them utilizing the term anthropology, the study of humankind:

a. "The quintessence of dust": biological anthropology;
b. "Infinite faculties": philosophical anthropology; and
c. "How like an angel…How like a god": theological anthropology.

Because I am a biologist, and because my purpose is to see where recent advances have taken this story, I will spend most of my time with biological anthropology. I will then examine aspects of the other two stories that are affected by these advances or that have something different and perhaps important to say.

Anthropology: The Study of Humankind

Of course, every human culture has asked the questions "who are we?" and "from where do we come?" In the case of the western Academy, the discourse can be traced to the earliest writings in both philosophy and theology. The conversation has included all of the great figures whose contributions have marked our path to the present. However, it was only after the rise of the scientific method for understanding nature that these questions began to take on a more quantitative nature. Thus, the Enlightenment approaches to these issues had a decidedly physical dimension.

The word "anthropology" was not used at these earliest times, but rather "natural history", reflecting much more of the cultural bent as opposed to the physical. That said, however, the burgeoning field did employ measurements, especially of anatomical differences, as part of the data gathering. During the "age of exploration" encompassing the 15th through 17th centuries, European scholars became increasingly aware of other human cultures, especially those of the indigenous peoples in the western hemisphere. As a result, questions about the nature of humankind were framed against the backdrop of these new encounters. Philosophers assumed that the "natural man" could be found existing still in the person of these indigenous cultures. Hobbes argued that they were bereft of the higher ethical states and thus lived in constant warfare.[1] Rousseau countered that these "primitives" lived in ultimate peace and tranquility.[2] Both of them focused on these non-European cultures as representative of humankind at the beginning of development, and therefore as viable models for asking such questions.

---

[1] Thomas Hobbes, *The Leviathan*, online at http://oregonstate.edu/instruct/phl302/texts/hobbes/leviathan-contents.htmlhttp://oregonstate.edu/instruct/phl302/texts/hobbes/leviathan-contents.html

[2] Jean-Jacques Rousseau, *Discourse on the Origin of Inequality*, online at http://www.constitution.org/jjr/ineq.htm

Along with the philosophical and historical investigations came the quantification of differences between cultures. Body measurements reached their apex with the application of techniques such as craniometry, the measurement of human skulls. Here the effort was not only to understand what constitutes humans, but also to quantify differences among human populations. The concept of "race" was firmly embedded into the presuppositions with which this work was done. Stephen Jay Gould, among others, has critiqued this enterprise. He focused his attention on the work of the great 19th century anthropologists Morton and Broca.[3] Morton, in particular, published voluminous studies of cranial capacity using his vast collection of skulls. He worked with the hypothesis that skull volume is related to intelligence. He concluded that the largest capacity, and therefore the highest intelligence, belonged to members of the Caucasian race, while the smallest and therefore lowest intelligence correlated with members of the Negroid race. American Indians were in the middle.[4] In spite of his meticulous work, Morton's presuppositions greatly influenced the outcome of his investigations, as Gould argues strenuously in *The Mismeasure of Man*.[5] As a result, the burgeoning field of anthropology would inherit, as part of its academic baggage, the concepts of race so firmly entrenched within the Euro-American mindset at the end of the 19th century.

In 1735, Carl von Linné, know to us by his Latinized name, Carolus Linnaeus, published the first edition of his *Systema Naturae*. It has been quipped that "God created Nature and Linnaeus gave it order". In his great classification system, still used in principle today, he placed humans among the animal kingdom, within the Mammalian class and the order of Primates. We are today designated *Homo sapiens*, in the classic binomial nomenclature of his system. Of course, making this proposal in the 18th century was not without criticism, especially within theological circles. Linnaeus remarked on these difficulties in a 1747 letter to the German botanist Johann Gmelin:

> It is not pleasing that I place Man among the primates, but man is intimately familiar with himself. Let's not quibble over words. It will be the same to me whatever name we use. But I request from you and from the whole world the generic difference between Man and Simian, and this from the principles of Natural History. I certainly know of none. If only someone might tell me just one! If I called man a simian or vice versa I would bring together all the theologians against me. Perhaps I ought to, in accordance with the law of the discipline [of Natural History].[6]

---

[3] Stephen Jay Gould, *The Mismeasure of Man* (1997, revised edition) (New York: W. W. Norton & Sons).

[4] Samuel G. Morton, *Crania Americanaor, Comparative view of the skulls of various aboriginal nations of North & South America* (1839), John Pennington, Philadelphia; *Crania Aegyptiaca; or, Observations of Egyptian Ethnography Derived From Anatomy, History, and the Monuments* (1844) John Pennignton, Philadelphia.

[5] Gould, op. cit., 82–104.

[6] Found in the Linnaean Correspondence, in Latin, on the web at http://linnaeus.c18.net/Letters/display_txt.php?id_letter=L0783.

Nonetheless, the biological classification of humans as a part of the living world became the centerpiece for naturalists from then on, not the least of whom would be Charles Darwin.

The November 1859 publication of *Origin of Species by Means of Natural Selection* had, of course, a tremendous impact on the culture of 19th century Europe and America. In fact, the model set forth in this publication, when coupled with the genetic laws uncovered by Mendel and the understanding of genes and mutations, set the stage for the current paradigm of biological science. Twelve years later, however, Darwin published another book, *The Descent of Man*, in which he tackled the question of our own origins in light of his theory. By the end of the 19th century the scientific discussion of what it means to be human was now being held in the developing language of biology.

"The Quintessence of Dust": Biological Anthropology

The question "from where did we come?" can be asked in a Darwinian sense as "what evidence can be found of our descent from a common ancestor?" The task, then, was to search the fossil record for clues to our evolutionary history. Could fossil remains be found that linked us to the classification scheme derived by Linnaeus? Would these clues fit into Darwin's theoretical framework? Beginning with discoveries in the late 19th century and continuing to this day, the answer to both of these queries is "yes."

The discovery of Neanderthal and then Cro-Magnon remains in the marvelous cave sites of Europe set the stage for the initial construction of our family tree. Findings such as Peking man added to this expanding database. Human paleontology reached its modern apex with the seminal work of the Leaky's at Oldavai Gorge in Africa. From this multitude of specimens a lineage could be proposed that followed from some as yet unidentified common ancestor off on one branch to our closest primate cousins and, on another, to us.

Are we indeed one family? Questions about "family" became quantitative with the work of Gregor Mendel, the Austrian botanical scholar and monk. Although his understanding of inheritance was published only nine years after *Origin of Species*, it was not appreciated until the beginning of the 20th century when DeVries, Correns, and Tschermak came to the same conclusions and resurrected the original publication. Soon after, the question "who are we?" could be asked as a specific genetics problem: "to whom are we related?"

With a new set of tools can come a new set of social issues related to their use. Just as Morton and Broca had pressed craniometry into the service of racial typographies, so too genetics came to be wielded as the weapon of choice in the battle to show the superiority or "divine right" of one group over another.

An early example of this focused on the discovery of human blood types at the beginning of the 20th century. There are many molecular attributes of human red blood cells that can be studied and utilized in the clinical setting to insure safe procedures during transfusions. Among them is the ABO grouping system. Humans have three versions of a gene that dictates this particular identification system. One version places an "A" molecular modification on the surface of our red blood cells. Another version of the same gene places, instead, a "B" modification on the cells. A third version, "O", sometimes called the null version, places neither "A" or "B" modification, but leaves the surface unmodified.

Because we carry two of each chromosome (one from each parent) we inherit genes in pairs. The result in terms of this system is that the three gene versions result in four possible blood types in our population: A, B, O, and AB. Both the A and B version are said to be dominant with respect to the O version. This means that when both the A and the O versions are present, the person has blood type A; likewise with pairing of B and O. But A and B are co-dominant with respect to each other, meaning that when both versions are present, both kinds of molecular modification take place, and the person has blood type AB. Finally, a person with both genes being the O version will have blood type O.

Anthropologists were very keen to study the population distribution of these gene versions throughout the world. Could this be a genetic indicator for what distinguishes one so-called "race" from another? Major studies were undertaken to chart the distribution of these gene versions in the world's human population. And, in fact, groupings were made based on these data that supposedly represented human "racial" descriptions. However, the genetic data forced certain conclusions that made no sense from the standpoint of actual human cultural groupings. For instance, based on the frequency of gene version, the people of Poland and the people of China were included within the same grouping (the Hunan category).[7]

It's certainly true that for human cultures where individuals tend to intermarry more often than not, the genetic representation, including blood group genes, tend to be less varied. However, there is no compelling evidence after over a century of work that blood groups have anything to do with racial identification. Instead, these are just part of a vast array of genetic markers that tend to distinguish individuals within the human family.

Over the course of the 20th century, the idea of race as a genetic category within anthropological investigations disappeared, thanks to the work of Ashley Montagu and others.[8] In its place we find the concept of ethnicity, with its overtones of language, cultural traditions, and, in some cases, geographic localization. This did not quell, however, the desire to seek greater details about our genetic roots and identification.

---

[7] Jonathan Marks, *What It Means to Be 98% Chimpanzee: Apes, People, and Their Genes* (Berkeley: University of California Press, 2003), 63.
[8] Ashley Montagu (ed.), *The Concept of Race* (New York: Macmillan, 1964).

The techniques of molecular biology have provided the tools necessary to probe our DNA, the locus of the informational content that forms the physical structure of who we are. Using these tools a great deal has been achieved over the last half of the 20th century.

For instance, we now understand that all currently living humans originated relatively recently in the history of the planet. In addition, we all descended from a small group of individuals and, as a result, share a common genetic heritage. The late Alan Wilson and his colleagues at Stanford University were the first to examine the genetic relationships of current human populations.[9] In order to do this, they exploited the biological fact that the mitochondria in our cells—the small organelles that are our energy factories and that contain their own genetic information—are inherited exclusively from our mothers. This matrilineal pattern of descent allowed them to ask the question: "how are we related with respect to the DNA of our mitochondria?" The answer, it turns out, is that we have all come from a few original human females. Wilson and his collaborators named this the "mitochondrial Eve" model, clearly a metaphorical and certainly not a literal nod to the Genesis account.

Soon after, another line of investigation resulted in a similar story with respect to patrilineal descent.[10] Each of us contains two sex chromosomes. In females, both of these are X. In males, on the other hand, one is X and the other is Y. The Y chromosome is provided by the man's father, and so DNA sequences of this chromosome mark patrilineal inheritance. By comparing Y chromosome data from current human populations, it has been concluded that we descended from a small population of males. As one might expect, this has been metaphorically called the "Y-chromosome Adam" model.

Both of these molecular investigations point to a special set of circumstances involving our biological origins. Our most recent common ancestors were a small population who had perhaps survived some kind of bottleneck or limiting event in their own history and from whom all modern humans descended. In addition to this, however, these conclusions support a single origin, or monogenesis, for all *Homo sapiens*, pointing to Africa as the geographical site from which human radiation took place. These DNA data, then, further eliminate the idea of "race" as a realistic genetic category in human physical anthropology.

The mitochondrial and Y chromosome studies were carried out against the backdrop of the Human Genome Project (HGP), the large, multi laboratory program to map the human genetic material at the level of the DNA sequences themselves. HGP was initiated by the U.S. Department of Energy after a

---

[9] Rebecca Cann, Mark Stoneking, and Allan Wilson, "Mitochondrial DNA and Human Evolution", Nature, 325, 1987, 31–36.

[10] Yuehai Ke, et al., "African Origin of Modern Humans in East Asia: A Tale of 12,000 Y Chromosomes", Science, 292, 2001, 1151–1153.

meeting held in 1984 at Alta, Utah.[11] Eventually, the funding would be administered by both DOE and the National Institutes of Health.

The goal of the HGP was to obtain the most detailed genetic map of the human chromosome complement. This meant deriving the base sequence of human DNA. Even with rapid sequencing techniques, the project goal was daunting until the decision was made to focus on those regions that actually encode protein information—so-called "expressed sequences". The decision to employ this strategy was, in large measure, stimulated by the formation of a private company, Celera Genomics, lead by Craig Venter. A combination of technological breakthroughs and the use of what is called whole-genome shotgun sequencing allowed HGP to reach its goal of publishing a first "working draft" of the genome in February 2001, nearly five years ahead of schedule.[12]

On the one hand, this achievement can be thought of as establishing the baseline of data that allows us to think about the structural pieces that make up the physical part of who we are. On the other hand, however, a kind of genetic essentialism, a reductionist view of what it means to be human, was certainly underlying some of this effort. As a result, the genomics data, when it was published, would lead some to conclude that we now know what it means to be human. As it turned out, it would immediately become apparent that this was not the case. The data itself would force this realization in a number of ways.

It had been assumed that humans contain about 100,000 genes that "define" us. When the database was published, it was found that we contain about 25,000 genes. While this number is much lower than expected, more disturbing was the fact that we have about the same number of genes as the fruit fly. Added to this shock was the complexity of the data itself that defied any kind of sum-of-the-parts approach. As a result, the fields of genetics and genomics began a 180° turn away from the atomization of humans to a much more holistic approach, utilizing the techniques of systems biology.

For biological anthropology, the 21st century is now the age of genetics and genomics. HGP has had, as spin-offs, two other projects. One is the cataloging of human genetic variations, in the form of what is called haplotype maps. Another is comparative genomics, in which complete genetic information for a large number of species have been obtained and are being analyzed for common themes.

The Hap Map Project is focused on the observation that very small DNA sequence differences (single nucleotide polymorphisms or SNPs) exist be-

---

[11] DOE funding for the project derives from that agency's interest in the effects of radiation on human biology. This research began as a part of the Manhattan Project in collaboration with the Japanese government after the nuclear bombing of Hiroshima and Nagasaki. The original organization, the Atomic Bomb Casualty Commission (ABCC), became a part of the Atomic Energy Commission, which morphed into the Nuclear Regulatory Commission under the DOE. In 1975, the ABCC became the Radiation Effects Research Foundation, a joint program of Japan and the U.S.

[12] J. Craig Venter, et al., "The Sequence of the Human Genome", Science, 291, 2001, 1304–1351.

tween individuals in a population and that such differences are often inherited in a set, called a haplotype. By examining DNA from large numbers of individuals, maps can be derived of such inherited sets.[13]

The positive outcome of these approaches has been the idea of customized medical care. It turns out that individual responses to medical treatment or drug therapies can vary dependent upon the person's genetics. Knowing this, a physician might be able to fine-tune the treatment to achieve the optimal result. On the negative side, however, has been the tendency to group haplotype data based upon racial categorizations.

While the medical goal is laudable, it is the potential anthropological outcome that I wish to explore. Recall that we had done away with race as a meaningful genetic category, although the concept is used loosely to mean ethnic, cultural, or even geographic identification. Currently we see the harvesting of haplotype data from what are described in the literature as racial groupings. As a result, there is the possibility of a reintroduction of these racial groupings as categories within anthropology. Troy Duster has identified this as a fallacy of misplaced concreteness, using Whiteheadian terms.[14] He concludes:

> If we fall into the trap of accepting the categories of stored data sets, then it can be an easy slide down the slope to the misconceptions of "black" or "white" diseases. By accepting the prefabricated racial designations of stored samples and then reporting patterns of differences in SNPs between those categories, misplaced genetic concreteness is nearly inevitable.

The other major outcome of the HGP has been the rise of comparative genomics. Once the techniques of rapid data acquisition had been developed, it was easy to apply these to the DNA of other organisms. As a result, databases have flourished which contain the complete genomes of a wide variety of species. Using sophisticated algorithms it is possible to compare these databases and ask questions about what is or is not similar or homologous.

Such comparisons have a great number of possible benefits for basic and medical science. For instance, much has been learned about human development by examining the genetics of this process in organisms such as the worm, the fly, and the mouse. This is because some of the basic control mechanisms for becoming complex, multicellular life forms have been conserved over evolutionary time. The potential outflow of new approaches to human biology and medicine is only just beginning to take place.

Among the genomic databases that have been created are those from our closest relatives in the biosphere, the great apes. It turns out that we share a great deal of sequence identity with the chimpanzee, with which we have

---

[13] A recent example of a data set such as this is the following: "A Haplotype map of the Human Genome", The International HapMap Consortium, Nature 437, 2005, 1299–1320.
[14] Troy Duster, "Race and Reification in Science", Science, 307, 2005, 1050f.

98.4 % homology. What does this mean? From a medical viewpoint, this close relationship has even more significance than comparative studies with more distantly related organisms. For instance, there are disease processes, such as Alzheimer's and heart ailments, that afflict humans but not chimpanzees. It will no doubt be instructive to learn why such differences exist.

With respect to anthropological definitions, however, this sequence similarity between species has led to what some consider a disturbing trend. We saw before that the natural historians of an earlier era looked to the Native Americans as and example of humans in their most natural or "primitive" state. Attention later turned to other indigenous peoples, including the Australian Aborigines or various African tribes. More recently, the focus has been on populations in South America, such as the Yanomamo, who have been living in relative isolation. With the information about the chimpanzee, however, there is a move to consider these animals as "humans" in the most basic form.

How plausible is this? Certainly, attempts to teach language to great apes has been an ongoing research project that has been received with mixed reactions. Some of the successes in this area have pushed the idea of chimpanzees as primitive and untrained humans. But the idea has reached a new level with the proposal that the great apes in general, and chimps in particular, should be granted the legal status of human personhood. At this writing, a case is in the Austrian court system in which the legal status of "personhood" is being claimed for a 26-year old male chimpanzee named Hiasl.[15] Jonathan Marks considers this a claim with no scientific merit. He says:

> Ultimately there is no self-evident meaning in the structural similarity of chimp and human DNA, any more than there is in the structural similarity of our phlegm or our little toes. We know that we are similar to chimpanzees and yet distinguished from them.[16]

Physical anthropology has become biological and ultimately molecular anthropology. Are we any closer to understanding what it means to be human? In one sense of the question, yes we are. We possess a detailed catalogue of our physical substructure, in the form of the human genome database. We also have, through comparative genomics, a validation of the Linnaean and Darwinian views that place us within a spectrum of life on the planet. We see ourselves even more finely described as part of our physical world—as creatures of the dust.

And yet we still want to know what distinguishes us, if anything? If not our DNA sequence or our set of genes, then what? Terrence Deacon has explored the evolution of humans and has concluded that, among other features,

[15] Story found on the web at http://observer.guardian.co.uk/world/story/0,,2047459,00.html and at http://www.foxnews.com/story/0,2933,270078,00.html. Last visited, May 10, 2007.
[16] Jonathan Marks, op. cit., 261.

it is our unique use of language that distinguishes us. He supports this so strongly in his now classic book, *The Symbolic Species*, that he would charge us with the possibility that we are, indeed unique:

> It is not just the origins of our biological species that we seek to explain, but the origin of our novel form of mind. Biologically, we are just another ape. Mentally, we are a new phylum of organisms. In these two seemingly incommensurate facts lies a conundrum that must be resolved before we have an adequate explanation of what it means to be human.[17]

Let's take our leave of biological explanations and, as Terry Deacon suggests, let's explore the question of the human mind. For this, we need to look into philosophical anthropology as a discipline.

"Infinite Faculties": Philosophical Anthropology

We are all aware of thinking. In fact, it was this realization that rescued René Descartes from ultimate systematic doubt in his *Meditations*. He realized that he was, in fact, thinking, and that this must mean that he, Descartes, existed:

> But I was persuaded that there was nothing in all the world, that there was no heaven no earth, that there were no minds nor any bodies: was I not then likewise persuaded that I did not exist? Not at all; of a surety I myself did exist since I persuaded myself of something (or merely because I thought of something). But there is some deceiver or other, very powerful and very cunning, who ever employs his ingenuity in deceiving me. Then without doubt I exist also if he deceives me, and, let him deceive me as much as he will, he can never cause me to be nothing so long as I think that I am something. So that after having reflected well and carefully examined all things, we must come to the definite conclusion that this proposition: I am, I exist, is necessarily true each time that I pronounce it, or that I mentally conceive it.[18]

The "I am, I exist" proposition here is often confused with a statement made in his earlier publication, *A Discourse on Method*, in which he said "I think, therefore I am" (*Je pense, donc je suis*). Nonetheless, it is clear that he associates the cognitive process with his existence, or, we might argue, with himself as a human person.

What does it mean to be a human in philosophical terms? Let me default to the Angelic Doctor, St. Thomas Aquinas for a statement on this issue. Jason Eberl, a Thomistic scholar, has provided a summary of this statement in his recent article "Aquinas on the Nature of Human Beings."[19]

Eberl begins his summary by recalling that Thomas, relying upon an earlier exposition by Boethius, defines a person as "an individual substance of a

---

[17] Terrence Deacon, *The Symbolic Species* (W. W. Norton & Co., New York, 1997) 23.

[18] René Descartes, *Meditations on First Philosophy*, E. S. Haldane and G. R. T. Ross, translators, 1952, Encylcopaedia Britannica (Chicago) 78.

[19] Jason Eberl, "Aquinas on the Nature of Human Beings", The Review of Metaphysics, 58, 2004, 333–366.

rational nature". Eberl then goes on to list the qualities that Thomas ascribes to the human person:

1. Having a rational nature distinguishes human beings from other material substances;
2. Human beings, however, have a material nature;
3. Human beings are rational animals, sharing a material nature with other animals;
4. Human beings have a rational soul that is responsible for the *esse* of humans, the actualization of humans, and the unity of existence of humans; and
5. The human body and soul are not separate substances, but "from these two is made one actually existing substance".

Thomas argued this position forcefully and successfully in a number of his writings. However, over time, as the scholastic movement that derived from and, in the process corrupted, his thinking took hold in Europe, the clarity of his conclusions was lost. Descartes became impatient with this and, in reaction, produced a new way of looking at the human person. As we saw above in his *Mediations* he had already concluded that his cognitive ability was proof of his own existence. How, then, to view the seat of this cognition, the mind, with respect to the body and the physical world? In the sixth part of his *Mediations*, Descartes came to the following understanding:

> And although possibly (or rather certainly, as I shall say in a moment) I possess a body with which I am very intimately conjoined, yet because, on the one side, I have a clear and distinct idea of myself inasmuch as I am only a thinking and unextended thing, and as, on the other, I possess a distinct idea of body, inasmuch as it is only an extended and unthinking thing, it is certain that this I (that is to say, my soul by which I am what I am), is entirely and absolutely distinct from my body, and can exist without it.[20]

Notice that his conclusion is exactly opposite from that of Thomas. His powerful separation of the *res cogitans* from the *res extensa* became the heart of what we now call Cartesian dualism. For Descartes, and for much of Enlightenment thinking that his work helped to precipitate, this *substance dualism*, as it came to be called, was assumed to be the case. While this provided a freedom for science to pursue that extended natural world in a logical series of experimental protocols, it also resulted in a logical inconsistency as that same science eventually began to ask questions about the nature of the human person. Exploring the features of the physical world and seeking natural causes as explanations became the central task of natural philosophy, as science was

---

[20] René Descartes, op. cit., 98.

originally called. But this came to mean the exclusion of supernatural explanations. Descartes' "thinking thing" ultimately fell into this category.

One solution to this problem has been to reconsider what dualism actually means. Rather than have two separate (and scientifically irreconcilable)
substances, why not have the mind become a property of the organization
of the body. That is, given the arrangement and interactions of the material
things that make up body, mind emerges. This is termed *property dualism*.
Such emergence might be considered epiphenomenal, or, as some thinkers
have more recently put it, be considered as an actual existing property of a
complex interacting system.

Another solution to the mind-body problem has been the position that,
while only one ontological category of substance exists, the way in which
we describe mind-related events cannot be reduced to this category. Thus
"thinking" is a language term that describes some function of physical brain
and central nervous system, and yet the concept itself is not reduced to those
physical parts. This is called *predicate dualism*.

The most common move, however, is to be a *monist*. This position assumes
that only one category of substance exists and that all explanations will ultimately rely upon the properties of this substance, namely, that which makes
up the observable material world. This theory of mind represents a materialist
position that may not be in concert with many theological frameworks. While
some philosophers and theologians have attempted to reconcile the materialist
or physicalist position with their particular faith system, most find this strict
ontological statement to be incompatible with notions of the non-material
aspects of human experience. As a result, a conceptual gap remains between
even the most non-reductionist scientific approaches and those of the theological community.

A recovery of the Thomistic notion of the human person could be used in
a way that serves the ends of science, philosophy, and theology. But, is that
merely asking for a return to substance dualism? After all, doesn't Thomas
state that human equals body plus soul?

Gyula Klima has argued, I believe persuasively, that Thomas's stance with
regard to the mind-body problem does not result in substance dualism or,
indeed, any kind of dualism, but rather in a strict monism.[21] Klima's view is
that Thomas only appears to be a dualist in light of the subsequent position
of Descartes. He holds that if one understands Aquinas's philosophical considerations in the light of the time in which they were written, and with the
proper conception of the assumptions being made at that time, then the statement that a human is a body plus a soul is not misconstrued as dualist.

---

[21] Gyula Klima, "Man = Body + Soul: Aquinas's Arithmetic of Human Nature", in: B. Davies
(ed.), *Thomas Aquinas: Contemporary Philosophical Perspectives* (Oxford University Press, Oxford, 2002).

Let me explore Klima's arguments in more specific detail. First, he points out that the word "body" can be understood in several senses. In one sense, the word "body" may indicate a three-dimensional object in the material world that occupies a certain space. It is in this sense, he argues, that Aquinas means the human is a body. A second sense of the word is understood as a living body, versus one that is not living. He argues that this is what Aquinas means when he says the human has a body.

The second issue that Klima raises comes from our modern, late Enlightenment, predilection for atomizing things we examine. We tend, in the reductionist mode popular with much of science, to take things apart. How we chose to do that is arbitrary, at best. Thus, when we speak of a cat, for instance, we tend to talk as scientists about the parts of the cat, rather than the whole. This does not mean, however, that the parts (the tail, the feet, the molecules that compose the cat) exist as "cat" separately from the whole. In fact, to make that assumption would be, for Aquinas, a serious mistake in logic. So it is, Klima argues, that when Thomas says that a human person has a body, he means that the whole person can only be defined by considering all of the parts, both the physical, three-dimensional parts, as well as the non-physical soul.

So, for the moment let's accept Klima's argument that Aquinas was not being dualist in asserting that a human consists of a body informed by a soul. What makes us willing to conclude that something like a soul actually exists as a part of our composition? If we consider, along with Thomas, the "perfections" or "completeness" or "purpose" of the human, we see that such perfections involve the end result of different contributions. For instance, that we are a body, in the spatio-temporal sense, is a perfection of the material substances that make up that body. On the other hand, that we have a body, in the living sense, is a perfection of the non-material form that gives this kind of completeness to the human. To say, in this way, that non-material form gives completeness should not be confused with a dualistic interpretation, such as the presence of some kind of *élan vital*. Rather, Thomas would argue, the non-material form, that is to say, the soul, gives to the human body what whiteness gives to something white.

Of course, having a prior ontological commitment to materialism prevents one from considering the possibility of the non-material. It is, therefore, no surprise that a completely physicalist description of mind, whether reductionist or holist, does not allow for the concept of soul in this sense. However, this is no reason to dismiss Thomas's description of the human person as substance dualism. That can only be said as a misunderstanding in retrospect, through the lens of the so-called Cartesian split.

For the purposes of continued discussion, let us assume some kind of concept such as a soul, in order to explore how a theologically informed anthropology might take shape.

"How Like an Angel...How Like a God": Theological Anthropology

> *Then God said, "Let us make man in our image, in our like-ness..."*
>   Gen 1:26 (NIV)

How exactly are we to interpret this passage from Genesis 1? What does it say about us, especially in light of God's reminder, two chapters later in Genesis 3, of our material origins? This phrasing of the *imago Dei* has formed a great deal of Christian thought about who we are and from where we have come.

It is virtually impossible to argue convincingly that this passage should be taken in a literal, physical sense. After all, Aquinas, among many others, took the position that we cannot, in principle, know anything in reality about God, especially God's physical appearance. And yet, this passage seems to be more than a simply analogy. The Yawhist author of Genesis 3 certainly did not quote God as saying "Let us make man in something like our image..." What aspects of the image of God do we have? What does this say about what it means to be human?

Interestingly, the World Council of Churches has released a study document (Faith and Order Paper #199) on the topic of theological anthropology from the Christian perspective. The paper concludes with ten affirmations about what it means to be human:

1. All human beings are created in the image of God and Jesus Christ is the one in whom true humanity is perfectly realized.
2. The presence of the image of God in each human person and in the whole of humanity affirms the essentially relational character of human nature and emphasizes human dignity, potentiality and creativity, as well as human creatureliness, finitude and vulnerability.
3. True humanity is most clearly seen in self-emptying (kenotic) love, the love expressed most profoundly in the person of Jesus of Nazareth: human beings are created to love and to be loved as Jesus loved.
4. Human beings are created to be in relationship not only with God and each other but with the whole of creation, respecting and being responsible for all living creatures and the whole created order.
5. All human beings, though created in the image of God, are inevitably affected by individual and corporate sin.
6. Sin is a reality which cannot be ignored nor minimized, for it results both in the alienation of humanity from God and in the brokenness of the world, its communities, and the individuals which make up those communities.
7. Sin can pervert or distort, but cannot finally destroy, what it means to be human.
8. Jesus Christ through his life, death and resurrection is victorious over sin and death, restores true humanity, empowers life, and brings hope for the end of inhumanity, injustice and suffering.

9. Christians, baptized into the Body of Christ and enlivened by the Holy Spirit, are called to be the new humanity, to grow into the likeness of God and, together, to carry on the work of Christ in the world. As the Church, Christians are the sign to the world of unity with God and with each other.

10. Humanity finds its ultimate fulfillment, together with the whole created order, when God brings all things to perfection in Christ.[22]

Let me glean four features from this anthropological statement upon which to focus: creativity, love, relationship, and sin. The last of these, of course, brings us back to the subject of this volume.

Philip Hefner writes that we are "created co-creators."[23] Implicit in this gloriously phrased description is something about God in which we share. Hefner proposes that humankind's God-given task—telos, in fact—is the creation, through the agency of free will, of a better world, a more "wholesome" world, to use his word. To be a human is to be charged with this task and to be actively engaged in carrying it out.

It is arguable whether humans have the capability at present to do this[24] or whether, indeed, we can see the creative results of their actions when we look at the state of our world in the light of current events and trends.[25] Nevertheless, Hefner has made a positive contribution to our understanding of a Christian theological anthropology by at least posing this as an ideal toward which we strive. In addition, his anthropological framing highlights what it might mean to be made in the image of God. As Westhelle concludes:

> [The] three aspects that are so succinctly put together in the concept of the created co-creator reflect three basic categories that are developed by Hefner. *Created* is expressed by the doctrine of the creation out of nothing (*creatio ex nihilo*). The prefix *co-* gives expression and wraps in itself the whole doctrine of the image of God (*imago Dei*). *Creator* reflects that in which we are immersed and are part of; it reflects participation in an ongoing creation, *creatio continua*.[26]

The ten affirmations cited above include the dictum that humans are created to love and be loved. It is traditional to connect the *imago Dei* concept with the selfless love termed *agape* in Greek. Thus, in the third affirmation, the

---

[22] The full text can be found on the web at http://www.oikoumene.org/en/resources/documents/wcc-commissions/faith-and-order-commission/christian-perspectives-on-theological-anthropology.html (last visited May 5, 2007).

[23] Philip Hefner, "Biocultural Evolution and the Created Co-Creator", in Ted Peters (ed.), *Science and Theology: The New Consonance* (Westview Press, 1998).

[24] William Irons, "An Evolutionary Critique of the Created Co-Creator", Zygon, 39, 2004, 773–790.

[25] Vítor Westhelle, "The Poet, The Practitioner, and the Beholder: Remarks on Philip Hefner's Created Co-Creator", Zygon, 39, 2004, 747–754.

[26] Ibid., 753.

self-emptying love of Christ is linked to what it means to be "truly human". I would argue that what it means to be human includes the other kinds of love, both *philia* and *eros*. It seems to me that to denigrate these two very human aspects is to leave something out of the final equation. True, each of these can be abused and found in perverted forms. Nonetheless, I would submit that being in the image of God includes the passion of *eros,* the fondness and loyalty implicit in *philia*, coupled with the selfless and unconditional love of *agape*. Each of these have a place in the theological response to the question of human meaning.

Both the created co-creator and the lover are involved in relationships. It would therefore seem that another aspect of our humanity resides in these interactions. In fact, it could be argued that we only know who we are by our relationships. The concept that we exist in a complex web of interactions has taken on new meaning with the rise of network science in the last few years. It is now scientifically apparent that at every level of life such webs are in operation, from the intricacies of the intracellular protein interaction network, to food webs, to the web of cultural interaction.[27] It is not a stretch to include in this analysis our relationship with the Creator. In fact, Beatrice Bruteau, reflecting on the way in which a contemplative Christian should approach creation, sees a trinitarian connection in these interactive webs:

> From elementary particles in the atom, through atoms in molecules, molecules in cells, cells in organisms, organisms in societies, to social actions and even ideas—all of them being organized as systems—the trinitarian image, as a Many-One, as a Community, has been present and growing.[28]

However, in an all too human way, relationships can fall apart. We can become separated from those we love, whether it is our companion humans or God. This latter separation is what the Christian means by sin. But this can only be accomplished by choice. Therefore, another facet of what it means to be human in the theological sense is the ability we have to act as moral agents. To act in this way implies that one aspect of being human is the exercise of free will.

The moral concept of free will is, of course, much debated in contemporary philosophical and theological circles. The modern discussion, especially after the rise of the scientific conceptual framework, focuses on the issues of freedom of action versus determinism. The polar positions consider free will and the deterministic nature of the universe to be either *compatible* or *incompatible*. In the former case, free will is seen as an unforced act that is separate from

[27] Albert-László Barabási, *Linked: The New Science of Networks* (New York: Perseus Books Group, 2002), Duncan Watts, *Six Degrees: The Science of a Connected Age* (New York: W.W. Norton and Co., 2003).

[28] Beatrice Bruteau, *God's Ecstasy: The Creation of a Self-Creating World* (New York: Crossroad Classic Publishing Company, 1997).

the causal laws of nature, but related to causality in some way, and therefore compatible with it. Incompatibilist traditions fall into two camps: libertarianism and strict or hard determinism. Libertarians deny the existence of determinism, while hard determinists deny the existence of free will. Without a detailed discussion, suffice it to say that each of these positions raises serious issues for theologians, and each of them tend to be either/or statements. I suggest that at least part of the problem here is the tendency to atomize or reduce the object or faculty being discussed.

It may be instructive here to look once again to Aquinas for some clarity in the conversation. Eleonore Stump has recently considered Thomas's understanding of what, in the modern discussion, is called "free will."[29] She sees in his writing a clear distinction between intellect and will, and discusses the interactions between these two. It is clear to me from her analysis, therefore, that Aquinas considers the entire concept of freedom of action as an emergent property of a complex system that is at the heart of what makes us human.

Aquinas regards our freedom to choose a particular action as an interaction between our intellect and our will. In this case, the will is considered not so much as the motive force of action but rather as a predilection for goodness. The intellect judges that a particular course of action will be good for us and presents this to the will. The result can be the choice of a particular action. Notice that the presentation of "goodness" by the intellect is not absolute, in the sense that only truly good things are represented. It may be that the intellect, by interaction with the passions, convinces the will that an act is potentially good when, in fact, it turns out not to be. This demonstrates the complexity of the interaction that Thomas proposes.

Because the freedom to choose cannot, in Aquinas's view, be influenced by any extrinsic cause, he would not be called a compatibilist in the modern sense. However, he is not a strict libertarian either, since, as Stump points out, he would differ from the modern tradition, which argues that for true freedom, the act is deemed free only if the person has alternative choices presented under exactly the same conditions. Thomas would not agree with this, maintaining that the will is subject to the intellect. In order to have another possibility of action, the intellect would have to be, by definition, in a different state. As such, Aquinas is not a libertarian.[30]

All of this leads to an understanding of the human person as a moral agent. If we accept any of these models of how we make choices, except for one that posits no freedom whatsoever, then it is apparent that with the process of decision making comes responsibility for that decision. As a result, we can argue that to be human is to be ultimately charged with the outcome of our choices.

---

[29] Eleonore Stump, "Aquinas's Account of Freedom: Intellect and Will", in: B. Davies (ed.), *Thomas Aquinas: Contemporary Philosophical Perspectives* (Oxford: Oxford University Press, 2002).
[30] Ibid., 290f.

In Pulverem Reverteris: Conclusion

As I write these comments, we sit in the middle of a world that seems to be overflowing with violent conflict. We have daily images from Iraq and Afghanistan. In America, we will never be far enough removed from 9–11 such that it is not a constant part of our awareness. And we have recently witnessed the horror at Virginia State.

All of these events would be called agent-caused evils. That is, they are all the result of the free choices of moral agents. Does this speak to us of how, in a world where we embrace creation as good, God could allow such evil to take place? The questions that drive theodicy arise from the battleground streets of Baghdad, from the ashes of the World Trade Center, and from the silent and bloodied classrooms of Norris Hall. Is this, then, what it ultimately means to be human? Are we only the sarcastic "quintessence of dust" that Hamlet hurls in the faces of Rosencrantz and Guildentstern?

Let me conclude with a somewhat eschatological view. We are a people in process. What we are to become has not yet been revealed. As such, we exhibit moments of incredible horror followed almost at once by shining beacons of beauty. What it means to be human is a complex acceptance of both of these possibilities.

Pioneer 10 and 11 were the first human made objects to leave the solar system. These deep space voyagers were launched in 1972 and 1973, respectively. It was realized that the chance exists, however remote, that these vehicles could one day be encountered by an extraterrestrial intelligence. Should that occur, it was reasoned that some message ought to be included. The plaques that were attached to the craft were designed by Carl Sagan, Frank Drake, and Linda Sagan.

Each plaque, made of gold-anodized aluminum, contains engraved symbols designed to reveal to another intelligence who made the craft and, more importantly, who and where we are. The information includes scientific data concerning hydrogen, in symbolic form, that would be understood by a sufficiently scientifically advanced civilization. The plaque has positional information about the location of our solar system. Finally, there are two figures, one male and one female, shown nude and against a silhouette of the spacecraft, for size reference. The male figure has his right hand raised, palm outward, in a gesture of peace.

To me, this plaque states who we think we are, or at least what we want the "others" to think about us. It encompasses all that we have considered in this discussion. We are creatures of the universe. We are self-conscious and self-reflective. We are rational beings. We are in relationship. And we can make the choice—in this case, the choice for peace.

Biology, Rhetoric, Genocide

Assembling Concepts for Theological Inquiry

Gaymon Bennett

Since the 19th century the biological sciences have been configured with political and ethical practices in such a way as to establish techniques for distinguishing favorable from unfavorable forms of human life. These techniques
and distinctions have functioned to orient various political and social interventions and to configure and realign political and social relations.[1] Biology
has contributed to "dividing practices" — producing classes of people through
techniques of segregation, such as eugenic techniques for dividing the fit from
the unfit. It has generated classifications whereby humans can be understood,
assigned stable identities, and worked on. Efforts in genomics have pushed
in this direction. They have helped produce categories of health and identity
through which individuals are encouraged to take responsibility for themselves as medical subjects. Consumer directed preventative medicine is an example of this.[2] Put briefly we might say that for two centuries biology has
contributed to modern forms of ordering life. The relations of biology and
life-ordering have often been directed to human abundance — vaccines, water
purification, bio-remediation, and the like. At its most paroxysmal, however,
this relation has consisted of the identification and attempted elimination of
individuals and groups found to be bad, problematic, undesirable, or defective, elimination to the point of genocide.

The problem I will focus on in this chapter is: what conceptual tools does
theology need in order to think adequately about the relations, or possible relations, of evolutionary biology and the problem of evil today? I will answer
that theology needs concepts that help analyze contemporary ways in which
evolutionary biology informs truth claims about human life and the ways in
which such truth claims function to justify specific ethical, political, and social interventions. I will suggest that as a means of orientation to the work
of developing such concepts theology can begin with a historical analysis of
relations between and among rhetoric, biology, and genocide. A sufficient
theological analytic for thinking about evolution and evil, however, should be

---

[1] See Ted Peters, "The Evolution of Evil", in this volume.
[2] Paul Rabinow, "Introduction", in: *The Foucault Reader* (New York: Pantheon Books,
1984), 12.

more than historical or even philosophical, as I hope to show. It should, as I have noted, be adequate to specific forms of these relations today.

This chapter consists of three major sections. In the first section I will situate the problem of evolution and evil as it functions in my analysis. This section will relate the problem of evolution and evil to the classical problem of salvation in philosophy and theology. It will introduce a series of concepts that help define the kind of object domain I wish to focus on, and it will introduce my rationale for focusing on the relations among rhetoric, biology, and genocide. The purpose of this first section is to orient the reader to some of the conceptual difficulties in thinking about evolution and evil as a conjoined and contemporary problem. In the second section I will introduce Michel Foucault's concept of *biopower* as a useful tool for analyzing historical relations among rhetoric, biology, and genocide. The term biopower has received considerable attention in recent years. My purpose in introducing it here is to draw attention to the kind of relations and interactions it brings into view. However, as I will point out, biopower may be more useful as a tool of historical than contemporary analysis. In the third section of the chapter I will introduce the concept of *authorization* as an analytic for contemporary thought. The purpose of this section is to point beyond biopower to other concepts for theological inquiry into contemporary relations of rhetoric, biology, and power.

Orientation: Situating the Problem of Evolution and Evil

In this section I want to situate the problem of evolution and evil as an object of analysis in this paper. I will do this first by connecting the problem of evil to the classical problem of salvation and describing how it is that evolutionary biology specifically, and the biological sciences more generally, affect this connection. Second, I will introduce the concept of *problematization* to help define the kind of object domain under consideration. Third, I want to identify a key dimension of the problem of evolution and evil—the problem of rhetoric, biology, and genocide—and position it in relation to this broader set of concerns.

The Problem of Evil and the Problem of Salvation
Three terms are central to this section of the paper. They bear definition from the outset. First is the term *problem*. The term problem as I am using it in this chapter has a specific technical meaning. A problem is a historical conjuncture, arising from a number of events and involving various difficulties or blockages, that not only raises challenges for thinking, but for ordering individual or collective life.[3] A problem always has conceptual and practical dimensions. It is

---

[3] Paul Rabinow, *Anthropos Today: Reflections on Modern Equipment* (Princeton: Princeton University Press, 2003) 54.

not just a matter of what one needs to know, though it is certainly this, but also of developing or fostering practices, experiences, and relations in conjunction with what one knows. The second is the term is *evil*. The term evil is used here to specify a particular domain of problems. As such, it is defined analytically as a domain of truth claims and associated actions concerning things taken to be morally depraved or bad, things troublesome or disagreeable, and things unsound, unwholesome, or defective. The third term *salvation* likewise designates a particular domain of problems, a domain broader than and inclusive of the problem of evil. The term salvation also has a range of meanings: being made to be secure, being rescued from danger, being preserved or protected. In addition it has a set of meanings having to do with the assurance of well-being or ensuring the good of someone or something. It is this second set that concerns me in this analysis. In sum, the problem of evil and the problem of salvation are not just matters of knowledge—knowledge of what constitutes things bad or things good. They involve the practical matter of what one must or can do to overcome the bad or to realize the good.

Classically the problem of evil was deeply connected to the problem of salvation. Thinking about what is depraved, troublesome, or unwholesome and how forms of life characterized by these things can or should be reformed, was pursued in the context of reflection on the good, God, logos, and the like. The integral relation between the two problems has been obscured in much contemporary thought. Since the work of Gottfried Leibniz in the 18th century, the problem of evil has usually been considered principally as a logical dilemma: how does one justify the existence of an all powerful good God in the face of evil in the world?[4] In addition, the problem of salvation, which was so central to classical philosophical as well as theological thought, generally (particularly in Protestant intellectual climates) became restricted to theological considerations of the state of the soul. It was thereby disconnected from broader considerations of the order of individual and collective human life.[5] The practical question of the good life and how it can be realized often was no longer the context for consideration of the problem of evil.

The problem of salvation (from the Greek *sōtēria*) in classical thought (e. g. in the work of Plato, Seneca, or Augustine) involved a shared basic supposition: such as the subject is, it is incapable of life lived in right relation to God (or the Truth, or the Good), but such as God is, God is capable of making the subject capable. The problem was both a matter of knowledge and practice. It involved the question of the truth of *anthropos*—the human creature—the

---

[4] Gottfried Leibniz, *Essais de Théodicée sur la bonté de Dieu, la liberté de l'homme et l'origine du mal.*

[5] Michel Foucault, *Hermeneutics of the Subject: Lectures at the College de France, 1981–1982,* Graham Burchell, trans., Frederic Gros, François Ewald, Alessandro Fontana, and Arnold David-son, eds. (New York: Palgrave MacMillan, 2005), 17 and 183.

truth of the cosmos or nature, and the truth of the divine; and it involved consideration of the forms of human life called for and made possible by knowledge of the self, God, and the world. Significantly, it also involved the practical question of what we can or must do if our lives, individual and collective,
are to be rightly ordered. Salvation was a problem of thought and practice.[6]

Salvation was given quite distinctive definitions in classical thought. For
Plato salvation could be found in the harmony of one's soul with the true
form of the Good; for Augustine it was the ordering of the soul to God.[7]
The Latin expression *salus augusta* meant that Augustus was the source of
the Empire's well-being, the source of the good.[8] Despite these differences
salvation generally referred to a particular dynamic between the subject and
the source of the good: it referred to a transformed way of being involving the
movement from a life marked by incapacity for the good, to a life marked by
capacity. Salvation named a life ordered to God, or truth, the *sunnum bonum*,
eudemonia, felicity, beatitude, and so on.

Whether Seneca's consideration of *apatheia* or Augustine's reflections on
original sin, the problem of salvation contained within it, explicitly or implicitly, the question of why it is that salvation is needed. Consideration of the
terms that make salvation necessary: this, broadly speaking, is the problem of
evil. The problem of evil is framed by the problem of salvation. It can be expressed variously: how is it the case that one experiences a difference between
life lived in relation to the good and life not lived in relation to the good?
How is it that one finds oneself in a situation where life needs to be given
right order? How is it that things human are depraved or bad, troublesome
or disagreeable, unsound, unwholesome, or defective? And, in the form of
theodicy, how is it that God can save, but yet suffering persists? Responses to
the problem of evil—understood in this way—have appealed to God's wrath,[9]
human sin,[10] cosmic disharmony,[11] human incompletion,[12] the unfolding of
history,[13] and the like. Such responses always animated the practical question:
what, if anything, can we, individually or collectively do about the state we
find ourselves in?

Developments in the biological and human sciences since the 19th century
have played a formative role in how the problems of salvation and evil have
been reformed and negotiated. Prominent examples of this have involved evo-

---

[6] Ibid., 182 f.
[7] Plato, *The Republic*, 500c/d; Augustine *The City of God*, V/18.
[8] Ibid., 183.
[9] E.g., Romans 2:1.
[10] E.g., *The City of God*, XIX/28.
[11] E.g. *The Republic*, 587.
[12] E.g. Aquinas, *Summa Theologiae*, 1a2æ2,7
[13] Immanuel Kant, "Idea of a Universal History with a Cosmopolitan Purpose".

lutionary biology and genetics.[14] Recently domains such as developmental biology, environmental biology, and other post-genomic specializations, which depend fundamentally on evolutionary biology and genetics, have played a role as well.[15] Informing conceptions of life generally and human life specifically, biology has been made to function to diagnose what is bad, problematic, or defective, and what, if anything, can be done.[16] Under the banner of scientific authority, such diagnoses have made specific interventions appear urgent and necessary.[17] These diagnoses have been taken up and considered in theology, political analysis, moral theory, sociobiology, legal debate, etc. These discursive domains have attempted to map out the difference between positive and negative states of human affairs and how it is that biology produces, relieves, or illuminates this difference.

For a century and a half biology has been linked to the question of evil as a conjoined problem. Biology has been authorized to help us think about and order our lives.

Object domain: Problematization
At present the problem of evolution and evil appears in and serves to connect a variety of domains. In the domain of popular philosophy, for example, Richard Dawkins has argued that truth claims in biology support and encourage atheism. While interventions into the family and into education appear both necessary and urgent, Dawkins thinks that religion is brainwashing our children. In the name of biological truths he calls for a reordering of pedagogical life.[18] In the Dover, Pennsylvania legal contest over Intelligent Design (ID), spokespersons for evolutionary biology argued that ID is a proxy for creationism and therefore not science, not even bad science, but rather religion. Religion, they insinuated, is dangerous for free inquiry. It is therefore unfavorable if not dangerously retrograde and should be barred from biology classes in public schools.[19] In theology a number of thinkers have wrestled with the apparent value-disvalue exchange at work in evolutionary processes. These thinkers have asked how traditional understandings of God's wrath and human enslavement to sin must be rethought in an evolutionary context.

---

[14] The most notorious example here is that of eugenics, as will be described in the next section of this chapter.

[15] A prominent example is the stem cell debate and the ways in which developmental biology has been scrutinized for answers to the question of what constitutes morally defensible human life. Other domains of scientific innovation such as synthetic biology are likely to play a critical role in such vital areas of contemporary life as energy, security, and health.

[16] The widely advertised promise of genomics to deliver anticipatory and highly personalized forms of medical intervention is an example of this.

[17] This will be the topic of the second section of this chapter.

[18] Richard Dawkins, *The God Delusion* (New York: Houghton Mifflin, 2006).

[19] See, for example, "Judge Rules Against 'Intelligent Design'", at http://www.msnbc.msn.com/id/10545387/

Proposals have been offered for how evolution might inform a reformation of core ethical practices.[20]

The problem of biology and evil in these cases is situated within the broader problematization of life and salvation that emerged in the 18th century. The term "problematization" was developed by historian Michel Foucault in order to describe the historically specific ways in which ensembles of discursive and non-discursive practices make something "enter into the play of true and false and constitute it as an object of thought."[21] In order for something to have entered into the play of true and false something must have happened to make prior ways of relating to them or understanding them unfamiliar, uncertain or otherwise unsatisfactory; that is, an event or a number of events combine to produce difficulties that are responded to in such a way as to make something once taken for granted an explicit object of thought.[22]

Several characteristics of problematizations are relevant to thinking about evolution and evil. First, a problematization is such that multiple solutions and responses are simultaneously possible. Second, a problematization is itself an event that emerges at a specific time and under specific conditions. Third, as anthropologist Paul Rabinow has pointed out, a problematization is "an event of long duration, one that sets events of a different scale in motion."[23] Problematization designates a historically broad and interconnected field within which other specific formations emerge and recede. Examples of problematizations include the Church Fathers' problematization of politics and Greek philosophy,[24] the Reformers' problematization of salvation and authority,[25] or the modern problematization of universal "man".[26] Among other things these characteristics tell us that problematizations are contingent, involve multiple elements, and are generative. Inquiry into them thus requires a patient, vigilant, and responsive *phronesis*.

Biology, Rhetoric, and Genocide

Even though their position in political and social fields is contested and unstable, evolutionary biology and related fields continue to produce knowledge about things human, such that unfavorable forms of human life are made visible and distinguished from favorable forms. A range of interventions into human life continue (in part) to be authorized by these truth claims. Authorized knowledge continues to play a role in the ways in which life is formed

---

[20] See for example Christopher Southgate's chapter in this volume.
[21] Michel Foucault quoted in *Anthropos Today*, 18.
[22] Ibid.
[23] Ibid., 55.
[24] An example of a work informed by this problematization is Augustine's *City of God*.
[25] An example of a work informed by this problematization is Luther's *On Secular Authority*.
[26] An example of a work informed by this problematization is Pannenberg's *Anthropology in Theological Perspective*.

and ordered today. If we are to characterize the relation between biology and the problem of evil today, it would be useful to attend to these relations. My proposal is thus to investigate the problem of evolution and evil in terms of the productive relations among and between biology, rhetoric, and power. These relations are illuminated by attention to the historical examples of biology, rhetoric, and genocide.

To the extent that an investigation of biology, rhetoric, and genocide is conducted in a mode informed by a Platonic definition of rhetoric, such an investigation will appear to be only a preliminary affair within the far-reaching and complex circuits of evolution and the question of evil—descriptive prolegomena to more substantive interpretive and explanatory work. Following Socrates' education of Gorgias, an investigation of biology, rhetoric, and genocide in such a mode might consist of demonstrating once again the indifferent relation between rhetoric and truth.[27] The investigation would seek to decode the deceptive language games played by genocidal regimes, codify patterns within the operations of these propagandistic language games, assess the role of these patterns within genocide in general, distinguish "good" and "bad" scientific claims, and develop critical truth-tools for the de-mystification of future genocidal ideologies. In sum, the study of biology, rhetoric, and genocide would aim at revealing the "real" mechanics of genocidal violence, flushing such truth from behind the dissimulating pretence of rhetorical justification.

A critical investigation of rhetoric and genocide that aims at demystification, however, can be limited in several respects. In the first place, it tends to treat rhetoric as merely instrumental. Rhetoric involves instrumentality to be sure; however, it is not clear that an analysis which focuses just on this aspect will be satisfactory. In the second place, it treats rhetoric as basically hostile to the truth. This suggests that rhetoric is more or less a tool of dissemblance such that truth can be opposed to it in the name of liberation. Third—and this is the vital point—such an approach may fail to carefully attend to how it is that it may fail to attend to the ways in which rhetoric is integral to the form of knowledge and thereby integral to the form and production of power relations. Rhetoric is integral to the assembly of things.

Essential to the German National Socialist rhetoric was the production of the Jew as contagion within the German social body.[28] This production fixed Jews within the logic of Nazi political networks in a way that authorized power to kill them. We might insist that Nazi rhetoric only produced a lie, that it worked a distortion of what was already really there, and laid an interpretive film over the humanity of a political object. While agreeing with such

---

[27] Plato, *Gorgias*, 462d.
[28] Robert Proctor, *Racial Hygiene: Medicine under the Nazis* (Cambridge, MA and London: Harvard University Press, 1988), 199.

protest, however, we must note how—from an analytic view—such insistence can remain insensitive to the productive capacities of political apparatuses. Such apparatuses are capable of producing figures of human life and working on those figures in direct and materially consequential ways. For example, racial hygiene persisted as a generative network of discursive and non-discursive practices which consisted of mutually productive relations among objects of study (e.g. the German race), authorized speakers (e.g. the doctor as judicial expert), truth claims (e.g. hereditary degeneracy), and strategies (e.g. programs of sterilization).[29] Rhetoric played a crucial role in this network.

The concept of problematization orients thinking to mutually productive and functionally integrated relations between discursive and non-discursive practices. It informs an analytic approach that displays the network of relations among objects of thought, authorized spokespersons, techniques for the ordering of individual and collective life, political rationalities, and the like. In other words, as a conceptual tool problematization facilitates an understanding of the strategic and mutually productive relations among the very elements that would appear to be at stake in an analysis of rhetoric and genocide.

Aristotle defined rhetoric as the art of public persuasion.[30] The three elements of this definition are crucial for an analysis of evolution and evil today. First as an object of analysis rhetoric names the ways in which discourse is given form.[31] It refers to the ways in which truth claims take form as authorized and thereby play a formative role in the assemblages within which they circulate. Rhetoric is no thing in addition to knowledge; it is form and mobilization, dynamic form. Second, as an object of analysis, rhetoric concerns and draws attention to specific publics.[32] This means that rhetoric is never simply an idiosyncratic production, even if truth claims vary in form from case to case. Third, rhetoric is a practice.[33] It names the practices whereby discourse is given form in relation to publics. The study of rhetoric is thus the study of how knowledge is given a form that can be recognized as authoritative by particular people at particular times.

Put another way, rhetoric is a mode of stylization that gives knowledge the form of authorization under specific arrangements. It is therefore closely related to the episteme of a particular time, place, and collectivity. Such authorization animates a number of crucial dynamics within an assemblage of relations, including the identification and characterization—figuration—of human life, the design of technologies by which such figures can be worked on, and the justifications by which the use of such technologies is made to ap-

---

[29] Ibid., 285–289.
[30] Aristotle, *The Art of Rhetoric*, trans. H.C. Lawson-Tancred (London: Penguin Books, 1991).
[31] Ibid., I/2.
[32] Ibid., I/3.
[33] Ibid., I/1.

pear necessary and even urgent. To study rhetoric is thus to study the relation between knowledge and authorization—the practices, forms, and publics of knowledge and power.

Inquiry into biology, rhetoric and genocide can be formulated as follows: How is it that the stylization of truth claims contributes to the production and maintenance of relations between those who are the subjects of power and those who are its objects? If the relations among biology, rhetoric, and genocide have historically been intrinsic, then any theological attempt to provide an analytically sufficient account of genocide must take as a primary domain of inquiry the relations of knowledge and power through which and within which truth claims about things human are produced, stylized, and authorized.

Genealogical Inquiry: Biopower as an Analytic for Historical Thought

The term "biopower" has gained widespread currency among theologians thinking about things political. Following trends in contemporary philoso phy, an increasing number of theologians take the term and its associated meanings as definitive of the politics of the present.[34]

First introduced by Michel Foucault to identify a specific set of political dynamics that emerged in the 19th century, the current prominence of "biopower" would seem to be due as much to the prominence of its recent interpreters and the generality with which these interpreters treat the term, as with its value as an analytic for historical and contemporary arrangements. Biopower is the central theme of two widely read works of political philosophy: Gorgio Agamben's *Homo Sacer* and Michael Hart and Antonio Negri's *Empire*.[35] Both books give the term broad conceptual rendering, positioning it as the "nature and essence of the present epoch."[36] Contemporary politics are portrayed as fundamentally oriented toward the domination and exploitation of the "vital existence" of political subjects. Biopower, it is suggested, describes the ways in which present politics bears on humans as mere living animals, a politics that finally drives toward death and elimination.[37] Such epochal definition effectively renders biopower as the single interpretive answer to the question of the nature of politics in the modern world. As with all such broadly cast concepts, biopower as rendered by these philosophical stars is misleading. It explains nothing by explaining too much. And so, as it has cir-

---

[34] See for example John Milbank's "Paul Against Biopolitics", at www.theologyphilosophycentre.co.uk/papers/Milbank_PaulAgainstBiopolitics.doc.

[35] Giorgio Agamben, *Homo Sacer: Sovereign Power and Bare Life*, trans. Daniel Heller-Roazen (Stanford: Stanford University Press, 1998); Michael Hardt and Antonio Negri, *Empire* (Cambridge, MA and London: Harvard University Press, 2001).

[36] Paul Rabinow and Nikolas Rose, "Biopower Today", BioSocieties, 2006, 1, 195–217.

[37] Ibid.

culated into wider and wider academic markets, biopower's symbolic capital
has compounded while its analytic value has plummeted.

Defining Biopower

Despite this decline, if given a more precise definition, biopower proves useful for thinking about the historical relations of biology, rhetoric, and genocide. It is useful in the first place for understanding in broad terms the ways
in which biology has been linked to a broad range of political practices. It is
useful in the second place because it helps us to be alert to the ways in which
authorized discourse is mobilized by and in turn serves to mobilize relations
of power. It bears noting in advance, however, that an analysis of evolution
and evil today will need to move beyond biopower. Despite the insistence of
its more famous interpreters, biopower describes a historically specific set of
conditions. While many of these conditions persist, they do not dominate.
Additional configurations of rhetoric, biology, and power characterize the
present—configurations that modulate, destabilize, and reposition apparatuses of biopower.

Biopower was introduced by Michel Foucault in his 1975–1976 lectures at
the Collège de France, *"Society Must Be Defended"*.[38] He further specified
the term in his next two courses *Security, Territory, Population*[39] and offered a
dense, if somewhat general, presentation of the concept in a key ten-page section of his first volume of the history of sexuality. Foucault promised to refine
this concept in one of the volumes of his projected six volumes of the *History
of Sexuality*. He died before this work could be done.[40]

The term was central to Foucault's effort to characterize the ways in which
life and governance were being problematized in the 19th and early 20th centuries. Employing rather cryptic phrasing, Foucault introduced the term biopower as a governmental rationality characteristic of modern forms of power and distinct from classical forms of state sovereignty. He argued that if the
sovereign power of the classical age can be characterized by the right to "let
live and make die", this new rationality can be characterized as the obligation
to "make live and let die."[41]

Though the practices and relations to which the term could be applied were
diverse, Foucault applied the term to a rather precise set of affairs. Biopower
designates a set of arrangements that brings two related but distinct objects—
the individual human body of the human species (populations)—into a single
political rationality through a set of norms. This set of arrangements works

---

[38] Michel Foucault, *"Society Must Be Defended": Lectures at the Collège de France, 1975–1976*,
trans. David Macey, Mauro Bertani and Alessandro Fontana (ed.) (New York: Picador, 2003).

[39] Michel Foucault, *Security, Territory, Population: Lectures at the Collège de France, 1977–1978*,
trans. Graham Burchell, Michel Senellart (ed.) (New York: Palgrave McMillan, forthcoming 2007).

[40] Rabinow and Rose, "Biopower Today."

[41] Foucault, *"Society Must Be Defended"*, 241.

to maximize the capacities of the first through regimes of discipline and the second through regulation and modulation.

Rabinow and Rose argue that biopower, as developed by Foucault, involves at least four elements: (1) a set of truth discourses about "the "vital" character" of individual and collective human life; (2) experts authorized to speak competently about such truth; (3) strategies and technologies of interventions advanced in the name of life and health; and (4) modes of subjectification by which individuals engage in self-formation, also in the name of life and health.[42] Within the strategic arrangement of these elements, human life is figured as a set of biological capacities which must be disciplined and regulated in order that vitality might be maximized and the life of society (by way of the life of the individual) ameliorated. Because it involves both the mandate to "make live" as well as the obligation to "let die", biopower concerns the problem of biology and evil and the practices by which the problem is worked on.

A Simplified Genealogy of Biopower
In the latter decades of the 18th century, Western Europe crossed a significant biological threshold. For the first time in European memory the interminable cycle of famine and epidemic was interrupted; death ceased to menace life so directly. Economic, particularly agricultural, development allowed the production of resources to outpace demographic growth. At the same time advances in fields of knowledge concerning human life allowed for an increasing control over the most immanent forms of death. As a space of relief was secured for human biological existence, a new political rationality emerged: in the name of health, well-being, and security, scientific knowledge and political power were conjoined, allowing modern society to take responsibility for organizing and optimizing life.[43] Human biological life was inserted into the workings of political rationalization. Knowledge and techniques of discipline and regulation were brought together for the sake of securing and improving human biological existence. The sciences of life were both produced by and productive of new social and political arrangements.

Power over life developed around two poles: the individual and the population. Within the logic of biopower the success of such socially vital mechanisms as criminal reform, education, healthcare, and economics all appeared to depend on the proper understanding of how individuals functioned under different arrangements and how those individuals could be made to function optimally. Population groups represented the site where the biological well-being of the human-as-species became visible. Problems such as birth and mortality rates, public health and hygiene, old age, race, and scarcity were ar-

---

[42] Rabinow and Rose, "Biopower Today."
[43] Foucault, *The History of Sexuality: An Introduction*, 142.

ticulated and addressed at the level of the population. As these problems were examined within the domain of the burgeoning sciences of life, they became available to strategies of government through series of regulatory mechanisms, forms of taxation, immigration control, insurance, and the like.[44]

In short, techniques of discipline and regulation depended on ever more finely detailed knowledge of individuals and populations under specific circumstances. This knowledge, provided by advancing scientific fields, was catalogued, interpreted, and arrayed in relation to norms against which deviations could be measured. These arrays, in turn, could then be put to use in designing effective techniques for overcoming socially dangerous deviations.[45] Biopower highlighted a simple logic: the underlying causes for social ills (such as criminality, public hygiene, etc.) could only be properly diagnosed and effectively remedied by the methodological tools of empirical science. Social ills needed to be rightly understood if they were to be effectively addressed. Once problems of governance were translated into technical terms, the tools of science could be put to use distinguishing social normality from social pathology and designing equipment for reducing the scope and prevalence of this distinction. Apparatuses for the organization and optimization of such equipment were constituted and mobilized.

With the entry of human biological life into the field of political and social relations, basic force relations could be ordered according to new normative models, new subject-roles could be created and correlated, new significations could be inscribed, and new strategies codified. All of this was facilitated by new scientific and discursive practices. Scientific, political, and social practices were articulated into functional apparatuses. If the knowledge of biology occasioned a new mechanics of power it is because relations of power had already begun the discursive process of fixing human bodies and populations as objects of investigation capable not only of being analyzed, ordered, and situated, but of being placed within interventionary strategies and worked on. Even as they remained distinct, any fundamental exteriority between "techniques of knowledge" and "procedures of discourse"[46] began to be eliminated. The mechanics of biopower relied on a new synthesis: "power-knowledge".[47]

Eugenics as an Example of Making Live and Letting Die
If biopower was characterized by the effort to maximize vital capacities, this effort also provided justification for the elimination of any individual or population that might diminish health and well-being. Biopower had a built-in

---

[44] Michel Foucault, *"Society Must Be Defended": Lectures at the Collège De France, 1975–76*, ed. Mauro Bertani, et al., trans. David Macey (New York: Picador, 2003), 241 ff.

[45] Foucault, *The History of Sexuality: An Introduction*. 144.

[46] Ibid., 98.

[47] Foucault, *Discipline and Punish*, 24–27.

potential for expulsion and elimination from the first. Just as the sciences of life could help identify the norms of health, they could also function to determine sites of pathology and provide technologies for working to control and eliminate those pathologies. This obligation to "let die" as part of "making live" showed itself most conspicuously in the logic of eugenics.

During the 19th century the study of heredity had emerged as a central concern of biological investigation. To quote historian of science Jean Gayon, by the 19th century, "heredity came to be treated as the most fundamental property of living beings."[48] The study of heredity seemed to draw into a single conceptual framework two vital processes: (1) the biological development of individual organisms; and (2) the biological development of species. Early biological investigators formulated heredity not as simply one biological property among others characteristic of living organisms, but the matrix for the possibility of life itself. The answer to the question as to whether the causes of social ills were propagated by nature or nurture appeared to fall directly within the purview of the hereditary sciences.

In the closing decades of the 19th century, Charles Darwin's theory of natural selection was mixed with the science of heredity to form what would become a socially infamous concoction: eugenics. The social chemist blending this concoction was British statistician and cousin of Darwin, Francis Galton. As historian Daniel Kevles points out, Galton, like others of his age, was confident that science and technology, as they had done in industry, could successfully engineer progress in human society. If, as Darwin had suggested, the mechanism of evolution was natural selection of the "fittest", and if science had uncovered the operation of that mechanism, then was it unreasonable to assume that humans could take charge of their own evolution future? Successes in 19th century breeding seemed to suggest that this was indeed possible. Plants and animals had been bred for specific traits. In 1865, the same year Mendel published on his peas, Galton asked: "Could not the race of men be similarly improved…Could not the undesirables be got rid of and the desirables multiplied?"[49]

Galton's eugenic proposal capitalized on the two-sided logic implied in the political mandate to take responsibility for life—in order for some to live others would have to be let to die. Galton coupled rhetoric of responsibility for improving the life of the species with the rhetoric of biological safety. In 1895 German scientist Alfred Ploetz sounded a eugenicist alarm: modern society was failing to work in concert with the processes of nature. Medi-

[48] Jean Gayon, "From Measurment to Organization: A Philosophical Scheme for the History of the Concept of Heredity", in: Peter Beurton, Raphael Falk, and Hans-Jorg Rheinberger (ed.), "The Concept of the Gene", in: *Development and Evolutin: Historical and Epistemological Perspectives* (Cambridge and New York: Cambridge University Press, 2000), 70.
[49] Daniel J. Kevles, *In the Name of Eugenics: Genetics and the Uses of Human Heredity* (Cambridge, MA and London: Harvard University Press, 1995), 3.

cal care for the weak, Ploetz argued, undercuts natural struggle for existence. Social welfare was allowing the poor and misfits to outbreed the more "fit" classes. Evolutionary "counter selection", warned Ploetz, was well underway.[50] In support of race-improvement, Galton and others took up the cry of Ploetz's evolutionary racism: cultural and social practices were leading to the evolutionary degeneration of the human species. Responsibility for securing and improving the life of the species required controlling the reproduction of "unfit" populations that were driving species degeneracy.

According to Galton and others, the trends of degeneracy could be reversed. Galton proposed to solve the problem of degeneracy through the development of a new empirical science of heredity—eugenics—and the linking of this science to technologies of social control. In the name of responsibility for the life of the species, eugenics, or "good birth", would investigate the factors that influence hereditary qualities so as to establish scientific criteria for who was fit to reproduce and who was not. By encouraging specific reproductive practices among certain categories of people, the human species could improve itself, favoring certain hereditary qualities and disfavoring others. As the Eugenics Health Foundation was to put it in 1930, "Eugenics is a new science which has as its object the betterment of the human race, and it embraces all forces and factors, whether hygienic, biologic, social, or economic, which are, or may be, influential in the uplifting and improvement of mankind".[51]

In the 1880s, German biologist August Weismann offered a theory of heredity that seemed to support Galton's nature over nurture view. Weismann argued that traits were passed between generations via "germ plasm", a hereditary substance present in the male and female gametes. Germ plasm seemed to provide an entity on which selection, natural or eugenic, could act.[52] The rediscovery and favorable reappraisal of Mendel's work in the early years of the 20th century seemed to bolster the nature over nurture conclusions drawn from Weismann's science. With the success of Mendelian genetics over the first decades of the 20th century, eugenic ideas concerning inheritance gained a borrowed scientific legitimacy. By the 1920s, particularly in the United States, eugenic apparatuses began to stabilize and spread.

Though propaganda explicitly denied it, eugenics reflected the racist and classist prejudices of those that promoted this brand of hereditary science. Characteristics of "good stock", those identified by the ecumenists as fit to reproduce, featured traits associated with the "best and the brightest" of the white (typically Anglo) middle and upper classes. All the same, leading eugenicists and prominent eugenics organizations saw themselves as fostering

---

[50] Ibid., 14.

[51] See archive materials on the Eugenics Health Foundation at the Eugenics Archive, http://www.eugenicsarchive.org/.

[52] Kevles, *In the Name of Eugenics: Genetics and the Uses of Human Heredity*, 19.

the public good. For the sake of health, well-being, and security, national germ plasm, or "protoplasm" as it came to be called, had to be protected.

Eugenicists promoted strategies of regulation in all areas of society. Working "hand in hand with nature", they published innumerable books and pamphlets concerning eugenic public health, and family planning. They offered incentives for the "fit" to have more children. In compliment to these strategies of "positive eugenics", eugenicists promoted programs of "negative eugenics" as well. They discouraged reproduction among the "unfit", a variable and ever changing catalogue of those that carried unfavorable, purportedly heritable, social traits, including criminals, alcoholics, the mentally ill, the retarded, feeble mindedness, the sexually deviant, the poor, the sick and members of selected "racial" groups.[53]

Biopower and Racial Hygiene

To the extent that eugenics represents its most infamous form, biopower was to achieve a pathological apex in the Nazi programs of Racial Hygiene. In 1930 the journal *National Socialist Monthly* published an article entitled "National Socialism as the Political Expression of Our Biological Knowledge". The article underscores the eugenic foundations of Nazi self-justification: National Socialism, the article argues, is nothing more or less than "applied biology"; its methods are "strictly scientific".[54] In the name of scientific care for the human race Ploetz and other German eugenicists had sought social reforms based on "principles of the optimal conditions for the maintenance and development of the race". Chief among these reforms was the transformation of traditional medicine. Traditional medicine, Ploetz argued, may help the individual, but in doing so it hurts the "race". A new kind of medicine, a new kind of public hygiene was needed that would allow medicine to care not only for the good of the individual, but the good of the race—racial hygiene.[55]

The National Socialists instituted far reaching programs for eugenic reform of German society. These programs included support for eugenics research (e. g. criminal and racial biology). Programs were instituted for public education in eugenic health. Incentives were offered to racially "fit" individuals to marry and reproduce. Medical schools began to train thousands of doctors in racial hygiene—"sick genetic lines" needed to be identified. Only science could "legitimately" distinguish between valuable forms of life and "lives not worth living", equipping politicians with the knowledge needed to reverse the alleged degeneration of racial stock.[56]

---

[53] Proctor, *Racial Hygiene*, 30.
[54] Ibid.
[55] Ibid., 25.
[56] Ibid., 93.

Nazi sterilization laws had been passed as early as 1933. Modeled largely
on U.S. laws, compulsory sterilization was instituted for "the Prevention of
Genetically Diseased Offspring."[57] By the end of the decade it was no longer
considered adequate to simply sterilize those on the growing list of the "unfit". Genetic deviants did not merely pose a threat to the well-being of future
generations; they represented a burden on current society. The violent trajectory of racial hygiene culminated with policies to destroy "lives not worth
living". The Nazi's designated 1939 as the year of "the duty to be healthy".
Under the auspices of this logic Hitler commissioned doctors to grant so-
called "mercy deaths" to those judged to be incurably sick. By 1941, the first
phase of "mercy" killings had been complete; 70,000 patients had been killed
in German hospitals. And as Proctor soberly concludes, these hospital mur-
ders, authorized in the name of science, were merely a "rehearsal for the subsequent destruction of Jews, homosexuals, communists, Gypsies, Slavs, and
prisoners of war."[58]

By and large mainline eugenicists were genetic fatalists. Genes, they held,
determined the most crucial aspects of who one was—intelligence, social conformity, morality, and so on; "blood will tell" so the eugenic mantra averred.
If an individual was the child of a criminal that individual was biologically
destined to the criminal life. And from the eugenicist's point of view, bad human stock was an evolutionary pathology. The only means of "curing" this
pathology was to intervene in human reproduction. Given such biological
fate, eugenicists held that the most charitable social policies were those informed by the biological Golden Rule: "Do unto both the born and the unborn as you would have both the born and the unborn do unto you." The
innocuous sounding rule provided rhetorical cover for willful neglect of the
socially disadvantaged. If we aid the "unfit" in this generation, so the Golden
Rule implied, we leave their offspring as a burden to future generations. Em-
bracing social policies of "survival of the fittest" could be rationalized as an
expression of altruism to the species. If modern state power sought to take
responsibility for life, then eugenics saw itself as an authorized apparatus of
that power.

Biology and Rhetoric Beyond Biopower
Following World War II, multiple events combined to reform the relationship
between biology and politics. Almost immediately upon the conclusion of
the war the moral and political rhetoric used to justify bio-scientific research
fundamentally shifted. Eugenics had been rationalized according to a racist
rhetoric of social progress. It was ostensibly concerned with securing and improving the biological life of the species. Politically translated, responsibility

---

[57] Ibid., 97.
[58] Ibid., 177.

for the life of the species meant responsibility for the life of selected "fit" population groups. In the name of saving the life of the species, eugenics justified allowing "unfit" population groups to die.[59] With revelations of Nazi barbarity, the rhetoric of eugenics no longer carried political and moral authority; the grand eugenic vision of improving the human species through race biology faded. Indeed, scientific accounts of race were politically discredited. The ten year old United Nations declared, "any doctrine of racial differentiation or superiority is scientifically false, morally condemnable, socially unjust and dangerous, and that there is no justification for racial division either in theory or in practice".[60]

Shifts in the articulation of genetics within political and social spaces, for example, reflected this turn from the biology of race. While continuing to operate in the name of health, well-being, and security, the rationalizing object of that operation was rarely the life of the human species. The rhetorical forms at work in nascent molecular biology increasingly positioned genetics as an instrument for improving the life of the human individual at the discretion of the individual. In many countries, including the United States, biopower shifted rhetorical concentration from the pole of populations to the pole of the individual. This shift, in turn, upset the eugenic moral calculus: if power is responsible for saving individual life, allowing certain groups to die becomes morally scandalous.[61]

Of course—and this must be under scored—biopower remained in force after World War II. Social welfare programs continued to develop unabated. Current debates over HPV vaccinations remind us that even in developed liberal societies like the U.S., states retain some measure of responsibility for the biological well-being of populations. More importantly, it would be a mistake to confuse biopower with eugenics. Eugenics is just one apparatus of biopower among others. Indeed, the paroxysmal form of biopower seen in Nazi programs of race purity have been described as tipping beyond biopower toward a "thanatopolitics"—a politics of death.[62] The assertion by Agamben and others that the truest manifestation of biopower can be seen in the death camps is certainly provocative, but analytically disingenuous. Nevertheless, with the emergence of a humanitarian logic, articulated by the United Nations, the Nuremburg investigators, and others, forms and practices of biopower shifted, and new authorizing rhetorics emerged.

---

[59] Foucault, *"Society Must Be Defended": Lectures at the Collège De France, 1975–76.*, 254.

[60] United Nations Declaration on the Elimination of All Forms of Racial Discrimination, http://www.unhchr.ch/html/menu3/b/9.htm.

[61] Michelle Condit Celeste, "The Meanings of the Gene: Public Debates About Human Heredity", in: David J. Depew, Deirdre N. McCloskey, John S. Nelson and John D. Peters (ed.), *Rhetoric of the Human Sciences* (Madison and London: The University of Wisconsin Press, 1999).

[62] "Biopower Today."

Archaeological Inquiry: Authorization as an Analytic of the Contemporary

Conventional political sociology has dealt with matters related to authorization in terms of "legitimation". Legitimation is typically defined as the processes by which particular power relations are not only institutionalized, but given moral grounding. Closely related to legitimation is "legitimacy". Legitimacy refers to the stabilization of power relations when they are considered morally valid.[63] Legitimation and legitimacy capture some of what I am interested in when thinking about rhetoric, biology, and genocide. However, I am not interested only in the ways in which power relations are given *moral* grounding. Rather I am interested in the ways in which they become *authorized* per se—a phenomenon that may or may not include moral validation. More specifically I am interested in analyzing the dynamics by which truth claims in biology (public truth claims) are given form as authorized and thereby are capable of playing a formative role in the wider assemblages within which they circulate.

Defining Authorization

"Authorization", as I want to develop it here, designates the ways in which public discourse contributes to connecting, animating, and giving form to a number of crucial dynamics and elements within an assemblage. These crucial dynamics and elements include the ways in which human life is identified and characterized, the design of technologies by which such figures can be worked on, and the justifications by which the use of such technologies are made to appear necessary and even urgent. To study biology, rhetoric, and genocide is to study the relation between knowledge and power, the form and dynamics of authorization.

Defined as the art of persuading publics, I noted above that rhetoric involves practice, form, and context—practices by which form is given to discourse such that it exists as more or less authoritative for a specific public. Taken together, the consideration of rhetoric as practice, form, and context can be thought of as consideration of the modality of discourse. Attention to rhetoric can thus analytically open up a complex operational dimension of language that may include, but which is by no means reducible to, the study of instrumentality. This analytic opening conceptually distinguishes modality from content within a concrete situation even while acknowledging that the separation of mode and content in relation to any given set of concrete arrangements is only a useful abstraction.

A sufficient investigation of biology, rhetoric, and genocide might fruitfully examine the modality of truth claims about human life in order to understand how they become effectively linked to and formative of power. The

---

[63] See, for example, Weber's *The Theory of Social and Economic Organization*.

modality of public truth claims helps determine the kinds of interventions that are likely to appear authorized and thereby likely to become elaborated and mobilized. For example, consider the modal difference between a logic of biopower and the humanitarian logic articulated by the United Nations at the close of the second World War. With biopower, humans are figured as forms of life endowed with natural capacities that must be regulated and maximized. There is no inherent principle of limitation with regard to the extent to which power can work on humans figured in this way; optimization is only limited by the restraints of capacity. With humanitarianism, the human is character- ized by an archonic dignity — a primordial value that can never be constituted, only recognized. There is a central principle of limitation at work such that the only authorized interventions are those which seek to respect and pro- tect and not actualize or realize value. The contrasts between biopower and humanitarian logics introduce an analytic question about the modality of dis- course: how is it that rhetoric functions to authorize optimization in the one case and protection in the other?

Archaeology of Knowledge
A sufficient response to this question (and hence the study of authorization) is likely to be neither philosophically generic nor deductive. Rather it will likely involve painstaking attention to peculiar conjunctions of relations, ob- jects, subject roles, concepts, strategic choices, truth claims, discourse, inter- ventions, and the like. At the same time, the study of authorization requires attention to how it is these elements push back on one's analytic, how these objects put the sufficiency of one's analytic into question. What conceptual tools can be adjusted to such work?

I propose considering Foucault's reformulation of Kant's archaeology of knowledge[64] as a preliminary step to thinking beyond biopower. Archaeology of knowledge is a method of analysis developed for the study of systems of thought, particularly the sciences, with attention given to the way in which these systems of thought are culturally, socially, and politically productive. *Philosophische Archäologie*, is "a phrase used by Kant to designate 'the his- tory of that which makes a certain form of thought necessary'" at a particular place and particular time.[65]

As Foucault developed the analytic approach, an archaeology of knowledge grants integrity to the specifics of a given assemblage of discursive materials. It is concerned not with the progressive or continuous evolution of ideas. It is concerned with emergence and transformation of discursive formations

---

[64] Michel Foucault, *The Archaeology of Knowledge and the Discourse on Language*, trans. A.M. Sheridan Smith (New York: Pantheon Books, 1972).
[65] David Macey, "Archaeology of Knowledge", in: *The Penguin Dictionary of Critical Theory* (London: Penguin Books, 2000).

and the underlying episteme that constitutes the logic of the relations among them. Archaeology attends not only to idiosyncratic performances of individual thinkers and scientists, but to the dynamics, forms and structures that make knowledge authoritative. Concentrating on "that which makes a certain form of thought necessary", an archaeology of knowledge facilitates an examination of how it is that certain discursive practices contribute to the authorization of biology as knowledge sufficient to intervening in human life.

It bears noting, however, that an archaeology of knowledge has particular, and therefore limited, analytic value. Foucault experimented with this approach as a means of testing the autonomy of discursive formations in relation to the social and political practices within which these formations were embedded, so as to identify the ways in which such formations were discursively formed.[66] As such this approach gives privileged attention to discursive over non-discursive practices. It is, therefore, finally insufficient (on its own) for assessing the formation and development of problematizations. Thus Foucault finally combines archaeological methods with genealogical methods in his later work on problematizations. Nevertheless, such focus on discursive practices is appropriate to a focus on rhetoric and authorization if its limitations are kept in view and monitored. Consonant with Aristotle's definition of rhetoric, an archaeology of knowledge concentrates attention on the modality of discourse in relation to assemblages.

Throughout the 18th and 19th centuries the developing human and biological sciences were established as stable and authoritative forms of discourse with proper rules for the formulation of statements, complex series of discursive relations that constituted and generated knowledge of the human thing as an object of scientific knowledge, susceptible to normative ordering, correlation, positioning, and optimization. These discursive practices helped establish the human social and individual body as objects of knowledge and intervention. They made varied, overlapping, sometimes incommensurable, claims about shared objects of study. Though they observed and calculated for particular and distinctive ends, they nevertheless appealed to the same objects as the factual arbiter of competing theories.

Such discursive formations can be thought of as being constrained and integrated by a shared *episteme*. Episteme refers to a contingent "historical set of relations uniting the various discursive practices and the discursive formations that generate the sciences and other forms of knowledge."[67] An episteme is not a body of knowledge per se; rather it is a field of relations that makes knowledge possible and thereby also constrains it. The episteme informing discourses about the human social and individual body as an object of scientific knowledge, for example, contributed to possible interactions and coordi-

---

[66] "Introduction", in: *The Foucault Reader*, 10.
[67] Macey, 101.

nation among the various experts, institutions, strategies, and technologies of biopower. Eugenicists claimed that, as a specified scientific enterprise, eugenics draws its materials from numerous sources (e.g. anthropology, biology, anatomy, sociology, political economy, statistics, genealogy, psychopathology, nosology, ethnology, and genetics) and organizes them into a "harmonious entity". Eugenics was able to attempt this synthesis, in part, because of the complex series of discursive relations that allowed the human as species and as individual bodies, both productive and reproductive, to be taken for granted as natural objects susceptible of observation, quantification, organization, manipulation, and transformation, that is, as objects of knowledge.

Inquiry into the fundamental discursive conditions that made eugenics not only possible or reasonable but authoritative can benefit by adjusting analytic attention such that it considers not only the "scientific" claims made by eugenicists, but the general orientation of the biological and human sciences toward the technical optimization of "society". Such adjustments help characterize relations between and among the particular content of eugenics, its rhetorical stylizations, and the political apparatuses within which eugenics was taken up as reasonable. Such characterization aims at the archaeological episteme—the set of positive conditions that tells us something about the ways in which discourse is productive of particular kinds of distinctions, relations, and interventions.

Archaeology and Authorization
The potential usefulness of an archaeology of knowledge for thinking about authorization is evidenced by a brief consideration of the historically situated character of eugenics.

Eugenic apparatuses no longer function authoritatively within contemporary discursive domains. They are not capable of strategically and stably informing contemporary assemblages. The term "eugenics" itself carries with it the weight of particular historical arrangements and a particular episteme. It is archived in the historical corpus of scientific and social thought according to specific sets of relations. The term only signifies as authorized within its proper historical archive. Eugenic social programs can only be considered meaningfully within contemporary discursive fields at a moral or historical distance. Current configurations of rhetoric, biology, and politics often work to dissociate from and guard present practices against the specter of eugenics. Eugenics has lost its prior claim to ethical and scientific authority.

Eugenics is rhetorically managed within the constraints of contemporary discursive practice through strategies of de-authorization. The objects of investigation and intervention that it historically took for granted—the plasmic root of social degeneration, feeblemindedness as hereditary contagion—are considered scientifically archaic. The particular subjective positions it formed and depended on—the relationship between the scientist as expert and the immigrant as degenerate, the clinician as guardian of hereditary health, the doctor as the master of the species' sexual future—have been reconfigured. The conception of favorable and unfavorable forms of human life that it formed—the fitter family, the hereditary imbecile, the ideal social future—have little political purchase. The strategic social choices it introduced—sterilization laws, immigration laws, interracial marriage laws, the statistical identification of groups, the internalizing of the individual into the strategic complex of hereditary health of the society—depended on political apparatuses that are no longer present. The rhetoric of eugenics is only authoritative as a displaced and dissociated stylization.

The logic of relations among rhetoric, biology, and power are malleable and open to intervention and change. They are specific to particular assemblages of things. And yet they persist, calling for renewed attention. Investigation of the public discursive formations being generated in relation to biology today is likely to focus attention on the modes in which life generally, and human life in particular is being rendered. These modes will resituate human life in relation to a broad range of institutions, processes, behaviors, norms, classifications, and the like. Although such resituating may not "define [the object's] internal constitution [as if it were a prior form awaiting content]", as Foucault wrote, but it will, no doubt, enable human life "to appear, to juxtapose itself with other objects, to situate itself in relation to them, to define its difference, its irreducibility, and even perhaps its heterogeneity, in short, to be placed in a field of exteriority."[68] Such exteriority, in turn, will call for and open human life up to new techniques of intervention. What form these interventions take cannot be known in advance; though they will, no doubt, exhibit the usual ambiguous confusion of blessings and curses. Whatever the case, truth claims about human life will likely be found to depend on emergent episteme, adapted interventions, and emergent forms of authorization.

In summary, the term *authorization* holds promise as a general concept that clarifies aspects of the ways in which truth and power work together to produce, integrate, modulate or disintegrate. It helps us focus on the place of rhetoric in these dynamics. As part of an archaeology of knowledge, the study of authorization should help identify how objects and relations are, in part, problematized, positioned, or produced by discursive practices. It should help us track the ways in which certain truth claims and interventions are linked and stabilized as axes—strategic axes—around which assemblages are, in part, ordered. Most important, it should help concentrate analysis on the ways in which human life is figured, becomes the site of coordination for a certain set of operations, and is thereby intervened on. Authorization consists of inquiry into how strategic axes between truth claims and interventions are given form, how certain figurations of things human are made authoritative for specific

[68] Foucault, *The Archaeology of Knowledge and the Discourse on Language*, 45.

publics, such that a range of practices can be mobilized in the name of what's right, desirable, necessary, defective, or evil.

Provisional Diagnosis: Authorization Beyond Biopower

Foucault demonstrated that biopower provides a useful analytic for genealogical work on the history of the life sciences and power in the 19th and early 20th centuries. But in what ways is biopower useful today as an analytic for thinking about biology and evil? To what extent is biopower helpful in developing an analytic of the contemporary forms of the problem of biology, rhetoric, and genocide, or even biology, rhetoric, and power more generally? With the rise of a humanitarian political logic and the deployment of that logic by bio-ethicists and others, biopolitical apparatuses for connecting biology, ethics, and politics, have been considerably modulated. Despite the claims made by the philosophical purveyors of biopower, even cursory empirical analysis demonstrates that we do not live in a biopolitical epoch. Things are in formation.

Paul Rabinow noted a range of risks associated with taking concepts useful for genealogical analysis as sufficient (without considerable adjustment) for thinking about the contemporary. The "contemporary" here means something quite specific. Rabinow defines the contemporary as a moving ratio of the recent past and the near future, a ratio in which one finds particular kinds of object domains and thus particular kinds of problems. These object domains are emergent—stylizations of old and new elements. As such, while many of the elements are familiar and well understood, their form, and therefore their significance and function, are not. Among other things, this means that the problems encountered are emergent as well.[69]

Contemporary Problems

To the extent that developments in evolutionary biology have contributed to fundamental reevaluations of theological concepts and approaches, this is in no small part because of the ways in which evolution poses challenges to an analysis of the contemporary.[70] Despite having first developed in the context of the great modern philosophies of history—philosophies that attempted to demonstrate the regular, necessary, and providential unfolding of historical dynamics—evolutionary biology has contributed to an understanding of the natural and human worlds as fundamentally contingent and emergent.[71] Such

---

[69] Paul Rabinow, *Marking Time: On the Anthropology of the Contemporary* (Princeton: Princeton University Press, 2007).

[70] For an example of how theology is adjusted in view of contingency and emergence—epigenesis as he calls it—see Ted Peters "Addressing the Post-Modern Person" in *GOD—The World's Future* (Minneapolis: Fortress Press, 2000).

[71] Among the many contemporary discussions on evolution and emergence, see as an example Terrence Deacon, "Emergence: The Hole at the Wheel's Hub", in: Philips Clayton and Paul Dav-

an understanding orients thinking. An approach to problems that takes the significance of configurations to be specific and that takes the future to be open is fruitful for pragmatic if not theoretical reasons. Problems in the contemporary might not be satisfactorily rectified by appeal to an unfolding history or a cosmos.

At the same time evolutionary biology has contributed to understandings of the interconnection and mutual formation of elements within dynamic systems. Such interconnection and mutual formation invites renewed attention to classic considerations of form as the site of significance—the meaning of elements is constituted, though perhaps not determined, by their place within the form of things. These considerations recommend the Deweyan proposition that the thinking subject is caught up in and formed by the milieu of problems on which the thinker works.[72] That is, it appears that we are situated in, and thereby partially constituted by, the emergent, specific, and interconnected problems that confront thinking.[73]

Although contemporary problems are often located within existing problematizations, their particular form and thus the particular ways in which one can usefully work on them cannot be fully known in advance. To quote Wolfhart Pannenberg, "a new situation demands new solutions."[74] Consider the theme of this volume for example. The problem of evil in relation to biology is not per se new. The challenges and opportunities connected to that problem, however, have been modulated in practical and specific ways. Development in sociobiology,[75] evolution and ethics,[76] and new theoretical models for how evolution functions,[77] for example, render past ways of dealing with this problem insufficient in practical and specific ways; new work is required.

The problem of evolution and evil cannot be adequately taken up today if we only employ materials developed under different arrangements, or materials that are too general in character. Historical modes and the conceptual tools developed under different arrangements are insufficient (e.g. Foucault's history of the present or biopower). Likewise the contemporary cannot be adequately worked on if we only employ the modes and conceptual tools of philosophy, a mode that emphasizes those features of knowledge and being that remain constant despite apparent change (e.g. Agamben's political philosophy or his conception of biopower). What theology needs today in

ies (ed.), *The Re-Emergence of Emergence: The Emergentist Hypothesis from Science to Religion*, (New York: Oxford University Press, 2006).

[72] John Dewey, "Introduction", in: *Essays in Experimental Logic* (New York: Dover Publications, 1953).

[73] Paul Rabinow, "Anthropologies Problems", Anthropos Today.

[74] Quoted in Ted Peters, *God—The World's Future* (Minneapolis: Fortress Press, 2000), 374.

[75] See James Haag's chapter in this volume, for example.

[76] See Christopher Southgate in this volume, for example.

[77] See Joshua Moritz in this volume, for example.

order to work on the problem of evolution and evil (or biology, rhetoric, and genocide in the case of my work) are modes and conceptual tools adequate to an analytic of the contemporary.

Biopower and the Contemporary

The term biopower proves to be a useful point of departure for the development of such an analytic. In the first place, and most simply, understanding of past forms of power helps us be alert to its contemporary iterations—the discipline of the human body and the regulation of populations still pervade many domains. In the second place, and more fundamentally, biopower displays ways (even if historically particular) in which scientific knowledge is saturated with power relations (consider the various kinds of authority at play in science from genre constraints to model based paradigms to the influence of granting institutions) and the ways in which power relations continue to rely on the objects, truth claims, and techniques provided by scientific knowledge.

Foucault famously suggested that power, defined as strategic relations of force, is everywhere and saturates everything.[78] His suggestion was both more benign and basic than many of his detractors and disciples think. In thinking about power Foucault wanted to draw out the kind of insights characteristic of systems thinking generally: within an assemblage of relations, the significance and productive functions of any given element is determined in part by its place within and by the form of the system. Form is a vector for constituting significance. Reflecting on biopower reminds us that the objects of knowledge, truth claims, and techniques for ordering life are interconnected and mutually productive. More crucially for the interests of this essay, it reminds us that the productive relations among these elements are dependent in basic ways on the operations of authorization. Biopower only emerged when shifts between objects and truth claims became authorized, when problematizations modulated relations.

The study of authorization as part of contemporary assemblages involves the work of characterizing how it is that a given event emerges within and works to modulate a prior set of elements, and also how such modulation both restricts and opens future possibilities. The stylization of a truth claim as authorized can "eventalize" an assemblage, repositioning a field of relations such that new kinds of practices are pursued and past practices abandoned or adjusted. An assemblage's recent past is never discrete and never stable. Additional authorized truth claims can emerge in a field of relations in such a way as to change the way in which any past knowledge persists in the broader corpus of authorization. Relations to prior ways of thinking may be modulated so as to produce association, dissociation, insufficiency or indifference. Of course no present truth-event so displaces past claims so as to eliminate them.

---

[78] Foucault, *History of Sexuality: An Introduction*, 93.

Rather, what is modulated is the status of these past claims relative to the logic of authorization in the contemporary.

Authorization often functions as simple declarative reference to the ostensibly self-evident (the human body, the population, the dignified human, and so on). Objects do become tacit and discursive practices become more or less stable—indeed apparatuses depend on the naturalization of the objects of truth discourse and the regularization of practices of intervention. Today, however, the relation between truth claims in biology and the range of interventions being proposed in the name of these truth claims is unstable and fragmented. The objects at stake and the relation of those objects to other domains of practice are not self-evident and, as such, no prescriptions for action are uncontested or broadly persuasive.

Innovations in the biological sciences are being assembled into key domains of human life and are thereby modulating the significance of past practices and the range of possible future practices. State run eugenics programs are no longer authorized. Indeed, prior forms of biopower appear to be under significant transformation in multiple domains. At the same time other possibilities are opening up. Knowledge taken to be authorized is shaping what we think is at stake from science education in public schools to our theories of God. There is a reciprocal relationship established by the modalities of authorization in the contemporary whereby new truth claims depend on and enter into existing problematizations and thereby modulate the significance of the past events which made such entrance possible. This stylization of the old and new is not yet stable and not yet fully authorized. As such, the ways in which biology will contribute to a dividing up of true and false in regard to things human and thereby to new practices of life-ordering remains to be seen. Theology must develop a pragmatic patience, adjusting its tools of analysis and proposals for intervention as things unfold.

Eugenics and the Question of Religion

Nathan Hallanger

As a Berkeley-educated molecular biologist, Wendy Northcutt knows something about evolution. As a best-selling author, she has done a great deal to popularize Darwinian thinking. Each year, Northcutt gathers submissions to her website, has visitors to her site vote on the submissions, and then awards the best submissions with a popular honor: the Darwin Awards. Northcutt's seemingly humorous awards—and her best-selling books—highlight the spectacular deaths of individuals who have removed themselves from the gene pool, and thus have done society a favor by assuring that such stupidity will not be bequeathed to the next generation. According to Northcutt (who in her capacity as the keeper of the Darwin Awards goes by the name "Darwin"), "The Darwin Awards honor those who improve our gene pool by removing themselves from it. We commemorate the actions of men and women who gave their all, in an effort to improve the human species. Of necessity, the honor is usually bestowed posthumously."[1]

Though meant to provide a healthy dose of black humor, the Darwin Awards are based on a curious assumption about intelligence and inheritance, and because of their popularity, no doubt reinforce this assumption. The Darwin Awards assume that the mental capacities of the award recipients are heritable genetic factors. One might surmise that the recipients of the Darwin Awards carried a stupidity gene, or perhaps failed to receive a fully functioning intelligence gene. Thus, stupidity that leads an individual to die in spectacular fashion can be eliminated from the population by the death of the genes that carry such lack of foresight. "Darwin" subscribes to this view. In an interview with Salon.com, Northcutt was asked if the awards "demonstrate how some people's stupid behavior may have a hand in keeping the rest of us smarter— by eliminating morons from the gene pool". She responded, "In an evolutionary sense, yes, people who die can't contribute to the gene pool any longer, so that those who die from their own stupid actions are preventing themselves from passing their unfavorable genes along to the next generation."[2]

---

[1] "The Darwin Awards", [online] (accessed May 11, 2003); available from http://www.darwinawards.com/.

[2] Wendy Northcutt, "We're With Stupid", interview by Carina Chocano, *Salon.com* [interview online] (January 3, 2000, accessed May 11, 2003); available from http://dir.salon.com/people/feature/2000/01/03/darwin/index.html?pn=1.

The Darwin Awards represent an instinct rooted in a movement begun a century ago, a movement that gained momentum in the United States and ultimately influenced the Nazi "final solution" in World War II: the eugenics movement. In the last thirty years, but particularly since the inception of the Human Genome Project, there has been increasing interest in the history of the eugenics movement, and much has been written on the subject. While many have noted the religious overtones of eugenics, few have offered an in-depth treatment of the interaction between religion and science in the eugenics movement. Eugenic scientists, who were largely naturalists, viewed eugenics as a religious endeavor, appealing to the highest aims and desires for humanity's future. Theologians and clergy, too, found in eugenics a scientific means for achieving a better society and for controlling sinful vices.

On both sides, then, the scientific and the religious, proponents viewed eugenics as a means for improving society; reducing the burden imposed by alcoholics, criminals, and the feeble-minded; and assuring the future success and prosperity of the nation. As a movement aimed at human betterment, eugenics appealed to the religious impulse of both scientists and clergy. Why was this the case? Why the widespread use of religious language among eugenicists? Did theologians and clergy accept eugenics as a new religion? If not, on what theological resources did they draw to reject it? The task of this chapter is to show the deep-seated nature of the eugenic scientists' religious impulse, and theology's reaction to eugenics. First, a brief survey of the genesis of eugenics will show Francis Galton's influence on later eugenicists. Next, an examination of a representative sample of eugenicists will demonstrate a distinct drive toward "scientific imperialism."[3] Then, an overview of the reception of eugenics among liberal Protestants in general and orthodox Protestants in the Deep South will show the theological rationale behind support of or opposition to eugenic measures. Finally, the paper will conclude with speculations about the appeal of eugenics and its relationship to teleology.

Origins: Galton and Eugenics

According to the movement's founding father Francis Galton, "eugenics", from the Greek meaning "good birth", was the human race taking control of its own biological destiny, or "the study of agencies under social control which may improve or impair the racial qualities of future generations."[4] In short, Galton, influenced by both his cousin Charles Darwin's theory of evolution by natural selection and the practice among farmers of selective breed-

---

[3] Ted Peters, "Science and Theology: Toward Consonance", in: Ted Peters (ed.), *Science and Theology: The New Consonance*, (Boulder, CO: Westview Press, 1998) 13 ff.

[4] Francis Galton, "Probability: The Foundation of Eugenics", in: *Essays in Eugenics* (New York: Garland, 1909) 81, quoted in Diane Paul, *Controlling Human Heredity: 1865 to the Present* (Atlantic Highlands, NJ: Humanities Press, 1995), 3.

ing, thought that humans should control the breeding of its own stock to encourage the best and discourage the worst. Reflecting on farmers' breeding practices, Galton asked, "Could not the race of men be similarly improved? Could not the undesirables be got rid of and the desirables multiplied?"[5] Moreover, Galton surmised that "human talent and character differed little from the more mundane traits discussed by Darwin to illustrate the selection and breeding of domestic animals and cultivated plants."[6] With careful planning, society could assure that men of talent would continue to be born.

In addition to believing that talent and character could be inherited, Galton recognized that even if evolution by natural selection had produced humanity, it was no longer operating in civilized society. In nature, the process of natural selection would eliminate the weak. In civilized societies, however, the weak and "feeble-minded" are cared for and provided for by society through charities, government programs, and religious groups. These efforts render the mechanism of natural selection inoperative. It is only right, therefore, that civilized human society take control of its own breeding practices. Only in this way can the human race—middle-class Protestants, at least—maintain its level of civilization and prevent the regression of humanity toward greater "feeble-mindedness" and greater physical weakness.[7]

Despite the enthusiasm of Galton and his successor Karl Pearson, the eugenics movement did not gain momentum until late in Galton's life, for it was not until after 1900 when the work of the Austrian monk Gregor Mendel was re-discovered that the true impact of heredity permeated both the scientific community and society. Mendel showed how individual characteristics such as height and pod color in pea plants could be inherited according to a regular pattern. Additionally, Mendel discovered that recessive traits could remain unexpressed in hybrids, only to reappear in later generations. To scientists concerned with human evolution and the apparent decline of industrialized societies, Mendel's work was proof that traits could be inherited according to certain statistical probabilities, and that by knowing the pedigree of an individual, one could predict the likelihood that a certain trait would appear in that individual's offspring. Equally important was the implication that traits are not muted or diluted from generation to generation but maintain their viability seemingly forever. An undesirable trait could thus continue to influence offspring generation after generation, even if an offspring's phenotype appeared unaffected by that recessive trait.

---

[5] Karl Pearson, *The Life, Letters, and Labours of Francis Galton*, 3 vol. in 4 (Cambridge: Cambridge University Press, 1914–1930) IIIA, 348, quoted in: Daniel J. Kevles, *In the Name of Eugenics: Genetics and the Uses of Human Heredity* (Cambridge, MA: Harvard University Press, 1995) 3.

[6] Nicholas Wright Gillham, *A Life of Sir Francis Galton* (Oxford: Oxford University Press, 2001), 156.

[7] Researching inheritance in pea plants and height in adult humans, Galton found that the data regressed to a mean value. See Gillham, 203 ff and 251–256.

The re-discovery of Mendel does not appear to have necessitated the movement toward eugenic measures, whether positive or negative, for the role of genetics remained a debated question. From early on, scientists cited the influence of environmental factors to refute claims of hereditary determinism. Aware of such criticism, Galton developed an ingenious method for determining the degree to which genetic factors and/or environmental factors determined traits.[8] In fact, it was Galton who coined the phrase "nature or nurture."[9] Indeed, Galton recognized the objection that environmental factors might play a greater role than heredity in the achievement of the eminent men of Britain whom he had examined in his book *Hereditary Genius*. He was pleased, therefore, to have developed an investigative tool "wholly free from this objection": twin studies.[10]

Galton had developed a seemingly perfect tool to establish the role of heredity in the transmission of traits. If monozygotic twins exhibited the same traits after being reared in different environments, Galton could prove that certain behaviors and traits were indeed hereditary. However, it seems that the proclivity to attribute behaviors solely to genetic factors led Galton to an unambiguous conclusion: "There is no escape from the conclusion that nature prevails enormously over nurture when the differences in nurture do not exceed what is commonly to be found among persons of the same rank of society and in the same country."[11] Galton used another method to mute the criticism of those who favored nurture. By looking at adopted sons of Roman Catholic officials, Galton could determine whether or not the traits necessary for success were environmental. He wondered, "Are, then, the nephews, etc., of the Popes, on the whole as highly distinguished as are the sons of other equally eminent men?" From his research, the answer was clear. "I answer decidedly not."[12]

With twin studies apparently proving that hereditary factors outweighed environmental ones, and with Mendel's experiments showing the persistence of heritable factors, scientists who shared Francis Galton's desire to take control of human evolution had scientific support for their proposals of positive and negative eugenics. But how to show which traits were heritable, and which traits should be targeted for eugenic measures?

---

[8] Gillham, 193 f. Galton was careful to distinguish between monozygotic and dizygotic twins.

[9] Gillham, 5.

[10] Francis Galton, "The History of Twins, as a Criterion of the Relative Powers of Nature and Nurture", *Fraser's Magazine* 12, 1875, 566, quoted in Gillham, 194.

[11] Ibid. Gillham notes that like many scientists after him, Galton used not only IQ tests to determine the role of nature and nature in mental ability but also told anecdotes about the similarity between twins' behaviors to reinforce apparent genetic influence, while simultaneously ignoring dissimilarities. See Gillham 5 f.

[12] Francis Galton, *Hereditary Genius: An Inquiry into its Laws and Consequences*, revised edition (New York: Appleton, 1879), 10, quoted in Gillham, 161.

Once again, the answer had its roots in Galton's work. In researching *Hereditary Genius*, Galton had analyzed pedigrees of eminent British men and had concluded that ability was indeed inherited.[13] Yet the inheritance of ability rested upon three separate traits: capacity, zeal, and vigour, each of which was required for a man to become eminent.[14] The exact results of Galton's research are not necessarily important, except in that they purport to show the inheritability of ability. What is important is the method of examining pedigrees to determine which traits were heritable.

With great success in the United States, eugenicists developed pedigree surveys and trained field workers to gather family pedigree information for hundreds of individuals. Charles Davenport, founder and director of the Eugenics Records Office at Cold Spring Harbor, New York, was keen to investigate the extended pedigrees of families to determine which traits were indeed hereditary. As Daniel Kevles notes, "Wherever the family pedigrees seemed to show a high incidence of a given character, Davenport concluded that the trait must be heritable and attempted to fit the heritability into a Mendelian frame."[15] It appears that for Davenport *correlation* between the incidence of a trait and familial relation was in fact *causation*. High incidence of a trait in a family pedigree meant that Mendelian inheritance was responsible.

The Mendelian explanation for the heredity of traits (after 1909 referred to as "genes"[16]) seemed to offer a concrete basis for eugenic impulses. After 1900, there existed a scientific and statistical means by which eugenicists could determine the inheritance of traits (both desirable and undesirable), and armed with an increasing library of pedigrees and previous studies of inheritance, eugenicists in America began to explore possible avenues by which eugenic ideas could be disseminated. And with the establishment of the Eugenics Records Office, eugenics had a firm base on which to build a future free of undesirable traits.

Apostles: Eugenics, Science, and Religion

From the beginning, Galton recognized the possible power of eugenic ideals and the necessary conditions for the spread and acceptance of eugenics. Indeed, "I take Eugenics very seriously, feeling that its principles ought to become one of the dominant motives in a civilized nation, much as if they were one of its religious tenets", Galton wrote.[17] As interpreted by the Eugenics

---

[13] Gillham, 163.

[14] Ibid.

[15] Kevles, 46.

[16] The term "gene" was coined by the Danish biologist Wilhelm Johannsen in 1909; Johannsen also created the terms "genotype" and "phenotype" to distinguish between genes and their expression. See Paul, *Controlling Human Nature*, 115 f.

[17] Francis Galton, *Memories of My Life* (London: Mehtuen, ³1909), 322, quoted in Gillham, 324.

Society of the United States of America, this meant that the "motive force for practical eugenics must be sound public opinion. In short, the effort should be not simply to impart information but to kindle earnest interest and establish a eugenic attitude and habit of mind. This is what Galton meant when he said that eugenics must become 'a religion.'"[18] "The eugenists", writes Donald Pickens, "were naturalists, but on occasion they could match the emotional heights of any fundamental evangelical. The eugenists considered themselves to be missionaries rescuing America from racial sin."[19]

These eugenic missionaries found that science offered a means to truly grasp concepts that previously were the province of theologians and philosophers. Once a topic included only in theological discussions of eschatology, immortality took on new force when eugenicists gave eternal life a scientific basis. Indeed, one of the widely-cited eugenic textbooks of the era was Paul Popenoe and Roswell Johnson's *Applied Eugenics*, which went through two editions (1918 and 1933) and a Japanese translation.[20] In a passage that waxes poetic about the long line of human descent, Popenoe and Johnson argued that one's genetic makeup is immortal because genes determine who we are and can be passed on to innumerable generations:

> Immortality, we may point out in passing, is thus no mere hope to the parent; it is a real possibility. The death of the huge agglomeration of highly specialized body-cells is a matter of little consequence, if the germ-plasm, with is power to reproduce not only these body-cells, but the mental traits—indeed, we may in a sense say the very soul—that inhabited them, has been passed on. The individual continues to live, in his offspring, just as the past lives in him. To the eugenist, life everlasting is something more than a figure of speech or a theological concept—it is as much a reality as the beat of a heart, the growth of muscles, or the activity of the mind.[21]

Immortality need no longer cause anxiety among religious believers, for the eugenicist has shown everlasting life to be a scientific fact alongside the physical operations of the human body. In some sense, one passes on one's soul from generation to generation by the propagation of the germ plasm. Religion has but speculated about the nature of the soul and its immortality; science has proven it.

---

[18] "Report and Program of the Eugenics Society of the United States of America" (Lancaster, PA: The Science Press, 1925), 7.

[19] Donald K. Pickens, *Eugenics and the Progressives* (Nashville: Vanderbilt University Press, 1968), 16.

[20] Paul Popenoe and Roswell Johnson, *Applied Eugenics*, revised edition (New York: Macmillan, 1933). The authors sounded a positive note in the 1933 preface, one that is eerily prescient in its linking of eugenics and the coming world war: "If the next decade or two can show as much progress, and at the same time avoid another world war, the eugenic welfare of the human race will be measurably advanced".

[21] Ibid., 41.

Immortality of the soul is not the only religious subject Popenoe and John-son address in *Applied Eugenics*. Indeed, they devote an entire chapter to the subject of eugenics and religion. Interestingly, Popenoe and Johnson begin their chapter on religion by asserting that "natural selection favors the altru-istic and ethical individual because he is more likely to leave children to carry on his endowment and his attitude" than the merely selfish, short-sighted in-dividual.[22] Once again, modern society has interfered with the operation of natural selection so that the selfish and short-sighted individuals are no longer weeded out. This creates problems for eugenicists since eugenics is based on placing the good of the race ahead of the good of the individual. Thus, as Popenoe and Johnson see it, the eugenics movement requires a structure for encouraging altruism and selflessness.

While recognizing that religion has often failed in this regard, Popenoe and Johnson credit religion with encouraging exactly the attitude that eugenics requires, "to cause men to foster lines of conduct that on the whole will be for the good of the race."[23] Religion can and must serve a key role in evangelizing for the eugenic cause. Though they hold what they feel is adequate scientific evidence, the eugenicists require a change in attitude that will assure soci-ety's acting on behalf of eugenic ends. "Since progress toward eugenic ideals is hampered by the present inadequate motivation toward eugenic conduct", the authors observe, "the eugenist looks with eager hope to religion for pos-sible aid."[24]

With that goal in mind, Popenoe and Johnson examine world history for examples of properly eugenic religions. The Near Eastern (Hebrews except-ed) and Greek religions were sufficiently dysgenic.[25] As a result, those civi-lizations collapsed. Roman religion was somewhat eugenic, but it collapsed when invading hoards diluted its emphasis on the family. On the other hand, Chinese religion has shown itself to be quite eugenic by large families and care of the children. Mormonism is quite eugenic, the authors think, because it encourages early marriages and large families to aid the eternal progres-sion of spirits hoping to enter the highest heaven. Finally, Hinduism also ap-pears to be a eugenic religion given that it—along with Chinese religion and Mormonism—"most effectively encourages a low rate of celibacy and a high rate of reproduction."[26]

Among all these examples, chastity has been one of religion's most impor-tant eugenic contributions. Chastity reduces venereal disease and encourages

---

[22] Popenoe and Johnson, *Applied Eugenics*, 212.

[23] Ibid.

[24] Ibid.

[25] Dysgenic is defined as "tending to impair the racial qualities of future generations". Popenoe and Johnson, *Applied Eugenics*, 395.

[26] Ibid., 218.

care in mate selection.[27] Here, as with immortality, religion would be more effective "if chastity were more clearly shown to be based on cogent rational grounds, rather than merely dogma."[28]

The discussion of chastity leads Popenoe and Johnson to consider Christianity. In short, they see Christianity as promoting four important eugenic principles:

(1) "its general emphasis on sound family life as the foundation for social welfare",
(2) "its social loyalty, which was such a prominent feature of Jesus' teachings",
(3) "its regard for children", and
(4) "its maintenance of high standards of personal chastity, making for better mate selection and more permanent and successful marriage."[29]

Yet science is beginning to offer a better, more quantitative basis for ethical behavior that has more nuance than religion's "plain black and white."[30] If religion cannot adjust itself to science, then it should avoid talking about ethical behavior at all.

The surrender of ethics to science is not a necessary course of action, however. Though they see the full retreat of religion from ethics as a possibility, Popenoe and Johnson suggest that it would be better were religion to adopt a more scientific attitude about ethics and take scientific research into account in ethical deliberations. Practically, churches should not encourage marriage for everyone but only for those who are most fit to have offspring. Likewise, churches should not encourage celibacy for all but only for those who are least fit to have offspring. In administering charity, the church should give it to those below a certain standard of fitness only if those individuals agree not to reproduce. In sum, the question for religion becomes, "Can it embrace a progressive and scientific code of ethics, rather than an over-crystallized and over-simplified code of ethics?"[31]

For Popenoe and Johnson, science can offer religion a firm basis for ethics, one amenable to eugenic ideals, as well as present a rational explanation for immortality and the soul. Religion need not retreat from the field of ethics, but it does need to re-examine its ethical groundings. Black and white moral injunctions are no longer tenable in a eugenic world. Popenoe and Johnson conclude:

---

[27] Ibid., 219.
[28] Ibid.
[29] Ibid., 220f.
[30] Ibid., 221.
[31] Ibid.

Eugenic progress is highly dependent on a motivation by which the individual will seek not merely his own good, but that of mankind in general, now and in the future. No agency seems better adapted to reach great masses of people with a eugenic ethics, and to infuse this with the necessary emotional basis that will result in action, than the church.[32]

Religion and the church can be a driving force behind eugenic change if they will but base their ethical systems on a firm scientific base.

Not surprisingly, Paul Popenoe and Roswell Johnson were not the only eugenic scientists interested in the religious dimensions of eugenic ideals. The 1925 "Report and Program of the Eugenics Society of the United States of America" points to the goals of the society and suggests the means by which the society's goals can be achieved. Far from being absent, religion plays a key role in the achievement of those goals.

The first target of the Eugenics Society was education and its effect on birthrate. A key contention among eugenicists was that the most successful members of society were breeding at low rates, while paupers and the feeble-minded were breeding at high rates. This disparity in birthrates was "race suicide."[33] To the Eugenics Society, religion appeared partly to blame for this disparity. As the Society believed, "Universities are still built somewhat on monastic ideas; their best fellowships are not open to married students."[34] The correlation between greater education and low birth rate could be attributed, at least in part, to the monastic history of higher education. Yet the report still framed the problem in terms of a question for which they had an apparent answer: "Are universities attracting the most intelligent elements in the population and virtually sterilizing them, both students and teachers?"[35]

In addition to examining the problem posed by education in lowering birthrates, the Society wondered whether the social value of religion could be used to further eugenic ends. No doubt, religion influenced dysgenic behavior by encouraging charity and social services. But like Popenoe and Johnson, both of whom sat on the Society's advisory council, the Society recognized religion's potential value in influencing individual behavior: "Research is needed to answer the question whether religion, philanthropy, modern sanita-

---

[32] Ibid., 227.

[33] *The Laws of Life, or Eugenics* (Marietta, Ohio: S. A. Muulikin, 1919), 207. "The birth-rate is so low among native Americans that it is feared by some that the native American stock will ultimately disappear. *An appeal* to patriotism has been made in this matter. Not only patriotism, but religion—our duty to God and man—also makes its appeal for larger families. It is quite clear that patriotism, our duty to God and the race, as well as the happiness of the family relation, demand larger families where both parents are physically, morally, intellectually, financially and hereditarily fitted for parenthood."

[34] "Report and Program of the Eugenics Society", 4.

[35] Ibid.

tion, and medical progress are really eugenic. If not, how can their vast *social* value be preserved and a *eugenic* value be added?"[36]

As should be clear, eugenic scientists embraced religious language even as they critiqued the eugenic impact of various religions. Still, they recognized religion's unequalled social power in influencing individual behavior and in urging action. Even as they criticized the dysgenic effects of unconditional religious charity and threatened to take over the entire field of ethics, eugenicists urged religion to incorporate supposedly scientific analyses into their ethical systems. The response by theologians and clergy presented a mixed bag, with Catholics generally opposing eugenics while Protestants generally favored eugenics. One religious group that seems to have been especially active in the eugenics movement were Protestants influenced by liberal theology.

The Liberals

Though not strictly defined, the Protestant liberals can be characterized by an affirmation of higher biblical criticism; a focus on ethics; a commitment to an immanent God over and against a strictly transcendent God; belief in some sort of progress; a recognition of the historical and cultural nature of creeds and traditions; and particularly after 1870, an adoption of the modernist project of adapting theology and religion to secular culture.[37] Additionally, the liberal Protestants of the late nineteenth and early twentieth century were concerned with the question of human nature. Indeed, "preoccupation with problems of human nature and destiny, and relative optimism about their resolution, pervaded all of liberalism, and especially marked its American form."[38] The discussion of human nature among liberals did not originate with Charles Darwin, but post-Darwin it seems to have taken on new urgency among theologians for whom science and secular society played an influential role. Liberal Protestant theologians began looking to science as the basis for theology, a move eugenicists would no doubt applaud. For example, Henry Ward Beecher argued in a lecture delivered at Yale in 1871 that

> we [preachers, ministers, and theologians] are in danger of having the intelligent part of society go past us. The study of human nature is not going to be left to the church or the ministry. It is going to be a part of every system of liberal education, and will be pursued on a scientific basis…And if ministers do not make their theological systems conform to facts as they are, if they do not recognize what men are studying, the time will not be far distant when the pulpit will be like the voice crying in the wilderness.[39]

---

[36] Ibid.

[37] William R. Hutchison (ed.), *American Protestant Thought in the Liberal Era* (Lanham, MD: University Press of America, 1968), 1–6.

[38] Ibid., 1.

[39] Henry Ward Beecher, "The Study of Human Nature", in: William R. Hutchison (ed.), *American Protestant Thought in the Liberal Era* (Lanham, MD: University Press of America, 1968), 43 f.

Fifty years later, Willard Sperry, a Boston minister who eventually became Dean of Harvard Divinity School, wrote that the doctrine of original sin needed updating, but not by theologians alone. Theologians might not even be best equipped to address the problem. Rather, what is required is a "full and candid use of all that modern science and modern literature have done to restate the doctrine of original sin in intelligible and credible terms, that we may press home to men their lost and needy state."[40] Sperry is referring specifically to Thomas Huxley's *Evolution and Ethics* of 1893 in which Huxley notes the immorality of evolution and suggests that "the science of biology had revealed in some new and terrible way the moral liability of every child of man."[41] For Huxley, ethical behavior is not aligning oneself with this "cosmic struggle" but rather "combating it."[42]

In short, liberal Protestants held scientific facts in high esteem and consequently altered their theology according to what science dictated, especially when the scientific issue at hand was human nature. It should come as no surprise, then, to find liberal Protestants among the most ardent supporters of eugenics. Harry Emerson Fosdick, pastor of the Riverside Church in New York and author of the famous sermon, "Shall the Fundamentalists Win?" sat on the advisory board of the American Eugenics Society.[43] Liberals were not the only group to respond to the growing movement. In the Deep South, Protestants looked to the resources unique to Southern religion for proper responses to eugenics.

"Pow'r in the Blood"

"Blood tells" was a common slogan in eugenics literature.[44] The imagery stems from previous theories of inheritance based on the transmission of blood from parent to child. Prior to the explanation offered by Mendel and clarified by Johanssen, Weismann, and others, scientists—including Darwin and Galton—thought that traits were carried as factors in the bloodstream. When a child was conceived, it received blood from its mother and blood from its father, who had in turn received blood from their parents. These factors carried in the blood determined the traits of the child. So by looking at the "bloodlines" of an individual, one could determine the kind of blood traits that one had inherited and prove that "blood tells". Clearly, belief in the determinism of heredity existed prior to a clear understanding of the mechanism of heredity.

---

[40] Willard Sperry, "A Modern Doctrine of Original Sin", in: Hutchison, 169.

[41] Ibid., 162.

[42] Thomas Huxley, quoted in Sperry, 162.

[43] "Report and Program of the Eugenics Society", 14.

[44] For example, see David Starr Jordan, *The Heredity of Richard Roe* (Boston: American Unitarian Association, 1911) 26–29, and the sermons available via the Eugenics Archive (http://www.eugenicsarchive.org). Nearly all the sermons expound on the theme of blood.

Still, even when the Mendelian explanation was re-discovered and traits were linked to genes, the old blood metaphors seem to have been taken onboard as eugenics swept through American and British society. Additionally, the new science of trait inheritance via genes seemed to affirm the prior instinct to assign success to one's pedigree. Genes had replaced blood as the factors of inheritance.

Though genes dominated, the power of the blood persisted. A sermon submitted to the Eugenics Society of the United States of American sermon contest was based on this theme. "Blood tells. It forever tells its story of shame or beauty, whether it flows in plants or animals, in the veins of beggars, poets or kings."[45] Another clergyman wrote, "We have learned that 'blood will tell', and 'sometimes the less it tells the better!'"[46] "Blood" continued to flow from the lips of scientists and theologians as a catchphrase for inheritance even after the gene had become the factor of heredity.

But blood is not only a scientific metaphor. Blood imagery figures prominently in Christian theories of atonement. The notion of a blood sacrifice had long been used to understand the work of Christ, and in Protestant thought, the cleansing power of God's grace through Jesus' sacrifice. Jesus Christ, the lamb who was slain, shed blood in order to cleanse the individual Christian believer. For Protestants, grace is God's gift received by unworthy sinners. In the Deep South where orthodox Christianity had a strong hold on society, atonement and grace offered a competing image of the power of blood, one that appears to have slowed the spread of eugenics.

According to Edward J. Larson, the religion in the Deep South was deeply influenced by the emotional power of religious song. Consequently, one can begin to understand the major themes of Southern religion by examining popular hymns. Larson, citing the southern historian Howard Odum, notes that a recurring theme in Southern hymns was the "power of Christ's blood sacrifice to redeem individual believers."[47] For example, the hymn, "There is Power in the Blood" asks, "Would you be whiter, much whiter than snow?" and "Would you be free from your passion and pride?" The refrain answers, "There is pow'r, pow'r, Wonder-working pow'r / In the precious blood of the Lamb." Blood here is a cleansing gift of God, something unmerited by lowly sinners. God acts on behalf of believers in the sacrifice of Jesus Christ, and believers should respond with gratitude, praise, and neighbor love as a result. Eugenics literature, in contrast, portrayed blood as a means of determining character and, for those with unfortunate pedigrees, a means of weed-

---

[45] "Sermon #2", American Eugenics Society Sermon Contest [online] (1926, accessed April 16, 2003); available from http://www.eugenicsarchive.org/eugenics/topics_fs.pl?theme=32&search=& matches=; Internet.

[46] Ibid., Sermon #36.

[47] Edward J. Larson, *Sex, Race, and Science: Eugenics in the Deep South* (Baltimore, MD: Johns Hopkins Press, 1995), 13.

ing out undesirable traits. The power of blood for eugenicists was as a tool to determine fitness or unfitness. For Christians in the Deep South, blood was a gift, a cleansing and saving power. And at least in principle, the life-giving gift of Christ's blood was available to all, both the fit and unfit. Larson concludes, "The concept of salvation and sanctification for all, solely by divine grace, challenged eugenic doctrines of fixed, inherited degeneracy and superiority."[48]

While a majority of eugenics supporters were liberal Protestants, orthodox Christians—at least in the South—strongly opposed eugenic measures. "At least in the Deep South", Larson writes, "values founded on traditional religion and concern for individual rights served as a more effective protection against the excesses of eugenics than did any internal regulatory mechanism within medicine or science."[49] Christianity *per se* did not align itself with eugenics, only particular strains of Christianity took as their mission the un-critical appropriation of contemporary culture, including science, into their theology. At least in the Deep South, those who held to a more orthodox Christianity were less likely to be in favor of eugenics. At the very least, they were slower in accepting positive and negative eugenics.

Conclusions

Despite the general attitude of liberal Protestants toward science, there appears to be something deeper at work in the appeal of eugenics. Eugenicists counted among their ranks not only materialist scientists and liberal Protestants but also Jews, social conservatives, socialists, and many others. As Diane Paul notes, "It is true that most eugenicists, and in particular those associated with the organized eugenics societies, were politically conservative and socially pessimistic. But eugenics also appealed to a wide range of reformers."[50] To what might one attribute the widespread appeal of eugenics?

One factor might be the plasticity of the term "eugenics" itself. In the minds of some advocates, eugenics served as a preventive measure and a means to return to the comfort of a previous *status quo*. Paul warns, however, that one "fail[s] to understand the appeal of eugenics to so many people…if [one] start[s] with the assumption that it was patently absurd."[51] For Paul the unifying force of eugenics was its promise to provide "technocratic solutions to social problems."[52]

One might also understand eugenics in terms of the deeper desire for a *telos*. Darwin's theory of evolution by natural selection, one might argue, removed

---

[48] Ibid.
[49] Ibid., 167.
[50] Paul, 20.
[51] Ibid., 21.
[52] Ibid.

from creation any notion of teleology. But during the scientific arguments following Darwin, there appeared room for competing interpretations of evolution that left room for teleology. By the turn of the century, however, Darwin appeared to be winning the day. The re-discovery of Mendel and the discovery of the mechanism of heredity via genes could be seen as driving a significant nail in teleology's coffin, particularly among liberal theologians for whom science set the theological agenda. But the problem of teleology was not new.

According to Charles Hodge, the famous Princeton theologian, the key point in Darwinian evolution is whether or not it excludes teleology. For Hodge, the lynchpins of Darwinian theory are evolution, natural selection, and "by far the most important and only distinctive element of his theory, that this natural selection is without design."[53]

Based on a careful analysis of Darwin's writings, his opponents' essays, and his supporters' texts, Hodge answers the question, "What is Darwinism?" with "It is atheism."[54] Denying teleology is tantamount to denying Christianity wholesale, and Darwin's theory had done just that, though Hodge is careful to note that Darwin himself never took such a position in his writings.

For Hodge and others, the denial or acceptance of teleology is the criterion by which one should judge any theory of evolution, be it Darwin's, Lamarck's, or Joseph LeConte's. This continuing controversy over the religious acceptance or rejection of Darwinian theory also influenced attitudes toward eugenics.

Both opponents and proponents recognized the connection between opposition to evolution and opposition to eugenics. Generally, the people who opposed one opposed the other. Alfred Wiggam, science writer and author of *The New Decalogue of Science* and *The Fruit of the Family Tree*, wrote in 1927 that "until we can convince the common man of the fact of evolution…I fear we cannot convince him of the profound ethical and religious significance of the thing we call eugenics."[55] In William Jennings Bryan, Wiggam's fears were realized. Bryan, whose nickname was "the great commoner", denounced eugenics and evolution in his speeches and argued that eugenics was one of the evil offshoots of evolutionary thinking.[56] In 1925, the trial of the century would make Bryan's position well-known.

The connection between evolution and eugenics influenced the trial of John T. Scopes in Dayton, Tennessee, and not simply because William Jennings Bryan served as on the prosecution. The textbook from which Scopes had allegedly taught evolution, George William Hunter's *Civic Biology*, in-

[53] Charles Hodge, *What is Darwinism?* (New York: Scribner, Armstrong, & Company, 1874), 48.
[54] Ibid., 177.
[55] Albert Edward Wiggam, *The Next Age of Man* (Indianapolis: Bobs-Merrill, 1927), 45, quoted in Edward J. Larson, *Summer for the Gods* (Cambridge: Harvard University Press, 1997), 28.
[56] Larson, *Summer for the Gods*, 28.

cluded Charles Davenport's research on the improvement of human heredity and concluded, "If such people were lower animals, we would probably kill them off to prevent them from spreading. Humanity will not allow this, but we do have the remedy of separating the sexes in asylums or other places and in various ways preventing intermarriage and the possibility of perpetuating such a low and degenerate race."[57] Furthermore, because he was a respected scientist, Davenport co-authored the AAAS resolution supporting Scopes and appeared with the young teacher at a New York publicity event prior to the trial.[58] However, in an interesting twist that reveals the difficulty of correlating attitudes toward eugenics with attitudes toward evolution, Clarence Darrow, an attorney for Scopes' defense, seems to have had difficulty getting expert testimony from evolutionary biologists because Darrow had expressed his opposition to eugenics as a violation of human rights. Six of the most well-known expert witnesses, one of whom was Davenport, were also leaders in the eugenics movement.[59]

What Darwinian evolution had taken away from both religion and science, eugenics returned: teleology. Eugenics allowed human society to understand the ultimate roots of social problems, and now that it understood, humanity could most certainly control. Under the watchful eye of the eugenic scientist, society could control marriage and breeding, taking the natural task too long inhibited by civilized society: weeding out undesirable traits and encouraging the propagation of desirable characteristics. True, many eugenicists adhered to conservative eugenics whose aim was to maintain a level of stability in a society apparently threatened by immigration, migration, and feeble-mindedness. But at least an equal number of eugenicists appealed to a higher aim and a future goal. The Eugenics Society's report from 1925 suggests an ultimate goal and a future-orientation. "Moreover, the ultimate fruits of any eugenic movement will, by the nature of the case, require many generations. The eugenic movement, therefore, can not be a short campaign like many political or social movements. It is, rather, like the founding and development of Christianity, something to be handed on from age to age."[60] The goal is future, and the present generation can rightly view itself as foundational. The trajectory of eugenics toward the betterment of society is clear. Eugenics provides not only the goal but also the means. All people hope for a better society, and eugenics can provide that better society via scientific means.

The eugenics movement achieved wide acceptance in the United States in the first thirty years of the twentieth century. Branching out from its begin-

---

[57] George William Hunter, *A Civic Biology: Presented in Problems* (New York: American, 1914), 263, quoted in Larson, *Summer for the Gods*, 27.

[58] Larson, *Summer for the Gods*, 113 ff.

[59] Ibid., 135.

[60] "Report and Program of the Eugenics Society", 10.

Nathan Hallanger

nings at places like the Eugenics Records Office at Cold Spring Harbor, New York, the movement gained momentum in science, politics, and religion. Though its adherents were largely white, middle-class, Protestants, eugenics permeated nearly every social group and category, from conservative to liberal, from atheist to believer.

For Protestants who were influenced by liberal theology, eugenics appeared alongside other progressive movements that garnered attention in the early decades of the twentieth century. Eugenics was unique among social movements, however, in that it promised a scientific solution to social problems. Religious people could affirm eugenics by saying that "The Bible is a book of eugenics", or that "It is a sin against God and a crime against humanity and the State for a child to be brought into the world diseased, or feebleminded."[61] Eugenicists saw in their new science the possibility to render religion's perceived role in maintaining moral behavior obsolete, or to provide a firm, scientific basis for religious ethics. According to Charles Davenport, "The biologist has his own idea of what is the word of God. He believes it to be the testimony of nature."[62] Having focused its sharp gaze inward on human nature, the all-knowing eye of science had penetrated the mystery of inheritance. Would not humanity be foolish to ignore this new knowledge and its potential for improving human stock?

Scientists saw the eugenic task in religious terms because they were, in part, treading on territory traditionally reserved for religion. Influenced by Galton's original hope that eugenics could become one of society's religious tenets, eugenic scientists examined morality, ethics, immortality, teleology, salvation, and sanctification. Most found they could explain these religious concepts better than theologians or clergy could. Their explanations were based on science, not on some rigid dogma that saw the world in black and white.

Liberal theologians who tried to uncritically appropriate science for theology agreed with eugenic scientists. Creeds and dogmas needed to be re-examined or even left behind if eugenics offered a better explanation for moral behavior than religion did. At the very least, religion needed to preach the eugenic gospel in order to assure the changes in attitude and behavior that eugenics required were accepted and practiced in society.

Finally, the connections between evolution and eugenics lead one to surmise that one of the major stumbling blocks to evolution might be one of the major hooks for eugenics: teleology. If Darwinian evolution had indeed removed teleology from nature and from the development of humans, then

---

[61] "Sermon #2", American Eugenics Society Sermon Contest [online] (1926, accessed April 16, 2003); available from http://www.eugenicsarchive.org/eugenics/topics_fs.pl?theme=32&search=& matches=; Internet.

[62] Charles Davenport, "Evidences for Evolution", *Nashville Banner*, June 1, 1925, 6, quoted in Larson, *Summer for the Gods*, 115.

eugenics sought to take control and put teleology back into human development. Clearly, the eugenicists had a future goal in mind toward which human control of its own evolution would lead. If eugenics were successful, then the seemingly aimless path of evolution would be aimless no more; moreover, the path would most certainly be prevented from heading downward toward greater degeneracy. If the aim was human betterment, then science had provided the answer: eugenics.

Sins of Commission, Sins of Omission

Girard, Ricoeur, and the Armenian Genocide

Derek Nelson

Addressing a group of his generals on August 22, 1939, just before launching his Death Head units into Poland, Adolf Hitler rationalized his plans by saying,

> Our strength consists of our speed and in our brutality. Genghis Khan led millions of women and children to slaughter—with premeditation and a happy heart. History sees in him solely the founder of a state. It's a matter of indifference to me what a weak western European civilization will say about me. I have issued the command—I'll have anybody who utters one word of criticism executed by a firing squad. Our war aim does not consist in reaching certain lines, but in the physical destruction of the enemy. Accordingly, I have placed my death-head formations in readiness—for the present only in the East—with orders to them to send to death mercilessly and without compassion, men, women, and children of Polish derivation and language. Only thus shall we gain the living space (Lebensraum) which we need. Who, after all, speaks today of the annihilation of the Armenians?[1]

Two features are particularly striking about this quotation. First is the unspeakable tragedy of the violence and death it both portends and attempts to justify. Most scholars date the beginning of World War II to the invasion of Poland a week or so after Hitler's statement, and the deadly efficiency with which the Nazis prosecuted their agenda is clearly evident here. Second is the nagging suspicion that somehow, in what he says above, Hitler was right. Who, after all, did remember the Armenians? Who saw in the attempted extermination of the Poles,[2] and later the victims of the Holocaust, a possible forerunner in the genocide of the Armenians at the hands of the Turks?

This book is a volume about evil. While "evil" is a concept that in many different valences, its most garish expressions are seen easily enough. The attempted extermination of the Armenian nation is about as clear an example of

---

[1] Kevork Bardakjian, *Hitler and the Armenian Genocide* (Cambridge, MA: Zoryan Institute, 1985), 6.

[2] That Hitler was here referring to wiping out the Poles, and not the Jews, is one of the primary ways modern-day Turks dismiss the relevance of this (in their minds, spurious) quotation. For my part, I do not regard the fact that Hitler did not carry out his intended genocide of the Poles as diminishing the relevance of his comment. It is symptomatic of a mindset which assumes the possibility of committing atrocities with impunity.

evil as we will ever see. The population of Armenians living in the Ottoman Empire before the massacres started was just over two million. At the end of the genocide, about 1923, the best estimates place the death toll at just over half that. The largest body of genocide scholars in the world, the Association of Genocide Scholars of North America, puts the likely number somewhere between 1.2 and 1.3 million.[3] This happened in broad daylight, just outside of technologically advanced Europe, to the peaceful Christian subjects of a modern nation-state. Neither the scope nor the brutality nor the senselessness of the killings escaped report while the events and their aftermath unfolded. In fact, the years 1915 and 1916 saw at least 150 articles about the Armenian genocide in the New York Times alone.[4] Relief agencies were mobilized to send aid, memoirs and first-person accounts were published, and a film detailing one young girl's survival story, *Ravished Armenia*, played to extensive American and international audiences. All this, and yet this event has been eerily excised from the collective memory of the West. Most Americans have never even *heard* of Armenia, let alone know the basics of the genocide that took place. That forgetfulness of tragedy, the relegation of the victims of genocide to the dustbin of history, constitutes an added angle of the evil of the genocide itself.

As a theologian, I have to interpret the Armenian genocide under the category of sin. In the following essay I want specifically to call to mind the ancient Christian distinction between sins of *commission* and sins of *omission*. Sins of commission occur when a freely acting moral agent commits an act that contravenes God's will, often, though not always, thereby harming neighbor, oneself, or creation. Sins of omission, on the other hand, result when actions commanded by God are not taken, though they should be and can be accomplished.[5] A common confession of sin in Christian churches goes something like, "We have sinned against you in thought, word, and deed; by what we have done, and by what we have left undone." This distinction captures some of the essence of the experience of the evil of the Armenian Genocide. One major aspect of the evil of the genocide was the simple fact that it took place. Millions were harassed, deported, robbed, raped, tortured and killed. Those are sins of commission. Though none of this was happening in secret, no one intervened to stop the massacres. Once it was over, the incident nearly disappeared, willfully or not, from our consciousness. Those are sins of omission.

This essay proceeds in three parts. First, I give an overview of the main features of the Armenian genocide, beginning with the events in the twenty

---

[3] Balakian, 195 f.

[4] Many of these are collected in the excellent, though by no means exhaustive, compilation of Richard Kloian, *The Armenian Genocide: News Accounts from the American Press 1915–1922* (Berkeley: Anto, 1980).

[5] Cf., Thomas Aquinas, *Summa Theologiae* Ia IIae q. 71.5.

years leading up to 1915. After outlining the genocide's salient elements, I engage one possible interpretation of the sins of commission. René Girard, the French philosopher and literary critic, has written profoundly on the phenomenon of scapegoating and religious violence, and his insights help us to understand the human desires and drives that can sometimes lead inexorably to violence. Then finally I develop some of the thoughts of the French philosopher Paul Ricoeur to look at the sins of omission of the genocide, especially its omission from the writing of the history of the World War I period. Offering interpretations of something as complex and unique as the Armenian genocide is hazardous. Insights ventured must always be viewed as preliminary and partial. But the work of Girard and Ricoeur can help at least by providing us with a vocabulary for discussing evil in more precise terms. Above all, I hope that this brief look at the Armenian tragedy can help open our eyes and memories, so that this "forgotten genocide" might remain no longer forgotten, and be never again repeated.[6]

The Armenian Genocide in Historical Context

Armenia was the first nation to adopt Christianity as its official religion, doing so in 301 AD. For centuries an independent kingdom, Armenia developed its own language, culture and theology. Largely isolated from their neighbors by the rough terrain of the Anatolian hinterland, Armenian culture took on a unique character. The rise to power of the Seljuk Turks in the 11th Century signaled the beginning of serious challenges to the safety of Armenian lands, and the Ottoman Turks' overthrow of Constantinople in 1453 instituted official subjugation for Armenians in the new Ottoman Empire. They were legally designated infidels, and were accorded significantly lower social status than their Muslim neighbors.[7] They had to pay higher taxes, were forced to pay obeisance to passing Muslims, and were generally looked down upon as gâvur.[8] By the 18th Century the Armenians were reorganized (through forced migrations) into regions called *millets*, and within the *millet* they were allowed limited self-government, such as control over the institutions of marriage and inheritance, and the building of churches and schools. But the price of this meager autonomy was often harsh, as Ottomans crushed any *millet* perceived to be gaining a threatening level of power.[9]

There are basically two schools of historiographical thought on how to approach the Armenian situation. In the first, the slaughter of the Armenians

---

[6] This is a reference to, among many other works, Dickran Boyajian, *Armenia: The Case for a Forgotten Genocide* (Westwood, NJ: Educational Book Crafters, 1972).

[7] Richard Hovannisian (ed.), *The Armenian Genocide: History, Politics, Ethics* (New York: St. Martin's Press, 1992), 45.

[8] A derogatory term for non-Muslims.

[9] Vahkan N. Dadrian, *The History of the Armenian Genocide: Ethnic Conflict from the Balkans to Anatolia to the Caucasus* (Providence, RI: Berghahn, 1995), 4ff.

is seen as the inevitable (though not necessarily just) response to decades of Armenian sedition and uprising, which is to be attributed to the Armenians' express wish for independence from Muslim rule. This is called the *provocation* thesis. The other perspective sees the genocide as the inevitable (and absolutely unjust) consequence of decades or even centuries of first Islamist, and then Pan-Turkic, ideology of domination. This view, called the *ideological* thesis, traces the roots of the genocide through the history of oppression and subjugation experienced by nearly all minority groups in the Ottoman Empire, including Kurds, Syrians, Georgians and especially the Armenian Christians.

I am operating under the assumption that the second of these theses ought to be followed. Documentary evidence recently uncovered has shown the provocation thesis to be a complete distortion of the historical record.[10] The Armenian genocide of 1915 was not provoked by Armenians, and the attempts of various Turkish governments to minimize the gravity of or to cover up completely the death tolls are based on fabrication of evidence, prevarication, and scapegoating. The Armenians never were in a powerful enough position to defend themselves against their oppressors, and the incidents cited as provocation by the Turks were actually attempts at self-protection in the face of systematic extermination. History had by the year 1915 no name for this horrifying phenomenon, and learned only later to call it genocide.

The story of violence begins earlier, however. At least twice before 1915 Armenians were the victims of large scale massacres at the hands of their rulers. The first of these took place in the mid 1890's, when the despotic sultan of the Ottoman Empire, Abdul Hamid II, ordered the extensive slaughter of Armenians all across the empire. The pathological hatred of one man is certainly not enough to "explain" the origins of a genocide. But similar to Hitler's hatred in the Holocaust, the intense personal hatred of Sultan Abdul Hamid II for the Armenians is a necessary starting point for understanding how the genocide was able to be undertaken. Until he was deposed in 1908, Hamid was so paranoid about the security of his kingdom,[11] so profligate in his spending, and so

---

[10] For translations and interpretations of such evidence and its distortion, see, among many others, Wolfgang Gust (ed.), *Der Völkermord an den Armeniern 1915/16: Dokumente aus dem politischen Archiv des deutschen auswärtigen Amts* (Springe: Zuklampen, 2005), Yair Auron, *The Banality of Denial: Israel and the Armenian Genocide* (New Brunswick, NJ: Transaction, 2003), as well as the recent republication of the important documents of Arnold Toynbee and James Bryce, *The Treatment of Armenians in the Ottoman Empire, 1915–1916: Documents Presented to Viscount Grey of Falloden by Viscount Bryce*, ed. Ara Sarafian (Reading, PA: Taderon, 2000).

[11] Peter Balakian aptly summarizes the Sultan's paranoia: "He declared numerous words and subjects taboo and illegal. Beyond his strict censorship of all words and references to Armenia, he ordered a ban on any form of expression that referred to regicide. The name of the deposed Sultan Murad V was banned; the king and queen of Serbia were reported to have died of indigestion, French president Carnot of apoplexy, and President William McKinley of anthrax. So far did his paranoia carry him that he ordered his censors to expunge all references to H_2O from science

consumed by hatred for Armenia that accounts of his life can seem implausible. Convinced that the Armenians were traitors who would assist Russia in a
takeover of the Ottoman Empire, he insisted that the word "Armenia" and its
derivatives be completely removed from all textbooks, road signs and official
documents, and that it never be uttered in his presence. He demanded that
the missionary school in Harput change its name from Armenia College to
Euphrates College. He disallowed Armenians from testifying in criminal and
civil courts, effectively making them victims of never-ending crime. Hamid
imposed *kishlak*, or winter-quartering responsibilities, for Armenians. This
meant that Kurdish and Turkish soldiers and workmen were allowed to quar-
ter themselves in Armenian homes during the winter. Since unarmed Armenians had neither physical nor legal recourse, this quartering invariably meant
the theft of the host's possessions, and the rape or kidnapping of the women
and girls of the household. Under Hamid, then, the traditionally subjugated
Armenians became the objects of public scorn, ridicule and savagery, whereas
they had hitherto been merely second-class citizens.[12]

Armenian frustration and resentment of the Sultan's mistreatment reached
a boiling point in the Eastern province of Sasun in late fall of 1894. Some
Armenian discontents staged demonstrations to protest against unfair legal
and taxation practices. Ottoman troops were quickly deployed to crush what
the Sultan referred to as the Armenian rebellion. Some 10,000 people in Sasun
were killed within two weeks of the demonstration (approximately 200 had
protested). The regular army then trained Kurds and Ottomans to be *zapit-
yes*, or military police, to go around to neighboring villages in the province
and to slaughter any and all Armenians they could find, irrespective of age or
sex. Tens of thousands were killed.

Public outcry ensued, and the Sultan was forced by world public opinion
to set up an investigation. The tribunal was a sham. It disallowed Armenian
testimony, and tried to show that the Armenians had incited open riots and
were involved in a conspiracy with Russia to overthrow the Empire. During
these months, reform parties in Armenian circles were able to organize themselves somewhat, spurred on by the fear of what the Ottomans would do if
they were not resisted. They staged a large protest on October 1, 1895 in the
capitol, then Constantinople, to bring world-wide attention to their plight.
Before the group (nearly 2000 people) had fully assembled, hundreds of *sof-
tas* (Islamic theological students) appeared on the streets of Constantinople
and began massacring Armenians.[13] The police and *zapitye*s who did not par-

---

textbooks because he feared the symbol would be read as meaning "Hamid the second is nothing".
The Burning Tigris: The Armenian Genocide and America's Response (New York: HarperCollins,
2003), 49.

[12] Cf. Dadrian, *The History of the Armenian Genocide*, 113–163.
[13] Balakian, *The Burning Tigris*, 57 ff.

ticipate in the slaughter only stood by and watched. When all 2000 protest-
ers were killed, the Ottomans continued to rape, arrest or slaughter nearly
every Armenian living in the city. The killings lasted for over a week, day and
night.[14] The Constantinople killings set off a new wave of violence throughout the empire, all the way to the Russian border. Towns were burned, houses
plundered, and thousands of Armenians killed. By the early spring of 1896,
the death toll reached 100,000 people, with at least that many others displaced
as refugees.[15]

The second major outbreak of massacres leading up to the full-blown genocide of 1915–6 took place in the Mediterranean region of Adana, this time
at the hands of a new government. Abdul Hamid was deposed in 1908, when
the rest of the Empire had had enough of his prodigal spending and his inability to rule effectively. In the ensuing power struggle, a group later called the
"Young Turks" took over the Ottoman Empire, replacing the broadly Islamic
ideology of isolationism with a Pan-Turkic expansionist spirit. Authority was
centralized in the Committee for Union and Progress (CUP), composed entirely of Turks. To be a "Turk" was now the only way to wield power in the
Empire (a Turk is generally defined as any Muslim whose native language is
Turkish). Coincidentally, Bulgaria, Serbia-Montenegro and some other European lands which had been under Ottoman rule declared their independence
from Turkish rule, and tried to align themselves with Austria-Hungary. The
Turks were outraged, and sent extra troops to the Balkans. Between 1909–12,
Turks massacred 25,000 Bulgarian, Kosovar, and Serbian citizens, in addition
to the number of casualties inflicted during the actual fighting of the war. The
Turks lost the wars, and ended up losing approximately 85% of their European holdings. With the humiliation of defeat and fear of the impending demise of the Empire the Turks turned even more hostile toward their Christian
subjects, the Armenians. In another unprovoked massacre, the Turks killed
untold thousands of people in the Mediterranean province of Adana. This
massacre, too, went unpunished and virtually unnoticed.

The stage was now fully set for a genocide to erupt. A long, long history of
scorn and hatred for the Armenians had been bred. Attacks against them were
proven to be followed with utter impunity. The years of killings of so many
Armenians from all over the Empire ensured that no critical mass of them
could rally together to resist Turkish domination. Artificial reasons for justifying the slaying of the Armenians had been conceived and disseminated. The
leaders of the CUP and many Turks in general began to convince themselves
that the only way to solve this so-called "Armenian Question" would be to
wipe out the entire social group altogether. The outbreak of World War I in
1914 provided the perfect pretext and cover-up for doing just that.

---

[14] Ibid., 59.
[15] Dadrian, *The History of the Armenian Genocide*, 153 ff.

The actual systematic extermination of the Armenians is usually dated to April 24, 1915. That evening, Turkish police rounded up hundreds of high profile Armenian intellectual and religious leaders, from Constantinople and across the whole of Asia Minor, and ordered them onto trains. They were told that they were being temporarily moved away from their homes. But nearly all of them were killed within the next few days. That started a wave of mass deportations all across the region. Hundreds of thousands of Armenians were driven from their homes, and forced to board railroad cars to unknown destinations.[16] Others, often women and children, were forced to form giant columns and were sent off to the wilderness, heavily guarded, where they were left to die of starvation, disease and thirst. In the desert heat, deportation meant almost certain death. Upon hearing what was happening, the American consul in Harput, Leslie Davis, wrote a letter to American Ambassador to the Ottoman Empire Henry Morgenthau, saying,

> The full meaning of such an order [to deport the Armenians] can scarcely be im agined by those who are not familiar with the peculiar conditions of this isolated region. A massacre, however horrible the word may sound, would be human in comparison with it. In a massacre many escape, but a wholesale deportation of this kind in the country means a longer and perhaps even more dreadful death…I do not believe it possible for one in a hundred to survive, perhaps not one in a thousand.[17]

Other mass deportations involved the killing of Armenians in a far more di-rect way. Crucifixion was a common method of murder, highlighting as it did the supposed impotence of the Armenians' faith to protect them.[18] Armenians who tried to convert to Islam, which had once meant an elevation in social standing and relative safety, did not fare any better.[19] An even more common method of killing involved mounted Turks herding masses of Armenians to the edge of steep ravines and pushing them off to their deaths. Many drowned in these killings. Walking along some such places, Leslie Davis wrote, "In some of the valleys there were only a few bodies. In others, there were more than a thousand."[20] Some had as many as fifteen hundred.[21] Armenians not killed by the heat or by being pushed over the cliffs were stabbed, stoned, or more rarely (due to the expense), shot. These deportations and their attendant

---

[16] Dadrian, *The History of the Armenian Genocide*, 220–225.

[17] Quoted in Balakian, *The Burning Tigris*, 232.

[18] Some of the most jarring accounts of this style of murder recount the lowering of Armenian women and girls onto sharpened spikes stuck in the ground, the spike entering through the vagina and extending up to the neck. Balakian, *The Burning Tigris*, 315.

[19] Mary Mangigian Tarzian, *The Armenian Minority Problem, 1914–1934: A Nation's Struggle for Security* (Atlanta: Scholar's Press, 1992), 39, 51, and 170.

[20] Leslie Davis, *The Slaughterhouse Province: An American Diplomat's Report on the Armenian Genocide, 1915–1917*, ed. Susan K. Blair (New Rochelle, NY: Aristide D. Carartazas Orpheus, 1989), 66.

[21] Balakian, *The Burning Tigris*, 245.

slaughters happened over a period of several years, from 1915 until as late as 1922–23, though the worst episodes were in the years 1915–16.

The accounts of survivors and witnesses are gut-wrenching. Ambassador Morgenthau later wrote of these months, "I do not believe that the darkest ages ever presented scenes more horrible than those which now took place all over Turkey."[22] Krikoris Balakian witnessed the carnage in and around Ankara. The slaughters were committed with "axes, cleavers, shovels and pitchforks". Children were killed by being smashed with rocks in front of their parents. The carnage was so ghastly outside of Ankara that the chief architect of the genocide, Talaat Pasha, ordered that over 40,000 corpses be buried in a huge pit outside of the city. His hopes of hiding the deaths failed, however, as Balakian recalled that "the stench of death and the mounds of bodies overwhelmed the landscape."[23]

The situation was the same all over the Ottoman Empire. Deportations, rapes, pillaging, murder. Violence and fear became the standard currency of the region. How could this possibly come about? What explanation are we to give for how humans could be capable of such palpable evil? We now turn from the history of the genocide itself to two possible interpretations of the experience of its evil.

René Girard and the Scapegoating of Victims

Few philosophers or theologians have written so extensively on the dynamics of violence than has the French philosopher and anthropologist René Girard. The centerpiece of his analysis of violence is what he calls the "scapegoat mechanism". The word scapegoat itself comes from William Tyndale, whose 1531 translation of the Bible into English rendered Leviticus 16's "Azazel" as "scapegoat", meaning the "goat that escapes" or departs.[24] The ancient Hebrew ritual at Yom Kippur, described in Leviticus, saw the high priest symbolically place all the sins of the people onto one goat, which was then released into the wilderness, and the same high priest would sacrifice another goat to God. The idea was that the community would then be purified of its sins and violence by casting them all onto these animals, which were then removed from the community, sins and all. Girard has written extensively about this ancient Jewish practice, identifying it as only one particularly vivid instance of a nearly universal phenomenon. For Girard, the scapegoat mechanism is the origin and sustenance of society, and provides insight into the dark

---

[22] Henry Morgenthau, *Ambassador Morgenthau's Story* (Detroit: Wayne State University Press, 2003), 305.

[23] Krikoris Balakian, *Armenian Golgotha*, 177, quoted in Peter Balakian, *The Burning Tigris*, 245.

[24] Most commentators believe Tyndale got this wrong. Azazel seems to refer to the name of a demon in the wilderness into whose hands the scapegoat was cast.

recesses of human nature. Humans are prone to violence, and when such violence threatens to destroy social relationships, a way of diverting that violence is needed. Girard's scapegoat theory is complex and highly nuanced. However, three salient features are especially helpful for analyzing the Armenian Genocide. The three aspects are *scarcity*, *desire*, and *violence*.

We live in a world where resources are scarce. This is the basic premise of such disparate fields as economics, politics, and evolutionary biology. What goods there are, from food to clothes to money to rights and responsibilities, are fundamentally finite. While there may be enough goods for everybody to have some of them, there is normally not enough for everyone to have all that they desire. We humans have a nearly insatiable appetite for the objects of our desire; we want more of what we already have and we wish to sample that which we do not have. Yet greed and scarcity are utterly at odds. This creates competition and struggle.

Many scholars look to greed and scarcity to explain human violence. Appeals to Darwinian accounts of scarcity, struggle, and survival of the fittest are prominent examples. However, Girard finds arguments from material scarcity insufficient. He points out that we do not just desire scarce goods as such. We also desire other subjects, as in the ancient conception of *eros*, and we also may desire that other subjects may desire us, as Hegel and others have pointed out. But most of all, Girard says, we desire *according* to another. That is, our conception of what is good and what is therefore desirable is largely determined by the desires *of* others. We see what they want, we see what they have, and our desires are conformed to theirs. The conception of the good is communal, not individual, and the shared view of the good is passed along.

Girard therefore links violence to the desire of a scarce communal good. "The principle source of violence between human beings is mimetic rivalry, the rivalry resulting from imitation of a model who becomes a rival or of a rival who becomes a model."[25] The violence will persist and intensify because, as Girard notes, "In imitating my rival's desire I give him the impression that he has good reasons to desire what he desires, to possess what he possesses, and so the intensity of his desire keeps increasing."[26] Violence erupts between the rivals, and this violence must be dealt with. One rival could kill another of course. That dynamic is common enough, as is illustrated amply by Girard's tireless philological work. But since no one is excepted from the risks of mimetic desire, this solution of the problem of mimetic rivalry can only end in the "war of all against all", of which Hobbes saw the awful secret.

Instead of one rival killing the other, which when multiplied across an entire society would lead to utter chaos, the rivals tend to unite with each other

---

[25] René Girard, *I See Satan Fall Like Lightning*, trans. James G. Williams (Maryknoll: Orbis, 2001).

[26] Ibid., 10.

against a common "enemy". "Suddenly the opposition of everyone against everyone else is replaced by the opposition of all against one. Where previously there had been a chaotic ensemble of particular conflicts, there is now the simplicity of a single conflict: the entire community on one side, and the on the other, the victim."[27] A society on the cusp of exploding into violence itself will try to alleviate the impending disaster by focusing its rage on just one component of the society. In Girard's writings the scapegoat mechanism is usually treated at the level of the individual's dynamics of willing, consciousness, and action. He has sometimes resisted translating these (relatively) individualistic dynamics of the scapegoat mechanism into non-individualistic terms. His hesitancy is understandable, as it is far from clear in what sense a group, such as a society or institution, may be said to "will" or "act". It seems at least plausible that a social group could be described according to the same conceptual scheme as is applied to individuals.[28] Yet either way, individually or corporately, the interrelation of desire, scarcity and violence is plain.

How does Girard's theory help us to understand the violent dynamics of the Armenian genocide? Ted Peters identifies three relevant factors of Girard's thought for understanding the large-scale collective violence exemplified in the Armenian genocide.

> The scapegoat mechanism is likely to kick in when (1) we are confronted by a cultural crisis, such as a plague or a war, that obliterates stable social differences; (2) we make symbolic accusation—that is, we identify the cause of the crisis with some representative of moral breakdown; and (3) we select certain *victims* who ostensibly embody this moral breakdown, usually people belonging to a minority and having distinctive marks such as color, sickness, madness, religious affiliation, or class status. The line between good and evil is drawn.[29]

All three of Peters' qualifications seem to apply in the case of Armenia just before 1915. Let us revisit some themes from the account of the genocide given above and read them through a Girardian lens.

As I pointed out, the full-blown genocide took place during a time of great social upheaval in the whole region. World War I, nominally dated to June 28, 1914, was the inescapable result of decades of mounting political tension and nefarious alliance making. The demise of the Ottoman Empire and the rise to power of the Young Turks in 1908–09 was accompanied with a surge in nationalism and the formation of a new "Turkish" identity. People who previ-

---

[27] Girard, *Things Hidden Since the Foundation of the World* (Stanford: Stanford University Press, 1987), 24.

[28] One scholar who has paid careful attention to this problem is John Searle, especially *The Construction of Social Reality* (New York: Free Press, 1995), and "Collective Intentions and Actions", in: Jerry Morgan, Philip R. Cohen, and Martha Pollack (ed.), *Intentions in Communication* (Cambridge, MA: MIT Press), 401–416.

[29] Ted Peters, *Sin: Radical Evil in Soul and Society* (Grand Rapids: Eerdmans, 1994), 184f.

ously had thought of themselves united merely as subjects under the rule of the same Sultan suddenly began to see themselves as part of a cohesive social whole, united in culture, language, and a new government. As Girard points out so poignantly, this kind of unity virtually always comes at the expense of a victimized other. Rome is founded on Romulus' murder of Remus, biblical civilization on Cain's murder of Abel, and so on, cross-culturally and trans-historically.[30] The Turkish historian Taner Akçam uses similar language about the formation of Turkey. In order to create a more homogenous corporate identity, the CUP leaders (especially Mustafa Kemal) authored a kind of "foundation myth", having thereby "created historical amnesia, and in conjunction with this a refusal to acknowledge that the new Turkish state had been built not from a war 'against imperial powers' but by expunging 'the Greek and Armenian minorities'".[31]

But why would the Armenians be a such a likely scapegoat candidate to be sacrificed on the altar of Turkish nationalism? There were certainly other possibilities, such as the Azerbaijanis, Kurds, or even the Greeks. But other facets of the region's history provide clues. In time of war a country can often justify its own violent actions as unsavory but necessary means to the desired end of social stability and peace. Turkey was constantly worried about its neighbor to the east, Russia. Russia was a Christian land, as was the Armenian homeland.[32] The Turks were able to blame the Armenians for their embarrassing military defeats by the Russians. The laying of this blame served to legitimate first the allegedly "retributive" slaughter, and then the genocide.

What is more, there is evidence that the Turks attributed the relatively stable social climate of the years between the two World Wars to the extermination of the Armenians. When there was social upheaval, the remaining Armenians were to blame. For example, after the Central Powers were defeated in World War I (for which the Armenians were partially blamed), Russia maintained authority in a relatively small region of northeast Turkey. They put surviving Armenians into some political positions. After the 1917 Bolshevik revolution, of course, Russia withdrew from the war, and took their support away from the few Armenians they had put into power. Some of these Armenians formed an irregular army of loose cannons bent on avenging the genocide. They attacked several Turkish villages in the area. When Turkey would later deny the

---

[30] For a reading of the Romulus and Remus myth, cf. René Girard, *The Scapegoat*, trans. Yvonne Freccero (Baltimore: Johns Hopkins University Press, 1987), 88–94.

[31] Taner Akçam, "The Genocide of the Armenians and the Silence of the Turks", in idem, *Dialogue across an International Divide: Essays towards a Turkish-Armenian Dialogue* (Toronto: Zoryan Institute of Canada, 2001), quoted in Balakian, *The Burning Tigris*, 370 f.

[32] I won't say that Armenia was a Christian nation, because so few cultural Armenians in 1915 lived in the actual territory now called Armenia. Diaspora had been the reality for many generations, and it was not until the formation of the Armenian Republic of the Soviet Union that a critical mass of Armenians was again centralized in that area.

reality of the genocide, these isolated incidents were marshaled as evidence that it was the Armenians who were the bloodthirsty killers at fault.[33] That so many Armenians were exterminated was named as the cause of social peace after the war, and the fact that not all the Armenians were killed was named as the cause of social unrest when the social atmosphere was stormier.

Girard's articulation of the scapegoat mechanism points out a nearly identical dynamic in ancient Greece. The Athenians often incarcerated and kept in reserve a number of people, often prisoners of war, called *pharmakoi*. When social unrest threatened, in the form of a famine, plague, invasion or the like, the *pharmakoi* would be brought out from prison, led around the city to be insulted, scorned and beaten, and then finally killed. It was thought that this ritual killing could purge the city of its contagion. The resultant social peace was attributed to their extermination, and, paradoxically, resultant social strife was attributed to their presence in the first place.[34] The very word *pharmakon* means, in Greek, both poison and the antidote to poison. So too, for the Young Turks, were the Armenians both the poison of the new Turkish society, and the antidote to the social ills which beset it. The confluence of all of these factors under cover of war at least helps us to understand how such atrocities could be committed.

Paul Ricoeur on the Forgetfulness of History

What about the sin of omission? How is it possible that something as significant as the Armenian Genocide could go basically unremembered in the consciousness of its international observers? That is of course a vast question, one involving so many factors as to be nearly unanswerable. But one philosopher who has thought hard about these kinds of problems is Paul Ricoeur, and he offers some helpful ways of thinking about the relationship between evil and its representation in history.

In a recent massive study, which turned out, incidentally, to be his final major scholarly work, Ricoeur analyzes at a very abstract level how it is that history comes to be written and remembered. To simplify an erudite and subtle work, Ricoeur locates history in the dialectic between memory and forgetting. The English word *memory* has, of course, two distinct senses. In one sense, the word (*memoire*, in French) refers to the ability every person has to call to mind, and thereby to make "present", something which has somehow passed, and therefore was "absent". In the other sense, a memory (*souvenir*) is that thing which is called to mind and made present. This process of memory calling to mind memories is not yet history however. Forgetting must also

---

[33] Cf. on this the preeminent American scholar of the genocide, Richard Hovannisian, *Armenia on the Road to Independence* (Berkeley: University of California Press, 1967), 114 f.

[34] René Girard, *Violence and the Sacred*, trans. Patrick Gregory (Baltimore: Johns Hopkins University Press, 1977), 94 f.

take place. As Ricoeur points out, "Our celebrated duty of memory is pro-
claimed in the form of an exhortation not to forget. But at the same time and
in the same fell swoop, we shun the specter of a memory that would never
forget anything. We even consider it to be monstrous."[35]

History emerges from this dialectical process between the memory of certain pieces of time and the actions taking place in them, and the forgetting of
others.[36] When I tell someone the "history" of my life, I must decide what
events from my past to include, and which to forget. I will be more likely to
remember and narrate extraordinary events, like graduations, deaths of loved
ones, or the day I fell in love, than I am ordinary days when nothing much
happens. Forgetfulness is therefore a prerequisite of narrative. As Ricoeur
says, "If one cannot recall everything, neither can one recount everything.
The idea of an exhaustive narrative is a performatively impossible idea. The
narrative necessarily contains a selective dimension."[37]

However, just as there are two aspects to memory, so too can forgetting be
understood in at least two ways. "Forgetting as effacement" implies the eras-
ure of all traces of memory. This can happen at many levels. In the individual,
one's brain might simply cease to maintain chemically the correct physical
arrangements required for memory to function. Or at the collective level, the
documentary history on which collective memory is based can be wiped out,
leaving no trace. Ricoeur cites King Henry IV's Edict of Nantes (legalizing
Protestantism in the French kingdom) to this effect. Henry wrote,

> Firstly, let the memory of all things that have taken place on both sides from the
> beginning of the month of March 1585 up to our arrival on the throne…remain ex-
> tinguished and dormant as something that has not occurred. It will not be admitted
> or permissible for our state attorneys nor any other persons public or private, at any
> time or for any reason, to make mention of […] them.[38]

This has obvious echoes of Sultan Abdul Hamid's criminalization of any reference to Armenia. It is also consonant with the attempt of the Young Turks' government to destroy evidence of the state-planned extermination of Armenians.
Forgetting through effacement is a frightful thing, for it virtually disallows the
emendation of history, once the historical narrative is told. Fortunately, for survivors, perpetrators, and all those affected by the Armenian genocide, forgetting
through effacement is not the kind of forgetfulness that plagues the omission of
the genocide from the dominant historical accounts of World War I.

---

[35] Paul Ricoeur, *Memory, History, Forgetting*, trans. David Pellauer (Chicago: University of
Chicago Press, 2004), 413.
[36] The limitations of the English word "history" show themselves again. Some German thinkers, such as Rudolf Bultmann, distinguish *Historie*, or objective, sequential history, from *Geschich-
te*, which involves more the subjective experience and sense-making aspects of history. Ricoeur
tries to include both aspects in his term *l'histoire*.
[37] *Memory, History, Forgetting*, 448.
[38] Ibid., 454.

Ricoeur also discusses "forgetting in reserve". Whereas forgetting through effacement involves the near eradication of memories, forgetting in reserve maintains the memory at a latent level. When prompted by some outside source, one who has forgotten in reserve may be able to recollect what had been forgotten. Documentary evidence of an event may exist that demands the reinterpretation of standard accounts of the event. Forgetting in reserve is temporary, whereas forgetting by effacement is virtually permanent.

None of this is strictly academic for Ricoeur, since the telling of a history is not simply the stuff of professional historians. On the contrary, the telling of a life history bears profound existential weight. My own personal identity simply is, in Ricoeur's view, my telling of my story. I *am* the story I tell others. When I tell the story well, I have conveyed who I am. So the process of the selection of what is to be remembered and what forgotten is crucial. It is not only important in the sense of getting the facts right, so to speak, but it also has an irreducibly *moral* dimension. As Ricoeur elsewhere emphasizes, there is no such thing as a morally neutral narrative.[39] The way a story is told always has a moral component.

Ricoeur's searching thoughts on forgetfulness and historical narrative apply to the history of the Armenian genocide in at least two ways. Most obviously, from the perspective of the historians, the decades-long Turkish denial of the genocide simply must be dealt with. Peter Balakian contends, for example, that much United States foreign policy, especially Middle Eastern oil policy, has become deeply interwoven with the contested interpretation of the Armenian genocide.[40] The impending entry of Turkey into the European Union complicates matter further. Some members of the EU are insisting that Turkey's accession to the group be contingent on Turkey acknowledging that the Armenian killings were not a product of "civil unrest" as they have claimed in the past, but rather part of a systematic attempt at state-mandated genocide. Other countries are asking only that Turkey admit that the widespread killings were "tragic", and therefore not the necessary punishment for sedition Turkey claims them to be.[41]

But Ricoeur's insistence that there is a moral imperative for a truthful telling of history, and therefore for truthful remembering and forgetting, is certainly not limited to the placement of blame on Turkey for the atrocities. Correlating the sinful act with its agent does of course imply blame, and Ricoeur

---

[39] Paul Ricoeur, *Oneself as Another*, trans. Kathleen Blamey (Chicago: University of Chicago Press, 1992), 140, and idem, *Time and Narrative*, trans. Kathleen McLaughlin and David Pellauer (Chicago: University of Chicago Press, 1984), 1:59.

[40] Balakian, *The Burning Tigris,* 363–372.

[41] This is the position of France, at least. Foreign Minister Michel Barnier said of the connection between EU entry and genocide recognition, "I think Turkey as a large country has a duty to remember". At least seven EU countries have already officially termed the killings a genocide, including Cyprus, Greece, Belgium, Sweden, Italy, Poland and France.

does think that the placement of blame is a condition for the possibility of genuine forgiveness.[42] Whether forgiveness or reconciliation is desirable, or even possible, is a separate matter. But more than that, as the Armenian theologian Vigen Guroian has asserted, the Armenian survivors and their descendants need to remember *well* the atrocities of the genocide in order to come to grips with their haunting past. Unable to deal with the realities imposed by the 1915 genocide, especially the resultant diaspora, Armenians have struggled to find a way to tell the history of the genocide in a way that might allow them to transcend it and cope with it. For example, Guroian argues that many Armenian Christians have looked to their history as the oldest Christian nation as a source of hope for their glorious future.

> Armenians persist in looking to this history as proof and encouragement that they as a people and church can overcome the devastation to the national and religious life wrought by the genocide and great dispersion of this century. Nevertheless, there also has been self-delusion in this sort of thinking that has prevented the Armenian Church from meeting the formidable challenges to its religious life posed by the new American host culture and society. Such thinking, in its self-delusion, has been symptomatic of the Armenian Church's refusal to come to terms with what actually happened in 1915.[43]

Here too we see an illustration of Ricoeur's chief insight: there is a moral and existential dimension to every narration of a story or history, and therefore to every remembering and forgetting. Guroian demonstrates that when Armenian survivors tell the story of the genocide as some kind of a test to their faith, or yet another chapter in the great unfolding plan of God for Armenian Christian nationhood, they blind themselves to the very real problems confronting them. They have not remembered well, he argues.[44] The selective forgetting and remembering of various aspects of the genocide ends up being an added dimension to the experience of its evil.[45]

---

[42] Cf. especially Ricoeur, *Memory History, Forgetting*, 457–506 for a beautiful meditation on the relationship of forgiveness to his three themes. Miroslav Volf makes similar points about the Croatian-Serbian "ethnic cleansing" situation in his *Exclusion and Embrace: A Theological Exploration of Identity, Otherness, and Reconciliation* (Nashville: Abingdon, 1996), esp. 119–125.

[43] Vigen Guroian, *Incarnate Love: Essays in Orthodox Ethics* (Notre Dame: University of Notre Dame Press, 2002), 191.

[44] Cf. also his essay "Church and Armenian Nationhood: A Bonhofferian Reflection on the National Church", in idem, *Ethics after Christendom: Toward an Ecclesial Christian Ethic* (Grand Rapids: Eerdmans, 1994), 102–129. The position he is criticizing seems like an analog to the position taken by Emil Fackenheim on the Holocaust; though the genocide is far from justifiable, the creation of a Jewish state was an imperative stemming from the reality of the Holocaust. Emil Fackenheim, *The Jewish Return into History: Reflections in the Age of Auschwitz and a New Jerusalem* (New York: Schocken Books, 1978).

[45] For further reflections on the shape of theodicy stemming from the experience of the genocide, cf. Vigen Guroian, "Armenian Genocide and Christian Existence", Cross Currents, 41, 1991, 322–343.

Concluding Remarks

Speaking about God in the face of, or even in the context of, such radical evil as a genocide is risky business. Giving "explanations" for how radical evil comes about can create more problems than it solves. First, many such theodicies are often rhetorically numb to the genuine cries of suffering from survivors. People who live through terrible tragedy should not have to hear that God has used their suffering for some other end, no matter how good that end is. God does not instrumentalize evil; God defeats it. Secondly, much philosophical reflection on the problem of evil ends up using conceptions of God drawn more from generic theism than from the biblical God who freely takes on a life of suffering. Approaches from philosophical theism end up being basically ir-relevant, even when relatively "successful", since they defend the existence of a God other than the triune God in whom most Christians believe.

Still, one has to say *something* about evil; silence in the wake of history's horrors, especially the Armenian genocide, is simply not an option. Girard's insights into human nature, focusing on desire, scarcity, and mimetic rival-ry, at least help us to understand the context out of which evil can emerge. And while I myself do not agree with the near neo-Gnosticism Girard can sometimes espouse as the remedy to evil,[46] I also cannot imagine seeing the Armenian genocide in terms fully divorced from the cycles of violence and scapegoating he exposes. Paul Ricoeur's insights into the nature of forgetting and forgiveness suggest a further strategy for dealing with the effects of evil, i. e., the moral imperative of their faithful remembrance, even as he shies away from "explaining" their origin.[47] I have tried to make use of the theological distinction between the sins of commission and the sins of omission to make this point; while evil is always finally inscrutable in its origin and nature, our experience of evil relentlessly prods us toward telling the story of what we have undergone. These dual aspects of the Armenian genocide, the tragic fact of its occurrence and the tragic story of its faulty recollection in history, de-mand ever deeper investigation and ever more faithful remembrance.

---

[46] "Once the basic mechanism is revealed, the scapegoat mechanism, that expulsion of violence by violence is rendered useless by the revelation. It is no longer of interest. The interest of the Gos-pels lies in the future offered mankind by this revelation [...] The good news is that scapegoats can no longer save men [...] The Kingdom of God is at hand." *The Scapegoat*, 189. Most Christians would say, *contra* Gnosticism, that revelation as such does not save; God does.

[47] The classic statement on the impossibility of explaining evil non-discursively is of course Ricoeur's own *The Symbolism of Evil*, trans. Emerson Buchanan (Boston: Beacon, 1967).

Violence, Scapegoating and the Cross

René Girard

During the first half of the last century, religious anthropology was very much alive and its method was essentially comparative. Many anthropologists were trying to show that the Christian story, in its main outline, is too similar to many myths of "death and resurrection" not to be one of them. Ever since Celsus, in the 2nd century after Christ, the opponents of Christianity have tried to show that, far from being unique, as it dogmatically claims, Christianity is merely one more mythical cult, similar to all archaic cults.

In the second half of the last century, the massive nihilism fostered by structuralism and deconstruction discouraged this effort. Comparative religion lost its appeal. The first and main reason for this skepticism was the researchers' inability to find the invariant without which no "science" of religion can be elaborated. In my opinion, the invariant really exists and it is not really difficult to discover. It is violence. But violence has long remained unmentionable. It was the object of a taboo which has long remained all powerful.

In the discussion of religion, the discretion on the subject of violence goes back to religion itself. It is this principle that led Plato to condemn Homer and other poets. What the philosopher found objectionable in their writings was the display of religious violence. The proclamation of the essential goodness and natural innocence of humanity by the Enlightenment was a powerful rejuvenation and reinforcement of the ancient taboo, which insured the failure of comparative religion.

Archaic religions represent mostly violence. Like the biblical creation story, they always begin with something that looks like "original chaos" and it is really a violent unraveling of the cultural order. This mysterious disaster is sometimes defined as an internal conflict, sometimes as a plague, or as a natural catastrophe, or even as a monster that demands more and more sacrificial victims. Whatever its definition, this crisis becomes so destructive that total annihilation threatens.

Fortunately for the community, as soon as this paroxysm is reached, the causes of the trouble are discovered and they are the nefarious activities of a single individual. Without further ado, the people kill or at least violently expel the presumed culprit; frequently, this violence takes the form of lynching. And lynching turns out to be the one effective medicine. Peace returns and the crisis is ended.

Archaic myths report the founding of their peaceful social orders by re-membering the lynched scapegoats from the perspective of the persecutors. What distinguishes the Bible with its Gospel accounts of the crucifixion is that the innocent victim is remembered. The cross reveals to us the self-delusion of myths of violence. The significance of the story of Jesus is that it moves us from self-delusion to the truth about who we are as human beings.

From Mimetic Rivalry to Violence

It is safe to assert, contrary to what Rousseau believed, that human beings have never lived in isolation from each other. But it is also true that they always had and still have a lot of trouble living harmoniously together.

The same malfunction affects human communities everywhere and it is their propensity to internal conflict. These conflicts are essentially rivalries between individuals who fight over the same object. The rivalry is mimetic rivalry, in other words a rivalry that results from an imitation that focuses not on mannerisms or customs but on something more fundamental, appetites, and appetites, with the help of this imitation, turn into what we call desire.

If people desire mimetically, we can well understand why neighbors always tend to desire the same objects and to clash with their models whom they transform into rivals. This type of conflict is so intense that, if allowed to grow unimpeded, it would destroy all human communities.

Mimetic rivalry already occurs in animals, especially when they first en-counter one another but the resulting combats quickly end with the surrender of the weaker animal to his stronger partner. This is how the stable dominance relations we call animal societies are established. Among human beings, be-cause the rivalries are more intense, dominance patterns become impossible and that is the reason, I believe, why human societies are built not on them but on this mysterious entity we call religion.

When mimetic rivalries begin, they tend to spread from imitators to models and then the models become the imitators of their initial imitators, while these imitators themselves become the models of their own models. All differences and distinctions unravel during this process, while rivalries keep intensifying.

Even death does not always end human rivalries since human beings re-sort to this terrifying custom that no animal species has ever invented which is called vengeance. Thanks to vengeance, violence transcends all individual limitations of time and space and becomes even more destructive.

In small archaic communities, mimetic rivalry and vengeance must have spread like wildfire and caused the generalized crises which we find at the be-ginning of myths and other foundational texts. When mimetic rivalry prolif-erates, it becomes so fierce that the desired objects ultimately are dropped or forgotten. This is "the war of all against all" greatly feared by Hobbes. Total destruction looms but a spontaneous change in the modality of the mimetic contagion can still prevent the ultimate catastrophe. Some conflicts are so intense that they absorb the mimetically less intense and, as a result, less "attractive" conflicts. A snowballing process now occurs that gradually eliminates all conflicts until only one final and terribly lopsided opposition remains, with only one single individual on one side, and everybody else on the other side.

This is the situation which the unanimous lynching of a single victim will immediately resolve and the community will thus be reconciled, at least for a brief moment. This evolution of the crisis explains the frequency of lynchings and collective violence in foundational myths. The mimetic nature of human relations is the cause not merely of the mimetic crises but of their spontaneous resolution through a single unanimous murder that reconciles everybody against one last victim.

When the violence that has long plagued a community suddenly ends in this way, the beneficiaries are so relieved and grateful that they see a divine savior in their victim whom they still regard, however, as the malefactor of the previous phase. This is why the archaic sacred is regarded as both good and bad, essentially unpredictable.

Violence, Myth, and Religion

When mimetic rivalries show up in a human community and they always do, the crisis portrayed in myths occurs and only the mimetic snowballing against one final victim can bring about a resolution. This is what determines the fundamentally religious nature of human society.

The final murder brings back the peace but not for very long. Mimetic rivalries ultimately reappear. What can be done to prevent the return of the painful crisis? This is a problem that all human communities have to face and they all solve it in more or less the same way. They re-enact the unanimous violence with substitute victims in the hope that the same cause will produce the same effect. In replacement of the original victim, they deliberately immolate sacrificial victims.

The sacrificers are so eager to succeed that, frequently, they reenact in their rituals even the mimetic crisis itself, which may be indispensable to the triggering of the victimage mechanism. This is why many sacrificial rites begin with a "mock crisis" which is a realistic copy of the real one.

Ritual must be the first specifically human technique, the origin of human culture. It is regarded as a precious gift of the god that first used it to solve the original crisis. And it is true, indeed that sacrifice is precious since, at the cost of only one single victim, it can prevent the mutual destruction of many members of the community. The power of sacrifice seems divine. All human communities do their best to turn it into a readily available instrument of peace and, ultimately, they regard it as some kind of panacea. With time, it looses all its effectiveness. One of the many paradoxes of this institution is that it fights fire with fire; it resorts to unanimous violence in order to strengthen the peace.

Lynching is highly characteristic of mythology. It can be traced behind countless distortions, disguises, mutilations, and transformations behind which it tries to hide. It also happens that lynching displays itself blatantly, insolently in other traditions such as the great dionysiac cycle of Greece which is literally nothing else but a vast collections of lynchings, reenacted by ritual sacrifices in all their gruesome details. The famous diasparagmos requires all participants to dismember small animals with their own hands, and then eat them raw.

In order to appreciate the importance of lynching in mythology, one must include among its many variations the myths, in Greece and all over the world, that substitute animals for the human lynchers. Wherever an animal species exists that happens to be gregarious and aggressive enough to play the role convincingly, they become the lynchers and this substitution must be interpreted, I believe, in conjunction with the substitution of animals for human beings as sacrificial victims. The role played by buffaloes among the Blackfoot Indians has its counterpart in Australia with kangaroos and other marsupials. These similarities cannot be fortuitous.

Freud on Founding Violence

Anthropological research depends on recurrent features and animal lynching is one of the most striking. The one powerful insight of *Totem and Taboo* is the one about the role of lynching in archaic religion. It is based on sound observations, I believe. It has remained sterile, however, because Sigmund Freud's specifically psychoanalytical obsessions prevented him from building a credible thesis around this genuine discovery.

If the real purpose and function of myth and ritual were, as Freud claims, the commemoration of one unique lynching situated in the distant past, some representation of it or allusion to it should figure in all myths and rituals. Lynching, however, is not universal, far from it. Many myths and rituals contain only individual violence or even no violence at all.

Freud was right nevertheless to regard lynching as highly significant. It figures in too many myths to be merely fortuitous. Each myth recounts the violent reconciliation of some real community who finally polarized unanimously against a single victim. The all-against-one pattern may or may not show up as actual lynching but unanimity against the victim is essential to the real reconciliation of the community, which is the ultimate reality behind archaic religion.

Rivalry Between Twins

Many features of mythical texts confirm the mimetic hypothesis. One of them is the curious religious role played by twins in many cultures in all parts of the

world. Biological twins are perceived as a visible manifestation of the conflictual uniformity produced by mimetic rivalries. As these rivalries keep spreading
and worsening, cultural differences erode and the rivals resemble each other
more and more. They seem to turn into enemy twins. In many communities,
the birth of twins is as feared as a deadly virus today. It seems to introduce into
the community a contagious germ of violent undifferentiation.

The crisis at the beginning of myths is often regard as due to the harmful
presence of twins. This is why a sizable number of myths have twins as their
protagonists instead of individual heroes, Eteocles and Polyneices in Greek
tragedy, Romulus and Remus in Rome, Jacob and Esau in the Bible, etc. The
mirror-like opposition of twins is a rivalry for some object they both desire
with the same intensity, the same throne, the same bride, the same inheritance.
In archaic thought, violent conflict is interpreted as a consequence not of what
we ourselves fear, too much difference but of the opposite, too much identity.

In twin dominated myths, one of the two, as a rule, kills the other and the
survivor becomes the king or even the god. One single murder proves as effective as the unanimous violence of other myths and it restores differences.
After killing Remus, the victorious Romulus is no longer a twin but the sacred king around whom the society structures itself.

The archaic cultures obsessed with biological twins are the ones which
confuse their physical resemblance with the undifferentiation generated by
reciprocal violence. The two phenomena are objectively independent. Biological twins are often prone to violence but so are ordinary brothers.

Incest, Parricide, and Witchcraft

In the light of the mimetic theory, the features of mythology that seem most
incongruous, such as the accusations of parricide and incest against Oedipus,
become intelligible. These accusations express the hostility of the whole community toward its single victim, as a result of a mimetic contagion that has
polarized against one individual who is essentially accused of destroying all
differences.

The victimization of Oedipus has less to do with his supposed crimes than
with his throne, with his foreignness and also with his limping. Many mythical heroes and gods are afflicted with physical infirmities which reflect, I believe, the tendencies of furious mobs to polarize, like animal predators, against
infirm and physically handicapped individuals.

Far from being an exceptional insight that would make the Oedipus myth a
uniquely inspired document, as Freud believed, the parricide and incest of the
hero, just like the bestialities of Zeus, are typical accusations that reappear in
countless myths all over the world.

The fact that, however unbelievable they are, these accusations are believed,
provides the careful observer with an important clue for the understanding of

mythology. The authors of the myth sincerely believe that the only way to cure the plague is to expel Oedipus. The authors of the myth are one with the community turned into a mimetic mob and that is why the mythical accusation is the one aspect of mythology that is almost always fantastic and unbelievable. This unreality does not entitle us to conclude that the collective violence is fictional as well.

In the 15th century, the madness of the accusations against supposed witches does not mean that the accused were not real human beings and that the persecution was not real. Just the opposite. Myths, like witchcraft stories, are rooted in episodes of collective violence which are inevitably distorted and slanted against the victims. Real persecution is distorted and fictionalized only in part, because it reflects the deluded perspective of real persecutors.

The difference in the case of myths is that the persecutors believe in their mad stories even more strongly than the medieval witch hunters and the final result is more transfigured than even the most deluded medieval nightmares, less easy to decipher therefore. The myth makers are not satisfied with turning their victims into bad witches, they finally turn them into something like archaic divinities.

The degree of transfiguration is higher and mythology plays in the structuring of social life a role that medieval persecutions can no longer play. As a result, the deciphering of medieval texts has become commonplace, whereas my interpretation of myth will still remain controversial for a while. A careful comparison reveals that witchcraft stories and archaic myths are two different stages of the same fundamental process of mimetic transfiguration.

Scapegoating in the Bible

The mimetic process that generates mythology is also visible in some well known biblical dramas, beginning with the Joseph story. Joseph is the innocent scapegoat of his twelve brothers and his being sold into slavery is a violent expulsion. In the execration psalms, the narrator often describes himself as a lonely individual surrounded by a crowd that seems to get ready for some collective violence against him.

Job finds himself in a very similar situation during the most original and longest part of the biblical book that bears his name, his strange "conversation" with his three "friends". What we learn from Job himself is that after many years during which he was the first citizen and unchallenged leader of his community, all of a sudden, the people, like one single man, turned against him. The language of the "friends" makes it clear they that represent the community turned into a mob and they agree with that mob. Job is on trial for his life. If condemned, everything he owns will be burned and he, himself, will be lynched.

Even though neither in this book nor in the Psalms does the violence ever becomes theriomorphic, in both Job and the execration psalms the threaten-

ing mob is often compared to packs of dogs, or to herds of bulls, or to boars –
to animals, in other words, that, in mythical texts, might substitute for human
lynchers.

The most spectacular lynching in the Jewish Bible is the murder of the Suffering Servant in Isaiah 52–53. When Jesus announces that he will die "like the
prophets" before him, he means that he, too, will die as a result of collective
violence. The crucifixion is a legal execution but it results from the mob's
victorious pressure on Pilate and it is a kind of lynching as well. Several times,
hostile crowds have already tried to stone Jesus and, if Pilate had refused to
give in, the crucifixion crowd might have stoned Jesus to death.

In addition to the crucifixion, the two gospels of Mark and Matthew contain one more quasi-lynching, the murder of John the Baptist which resembles
the murder of Jesus in a very real sense. The chief murderer, Herod, orders
the beheading of John only because, like Pilate, he does not dare resist the
unanimous demand of a blood-thirsty crowd. John is defined as "the last of
the prophets". His quasi-lynching is a significant link between the many Old
Testament lynchings and the quasi-lynching of Jesus.

Is the Bible Unique?

When the first anti-Christian writers appeared, they interpreted the similarities between myths and Gospels as an argument against the uniqueness of
Christianity. In the 19th century, this same interpretation reappeared, powerfully strengthened by the discovery of many archaic myths characterized by
the tripartite structure I am talking about: 1) a community-wide crisis, 2) the
lynching or quasi-lynching of a single victim, 3) the return of peace and order
under the aegis of this victim.

The fact that the central dramas of many myths, many Old Testament stories, and finally the Crucifixion have the same basic structure has always convinced most anthropologists that the biblical religions cannot be significantly
different from archaic religions.

To the Christians the fact that the Gospels have the same basic structure as
most myths constitutes a challenge which, unfortunately, is always eluded. In
the last two centuries, however, the rarefying of the Christian faith certainly
owes something to the widespread awareness of the structural similarities between myths and Christianity.

In the Catholic Church, the first open rebellion against the dogma of
Christian uniqueness was the "modernist movement" in the early nineteen-
hundreds. It never fully subsided and, after Vatican II, it became dominant
in most churches. The "triumphalism" which the progressive clerics always
advise the faithful to renounce is really a coded reference to the traditional
belief in Christianity's uniqueness, which the Christians are discreetly advised
to forget.

Most educated Westerners take for granted that the dogma of Christian uniqueness is the fruit of "Western ethnocentrism". Even sincere Christians nowadays are convinced that the scientific evidence in favor of the mythical nature of Christianity is overwhelming.

For more than twenty years, now, I have been trying to show that the opposite is demonstrably true. It is true that, between myths on the one hand and the Bible and Gospels on the other hand, the similarities are striking, but they do not prove what everybody thinks they must prove. They prove the very opposite.

Most people think that when I speak as I just did, I must twist the textual evidence in favor of Christianity. They are absolutely certain that an unbiased confrontation of mythology and Christianity must turn to the advantage of the former.

I shall now summarize once again the argument I have made many times in favor of the uniqueness of the gospels and the whole biblical tradition. It contains absolutely nothing that could be regarded as slanted in favor of the Christian and Judaic Scriptures. As a matter of fact, it has nothing to do with religion or religiosity properly speaking. It is purely commonsensical. The readers will be the judge.

The Story of Jesus and its Significance

In the case of the Gospels, the equivalent of the mythical crisis is the crisis of the small Jewish state that will be utterly destroyed by the Romans only a few years later. The historical reality of this crisis is unquestionable of course.

Like all myths, the Gospels culminate in the drama of a single victim, Jesus, who is condemned not only by all the authorities, Jewish as well as Roman but by the Jerusalem crowd which had been favorable to him until then. Jesus is the unanimous victim of his entire community. In the Gospel of John, a famous observation of Caiphas, a former High priest, makes the link quite explicit between the historical crisis and the single drama: "It is better that one man die and that the whole people do not perish." Jesus became the scapegoat.

Scapegoating originally designates the victim of the ritual in Leviticus 16. There is a modern sense of the word which has nothing to do with the Hebrew ritual, at least directly. It signifies the collective persecution of individuals whose selection is partly or wholly unjustified, arbitrary. The mimetically unified crowd is unaware that its scapegoat is innocent of the crises of which it is accused.

Jesus is a scapegoat in the modern sense of the word. The New Testament itself says so in its own vocabulary which is more appealing and respectful than the word scapegoat. The expression is the lamb of God.

The problem with modern Christians is that, just like their opponents, they assume that, in order to differ significantly from myths, the Gospels should talk about something different, something unique. It should have a different story line.

This makes no sense whatever. A change in thematic content would imprison us in the indifferent type of difference so beloved by the nihilistic deconstructors. It would have no more significance than the difference between the two different plot lines of two works of fiction.

We need something more essential than this indifferent difference. The Bible and Gospels are significantly different because they talk about the same type of victims as myths, but they treat these victims most differently.

Jesus' death becomes inevitable when the Jerusalem crowds which, until then, had been favorable to him, suddenly and inexplicably turn hostile. As in the case of Job's villagers, this about-face is purely mimetic. The hostile contagion against the formerly beloved holy man is so sudden and powerful that it influences Peter himself. The apostle's denial of Jesus spectacularly illustrates the dreadful power of the mimetic contagion over any individual suddenly plunged into a crowd mimetically polarized already against its single victim, in this case Jesus who has just been arrested.

Even Peter, the strongest disciple, succumbs to the mimetic contagion. He is the most significant example of this very human weakness that mimetic contagion always is. Even the one disciple most faithful to Jesus briefly surrenders to it. If Peter cannot withstand the pressure, who will? And indeed no one does; no one stands on Jesus' side during the crucifixion, except for the "holy women" who are not influential enough from a societal standpoint to affect the course of events.

During the crucifixion itself, the mimetic contagion is very much in evidence. Not Peter alone but everybody surrenders to it. Everybody vociferates against Jesus, even the two thieves crucified with him, (only one in Luke). This example is tragically caricatural, but in the case of Pilate, who is situated at the top rather than the bottom of the social scale, things are very much the same. Because he fears a riot, the Roman procurator is swayed by the mob. That is why he orders the crucifixion. Most politicians in the end follow the crowds that they pretend to lead.

Everything in the crucifixion seems calculated to reinforce the old anti-Christian conclusion that the Gospels are the same thing as a myth. It is obviously the same process, the same contagion that leads to the same unanimous lynching or quasi-lynching that generates mythology.

Are the gospels another myth, therefore? The answer is a resounding no. When we shift from the mythical to the biblical, we discover one great difference in the representation of the victim. Even though in myths the victims normally end up as saviors and as gods, they are perceived as authentic criminals to begin with, guilty of parricide and incest or of similar crimes, and all this still characterizes the archaic divinities generated by mythology.

In myths such accusations always seem justified. In the Bible and Gospels, the equivalent accusations are mentioned as an illusion of the lynchers which must not be believed. The few disciples who are behind the writing of the Gospels know that Jesus is innocent and the Gospels forcefully affirm this innocence against the slanderous mob. It is simply not true that Jesus is a blasphemer; it is not true that Jesus has violated the Law. The Gospels understand that Jesus is falsely accused by a crowd that "does not know what it is doing".

The Gospels and many biblical dramas deny the guilt of victims that in myths would seem warrented, because mobs always regard their victims as guilty and myths are the voice of lynching mobs. The victims are represented just as the lynchers see them. They are ultimately regarded as divinities but, first and foremost, they are viewed as authentic criminals.

Interpreting the Myth

Something, of course, remains constant in all the texts we have been talking about, in myths first and then in the biblical texts and in the Gospels. The event represented is always the same type of event, the arbitrary polarization of an entire community against a single victim, the mimetic contagion that leads to lynching. The difference, as Nietzsche observed, lies in the interpretation. In mythology, however, the victims of this violence are represented as guilty not because they are but because the perspective is that of the deluded crowd. Myths reflect uncritically the mimetic delusion that leads to lynching. That is why they always show us only one perspective upon the violence, the perspective that justifies it which is regarded as true. This perspective is that of the lynchers themselves who believe they are acting justly whereas in reality, they are deluded, but they never find out.

In the Gospels, we are told repeatedly Jesus has not committed the crimes of which he is accused. The crowd believes these accusations and even the disciples, as we found out, are swayed at first by the mimetic contagion against Jesus. But their final perspective, which is the perspective of the Gospels as a whole, is that Jesus is innocent.

The non-mythical truth finally triumphs only because God himself sends his Spirit himself to enlighten the disciples and enable them to resist all forthcoming persecutions. The Spirit of Truth is also called the *Paraclete,* a Greek work with a highly significant meaning. It simply means the lawyer for the defense, the defender of unjustly accused victims.

In addition to the crucifixion scene, there are many statements in the Gospels that confirm the nature of the entire process and its radical break with mythical illusions. Jesus is playing the same role as the mythical heroes who were ultimately turned into gods as a result of being violently expelled from their communities. But the process here is based not on a false accusation but on the true assertion of the innocence of Jesus. One sentence that Jesus, himself, extracts from a psalm amounts to a quasi explicit definition of what is happening: "The stone that the builders rejected has become the keystone." Many statements represent Jesus as the rejected one, an unjustly sacrificed victim, "the lamb of God". And the definitions of the Word in the prologue of John represent him as an unjustly excluded: "He was in the world and the world was made through him, yet the world knew him not. He came to his own home, and his own people received him not" (John 1:10).

Even if the pertinence of these statements impresses us, we may fail to realize why they make the gospel so different from a myth. The Gospels are not merely a more detailed and explicit version of what myths also describe. It is a mistake to believe that because myths and biblical texts talk about the same violence and the same type of victims, they are equivalent. The event which is recounted is the same, I repeat; it is a unanimous ganging up against the victim. But instead of going along with the mythical version of the event, instead of merely repeating the lies of the persecutors, the Gospels proclaim the innocence of Jesus. And no other religion does this except some biblical texts. The Gospels truly reveal a truth that has remained hidden, "since the foundation of the world".

From Distortion to Truth

In all the dramas we have discussed, biblical as well as mythical, the victims may be called scapegoats in the modern sense of victims universally condemned as guilty even though they are innocent.

In order to understand mythology, we had to do some guessing and the most hazardous guess consisted in interpreting the crimes, mistakes, or faults attributed to the victim as spurious accusations, as a false indictment, really, due to the frustrated crowd's appetite for violence. The mimetic theory asserts that the often fantastic guilt attributed to the victim, the parricide and incest of Oedipus for instance, are nonsensical accusations invented by the crowd in order to satisfy its appetite for violence.

The myths do not acknowledge this truth and that is why, in order to decrypt them, we have to guess that they are distorted by the perspective of the persecutors. But the Gospels are not distorted and they lead us directly to the truth. They confirm the validity of our guessing but they put an end to it. They introduce into the world a truth that had never been there before. Even a victim who is universally accused by a community may be innocent. This discovery the only true deconstruction or demystification of mythology.

The difference between the mythical and biblical inspiration is made obvious in the Gospels by to the dual perspective we have on the same event, the crucifixion of Jesus. The first perspective is that of the crowd, of the vast majority of witnesses who call loudly for the crucifixion because like all myth-makers, they believe in the guilt of the victim. This mythical perspective which meets with the quasi-universal approval of the crowd, even though it is false, is a product of the mimetic contagion and nothing more.

Myths fail to understand the victimage mechanism and they merely reflect its operation which they do not disturb. In order to operate efficiently and reconcile the community, the victimage mechanism must be misunderstood. Archaic cults never reveal the mimetic cycle of order and disorder which they reactivate and they powerfully reinforce through the simultaneous demonization and divinization of the victim and through the ritual reenactment of the lynching which is called sacrifice.

The biblical inspiration reveals the victimage mechanism and, even if it takes a very long time for this revelation to become conscious of itself, even if this revelation long remained and still remains as if unrevealed, it has not been without effect on the actual life of Christian communities. In our world, the operation of the victimage mechanism has become progressively more visible, controversial and precarious.

As a result of becoming slowly more visible this mechanism is being progressively weakened and we live a world infinitely more free and more knowledgeable than the archaic world. But more exposed as well to dangers no previous world had ever had to face, dangers that result from the end of all sacrificial protection, from unleashed human violence.

In our world, many prophecies formulated in the Gospels are becoming true, even the ones that sound most unbelievable to the unbelievers, the one for instance, according to which "the blood shed since the foundation of the world,…shall be required of this generation" (Luke 11:52).

This is the one decisive textual difference between the Gospels and mythology. Whereas Jesus is innocent, and so is the Suffering Servant in Isaiah, and many other biblical heroes, mythical heroes are, first and foremost bona fide culprit. Oedipus is supposed to have really killed his father and married his mother. Oedipus is portrayed as a justly punished criminal.

What Difference Does This Make?

What characterizes mythology in general is that the single victim is guilty. In the biblical tradition only, and above all in the Gospels, this same victim is innocent.

What can that difference really mean in the context of the mimetic process I have outlined? In myths, the persecuting community is unanimously convinced that its victim is guilty and myths reflect this conviction which, of course, is false.

According to our previous analysis, the mimetic contagion triumphs so completely in myths that it is unanimous and this can be verified in the fact that the victims are always guilty. Oedipus for instance is represented as unquestionably guilty. But, even though the possibility of a judicial error is never envisaged, this unshakeable conviction is really the product of mimetic contagion.

Instead of being deceived by the mimetic mechanism of the single victim, the biblical authors and the authors of the Gospels see through the self-deception of the crowd and denounce it as the collective self-deception that it is. They understand that the common people, the Jerusalem authorities, Herod and Pilate (in other words, everybody) have joined the mob against Jesus. Yet the Gospel authors refuse to follow and they reveal the truth which a myth would hide.

We are used to regarding Jesus as so visibly innocent and truthful and so full of good will that his innocence should strike everybody as obvious. Therefore we feel certain that, had we been there at the time, we would have been on his side. This is an illusion. We resemble these Pharisees whom Jesus mocks because they build tombs to the prophets who were killed by their ancestors, and they say: If we had lived in our fathers' days, we would not have joined them to kill the prophets.

What Jesus is describing in this sentence is not some weakness characteristic of the Pharisees exclusively but something universally human, our tendency always to join the current mob, the current fashion, and therefore not to realize we would have done the same thing in the past with different mobs and different victims.

Jesus is an exception in a world where human beings are very different from him. But, in the context of myths, in other words in the context of the victimage mechanism, there is another aspect to the proclamation of Jesus' innocence by the disciples.

It is a reversal of what happens in myths. It is a momentous departure from mythology since instead of representing the viewpoint of the crowd which is just as convinced of Jesus' guilt as the Theban crowd in the Oedipus myth, the Gospels represent the innocence of the victim falsely convicted by the crowd. The Gospels, therefore, reveal what no myth ever has ever revealed, the whole process of mimetic contagion through which the crowd has deceived itself and spuriously convinced Jesus to death. In other words, instead of being victorious in the Gospels, the process that generates mythology, is represented as the process of collective self-deception that it really is, the process that I have just defined, the process which myths cannot represent because they embody its successful fulfillment and therefore are so engrossed in it that they cannot see themselves as self-deceived. The nature of self-deception is precisely that you cannot uncover it as self-deception and you represent it as truth. The four accounts of the Passion are the only texts that reveal the genesis of mythology such as it really happens and that is why they are not mythical.

Mythology is a process of collective self-delusion which is so unanimous that, when it tries to give an account of itself, it cannot reveal the self-delusion which it is and we can well understand why: each individual witness is individually deluded, is a part of the total self-delusion. The unanimity is such that no one is left in the community, who could report the truth. In the case of the Gospels, what we have is that same process of collective self-delusion but, this time, it is reported as the self-delusion that it really is.

Against Celsus

In his polemic against Christianity, the pagan Celsus resorts to the following argument: the pattern of many pagan cults and the pattern of the Christian story are too much the same not to discredit Christianity's claim of being unique.

This is the conclusion to which my own analysis seems to lead: the pattern of many archaic cults and the pattern of Jesus' crucifixion are strikingly similar. In a world much better acquainted with archaic religions than Celsus was, these similarities seems more relevant than ever and this relevance certainly plays a role in the ever widening religious skepticism of our time.

Our world has no appetite for Christian literature but, even though it loves to call itself post-Christian, it still hungers for anti-Christian literature. Celsus is more widely read today than Origen's *Contra Celsum*, the source of our knowledge about him. The Christian apologist quotes Celsus so abundantly that, a few years ago, an enterprising editor published a book under the name of Celsus, simply by assembling all these quotes together into a little book that completely disregards Origen, even though the entire material in it comes from the Christian apologist. Thanks to this publication, contemporary readers can enjoy their Celsus undiluted by Christian counter-arguments. Origen is completely ignored and forgotten.

At this very moment, more people are inclined to agree with Celsus, obviously, than at any previous time in Christian history. Even many Christians today are beginning to assimilate the lessons of "comparative religion" and they suspect that Christianity must be a death and resurrection myth quite similar to all others in the archaic world.

Was Celsus right after all? Is it not true that the similarities between the mythical and the biblical are too perfect not to discredit irremediably all possible belief in the uniqueness of Christianity? My answer is a resounding: no. Christianity seems equivalent to the mythical "cults of death and resurrection" only because we remain blind to the obvious, to a difference so enormous that it becomes invisible: the difference between the mythical and the biblical, separated by an unbridgeable gulf.

Unlike mythology, the Bible with its Gospels demystifies scapegoating. Unlike mythology, the biblical tradition as a whole truly deserves to be regarded as uniquely true. The biblical tradition is the first and only real challenge to the systematic lie that the archaic world mistakes for the truth.

This is so important and so universally misunderstood that I will reformulate it: all archaic religions are founded upon blind scapegoating and they uncritically agree with the violent mobs. They are totally dependent upon their foundational illusion from which they derive all their themes, the false unanimity of scapegoating.

Only the Bible and Christianity try to discredit mythical scapegoating and make it intelligible by proclaiming the innocence of its victims. For the first time in human history, scapegoating is universally acknowledged as the collective self-delusion that it could not be in archaic cultures.

"Were you there when the crucified my Lord?" asks the familiar Lenten hymn. The answer should be "yes". And we will be there again and again.

Cross, Evolution, and Theodicy

Telling It Like It Is

George Murphy

> *"A theologian of glory calls evil good and good evil. A theologian of the cross calls the thing what it actually is."*
>
> Martin Luther[1]

Any attempt to "justify the ways of God to men" in Milton's classic phrase, is confronted at the outset by some basic theological questions. What "God" is it who is to be justified? What is the character of that deity? Where do we get the standards that this God supposedly must meet in order to be justified? And if it turns out that God fails to measure up to our standards, is that God's problem or ours?

Those obvious questions have not always been asked. If we try to explain certain aspects of the world in relation to a God who is described in terms of abstract divine attributes such as omnipotence and beneficence then our enterprise will be limited by the fact that we know nothing specific about God's will for the world. If God is assumed to be impassible then we will not be able to consider the possibility that God participates in any way in the sufferings of the world. It is not surprising that attempts at theodicy on the basis of philosophical theism alone have often been unsatisfying.

Furthermore, the statement of Luther with which I began, and to which we will return, reminds us that we need to ask where we get our criteria for good and evil. If all suffering is some form of evil then the problem of theodicy differs considerably from what it is if we are more realistic and recognize that suffering sometimes has beneficial results. In the context of his theology of the cross this is just the point that Luther was making with that statement.

For our present task, that of considering theodicy in connection with biological evolution, there are also scientific issues that have to be addressed. If we are to try to understand God's actions, or at some points lack of action, in connection with evolution then we must deal with evolution as it really takes place. That may seem obvious but the history of the subject is replete with attempts to explain evolution in ways that are more pleasing to our sensibilities

---

[1] Luther, Martin, "Heidelberg Disputation", in: *Luther's Works*, vol. 31 (Philadelphia: Fortress, 1957) 53.

than the rather harsh ways in which it often takes place in reality. It will do no good to justify God's actions in an evolution which operates by some system of rewards and punishments or to ensure some sort of progress, if evolution in the real world has nothing to do with those categories.

Since I have referred to reality, it will be well to bear in mind that for many conservative Christians it is evolution, not God, which seems to be in need of justification. The fact that evolution, and the long ages of earth history that go with it, imply that death was present in the world long before human sin occurred is for them a definitive argument against evolution. How can an utterly good God have created a universe in which death is (as the idea of natural selection implies) a necessary part of the development of living things? These presuppositions mean that if evolution cannot be reconciled with traditional beliefs in the goodness and power of God then it is evolution, not God, which must be rejected.

Unless such people can be shown that there is a way to understand biological evolution within the context of a theology that maintains the central elements of the historic Christian faith then evolution will be ruled out of court and divisive creation-evolution battles will continue. And this will be the case in spite of the tremendous weight of scientific evidence that indicates that evolution has in fact been taking place.

It is not difficult to see that these basic questions, the theological and the scientific, are related. Certain ideas about God may encourage those who hold them to understand evolution in ways that the God in whom they believe would work. On the other hand, the old but debatable tradition of natural theology may lead others to develop a view of God from their understanding of the world. Or it may be that the result will be a natural anti-theology in which (as the subtitle of one book puts it), "the evidence of evolution reveals a universe without design."[2]

Is Theodicy a Legitimate Enterprise?

When Saint Paul considered a challenge to the justice of God's election (a subject which, as we will see, is related to evolution), his response was straightforward: "But who indeed are you, a human being, to argue with God?" (Romans 9:20)[3] While that could in itself be considered a type of theodicy, it is a rejection of any attempt to insist that God's actions be justified in terms of merely human criteria. If God really is the creator of the universe, if "it is he that made us, and not we ourselves", (Psalm 100:3 NRSV margin), then it is presumptuous for us to take upon ourselves the job of justifying God.

---

[2] Dawkins, Richard, *The Blind Watchmaker: Why the Evidence of Evolution Reveals a Universe without Design* (New York: W. W. Norton, 1987).

[3] Biblical citations are from the *New Revised Standard Version*.

If we are to discuss the justice of the creator of the universe then we must try to look at matters from God's standpoint, which means that we must consider God's own self-revelation. This does not mean simply to assert that God can do whatever God pleases, and that we have to accept the arbitrary decrees of an absolute monarch. It is rather that God will be seen to be justified when God's own character and God's purpose for creation are understood. We return to the point made at the beginning of this chapter, that we must know what God we are talking about.

Theodicies, if they are not just academic exercises, are generally developed as part of an apologetic for a religion—in our case, for Christianity. In order to persuade people to consider the claims of the Christian faith, it may be felt necessary to defend God against the charge that the divine governance of the world is unjust. The practice of apologetics came under strong attack by Karl Barth and other theologians of neo-Orthodoxy because it seemed to concede too much to non-Christian presuppositions. The ideas that might be used for the purpose of defending the faith could turn out to undermine important parts of it.

But this need not happen. Instead of appealing to supposedly common sense ideas that non-believers will accept, we can begin by reminding them that modern science should have taught us to be wary of common sense. A theory is not to be judged by the *a priori* plausibility of its postulates but by its success in enabling us to understand our experience of the world. For example, the second postulate of Einstein's special relativity, that the speed of light is the same for all observers, regardless of their velocity, clashes violently with common sense.

In a similar way, the claim that God is revealed in a first century Jew suffering and dying on a cross is not common sense. Instead of pretending that it is, we invite non-believers to consider their experiences of the world and their own lives from that standpoint, and try to help them to see that it better explains those experiences than do other religious or philosophical claims.[4]

Luther's theologia crucis *and its extensions*

My fundamental thesis is that God's actions in the world, and specifically in the processes of biological evolution, should be viewed in the context of a theology of the cross.[5] While we will not be able to restrict ourselves to a particular sixteenth century formulation, we will find it most helpful to begin with Luther's *theologia crucis* as he set it out in his theological theses (or, as he called them, "theological paradoxes") for the Heidelberg Disputation of

---

[4] Murphy, George L., "Cross-Based Apologetics for a New Millennium", Perspectives on Science and Christian Faith 52, 2000, 190–193.

[5] Murphy, George L., *The Cosmos in the Light of the Cross* (New York: Trinity Press International, 2003).

1518.[6] One reason for this is the claim expressed in the twenty-first of the theses with which I have prefaced this chapter: In modern parlance, a theologian of the cross tells it like it is. If we are to talk about God's activities in the real processes of evolution as science describes them, and not only about ancient creation stories or ways in which we would like evolution to work, then we need a realistic theology. In the Heidelberg theses we are told how we can expect to know who God is, where God is present for us, and what constitutes good theology and bad theology.

We need to keep in mind Luther's primary interest in his formulation of a theology of the cross. It should go without saying that he knew nothing of modern evolutionary theories. His concern was with the central issues of the Reformation—law and gospel, sin and salvation. This certainly does not mean that what he has to say is of no help for our reflections on evolution, but we must expect to do some work if we are to draw out implications of his theology which are useful for our discussion.

Earlier we posed the question, "What 'God' is it who is to be justified?" A common belief which underlies many attempts at theodicy is that we can know who God is from our experiences of the world and of our lives and reflection upon them. Romans 1:18–31 is often appealed to in support of such a natural theology but that misses the point of that passage. In Romans 1:18–3:20 Paul is intent on showing that all people are sinners. In 1:18–31 he describes the problems of idolatry to which bad natural theologies give rise. The difficulty is not that people believe in no God at all but that they do not know who the true God is.

Thus Luther argues forcefully against trying to know God from our experience of the world and reason in Thesis 19:[7] "That person does not deserve to be called a theologian who looks upon the invisible things of God as though they were clearly perceptible in those things which have actually happened." Comparison of Luther's Latin with the Vulgate of Romans 1:20 makes it clear that he has that verse in mind here.

Our idols tend to be the types of God that we would be if only we could be God, a deity present in the beautiful and glorious things of the world, one who is immune from suffering and loss. And it is that kind of God sought by what Luther will call the "theologian of glory" that theodicies usually try to justify.

Thesis 20, on the other hand, tells us how the true God is to be known: "He deserves to be called a theologian, however, who comprehends the visible and manifest things of God seen through suffering and the cross."[8]

The cross of Christ is the supreme revelation of God. We will be talking about the implications of this claim for the way we understand God's involve-

---

[6] Luther, "Heidelberg Disputation".
[7] Ibid., 40.
[8] Ibid.

ment in all the suffering of the world, and especially that of evolution, but it is first of all a claim about what happened to Jesus of Nazareth "under Pontius Pilate". As Luther says in his proof of this thesis, "true theology and recognition of God are in the crucified Christ".[9]

The true God is to be known in a situation of abandonment, suffering and death, and the supreme divine work of saving the world is accomplished there. If we take this claim seriously then the common assumptions that underlie many theodicies are challenged. So we come to the statement with which we began, Thesis 21: "A theologian of glory calls evil good and good evil. A theologian of the cross calls the thing what it actually is."

This means in particular that suffering is not always evil. Of course it is sometimes, and sometimes suffering is the result of evil, but every athlete knows the cliché "No pain, no gain." Many good things could not be accomplished without physical and/or emotional pain, and the theology of the cross sets before us the passion of Christ as the supremely good work of God. "The problem of suffering should not just be rolled up with the problem of evil", Forde comments on this thesis. "Only false speaking lures us into doing that."[10]

The very term "theology of the cross" can give an impression of a system which deals only with suffering and death. Thus it is important to realize that the resurrection is an essential part of this theology. If it were not for Easter then there would be no proclamation of Christ crucified and no corresponding theology. Jesus of Nazareth would be just one more prophet ground under by the oppressive forces of the world. On the other hand, the Easter message is a proclamation that "Jesus of Nazareth, who was crucified...has been raised" (Mark 16:6). The resurrection does not cancel out what Paul called the "stumbling block" and "foolishness" of the cross (I Corinthians 1:23). In fact it intensifies the offence of the cross because it means that the crucified One is to be confessed as Lord.[11]

Luther's concern in formulating his *theologia crucis*, as I noted, was with central Reformation issues of sin, law and the justification of sinners. Evolution may seem to have little to do with those issues, though we will see later that some of the theological disagreements over them surface in different form in the types of evolutionary theories that people prefer. But at this point we need to ask a question of another type. If the true God is indeed known first of all and most clearly in the cross of Christ, how might we expect that God to work in the world?

---

[9] Ibid., 53.

[10] Forde, Gerhard O., *On Being a Theologian of the Cross: Reflections on Luther's Heidelberg Disputation, 1518* (Grand Rapids, MI: William B. Eerdmans, 1997) 84.

[11] Cousar, Charles B., *A Theology of the Cross: The Death of Jesus in the Pauline Letters* (Minneapolis: Fortress, 1990) 104.

We need not at this point try to develop an understanding of divine action from scratch because a great deal of thought has gone into this question over the centuries, with a resurgence of interest in it in recent science-theology dialogue. Ian Barbour has given a helpful typology of theologies of divine action with corresponding models.[12] An appropriate combination of these models will meet our needs.

We can begin with what Barbour calls a "Neo-Thomist" theology of divine action, the idea that God as First Cause acts through created agents as second causes. The model of a human worker using instruments to accomplish some piece of work illustrates this view. What science has shown us about the world then tells us something about the way in which God acts. The near-complete uniformity of natural processes that are described by our scientific theories indicates that God does not work with these created instruments in arbitrary ways. Divine action seems to be limited, at least in the vast majority of situations, to regular patterns.

A *kenotic* view of divine action provides the necessary limitation. This is the distinctive contribution of a theology of the cross to the doctrine of creation. The concept of kenosis has its origin in the Christ hymn of Philippians (2:5–11), in which the one who was in the form of God "emptied (*ekenōsen*) himself", limited himself, in the Incarnation and death on the cross. If the cross is indeed a true revelation of God, and not merely a temporary tactic that God used to accomplish some purpose, then willingness for such self-limitation is an important aspect of the divine character.

Kenosis in creation means that God normally limits divine action to what can be accomplished in accord with the natures of created agents. (The qualification "normally" means that we cannot rule out miraculous divine action beyond the capacities of creatures.) Because of this, natural processes operate in regular ways that can be understood by scientific investigation so that rational beings can understand the world. This divine limitation is a gift because it enables us to understand our world and grow to maturity, just as wise parents refrain from doing everything for their children but enable them to learn to do things for themselves. But this also means that God does not act beyond the capacities of created agents to prevent the extinction of species or the growth of cancers.

Kenosis is a concept that is easily misunderstood. It is not nihilism but rather self-limitation for the sake of the other. (Paul quotes the Christ hymn in Philippians as pattern to be followed by his readers.) The Son of God took on human form and accepted the death of the cross in order to save the world.

---

[12] Barbour, Ian G., *Religion in an Age of Science: The Gifford Lectures 1989–1991, Volume One. San Francisco* (San Francisco: HarperCollins, 1990) 244. The revised edition, *Religion and Science: Historical and Contemporary Issues* (San Francisco: HarperCollins, 1997) omits the existentialist type.

God limits divine action to enable the universe to develop freely, and so that the rational beings who evolve can become adult citizens of the world.

Kenosis also does not mean that God is absent from some situations or inactive in certain phenomena.[13] Instead, it means that God's ever-present cooperation with creatures will not exceed their natural capacities. God is active in everything that takes place but not by overpowering the created entities which act along with God.

A combination of the Neo-Thomist and kenotic views of divine action enables us to understand how God acts in the natural world, but we need to remember that theology is not physics. What we observe in the world is the operation of natural processes, not the God who cooperates with them. We believe that the God revealed in Christ is acting through those processes, and this is the element of truth in what Barbour described as the "existentialist" theology of divine action. Understanding of creation as well as of salvation requires an act of faith, for while science enables us to understand the world, it does not tell us that the world is God's creation or that God is at work in it.

Because we do see only the instruments with which God works, those instruments conceal God from our direct observation. This means that they can be described by another metaphor as well: The created things with which God works are not only God's instruments but are in Luther's phrase "the masks of God behind which He wants to remain concealed and do all things."[14]

The Free Process Defense of Evil

With this understanding of the way in which God works in the world we are now in a position to invoke John Polkinghorne's "free process" defense for the existence of natural evil in the world.[15] Viruses which cause suffering and death and environmental changes which bring about extinctions are consequences of the fact that God, choosing to act within the capacities of creation, grants it freedom and "functional integrity."[16] But having developed the argument in this way, we see that the free process defense is not an independent claim but one founded in a theology of the cross.

Up to this point our discussion of the theology of the cross and its implications for God's relationship with the world could be understood in terms of traditional ideas about the impassibility of the divine nature and Chalcedonian christology. God would be revealed in the human sufferings of Christ, and while we could speak of them as the sufferings of the divine person of the

---

[13] Ted Peters and Martinez Hewlett, *Evolution from Creation to New Creation: Conflict, Conversation, and Convergence* (Nashville: Abingdon, 2003) 142f.

[14] Luther, Martin, "Psalm 147", in: *Luther's Works*, Vol. 14 (St. Louis: Concordia, 1955) 114.

[15] Polkinghorne, John, *Science and Providence* (London: SPCK, 1989) 65ff.

[16] Van Till, Howard J., "Basil, Augustine, and the Doctrine of Creation's Functional Integrity", Science and Christian Belief, 8, 1996, 21–38.

incarnate Word, we would also have to maintain that the divine nature itself is impervious to suffering and perishability.

But if it is really true that God is revealed in the fullest sense in the crucified Christ then we have to ask if this insight is profound enough. Luther in some places seems to go beyond its limits so that it is possible to speak of the "Dei-passianism" of some of his statements.[17] These ideas have been explored more explicitly and more fully by recent theologians. Jürgen Moltmann argues that God takes suffering and death into the divine being, so that we can speak of "death in God."[18] Kazoh Kitamori insists that it is necessary to speak of the "pain of God",[19] while Eberhard Jüngel develops a "theology of the crucified One" which uses the language of God's "unity with perishability."

> Based on the word of the cross, which emphatically proclaims that the one *who was raised from the dead is the Crucified One*, we answer that the being of God is first revealed as creative being in the struggle with the annihilating nothingness of nothing. This means hermeneutically that we are not to expound the word of the cross on the basis of the biblical statements about the imperishability of God, which are directed toward God the Creator. Rather, conversely, we learn how to understand who God the Creator is on the basis of the biblical statements directed toward the Crucified One, which statements force us to think God in unity with perishability.[20]

Our understanding of creation, including the ways in which God acts in evolution, begins at Calvary.

This concept of the suffering of God is not meant as a general truth of which the cross may be one example, as in process theology. It is rather something we know *from* the cross. It is only at Calvary that we really know what it means to say, in the words of a controversial seventeenth century hymn, that "God himself lies dead."[21] But having been brought to recognize the presence of the true God in the event of the cross, we can look for that God's presence and activity throughout the world. "The Son of God was crucified for all and for everything", Irenaeus said, "Having traced the sign of the Cross on all things."[22]

The Evolutionary Process

Biological evolution by itself, "descent with modification", would not necessarily raise any questions about the goodness, justice, or power of God. With

---

[17] Lienhard, Marc, *Luther: Witness to Jesus Christ* (Minneapolis: Augsburg, 1982) 171.
[18] Moltmann, Jürgen, *The Crucified God: The Cross of Christ as the Foundation and Criticism of Christian Theology* (New York: Harper & Row, 1974) 207.
[19] Kitamori, Kazoh, *Theology of the Pain of God* (Richmond, VA: John Knox, 1965).
[20] Jüngel, Eberhard, *God as the Mystery of the World: On the Foundation of the Theology of the Crucified One in the Dispute between Theism and Atheism* (Grand Rapids, MI: Eerdmans, 1983) 218.
[21] Ibid., 64 ff.
[22] This statement from Irenaeus' *On the Apostolic Preaching* is quoted in this form in Evdokimov, P. "Nature", Scottish Journal of Theology, 18, 1965, 11.

a little effort we could imagine a "peaceable kingdom" in which God directed things so that species would slowly change over the course of time, giving rise to new forms of life which were always in harmony with one another. Creatures in such a scenario could end their lives "old and full of years" or perhaps (as in some naïve versions of eschatology) be translated to a spiritual realm in which there was no danger of overcrowding. But such pictures are indeed the products of imagination.

For the history of life on earth has been far from peaceable. There have been deaths of individuals and extinctions of species, predators and prey, disease and starvation, for millions of years before humanity ever came on the scene, and those processes have not abated since the advent of *Homo sapiens*. Just to describe the way evolution works provokes many people to ask questions about the goodness of the process and of any deity who is supposed to be at work in it.

The relative importance of various factors involved in the evolutionary process are, of course, debated by scientists who work in the field. For our purposes here it is more important to look at broad outlines of evolutionary theories than to consider their details. It is illuminating to compare and contrast the predominant neo-Darwinian understanding of evolution with two other ways in which the evolutionary process has been understood. They are ways which, in spite of their scientific drawbacks, are often what the man or woman in the street means by evolution.

The concept of natural selection proposed by Darwin and Wallace is at least a major factor in the development of new species. There will always be variations among members of a species and not all of them will be equally suited for survival in a given environment. There will be competition for food, opportunities for reproduction and other things that are needed for an organism's genes to be passed on. Those that are better suited in that environment will, on the average, be more likely to survive (by obtaining food, avoiding predation, or whatever is necessary) and produce offspring which will inherit their favorable characteristics.

This does not mean that organisms which survive and reproduce have any type of absolute superiority. Fitness is relative to the environment, and if the environment changes, the properties which suit organisms for survival may change significantly. In particular, catastrophic environmental changes such as those associated with the asteroid impact some sixty-five million years ago, may be of a nature that no species could be prepared for.

Natural selection in this sense is thus very different from the way in which "survival of the fittest" is often popularly understood. As Stephen Jay Gould has pointed out,[23] the common pictures of evolution as a linear transition

---

[23] Gould, Stephen Jay, *Wonderful Life: The Burgess Shale and the Nature of History* (New York: W. W. Norton, 1989) ch. 1.

from a fish crawling out the sea through slouching apelike animals to upright modern *Homo sapiens* present evolution as an inevitable progress from earlier forms of life to ourselves. We might borrow a term from nineteenth century American history and describe this as a "manifest destiny" view of evolution. Just as some Americans claimed that the United States was clearly ordained to occupy the entire North American continent, so those who see evolution in this way think that higher forms of life were manifestly destined to develop and eventually win out in the struggle for survival. (And it is worth noting that the political idea of manifest destiny eventually found social Darwinism a convenient ally.[24])

Lamarck's concept of the transmission of acquired characters is another, and earlier, alternative to Darwin's and Wallace's idea. Properties which an organism acquires during the course of its life, such as increased strength or endurance, are supposed to be passed on to its offspring. Organisms according to this theory are more active in determining the course of evolution than they are with natural selection.

On closer investigation neither of these latter theories of evolution works. Manifest destiny tends to omit the crucial role of the environment and its changes, and implies that evolution would have worked out in much the same way even if the environment had changed in different ways. If the dinosaurs had not become extinct when they did, something else would have happened to remove them in order to create niches into which mammals, and eventually hominids, could expand. This ignores the historical contingency of the whole process that led to us[25]. If (among other events) an asteroid impact had not led to the demise of the dinosaurs, the course of evolution would have been quite different. Some intelligent species might have eventually arisen but it could have been very different from us.

Lamarck's version of evolution has failed to stand up to many experimental attempts to confirm the transmission of acquired characters. The children of blacksmiths are not born with larger biceps than those of lawyers. Nor is this surprising in light of modern genetics. The so-called "central dogma" of genetics is that information passes from the germ line to body cells but not the reverse, and while we do not need to give this claim as absolute a status as the word "dogma" implies, it is certainly very hard to see how gross anatomical changes in the parent generation could affect corresponding regions of the organism's DNA and thus be passed on to offspring.

But our point here is not simply to dismiss these theories as scientifically inadequate. In spite of their scientific weaknesses they continue to be common understandings of evolution, especially among the general populace.

---

[24] Pratt, Julius W., *A History of American Foreign Policy* (Englewood Cliffs, NJ: Prentice-Hall, 1955) 368–372.
[25] This is the basic argument of Gould, *Wonderful Life*.

This may be because those views are easier to understand than natural se‑lection, but both transmission of acquired characters and manifest destiny are ways in which people would *like* evolution to take place. They also ex‑press ways in which people naturally expect God to make evolution work. A common understanding of Lamarck's view (though Lamarck himself did not speak in this way) is that species whose members work hard to succeed will survive. Effort is rewarded. Lamarckian evolution is a kind of biologi‑cal works righteousness—"God helps them who help themselves." (Many Americans think that comes from the Bible but it is from Benjamin Franklin's *Poor Richard's Almanac.*[26]) The preference for Lamarckian evolution by peo‑ple with viewpoints as different as the Roman Catholic Teilhard de Chardin and the Marxist Lysenko illustrates this fact.[27]

Manifest destiny, on the other hand, would mean that some species sur‑vive and propagate because of their intrinsic superiority. It corresponds to the belief that God saves pious and morally upright people, in contrast to Paul's statement in Romans (4:5) that God "justifies the ungodly". In the last of the theological Heidelberg theses Luther makes it clear that God does not look for people who are already just. Instead, justification is an act of divine creation: "The love of God does not find, but creates, that which is pleasing to it."[28]

In studying evolution in the real world our attention is not focused on the inherent superiority of some organisms or of their efforts to survive. We see competition for resources, privation and death. Extinction is forced on our attention even as new species come into being. And, as we will discuss later, there is something corresponding to the theological concept of election.

The violent aspects of the history of life need not be overstated. It has not always involved actual combat, and has often been a matter of slow declines of populations due to shortages of food or other resources. The well-known description of the world of evolution as "nature red in tooth and claw" is hyperbolic. But competition, death, and extinction have been essential to the process.

Evolution as Divine Action

The traditional problem of theodicy is, "If God is all-good and all-power‑ful, why do bad things happen?" Waiving for now the question of what we should call "bad", we note that this traditional formulation makes the prob‑lem one of God's apparent inaction in the face of evil: "Why doesn't God do something?"

---

[26] *Poor Richard's Almanack.* Mount Vernon, NY: Peter Pauper Press, n.d., no page numbering.

[27] Teilhard de Chardin, Pierre, *The Phenomenon of Man* (New York: Harper & Row, 1959) esp. 149f. Medvedev, Zhores, A., *The Rise and Fall of T. D. Lysenko* (New York: Columbia University, 1969).

[28] Luther, "Heidelberg Disputation", 41.

That suffices as a challenge to the God of Deism but the difficulty for a
biblical view of God's involvement with the world is more serious. Job's com-
plaint is not that God simply allows his suffering but that God is actually
doing something to him—"multiplies my wounds without cause" (Job 9:17).
God is, according to a traditional view of providence, involved in everything
that happens in the world. God as the primary cause "cooperates" or "concurs" with created agents as secondary causes.[29] Thus when bad things happen we can ask not just "Why does God let this happen?" but "Why is God
doing this?" Heinrich Schmid described a specific instance of this problem,
"exhibiting the method of the divine concurrence in the evil actions of men,
without at the same time in any wise throwing the blame of the evil upon the
first cause, *i.e.*, upon God", as "The most difficult problem in the science of
theology."[30]

(The way in which such issues were dealt with by protestant scholasticism
is illustrated by the two solutions which Schmid goes on to cite from, respectively, Quenstedt and Hollaz: "God concurs in producing the effect, not the
defect; God concurs as to the materials, not as to the form." Both are purely
philosophical. Schmid's compendium of the theology of Lutheran Orthodoxy
has no reference to Luther's theology of the cross)

But the mechanism of evolution proposed by Darwin and Wallace, natural
selection, makes the problem still more difficult. If we are to understand this
type of evolution as God's way of creating life then we must say that God is
not only active in processes which bring about results that we see as evil but
also makes use of things like privation, suffering, loss, death and extinction
in order to create new forms of life, including humanity. God has apparently
chosen to create life by means of things that we see and experience as bad.

Those who want to reconcile the scientific reality of evolution with some
type of theistic belief have often followed the nineteenth century American
historian John Fiske in saying that evolution is "God's way of doing things."[31]
God creates through the evolutionary process. That is true as far as it goes,
but that way of "doing things" is what raises the theodicy issue for many
people, for it means that God creates life by using the processes of privation,
death and extinction.

God's willingness to give of self for the sake of creation, something that we
have seen in self-emptying of Christ, suggests that God does not withhold
anything from the world. "For God is good, or rather is essentially the source
of goodness:" said Athanasius. "Nor could one that is good be niggardly of

---

[29] Heinrich Schmid, *The Doctrinal Theology of the Evangelical Lutheran Church* (Minneapolis,
Augsburg, ³1961) 170–194.

[30] Ibid., 185.

[31] Quoted in Abbott, Lyman, *The Theology of an Evolutionist* (Boston and New York:
Houghton, Mifflin, 1897), 3.

anything: whence, grudging existence to none, He has made all things out of nothing by His own Word, Jesus Christ our Lord."[32] Thus we should understand God to have given the world not bare existence alone but fullness of being, including functional integrity and relative autonomy.

Time and history are part of the universe which God has created. "The world was made", Augustine said, "not in time, but simultaneously with time."[33] Christians have sometimes understood God's initial creation of the world to be a state of static perfection but a phrase like "Be fruitful and multiply" would make no sense if that were the case. God has made a universe which is able, with divine cooperation, to move toward the goal which God wills. Both God and natural processes are genuine causes in this motion.

But what is God's purpose in all of this? Answering that question requires a certain amount of speculation and any attempt to do so is rather presumptuous because it puts us in danger of claiming that God was required to do something in order to accord with our understanding of the divine plan. But while we should proceed with humility, it is necessary to say something about this because otherwise we have no way of knowing what purpose the sufferings of the world may serve from a theological standpoint. Fortunately we do have some hints that go beyond mere guesswork.

To begin with, Ephesians 1:10 speaks of speaks of God's "plan for the fullness of time, to gather up all things in him [Christ], things in heaven and things on earth". This suggests that the Incarnation was not simply contingent upon human sin but was part of God's intention in the beginning. The controversial anthropic principles of cosmology can be subsumed in theology by a theanthropic principle. The universe has been given properties which make it possible for intelligent life to evolve. But the goal of the universe is not merely the evolution of that type of life but such life indwelt by the Word of God in order to unite all things in himself.[34]

If God was to act kenotically in the development of life, respecting the properties with which the world was endowed in creation, there would be divine cooperation with created agents but in ways limited to their natural capacities—which is to say, in accord with what we approximate by our scientific laws. And with our current understandings of natural processes we are unable to see how something radically different from neo-Darwinian evolution could work to develop new forms of life. It is not just that acquired characters aren't transmitted but that it's very hard to see how acquired characters *could* be transmitted.

---

[32] St. Athanasius, "On the Incarnation of the Word", in: *The Nicene and Post-Nicene Fathers*, Second Series, Vol. 4, 37.

[33] St. Augustine, "The City of God", Book XI, ch. 6, in: *The Nicene and Post-Nicene Fathers*, First Series, vol. 2, 208. Murphy, George L., "Time, Thermodynamics, and Theology", Zygon, 26, 1991, 359–372.

[34] Murphy, *The Cosmos in the Light of the Cross*, 182 ff.

This suggests that if God wanted to create a free universe, it would have to have the kind of character it does, including natural selection. Pain and death are thus an inevitable concomitant of God's choice to allow creation to be itself, to possess its own integrity and freedom. While there is "natural evil" in such a world there need not be any "moral evil" if there are no moral agents among the world's inhabitants.

But if moral agents developed through the processes of natural selection then it seems very likely that it was inevitable (though not a strict logical necessity) that moral evil would occur. Deception, theft, sexual promiscuity and the killing of fellows were not sins for our pre-human ancestors. But the first hominids among whom moral agency did develop (and here we do not need to try to discern when and how that took place), and for whom such activities would have been sinful, would have had a long history which predisposed them to such behaviors.[35]

If this is the case, and if (as we must suppose) God knew that sin was an inevitable consequence of a free creation, then it would seem that not only the Incarnation but also the cross was part of God's intention from the beginning. There are suggestions of this in I Peter 1:19–20 and Revelation 13:8 which speak of Christ as a sacrificial lamb "destined before" or "slaughtered from" (respectively) "the foundation of the world."[36]

There is suffering which is clearly a consequence of human sin—all the wars and oppressions and injustices that human beings have caused, and all of the destructive impact upon nature brought about by human greed and carelessness—but the world would not always have been a peaceable kingdom even without that. All of this means that "nature" must pay a price for its integrity and relative freedom, and that that price becomes higher the farther living things have advanced toward sensitivity, consciousness, and moral agency.

God Share's in the World's Suffering

The distinctive insight of a theology of the crucified One is that God shares in paying that price. God gives to creation not only fullness of being but God's own life. The God who is made known in the cross and resurrection of Jesus is not an impassible cosmic dictator or puppet master who drives living things through millions of years of competition, suffering, death and extinction in order to reach some goal. The true God becomes a participant in the evolutionary process.

---

[35] Murphy, George L. "Roads to Paradise and Perdition: Christ, Evolution, and Original Sin", Perspectives on Science and Christian Faith, 58, 2006, 109–118.

[36] This rendering of Revelation 13:8 is that of NRSV margin. Caird, G. B. The Revelation of St. John the Divine (New York: Harper & Row, 1966), 168 makes the case for it.

We should pause at this point to realize that that last sentence means exactly what it says. If we are the result of a long process of evolution, closely related to chimpanzees and the extinct australopithecines and more distant relatives of all living things on earth, then the genuine humanity of God Incarnate means that he too shared the same evolutionary history and those same relationships. Just as we can call Mary *theotokos*, "Mother of God", we can properly say that God is a cousin of apes and a distant relative of the extinct creatures of the Cambrian.

God becomes a participant in the evolutionary process not to overcome all competitors in the "struggle for survival" but to be on the side of the losers. In the short term it is those who will do anything to maintain their grasp on power, Caiaphas and Pilate, who survive. Of course in the larger evolutionary scheme it is species, not individuals, whose extinction or survival are at issue. But in the event of the cross God dies the death that faces all living things because he has entered into their evolutionary history.

And as an old christological axiom has it, "What has not been assumed has not been healed."[37] Christ's resurrection means that there is hope for the losers in evolution. This is a hope not just for individual human beings but one of "a new heaven and a new earth" (Revelation 21:1). This is the eschatological promise in which the world was created. "From the beginning", Bonhoeffer said, "the world is placed in the sign of the resurrection of Christ from the dead."[38]

But the fundamental justification of God (if it must be called that) presented here is not that there is a happy ending. That is indeed the promise of the resurrection, and it is a promise which should not be ignored when suffering and evil in the world are considered. We do not need to be timid about the reality of Easter and its implications simply for fear of being accused of peddling pie in the sky. But we are also assured that here and now, and throughout the history of the world, God is a participant with us in evolution, sharing in suffering and in the effects of natural and moral evil.

Even that is not the last word. The point is not just that misery loves company, but that God is God. The spirit in which we should approach these matters is that of C. S. Lewis when he reflected on the hope of everlasting life in a letter to a friend:

> I believed in God before I believed in Heaven. And even now, even if—let's make an impossible supposition—His voice, unmistakably His, said to me, "They have misled you. I can do nothing of that sort for you. My long struggle with the blind forces is nearly over. I die, children. The story is ending"—would that be a moment

---

[37] Cited in Grillmeier, Aloys, *Christ in Christian Tradition*. vol. 1 (Atlanta: John Knox) 321 and 531.

[38] Bonhoeffer, Dietrich, *Creation and Fall/Temptation* (New York: Macmillan, 1959) 19.

for changing sides? Would not you and I take the Viking way: "The Giants and the Trolls win. Let us die on the right side, with Father Odin."[39]

Who is in Charge?

Even though the somewhat speculative sketch in the previous section of God's involvement in the evolutionary process may have sounded plausible, questions will arise about how God could actually carry out this program if divine action takes place in accord with a theology of the cross. After all, the pattern of that action is one of weakness and passivity, a man dying on the cross. How can God then exert enough control over the process to accomplish any purpose for the world? If environmental contingencies affect the course of evolution so strongly, how could any long-term goal be accomplished? After all, we have insisted that the manifest destiny view of evolution is inadequate on both scientific and theological grounds.

It is hard to see how God's statement to Paul, "Power is made perfect in weakness" (II Corinthians 12:9), can make any sense. Effective applications of nonviolent resistance or martial arts like aikido may help us to see how things can be accomplished through appropriate types of weakness. But it is essential to realize that God's limitation of divine action to what can be accomplished through natural processes does not mean that God is not doing anything at all. Created agents and their interactions would not exist and would do nothing without God.

It is also essential to realize that that limitation on God's actions is not so tight that God is locked into a single course of action that can be described by deterministic laws. Both the sensitivity to initial conditions of many physical processes ("chaos theory") and quantum mechanics mean that the laws of physics are not deterministic in the way that many people thought during the dominance of the Newtonian worldview.[40] This means that even when God chooses to restrict action kenotically there is a certain amount of freedom in what can be done. (And *a fortiori* this is so if God would choose to act beyond the capabilities of created agents.)

Thus God could act on relatively small scales, but precisely the uncertainties which chaos and quantum theories point to raise questions about any "long term planning" on God's part. The idea that evolution has from the beginning been aimed at the emergence of intelligent bipedal mammals like ourselves is precisely the sort of thing that Gould's emphasis on the contingency of evolution was directed against. How can we talk about any sort of divine election in this context?

---

[39] Lewis, C.S. Prayer, *Letters to Malcolm* (Glasgow: William Collins Sons, 1966) 120.
[40] Murphy, *The Cosmos in the Light of the Cross*, ch. 4 (Polkinghorne, Science and Providence).

The primary object of election, however, is not individual humans, or the species *Homo sapiens*, or any other species. It is Jesus Christ. People have been chosen "in Christ" and he is the one in whom God intends "to gather up all things" (Ephesians 1:4 and 10). The election of all others is in him. The universe might have brought forth an intelligent species quite different from ourselves in order to accomplish the divine plan.

A hundred million years ago there was nothing to indicate that mammals rather than the dominant reptiles would give rise to the species that would inherit the earth. That they did corresponds to the fact that in scripture the election of people does not depend on their actions or merit. Scripture reminds the people of Israel that they were not the most obvious candidates for election:

> It was not because you were more numerous than any other people that the LORD set his heart on you and chose you—for you were the fewest of all peoples. It was because the LORD loved you and kept the oath that he swore to your ancestors, that the LORD has brought you out with a mighty hand, and redeemed you from the house of slavery, from the hand of Pharaoh king of Egypt. (Deuteronomy 7:7–8)

Christ is the elect one. But, as Barth emphasized with his distinctive version of double predestination, he is also the one chosen for reprobation.[41] God is the one chosen by God to bear the sufferings of the world. Luther said that "the CROSS alone is our theology".[42] We can add the cross is also the only firm basis for theodicy.

---

[41] Barth, Karl, *Church Dogmatics*, vol. II.2 (Edinburgh: T. & T. Clark, 1957).

[42] "CRUX sola est nostra theologia". *D. Martin Luthers Werke, Kritische Gesammtausgabe*, Bd. 5. (Weimar: Hermann Böhlau, 1892) 172. The capitalization is in the original.

Contributors

Gaymon Bennett is Director of Ethics at the Synthetic Biology Engineering Research Center at U.C. Berkeley.

William A. Dembski is Research Professor in Philosophy at Southwestern Baptist Theological Seminary in Ft. Worth and a senior fellow with Discovery Institute's Center for Science and Culture in Seattle.

René Girard is the retired Andrew B. Hammond Professor of French Language, Literature, and Civilization Emeritus at Stanford University and a member of the Académie Française.

James W. Haag recently finished his Ph.D. at the Graduate Theology Union in Berkeley, California and is now Postdoctoral Visiting Scholar at the Center for Theology and the Natural Sciences in Berkeley.

Nathan Hallanger is a doctoral candidate at the Graduate Theological Union in systematic and philosophical theology, and currently serves as Program Director at the Center for Theology and the Natural Sciences.

John F. Haught is Senior Fellow, Science & Religion, Woodstock Theological Center, Georgetown University, and was previously Chair and Professor in the Department of Theology at Georgetown.

Peter M.J. Hess is the Faith Project Director of the National Center for Science Education and an adjunct faculty member at Saint Mary's College, Moraga.

Martinez J. Hewlett is Professor Emeritus at University of Arizona and Adjunct Professor at Graduate Theological Union in Berkeley, California.

Joshua Moritz is a doctoral student at the Graduate Theological Union, Berkeley, and Managing Editor of *Dialog: A Journal of Theology*.

George Murphy, a physicist and Lutheran pastor, is adjunct faculty at Trinity Lutheran Seminary in Columbus, Ohio.

Derek Nelson is Assistant Professor of Religion at Thiel College in Greenville, Pennsylvania and author of numerous articles on topics in systematic and historical theology and the philosophy of religion.

Ted Peters is Professor of Systematic Theology at the Pacific Lutheran Theological Seminary and the Graduate Theological Union.

Michael Ruse is the Lucyle T. Werkmeister Professor and Director of the History and Philosophy of Science Program at Florida State University.

Robert John Russell is the Ian G. Barbour Professor of Theology and Science in Residence, The Graduate Theological Union, and Founder and Director, the Center for Theology and the Natural Sciences, Berkeley.

Christopher Southgate trained originally as a biochemist, and is now a poet and editor, and Research Fellow in Theology at the University of Exeter, UK.

Patricia A. Williams is a philosopher of science and a philosophical theologian who writes at the interface of science and religion.